HARBINGER

DEATH OF A
RENEGADE

JOSHUA DYSART | CLAYTON HENRY | KHARI EVANS | BRIAN REBER

CONTENTS

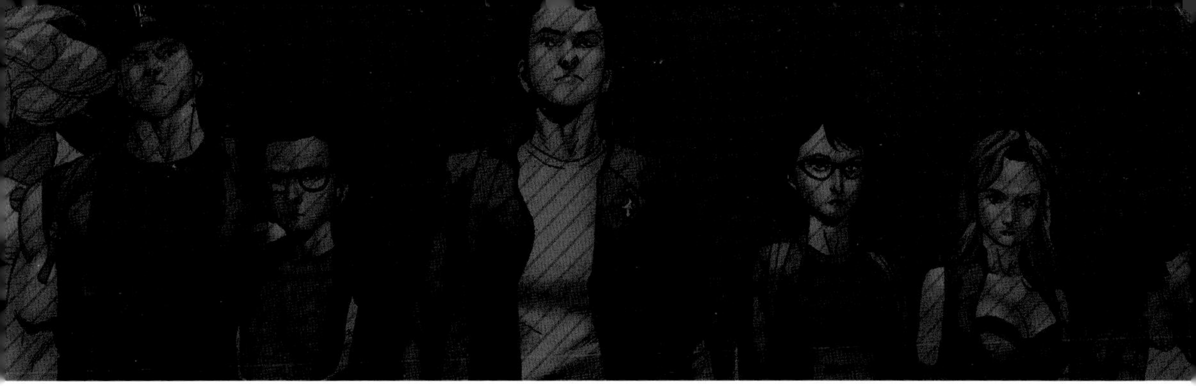

Assistant Editor: Josh Johns
"A Hero's Mission" Editor: Alejandro Arbona
Editor-in-Chief: Warren Simons
Collection Cover Art: Michael Walsh

VALIANT.

Peter Cuneo
Chairman

Dinesh Shamdasani
CEO and Chief Creative Officer

Gavin Cuneo
CFO and Head of Strategic Development

Fred Pierce
Publisher

Warren Simons
VP Editor-in-Chief

Walter Black
VP Operations

Hunter Gorinson
Director of Marketing, Communications
& Digital Media

Atom! Freeman
Sales Manager

Travis Escarfullery
Production and Design Manager

Alejandro Arbona
Associate Editor

Josh Johns
Assistant Editor

Kyle Andrukiewicz
Assistant Editor

Peter Stern
Operations Manager

Robert Meyers
Operations Coordinator

Ivan Cohen
Collection Editor

Steve Blackwell
Collection Designer

Rian Hughes/Device
Trade Dress and Book Design

Russell Brown
President, Consumer Products,
Promotions and Ad Sales

Jason Kothari
Vice Chairman

Harbinger®: Death of a Renegade. Published by Valiant Entertainment, LLC. Office of Publication: 424 West 33rd Street, New York, NY 10001.
Printed in the U.S.A. First Printing. ISBN: 9781939346339.

THE ORIGIN OF HARBINGER

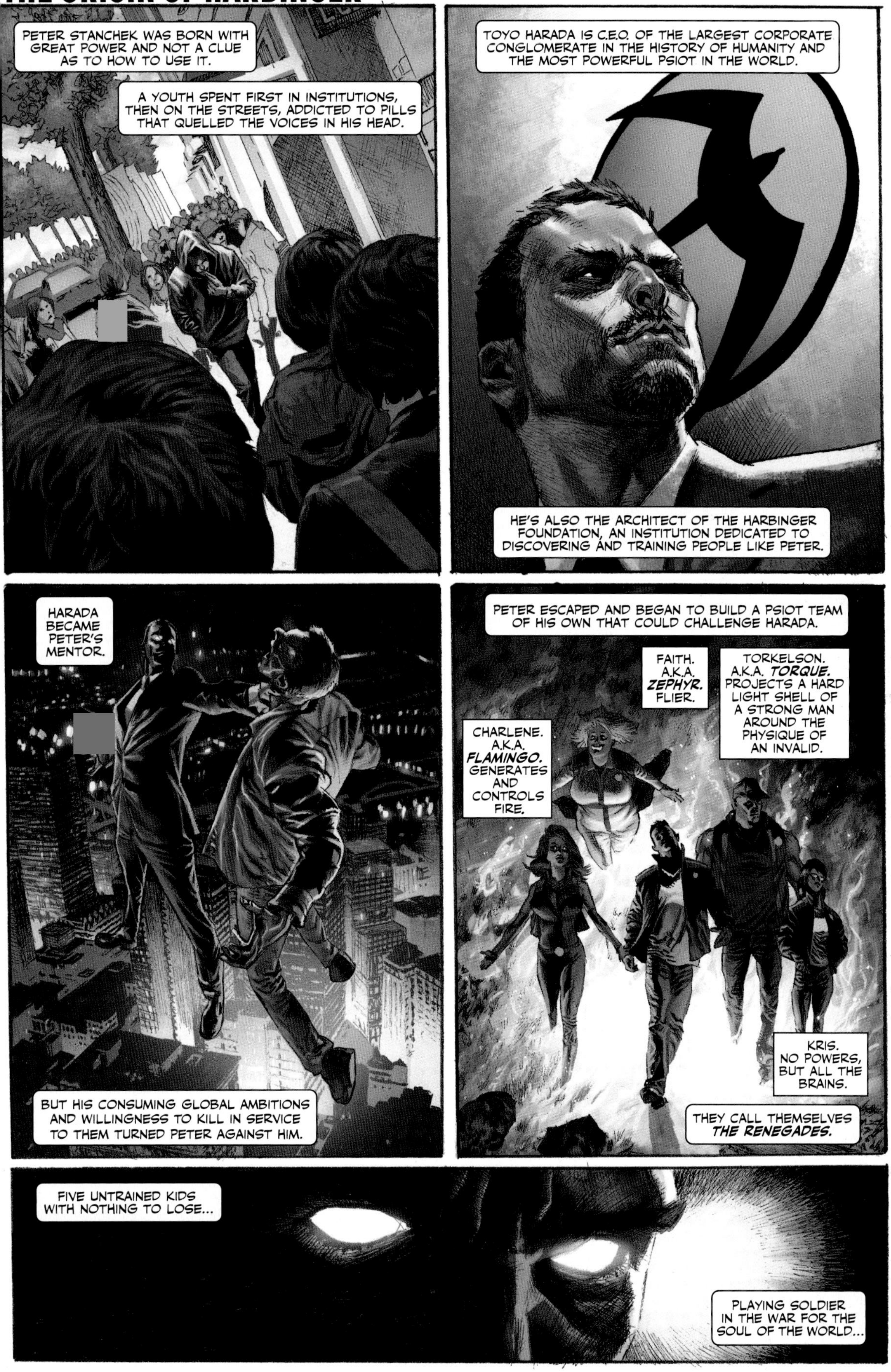

PETER STANCHEK WAS BORN WITH GREAT POWER AND NOT A CLUE AS TO HOW TO USE IT.
A YOUTH SPENT FIRST IN INSTITUTIONS, THEN ON THE STREETS, ADDICTED TO PILLS THAT QUELLED THE VOICES IN HIS HEAD.
TOYO HARADA IS C.E.O. OF THE LARGEST CORPORATE CONGLOMERATE IN THE HISTORY OF HUMANITY AND THE MOST POWERFUL PSIOT IN THE WORLD.
HE'S ALSO THE ARCHITECT OF THE HARBINGER FOUNDATION, AN INSTITUTION DEDICATED TO DISCOVERING AND TRAINING PEOPLE LIKE PETER.
HARADA BECAME PETER'S MENTOR.
BUT HIS CONSUMING GLOBAL AMBITIONS AND WILLINGNESS TO KILL IN SERVICE TO THEM TURNED PETER AGAINST HIM.
PETER ESCAPED AND BEGAN TO BUILD A PSIOT TEAM OF HIS OWN THAT COULD CHALLENGE HARADA.
CHARLENE. A.K.A. *FLAMINGO.* GENERATES AND CONTROLS FIRE.
FAITH. A.K.A. *ZEPHYR.* FLIER.
TORKELSON. A.K.A. *TORQUE.* PROJECTS A HARD LIGHT SHELL OF A STRONG MAN AROUND THE PHYSIQUE OF AN INVALID.
KRIS. NO POWERS, BUT ALL THE BRAINS.
THEY CALL THEMSELVES *THE RENEGADES.*
FIVE UNTRAINED KIDS WITH NOTHING TO LOSE...
PLAYING SOLDIER IN THE WAR FOR THE SOUL OF THE WORLD...

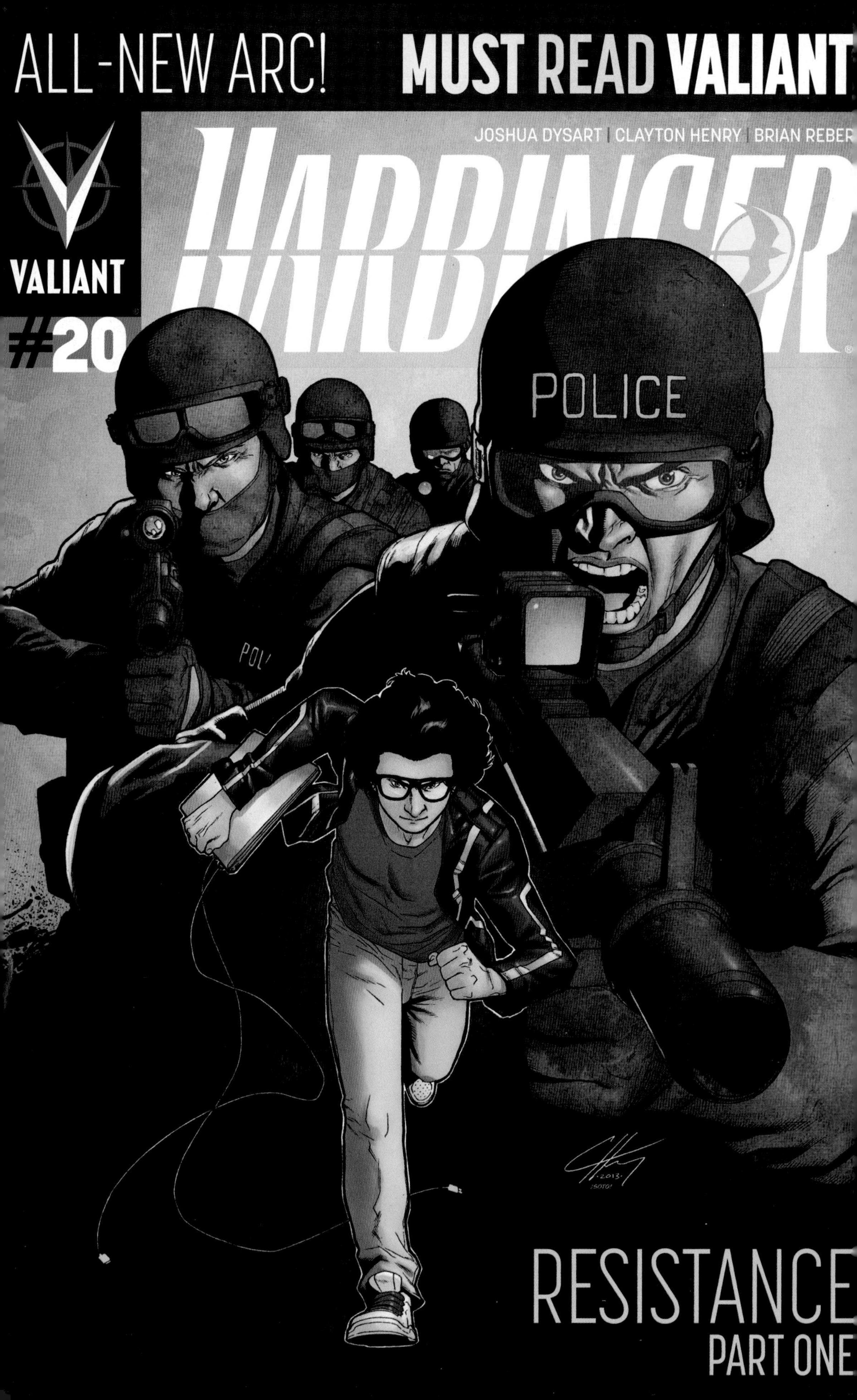
ALL-NEW ARC!
MUST READ VALIANT
VALIANT
#20
JOSHUA DYSART | CLAYTON HENRY | BRIAN REBER
HARBINGER
POLICE
POL
RESISTANCE
PART ONE

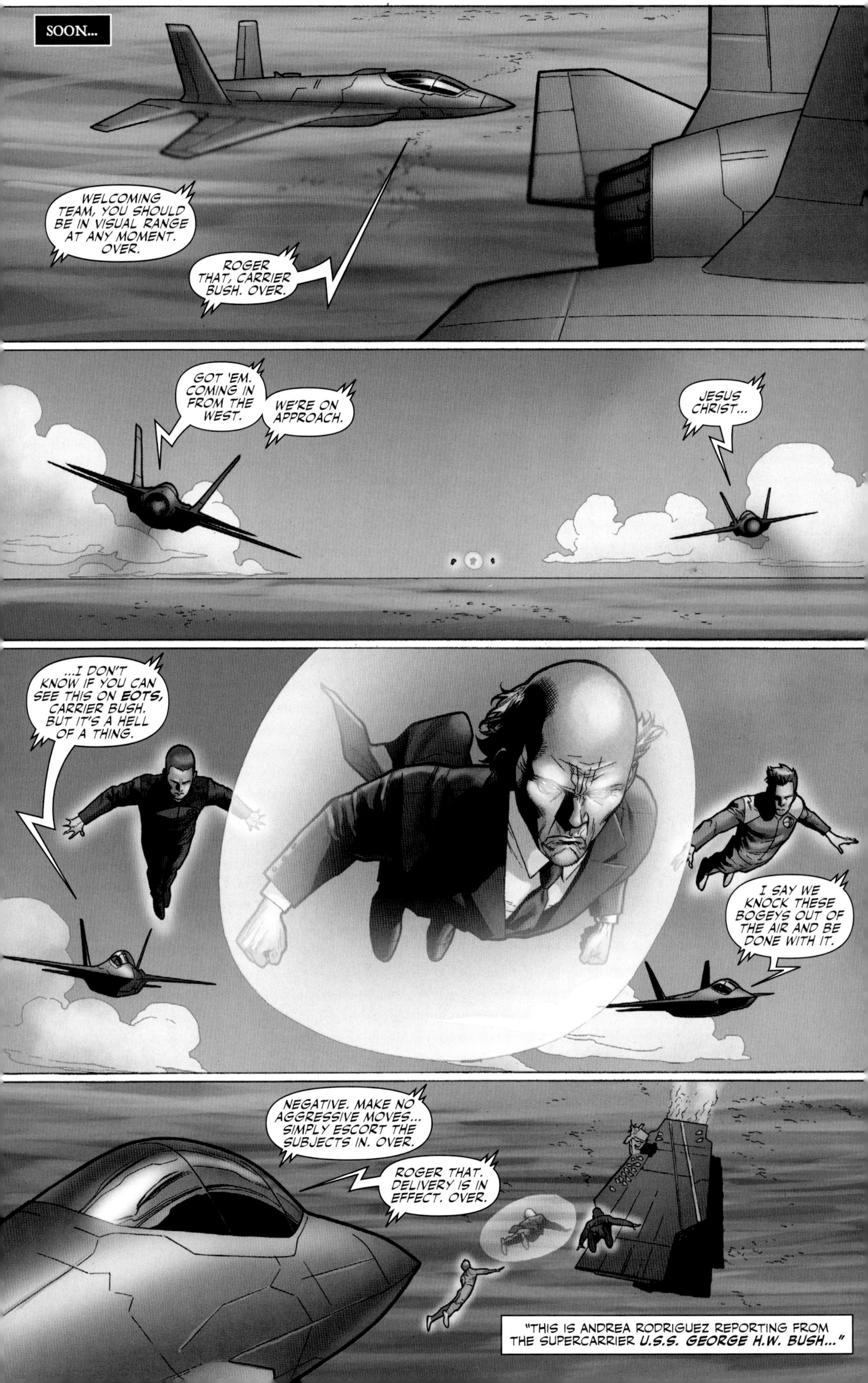
SOON...
WELCOMING TEAM, YOU SHOULD BE IN VISUAL RANGE AT ANY MOMENT. OVER.
ROGER THAT, CARRIER BUSH. OVER.
GOT 'EM. COMING IN FROM THE WEST.
WE'RE ON APPROACH.
JESUS CHRIST...
...I DON'T KNOW IF YOU CAN SEE THIS ON EOTS, CARRIER BUSH. BUT IT'S A HELL OF A THING.
I SAY WE KNOCK THESE BOGEYS OUT OF THE AIR AND BE DONE WITH IT.
NEGATIVE. MAKE NO AGGRESSIVE MOVES... SIMPLY ESCORT THE SUBJECTS IN. OVER.
ROGER THAT. DELIVERY IS IN EFFECT. OVER.
"THIS IS ANDREA RODRIGUEZ REPORTING FROM THE SUPERCARRIER U.S.S. GEORGE H.W. BUSH..."

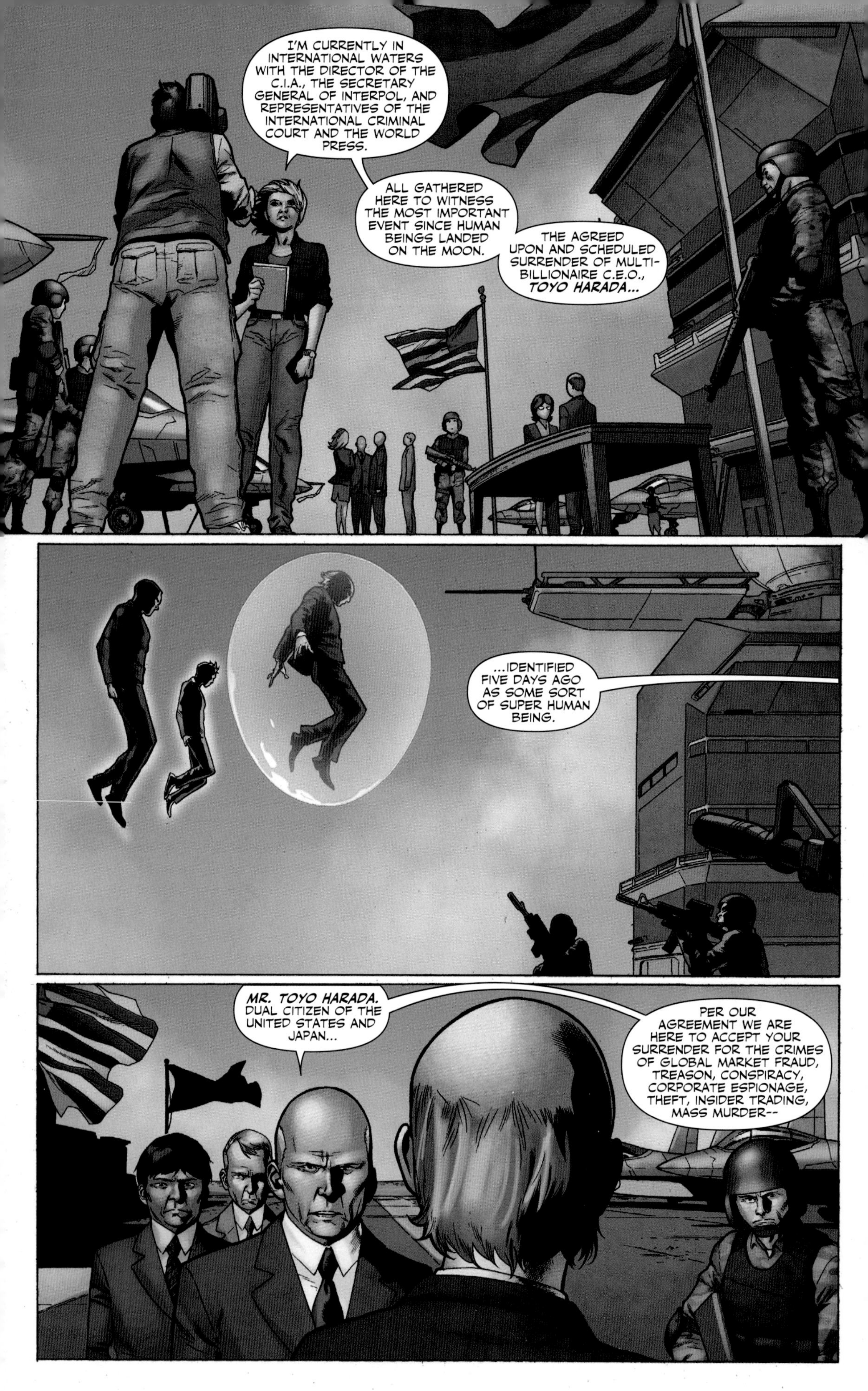
I'M CURRENTLY IN INTERNATIONAL WATERS WITH THE DIRECTOR OF THE C.I.A., THE SECRETARY GENERAL OF INTERPOL, AND REPRESENTATIVES OF THE INTERNATIONAL CRIMINAL COURT AND THE WORLD PRESS.
ALL GATHERED HERE TO WITNESS THE MOST IMPORTANT EVENT SINCE HUMAN BEINGS LANDED ON THE MOON.
THE AGREED UPON AND SCHEDULED SURRENDER OF MULTI-BILLIONAIRE C.E.O., *TOYO HARADA*...
...IDENTIFIED FIVE DAYS AGO AS SOME SORT OF SUPER HUMAN BEING.
MR. TOYO HARADA. DUAL CITIZEN OF THE UNITED STATES AND JAPAN...
PER OUR AGREEMENT WE ARE HERE TO ACCEPT YOUR SURRENDER FOR THE CRIMES OF GLOBAL MARKET FRAUD, TREASON, CONSPIRACY, CORPORATE ESPIONAGE, THEFT, INSIDER TRADING, MASS MURDER--

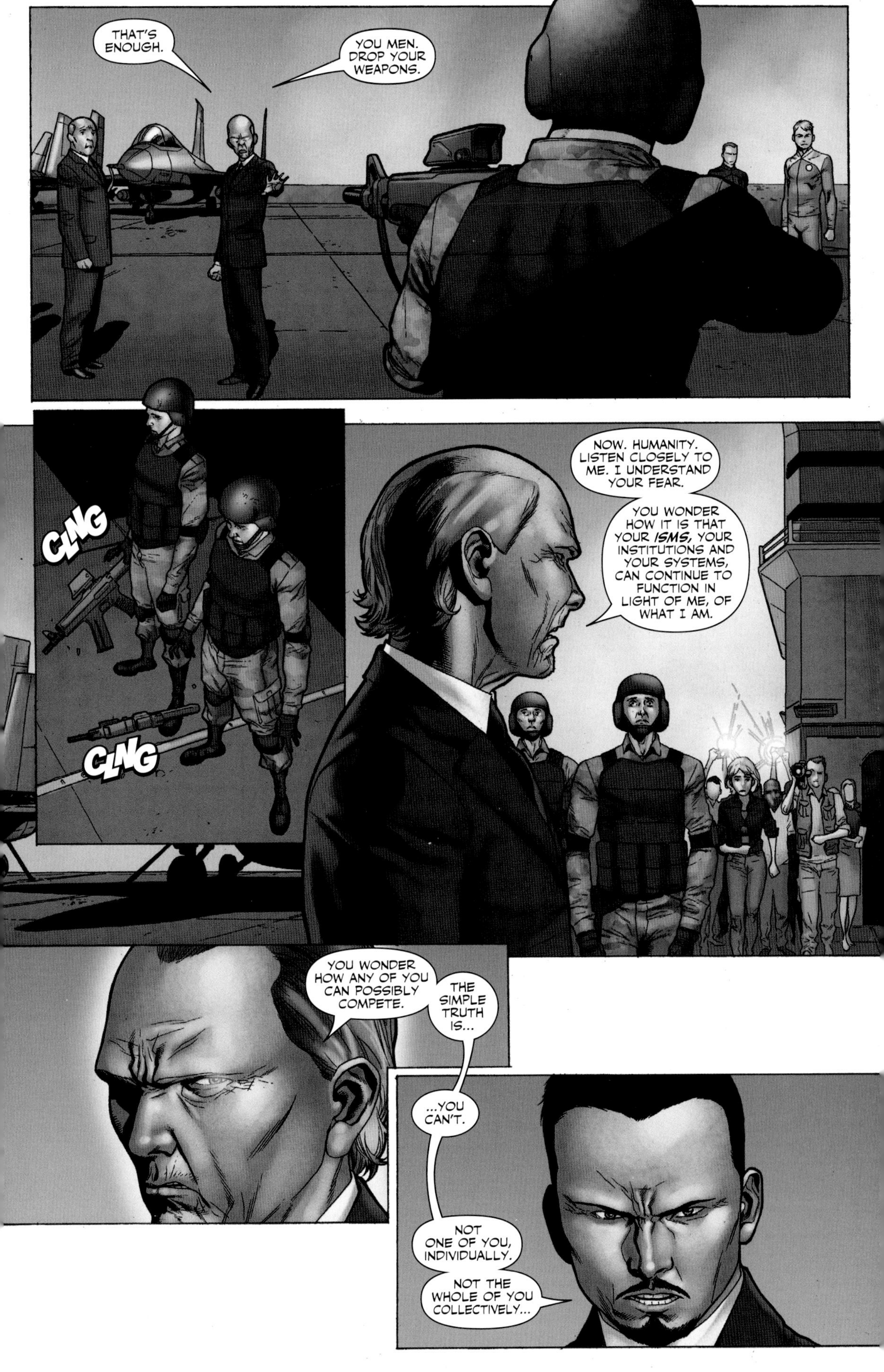
THAT'S ENOUGH.
YOU MEN. DROP YOUR WEAPONS.
CLNG
CLNG
NOW. HUMANITY. LISTEN CLOSELY TO ME. I UNDERSTAND YOUR FEAR.
YOU WONDER HOW IT IS THAT YOUR ISMS, YOUR INSTITUTIONS AND YOUR SYSTEMS, CAN CONTINUE TO FUNCTION IN LIGHT OF ME, OF WHAT I AM.
YOU WONDER HOW ANY OF YOU CAN POSSIBLY COMPETE.
THE SIMPLE TRUTH IS...
...YOU CAN'T.
NOT ONE OF YOU, INDIVIDUALLY.
NOT THE WHOLE OF YOU COLLECTIVELY...

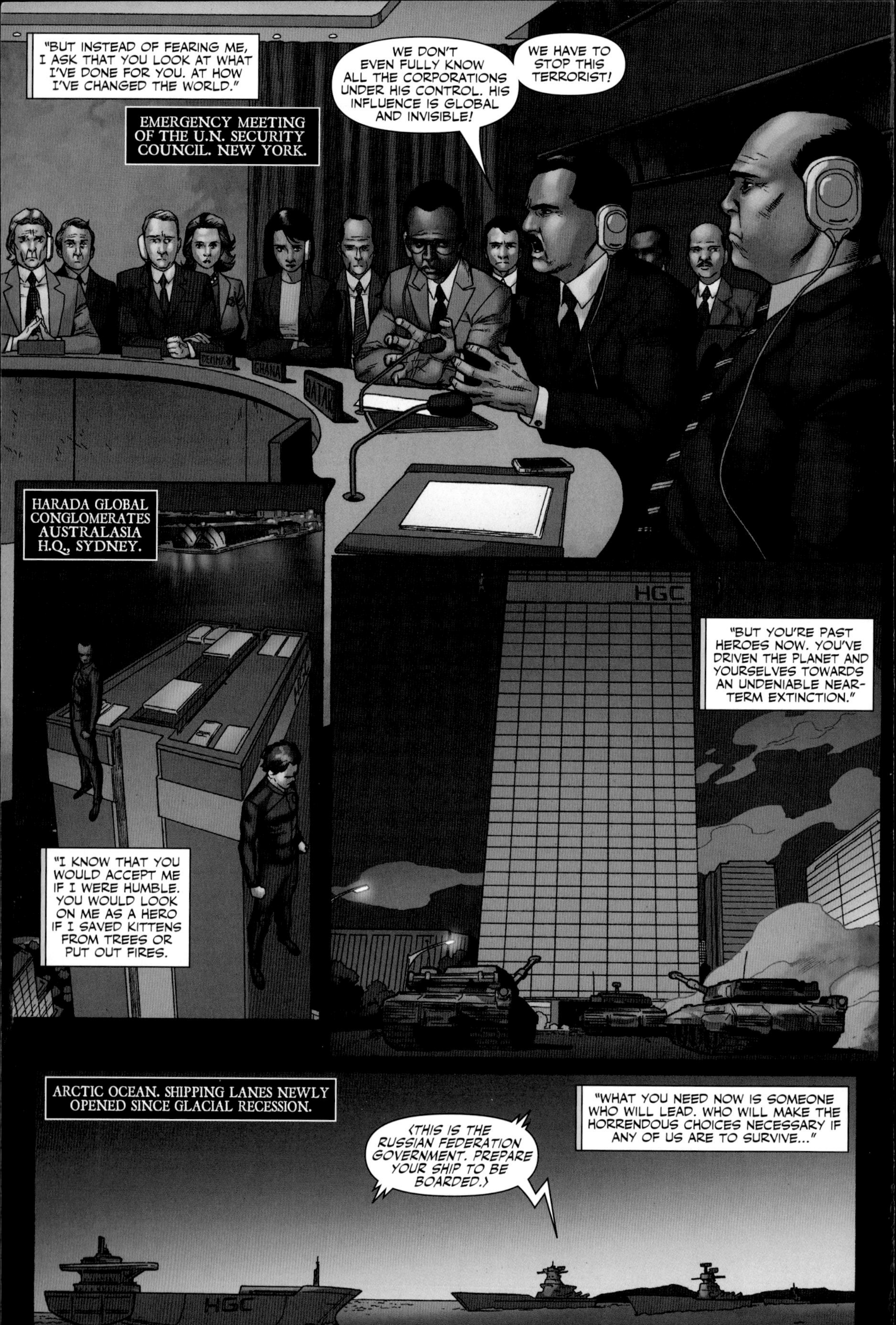
"BUT INSTEAD OF FEARING ME, I ASK THAT YOU LOOK AT WHAT I'VE DONE FOR YOU. AT HOW I'VE CHANGED THE WORLD."
EMERGENCY MEETING OF THE U.N. SECURITY COUNCIL. NEW YORK.
WE DON'T EVEN FULLY KNOW ALL THE CORPORATIONS UNDER HIS CONTROL. HIS INFLUENCE IS GLOBAL AND INVISIBLE!
WE HAVE TO STOP THIS TERRORIST!
GHANA
QATAR
HARADA GLOBAL CONGLOMERATES AUSTRALASIA H.Q., SYDNEY.
"I KNOW THAT YOU WOULD ACCEPT ME IF I WERE HUMBLE. YOU WOULD LOOK ON ME AS A HERO IF I SAVED KITTENS FROM TREES OR PUT OUT FIRES.
HGC
"BUT YOU'RE PAST HEROES NOW. YOU'VE DRIVEN THE PLANET AND YOURSELVES TOWARDS AN UNDENIABLE NEAR-TERM EXTINCTION."
ARCTIC OCEAN. SHIPPING LANES NEWLY OPENED SINCE GLACIAL RECESSION.
‹THIS IS THE RUSSIAN FEDERATION GOVERNMENT. PREPARE YOUR SHIP TO BE BOARDED.›
"WHAT YOU NEED NOW IS SOMEONE WHO WILL LEAD. WHO WILL MAKE THE HORRENDOUS CHOICES NECESSARY IF ANY OF US ARE TO SURVIVE..."
HGC

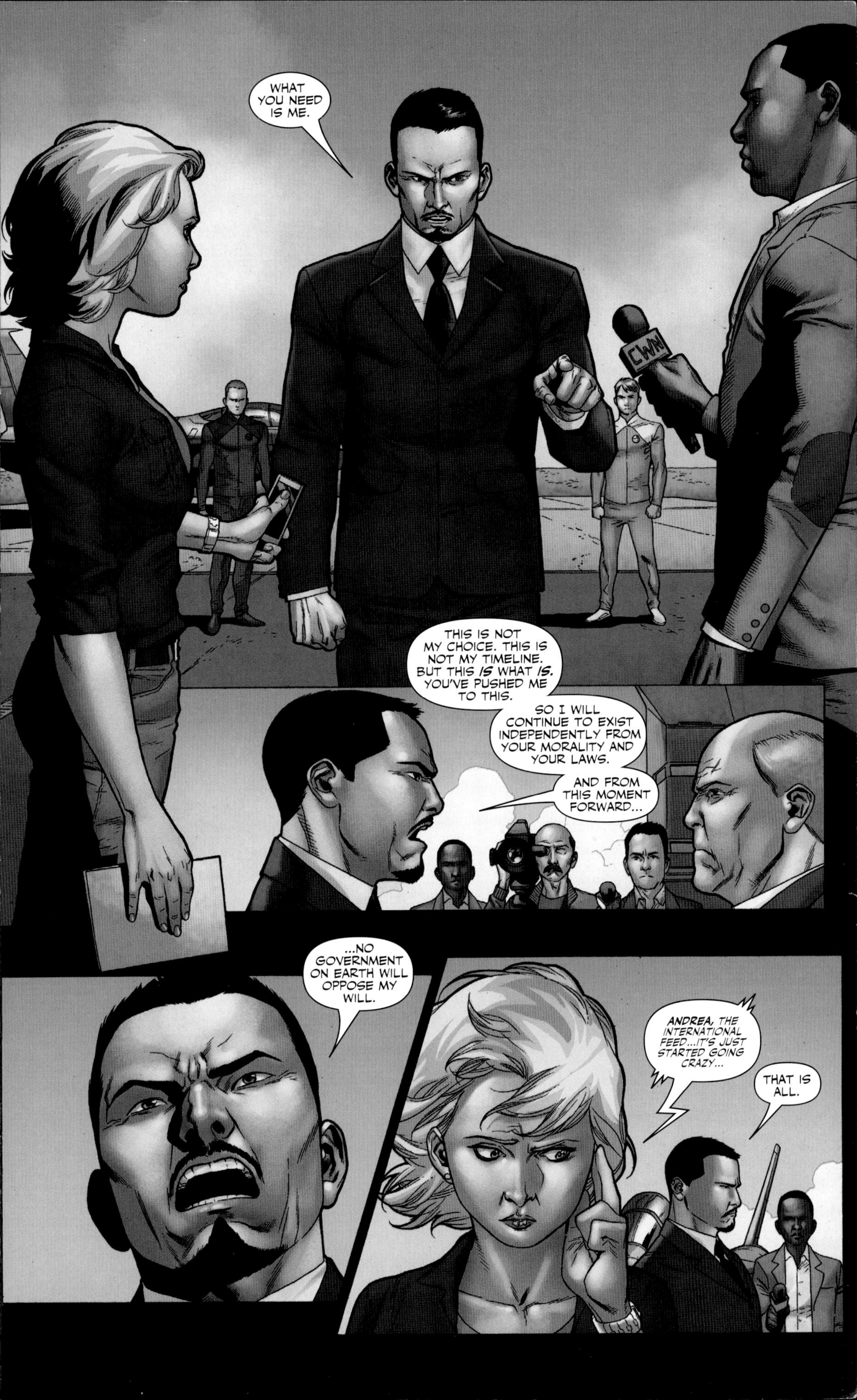
WHAT YOU NEED IS ME.
THIS IS NOT MY CHOICE. THIS IS NOT MY TIMELINE. BUT THIS *IS* WHAT *IS.* YOU'VE PUSHED ME TO THIS.
SO I WILL CONTINUE TO EXIST INDEPENDENTLY FROM YOUR MORALITY AND YOUR LAWS.
AND FROM THIS MOMENT FORWARD...
...NO GOVERNMENT ON EARTH WILL OPPOSE MY WILL.
ANDREA, THE INTERNATIONAL FEED...IT'S JUST STARTED GOING CRAZY...
THAT IS ALL.

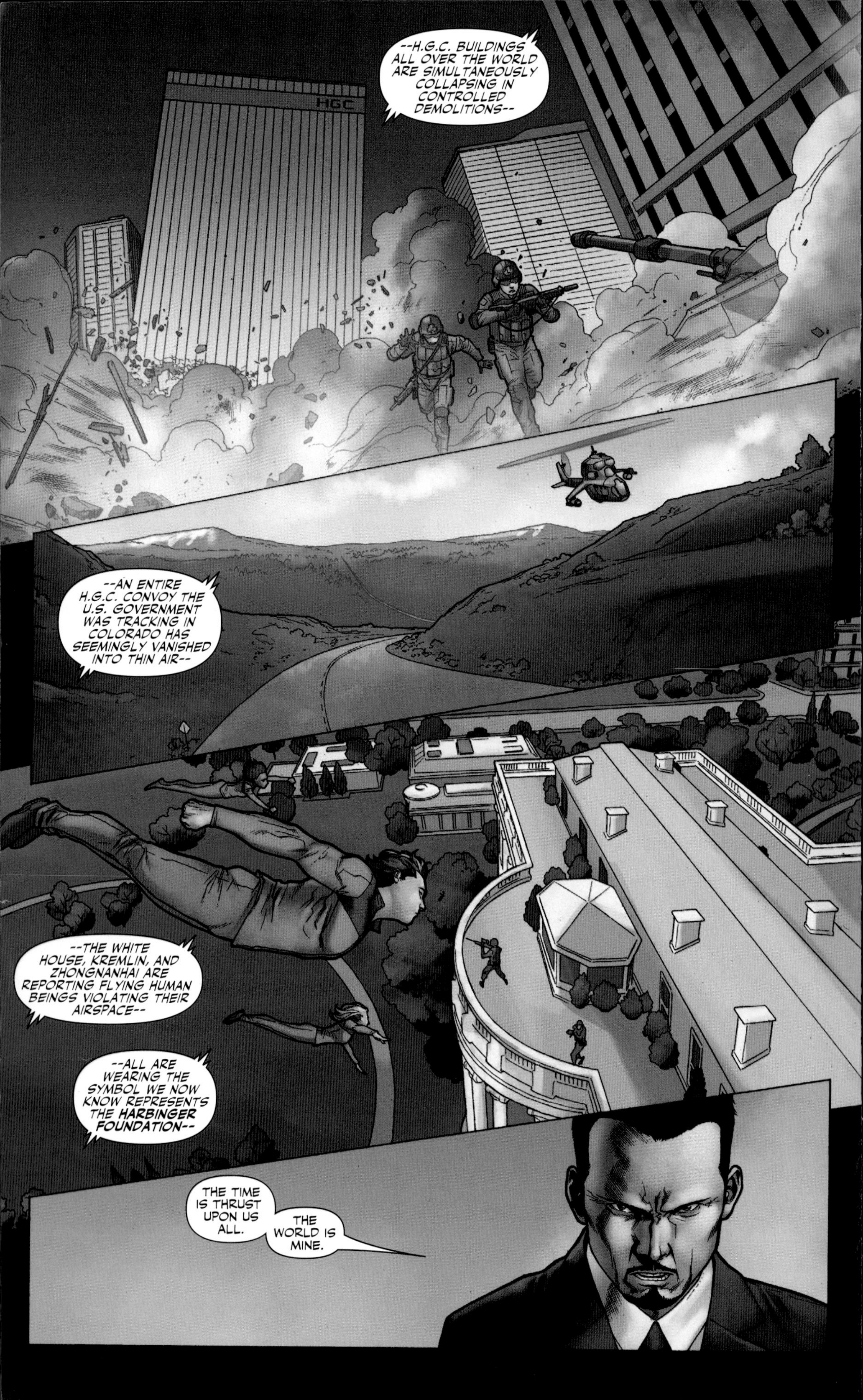
--H.G.C. BUILDINGS ALL OVER THE WORLD ARE SIMULTANEOUSLY COLLAPSING IN CONTROLLED DEMOLITIONS--
HGC
--AN ENTIRE H.G.C. CONVOY THE U.S. GOVERNMENT WAS TRACKING IN COLORADO HAS SEEMINGLY VANISHED INTO THIN AIR--
--THE WHITE HOUSE, KREMLIN, AND ZHONGNANHAI ARE REPORTING FLYING HUMAN BEINGS VIOLATING THEIR AIRSPACE--
--ALL ARE WEARING THE SYMBOL WE NOW KNOW REPRESENTS THE **HARBINGER FOUNDATION**--
THE TIME IS THRUST UPON US ALL.
THE WORLD IS MINE.

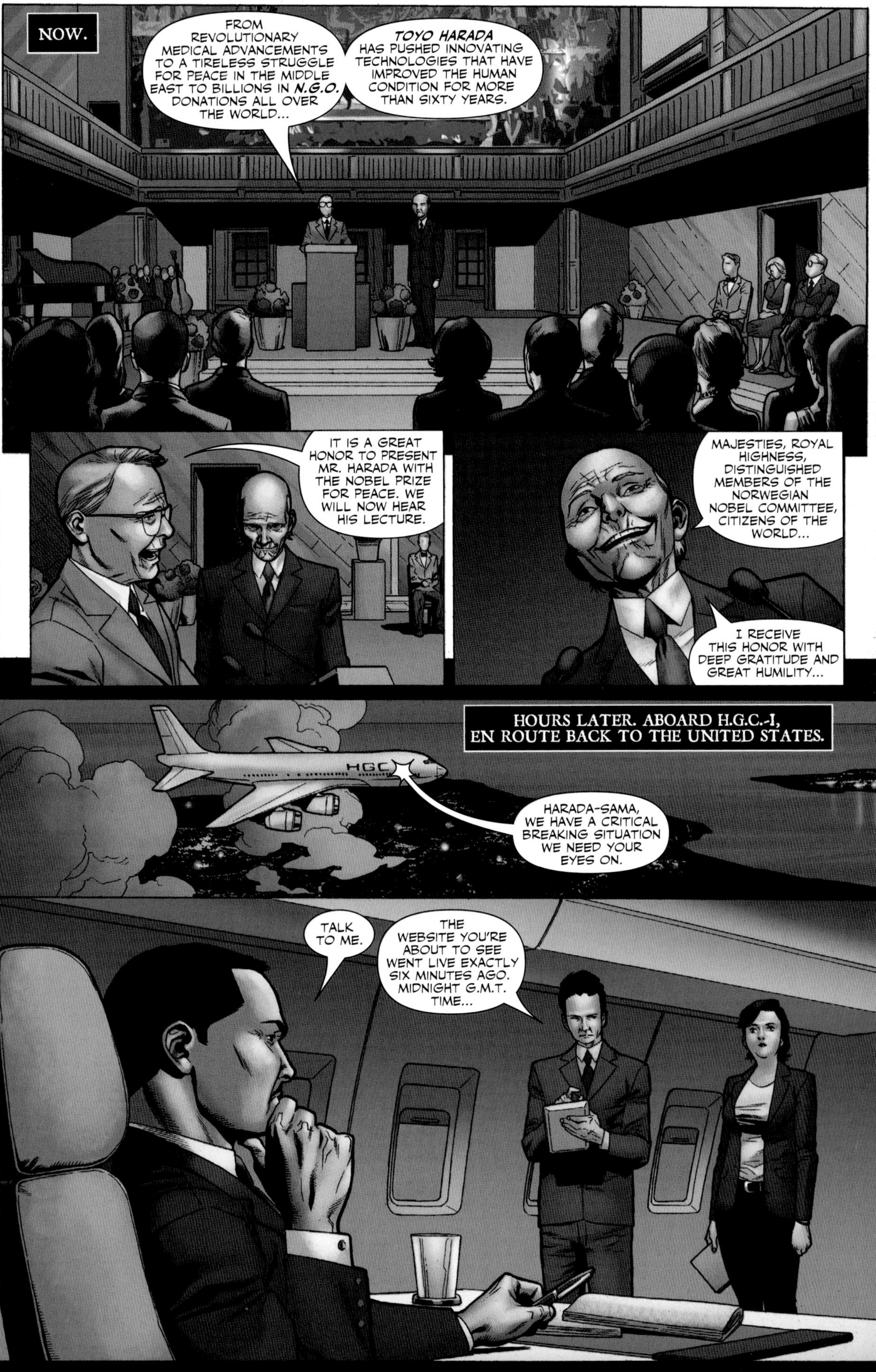
NOW.
FROM REVOLUTIONARY MEDICAL ADVANCEMENTS TO A TIRELESS STRUGGLE FOR PEACE IN THE MIDDLE EAST TO BILLIONS IN N.G.O. DONATIONS ALL OVER THE WORLD...
TOYO HARADA HAS PUSHED INNOVATING TECHNOLOGIES THAT HAVE IMPROVED THE HUMAN CONDITION FOR MORE THAN SIXTY YEARS.
IT IS A GREAT HONOR TO PRESENT MR. HARADA WITH THE NOBEL PRIZE FOR PEACE. WE WILL NOW HEAR HIS LECTURE.
MAJESTIES, ROYAL HIGHNESS, DISTINGUISHED MEMBERS OF THE NORWEGIAN NOBEL COMMITTEE, CITIZENS OF THE WORLD...
I RECEIVE THIS HONOR WITH DEEP GRATITUDE AND GREAT HUMILITY...
HOURS LATER. ABOARD H.G.C.-I, EN ROUTE BACK TO THE UNITED STATES.
HGC
HARADA-SAMA, WE HAVE A CRITICAL BREAKING SITUATION WE NEED YOUR EYES ON.
TALK TO ME.
THE WEBSITE YOU'RE ABOUT TO SEE WENT LIVE EXACTLY SIX MINUTES AGO. MIDNIGHT G.M.T. TIME...

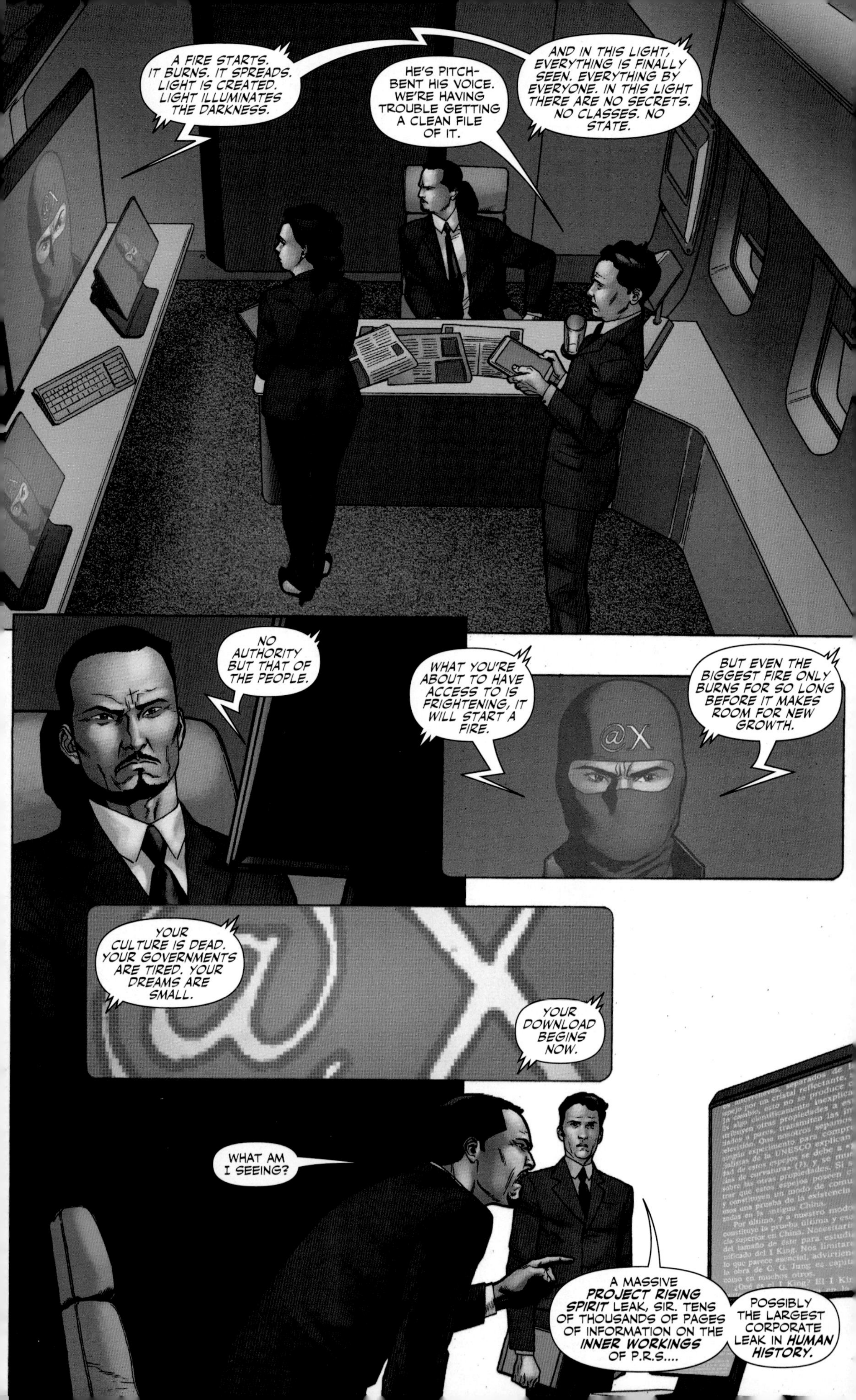
A FIRE STARTS. IT BURNS. IT SPREADS. LIGHT IS CREATED. LIGHT ILLUMINATES THE DARKNESS.
HE'S PITCH-BENT HIS VOICE. WE'RE HAVING TROUBLE GETTING A CLEAN FILE OF IT.
AND IN THIS LIGHT, EVERYTHING IS FINALLY SEEN. EVERYTHING BY EVERYONE. IN THIS LIGHT THERE ARE NO SECRETS. NO CLASSES. NO STATE.
NO AUTHORITY BUT THAT OF THE PEOPLE.
WHAT YOU'RE ABOUT TO HAVE ACCESS TO IS FRIGHTENING, IT WILL START A FIRE.
BUT EVEN THE BIGGEST FIRE ONLY BURNS FOR SO LONG BEFORE IT MAKES ROOM FOR NEW GROWTH.
@X
YOUR CULTURE IS DEAD. YOUR GOVERNMENTS ARE TIRED. YOUR DREAMS ARE SMALL.
YOUR DOWNLOAD BEGINS NOW.
WHAT AM I SEEING?
A MASSIVE PROJECT RISING SPIRIT LEAK, SIR. TENS OF THOUSANDS OF PAGES OF INFORMATION ON THE INNER WORKINGS OF P.R.S....
POSSIBLY THE LARGEST CORPORATE LEAK IN HUMAN HISTORY.

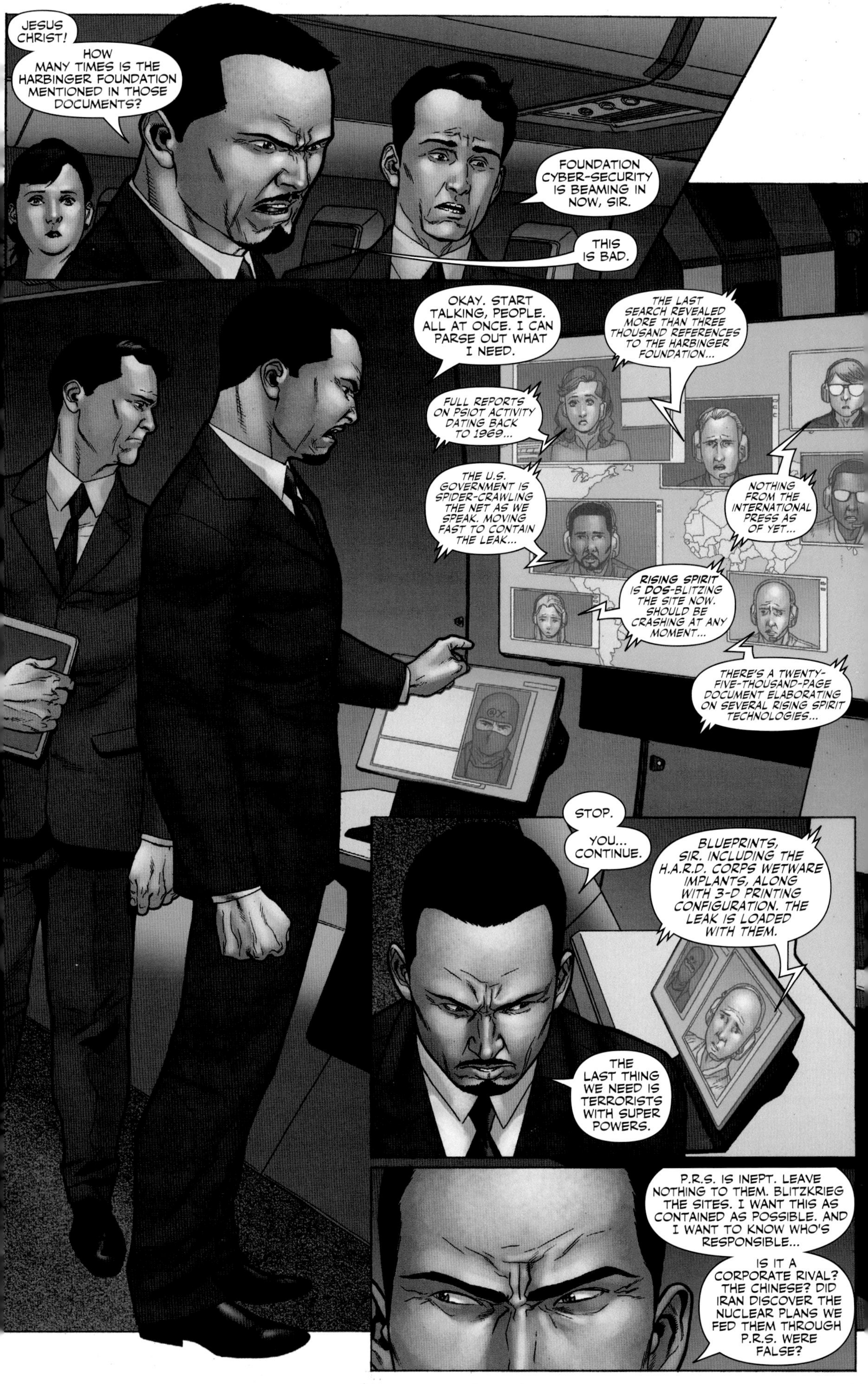
JESUS CHRIST!
HOW MANY TIMES IS THE HARBINGER FOUNDATION MENTIONED IN THOSE DOCUMENTS?
FOUNDATION CYBER-SECURITY IS BEAMING IN NOW, SIR.
THIS IS BAD.
OKAY. START TALKING, PEOPLE. ALL AT ONCE. I CAN PARSE OUT WHAT I NEED.
THE LAST SEARCH REVEALED MORE THAN THREE THOUSAND REFERENCES TO THE HARBINGER FOUNDATION...
FULL REPORTS ON PSIOT ACTIVITY DATING BACK TO 1969...
THE U.S. GOVERNMENT IS SPIDER-CRAWLING THE NET AS WE SPEAK. MOVING FAST TO CONTAIN THE LEAK...
NOTHING FROM THE INTERNATIONAL PRESS AS OF YET...
RISING SPIRIT IS DOS-BLITZING THE SITE NOW. SHOULD BE CRASHING AT ANY MOMENT...
THERE'S A TWENTY-FIVE-THOUSAND-PAGE DOCUMENT ELABORATING ON SEVERAL RISING SPIRIT TECHNOLOGIES...
STOP.
YOU... CONTINUE.
BLUEPRINTS, SIR. INCLUDING THE H.A.R.D. CORPS WETWARE IMPLANTS, ALONG WITH 3-D PRINTING CONFIGURATION. THE LEAK IS LOADED WITH THEM.
THE LAST THING WE NEED IS TERRORISTS WITH SUPER POWERS.
P.R.S. IS INEPT. LEAVE NOTHING TO THEM. BLITZKRIEG THE SITES. I WANT THIS AS CONTAINED AS POSSIBLE. AND I WANT TO KNOW WHO'S RESPONSIBLE...
IS IT A CORPORATE RIVAL? THE CHINESE? DID IRAN DISCOVER THE NUCLEAR PLANS WE FED THEM THROUGH P.R.S. WERE FALSE?

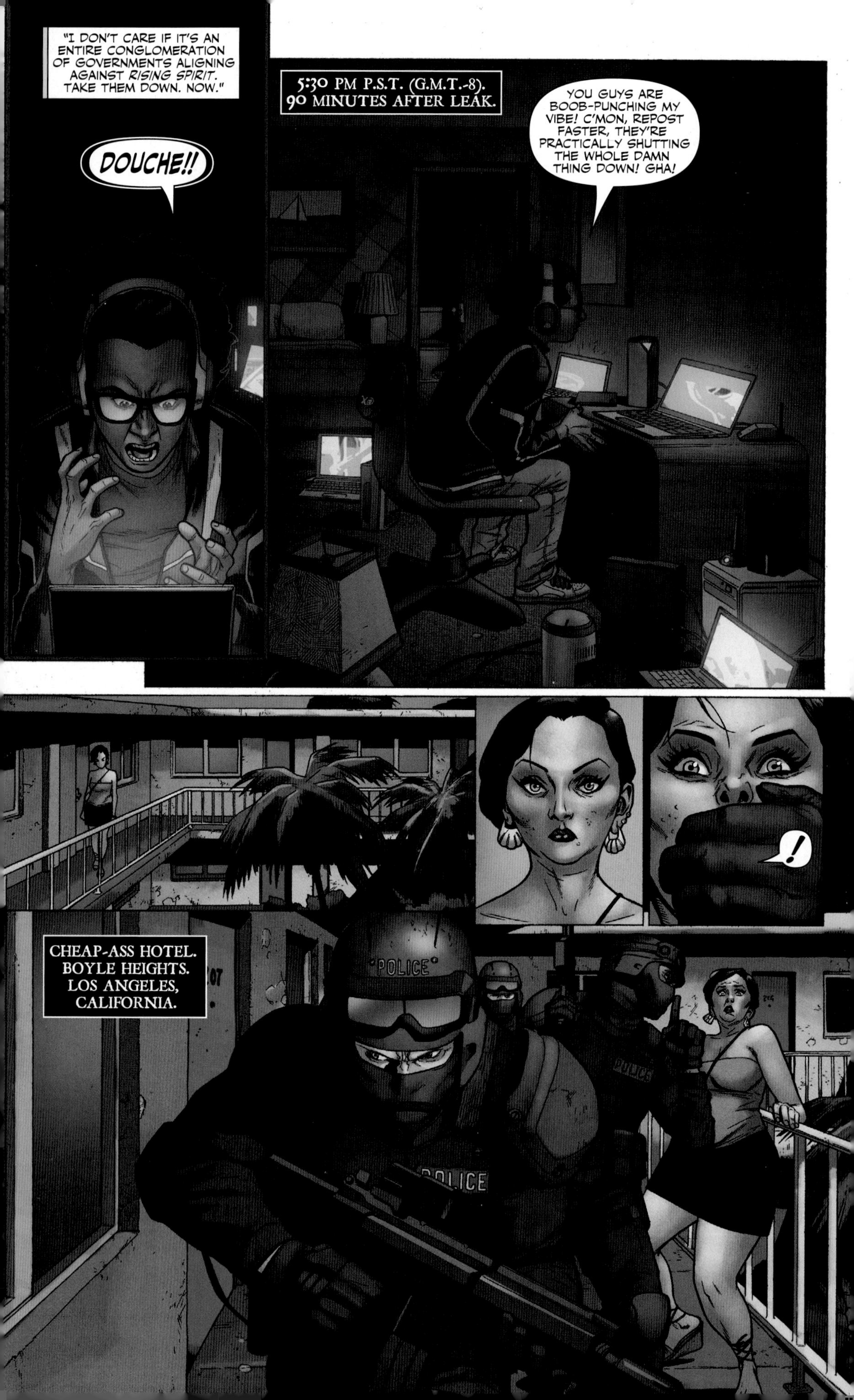
"I DON'T CARE IF IT'S AN ENTIRE CONGLOMERATION OF GOVERNMENTS ALIGNING AGAINST *RISING SPIRIT*. TAKE THEM DOWN. NOW."
DOUCHE!!
5:30 PM P.S.T. (G.M.T.-8). 90 MINUTES AFTER LEAK.
YOU GUYS ARE BOOB-PUNCHING MY VIBE! C'MON, REPOST FASTER, THEY'RE PRACTICALLY SHUTTING THE WHOLE DAMN THING DOWN! GHA!
!
CHEAP-ASS HOTEL. BOYLE HEIGHTS. LOS ANGELES, CALIFORNIA.
POLICE
POLICE

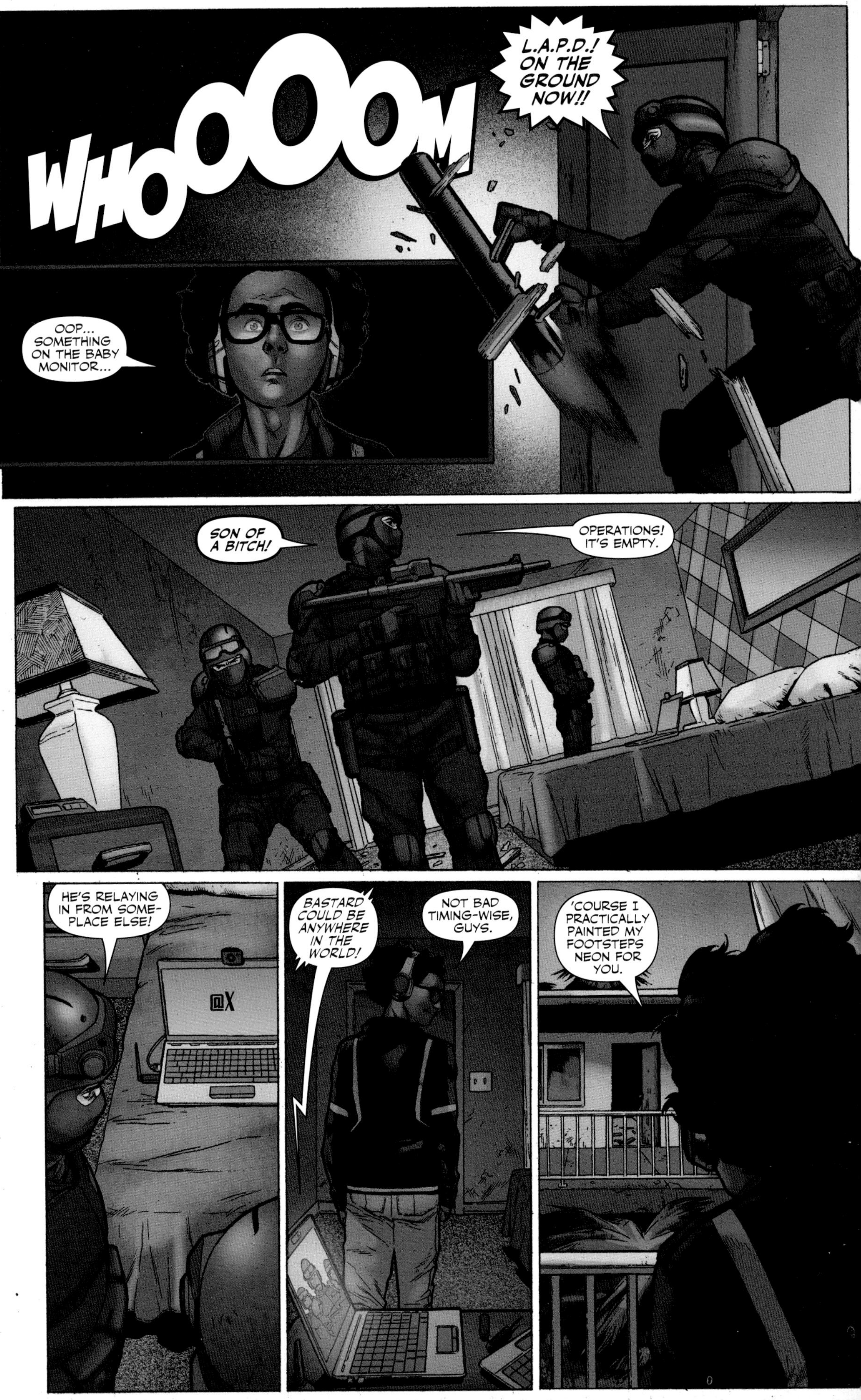
WHOOOOOM
L.A.P.D.! ON THE GROUND NOW!!
OOP... SOMETHING ON THE BABY MONITOR...
SON OF A BITCH!
OPERATIONS! IT'S EMPTY.
HE'S RELAYING IN FROM SOME-PLACE ELSE!
@X
BASTARD COULD BE ANYWHERE IN THE WORLD!
NOT BAD TIMING-WISE, GUYS.
'COURSE I PRACTICALLY PAINTED MY FOOTSTEPS NEON FOR YOU.

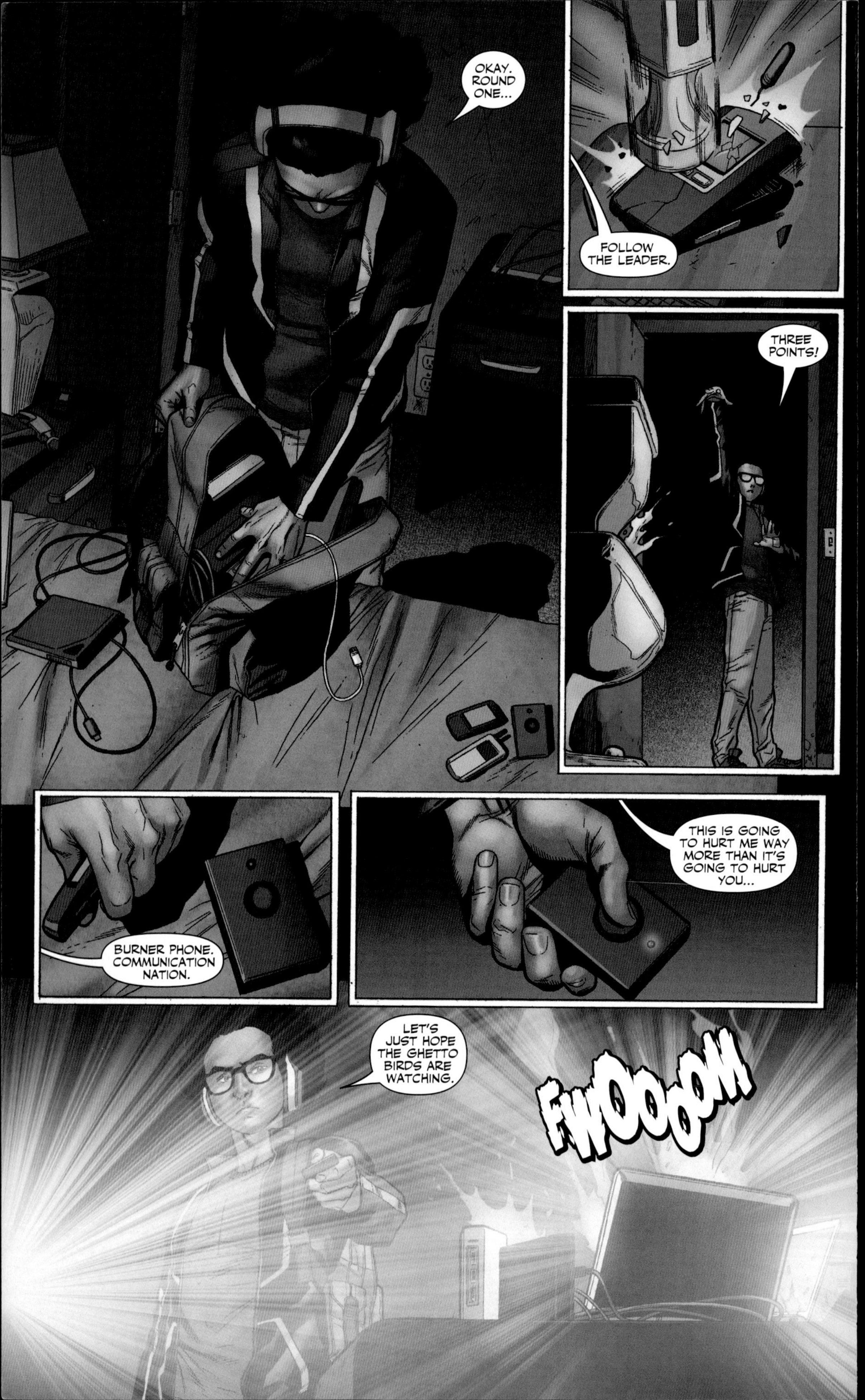
OKAY. ROUND ONE...
FOLLOW THE LEADER.
THREE POINTS!
BURNER PHONE. COMMUNICATION NATION.
THIS IS GOING TO HURT ME WAY MORE THAN IT'S GOING TO HURT YOU...
LET'S JUST HOPE THE GHETTO BIRDS ARE WATCHING.
FWOOOOOM

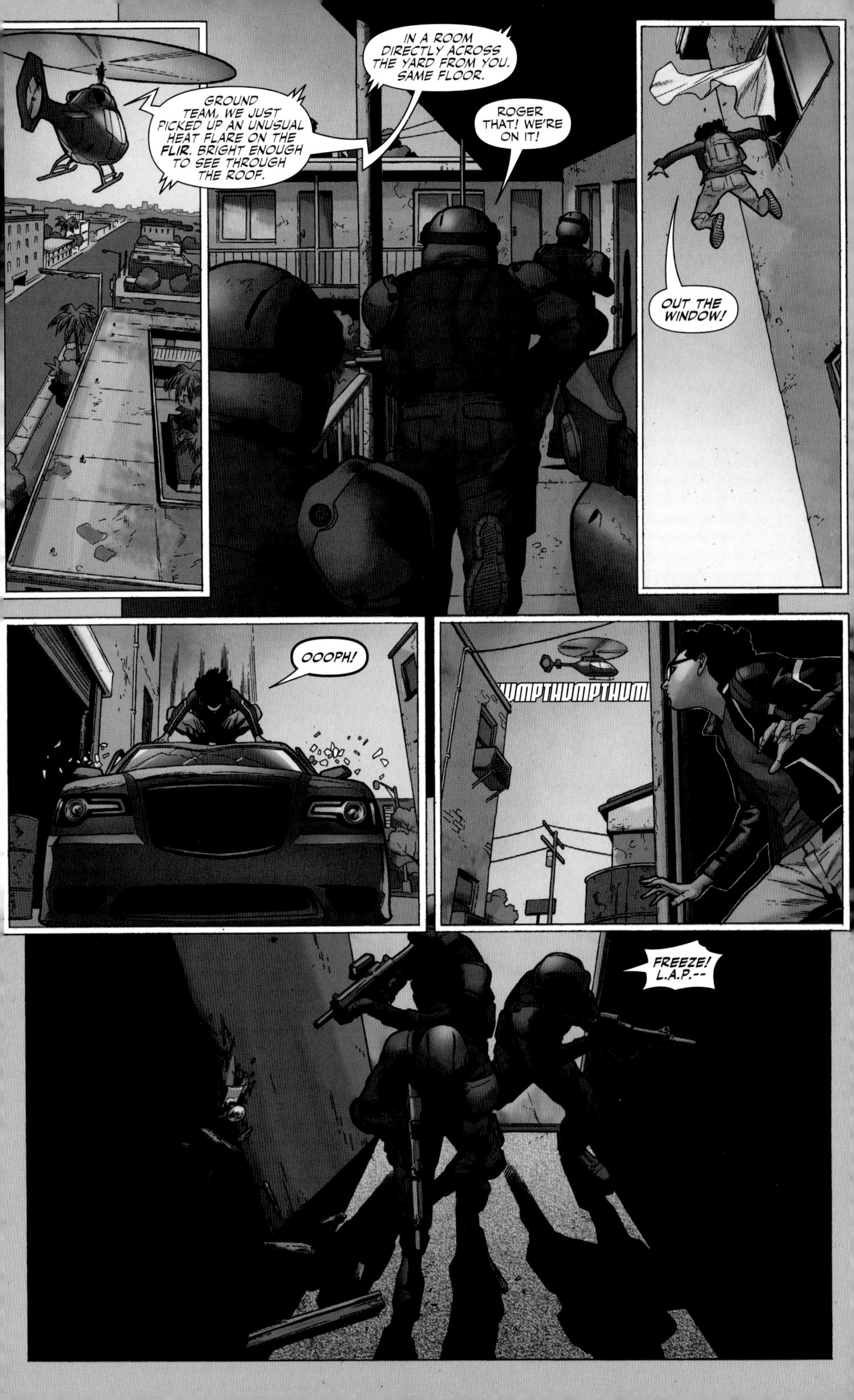
GROUND TEAM, WE JUST PICKED UP AN UNUSUAL HEAT FLARE ON THE FLIR. BRIGHT ENOUGH TO SEE THROUGH THE ROOF.
IN A ROOM DIRECTLY ACROSS THE YARD FROM YOU. SAME FLOOR.
ROGER THAT! WE'RE ON IT!
OUT THE WINDOW!
OOOPH!
HUMPTHUMPTHUM
FREEZE! L.A.P.--

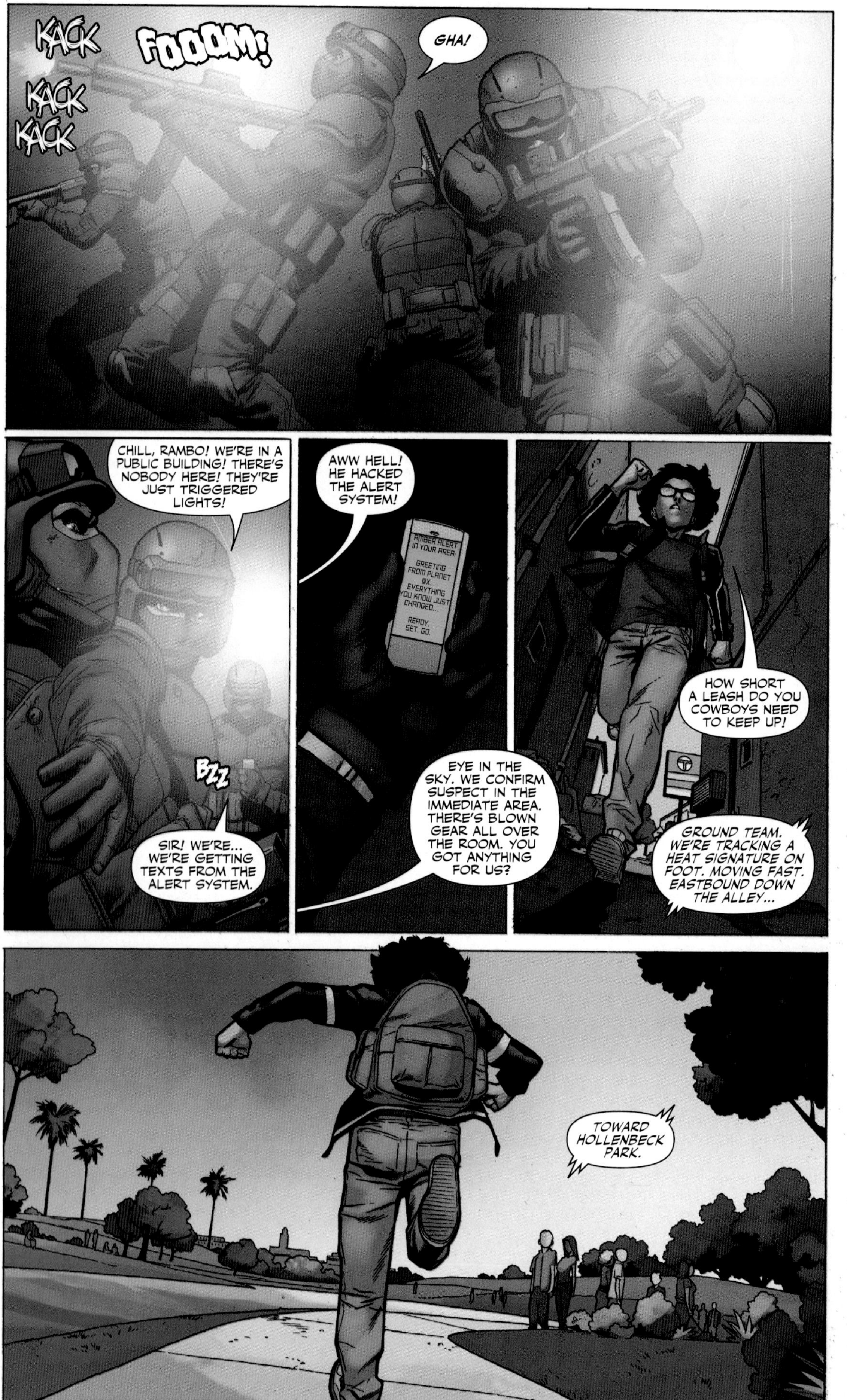
KACK
FOOOM!
KACK
KACK
GHA!
CHILL, RAMBO! WE'RE IN A PUBLIC BUILDING! THERE'S NOBODY HERE! THEY'RE JUST TRIGGERED LIGHTS!
BZZ
SIR! WE'RE... WE'RE GETTING TEXTS FROM THE ALERT SYSTEM.
AWW HELL! HE HACKED THE ALERT SYSTEM!
AMBER ALERT IN YOUR AREA.
GREETING FROM PLANET ØX.
EVERYTHING YOU KNOW JUST CHANGED...
READY. SET. GO.
EYE IN THE SKY. WE CONFIRM SUSPECT IN THE IMMEDIATE AREA. THERE'S BLOWN GEAR ALL OVER THE ROOM. YOU GOT ANYTHING FOR US?
HOW SHORT A LEASH DO YOU COWBOYS NEED TO KEEP UP!
GROUND TEAM. WE'RE TRACKING A HEAT SIGNATURE ON FOOT. MOVING FAST. EASTBOUND DOWN THE ALLEY...
TOWARD HOLLENBECK PARK.

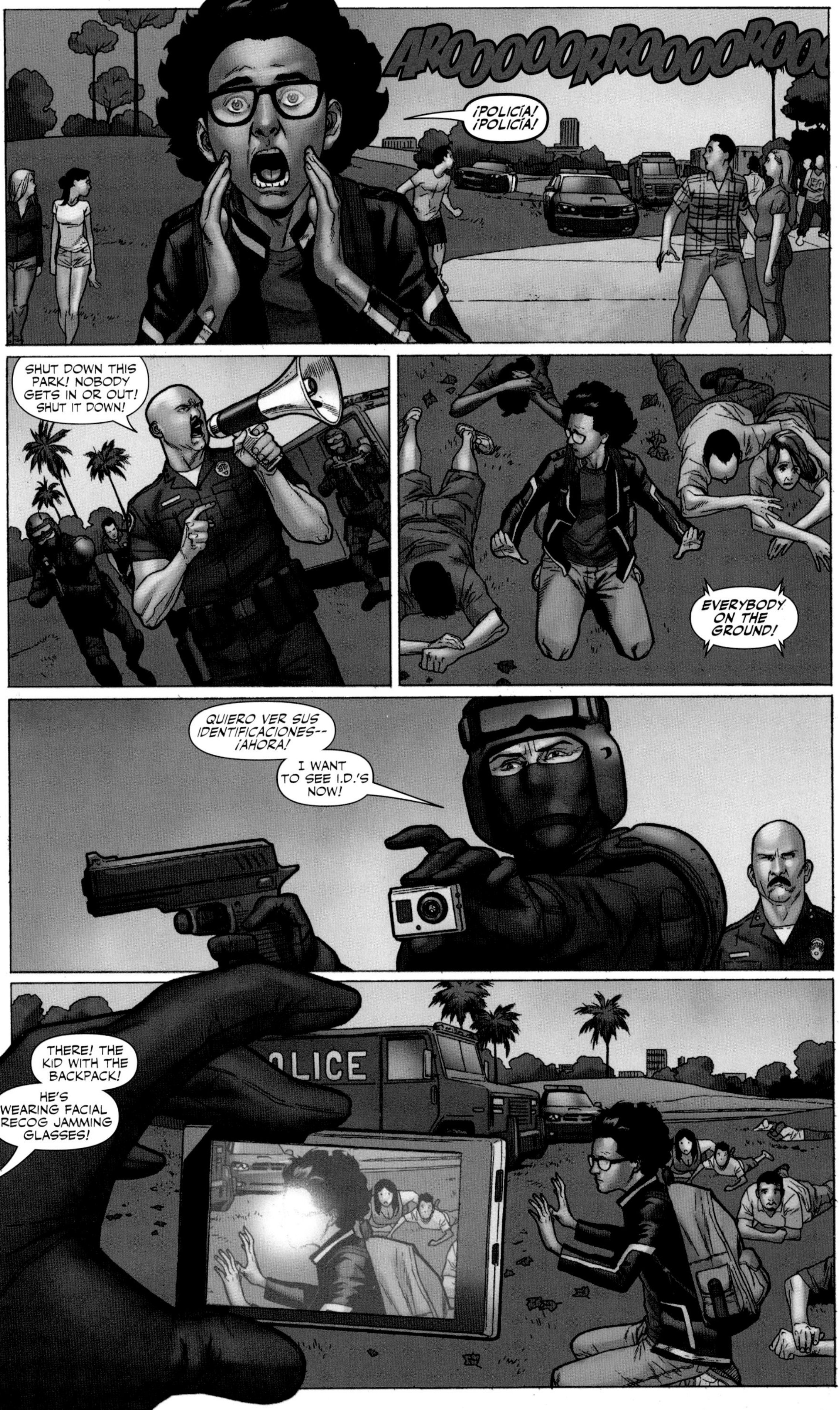
AROOOOORROOOOOROO
¡POLICÍA! ¡POLICÍA!
SHUT DOWN THIS PARK! NOBODY GETS IN OR OUT! SHUT IT DOWN!
EVERYBODY ON THE GROUND!
QUIERO VER SUS IDENTIFICACIONES-- ¡AHORA!
I WANT TO SEE I.D.'S NOW!
POLICE
THERE! THE KID WITH THE BACKPACK!
HE'S WEARING FACIAL RECOG JAMMING GLASSES!

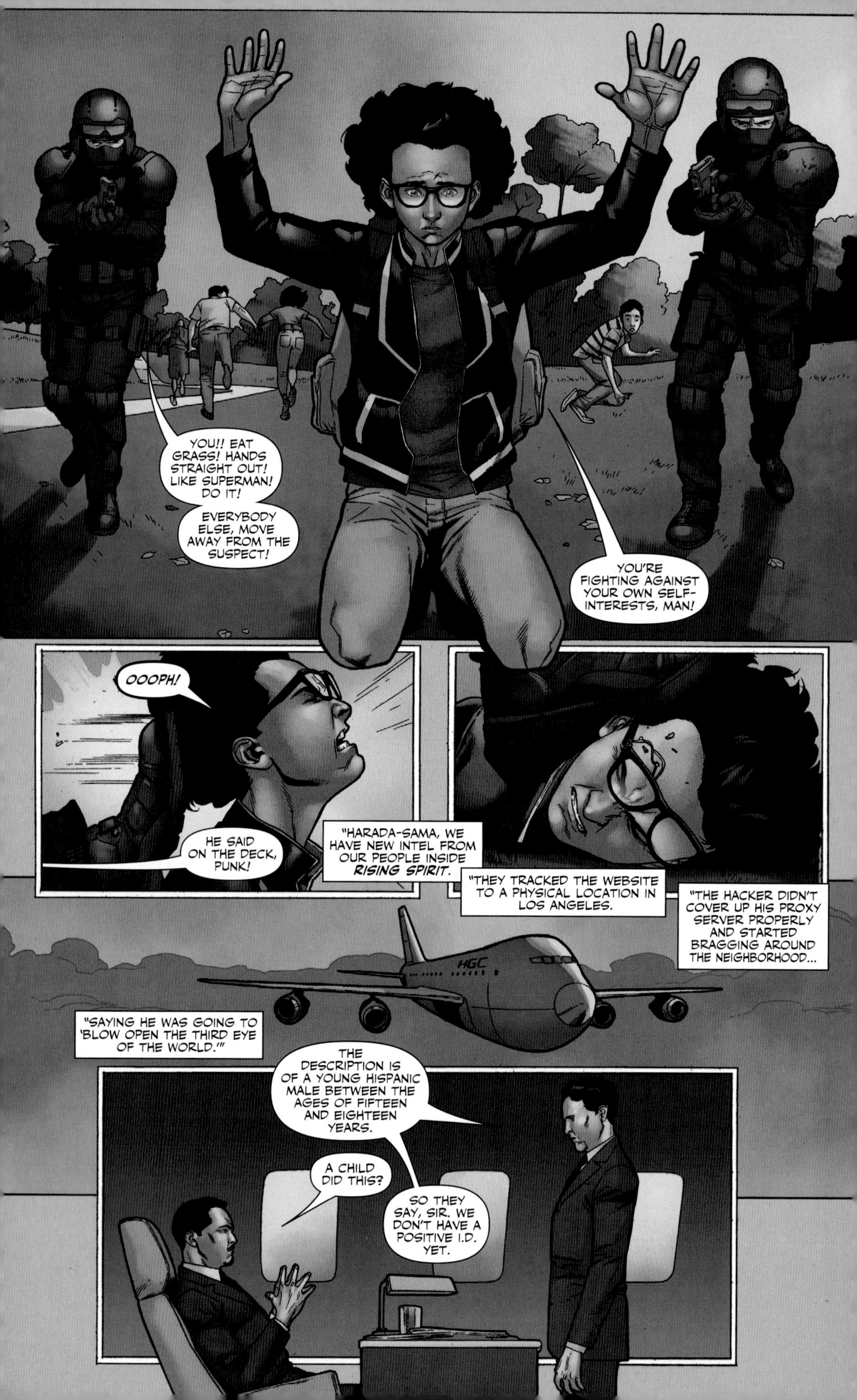
YOU!! EAT GRASS! HANDS STRAIGHT OUT! LIKE SUPERMAN! DO IT!
EVERYBODY ELSE, MOVE AWAY FROM THE SUSPECT!
YOU'RE FIGHTING AGAINST YOUR OWN SELF-INTERESTS, MAN!
OOOPH!
HE SAID ON THE DECK, PUNK!
"HARADA-SAMA, WE HAVE NEW INTEL FROM OUR PEOPLE INSIDE *RISING SPIRIT*.
"THEY TRACKED THE WEBSITE TO A PHYSICAL LOCATION IN LOS ANGELES.
"THE HACKER DIDN'T COVER UP HIS PROXY SERVER PROPERLY AND STARTED BRAGGING AROUND THE NEIGHBORHOOD...
HGC
"SAYING HE WAS GOING TO 'BLOW OPEN THE THIRD EYE OF THE WORLD.'"
THE DESCRIPTION IS OF A YOUNG HISPANIC MALE BETWEEN THE AGES OF FIFTEEN AND EIGHTEEN YEARS.
A CHILD DID THIS?
SO THEY SAY, SIR. WE DON'T HAVE A POSITIVE I.D. YET.

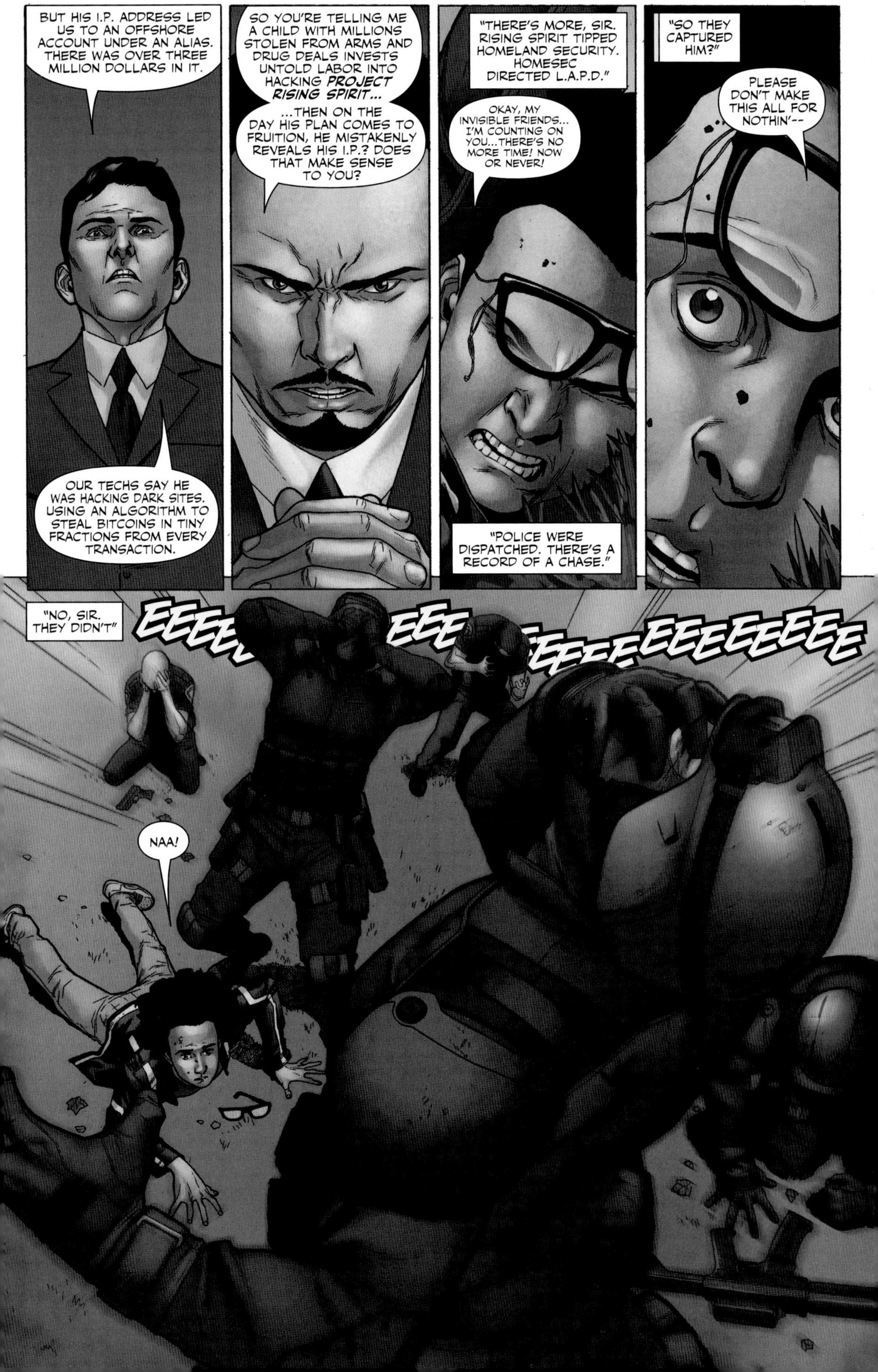
BUT HIS I.P. ADDRESS LED US TO AN OFFSHORE ACCOUNT UNDER AN ALIAS. THERE WAS OVER THREE MILLION DOLLARS IN IT.
OUR TECHS SAY HE WAS HACKING DARK SITES. USING AN ALGORITHM TO STEAL BITCOINS IN TINY FRACTIONS FROM EVERY TRANSACTION.
SO YOU'RE TELLING ME A CHILD WITH MILLIONS STOLEN FROM ARMS AND DRUG DEALS INVESTS UNTOLD LABOR INTO HACKING PROJECT RISING SPIRIT...
...THEN ON THE DAY HIS PLAN COMES TO FRUITION, HE MISTAKENLY REVEALS HIS I.P.? DOES THAT MAKE SENSE TO YOU?
"THERE'S MORE, SIR. RISING SPIRIT TIPPED HOMELAND SECURITY. HOMESEC DIRECTED L.A.P.D."
OKAY, MY INVISIBLE FRIENDS... I'M COUNTING ON YOU...THERE'S NO MORE TIME! NOW OR NEVER!
"POLICE WERE DISPATCHED. THERE'S A RECORD OF A CHASE."
"SO THEY CAPTURED HIM?"
PLEASE DON'T MAKE THIS ALL FOR NOTHIN'--
"NO, SIR. THEY DIDN'T"
EEEEEEEEEEEEEEEEEEEEEEEEE
NAA!

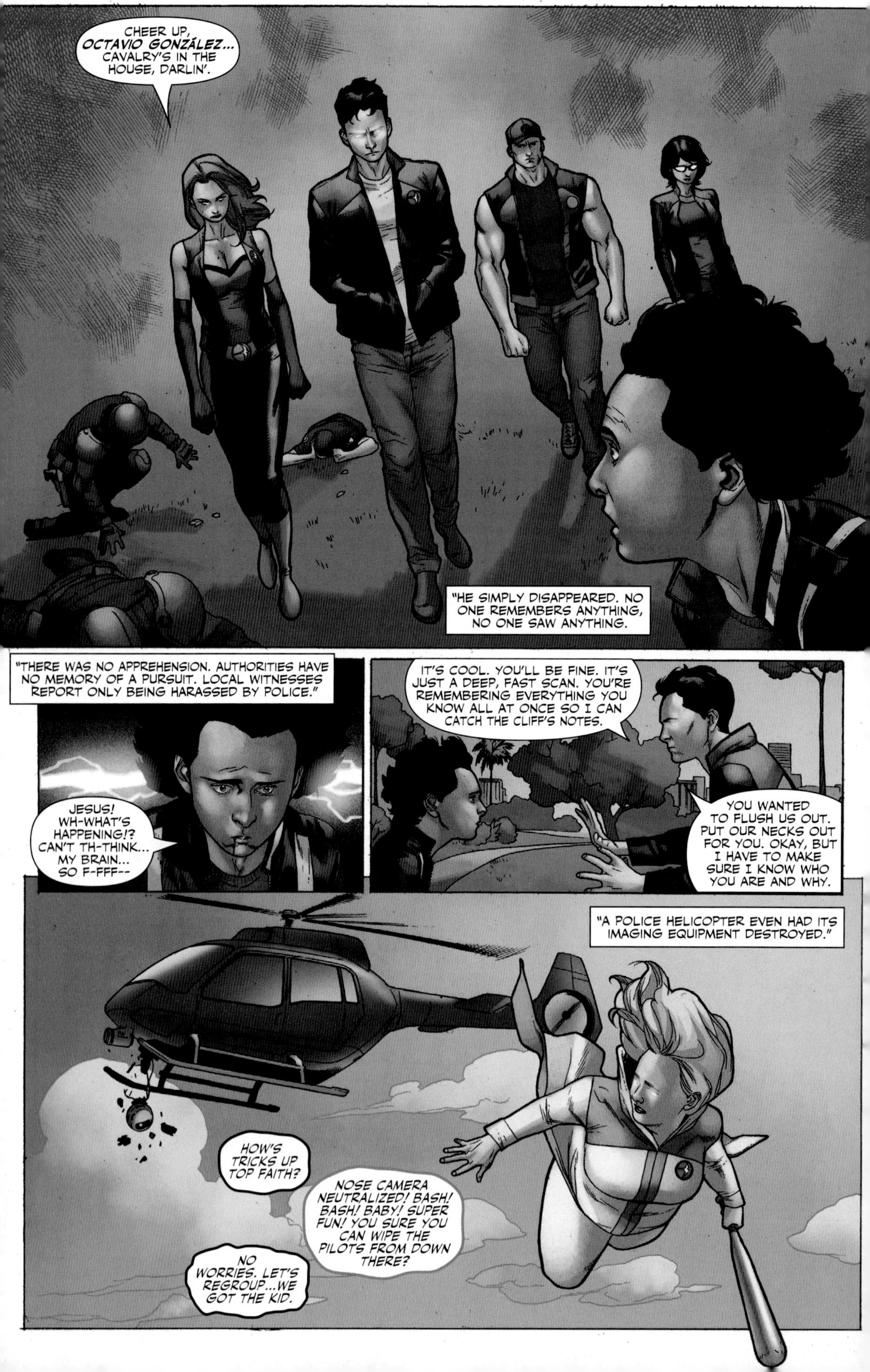

CHEER UP, OCTAVIO GONZÁLEZ... CAVALRY'S IN THE HOUSE, DARLIN'.
"HE SIMPLY DISAPPEARED. NO ONE REMEMBERS ANYTHING, NO ONE SAW ANYTHING.
"THERE WAS NO APPREHENSION. AUTHORITIES HAVE NO MEMORY OF A PURSUIT. LOCAL WITNESSES REPORT ONLY BEING HARASSED BY POLICE."
JESUS! WH-WHAT'S HAPPENING!? CAN'T TH-THINK... MY BRAIN... SO F-FFF--
IT'S COOL. YOU'LL BE FINE. IT'S JUST A DEEP, FAST SCAN. YOU'RE REMEMBERING EVERYTHING YOU KNOW ALL AT ONCE SO I CAN CATCH THE CLIFF'S NOTES.
YOU WANTED TO FLUSH US OUT. PUT OUR NECKS OUT FOR YOU. OKAY, BUT I HAVE TO MAKE SURE I KNOW WHO YOU ARE AND WHY.
"A POLICE HELICOPTER EVEN HAD ITS IMAGING EQUIPMENT DESTROYED."
HOW'S TRICKS UP TOP FAITH?
NOSE CAMERA NEUTRALIZED! BASH! BASH! BABY! SUPER FUN! YOU SURE YOU CAN WIPE THE PILOTS FROM DOWN THERE?
NO WORRIES. LET'S REGROUP...WE GOT THE KID.

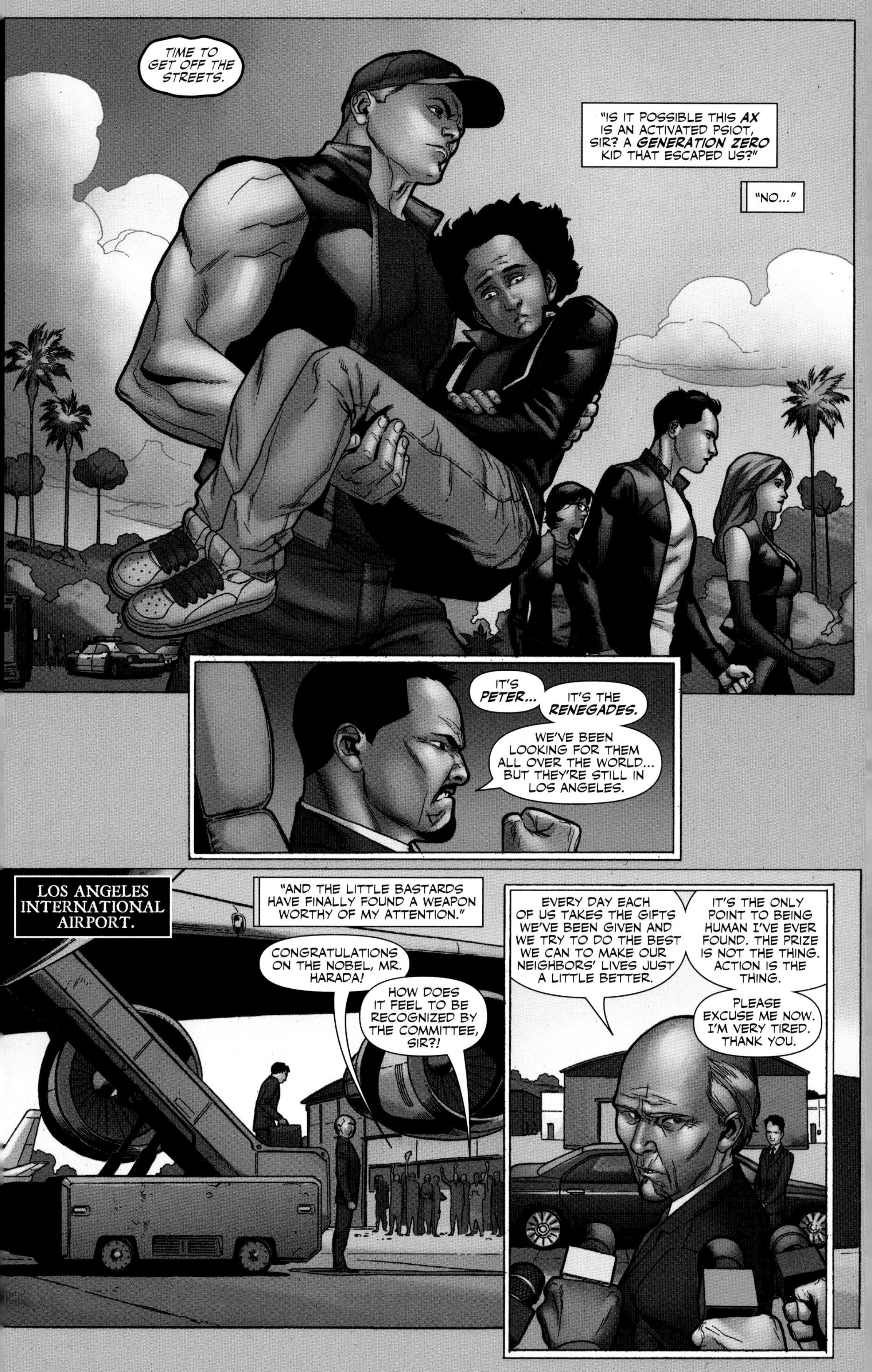
TIME TO GET OFF THE STREETS.
"IS IT POSSIBLE THIS AX IS AN ACTIVATED PSIOT, SIR? A GENERATION ZERO KID THAT ESCAPED US?"
"NO..."
IT'S PETER...
IT'S THE RENEGADES.
WE'VE BEEN LOOKING FOR THEM ALL OVER THE WORLD... BUT THEY'RE STILL IN LOS ANGELES.
LOS ANGELES INTERNATIONAL AIRPORT.
"AND THE LITTLE BASTARDS HAVE FINALLY FOUND A WEAPON WORTHY OF MY ATTENTION."
CONGRATULATIONS ON THE NOBEL, MR. HARADA!
HOW DOES IT FEEL TO BE RECOGNIZED BY THE COMMITTEE, SIR?!
EVERY DAY EACH OF US TAKES THE GIFTS WE'VE BEEN GIVEN AND WE TRY TO DO THE BEST WE CAN TO MAKE OUR NEIGHBORS' LIVES JUST A LITTLE BETTER.
IT'S THE ONLY POINT TO BEING HUMAN I'VE EVER FOUND. THE PRIZE IS NOT THE THING. ACTION IS THE THING.
PLEASE EXCUSE ME NOW. I'M VERY TIRED. THANK YOU.

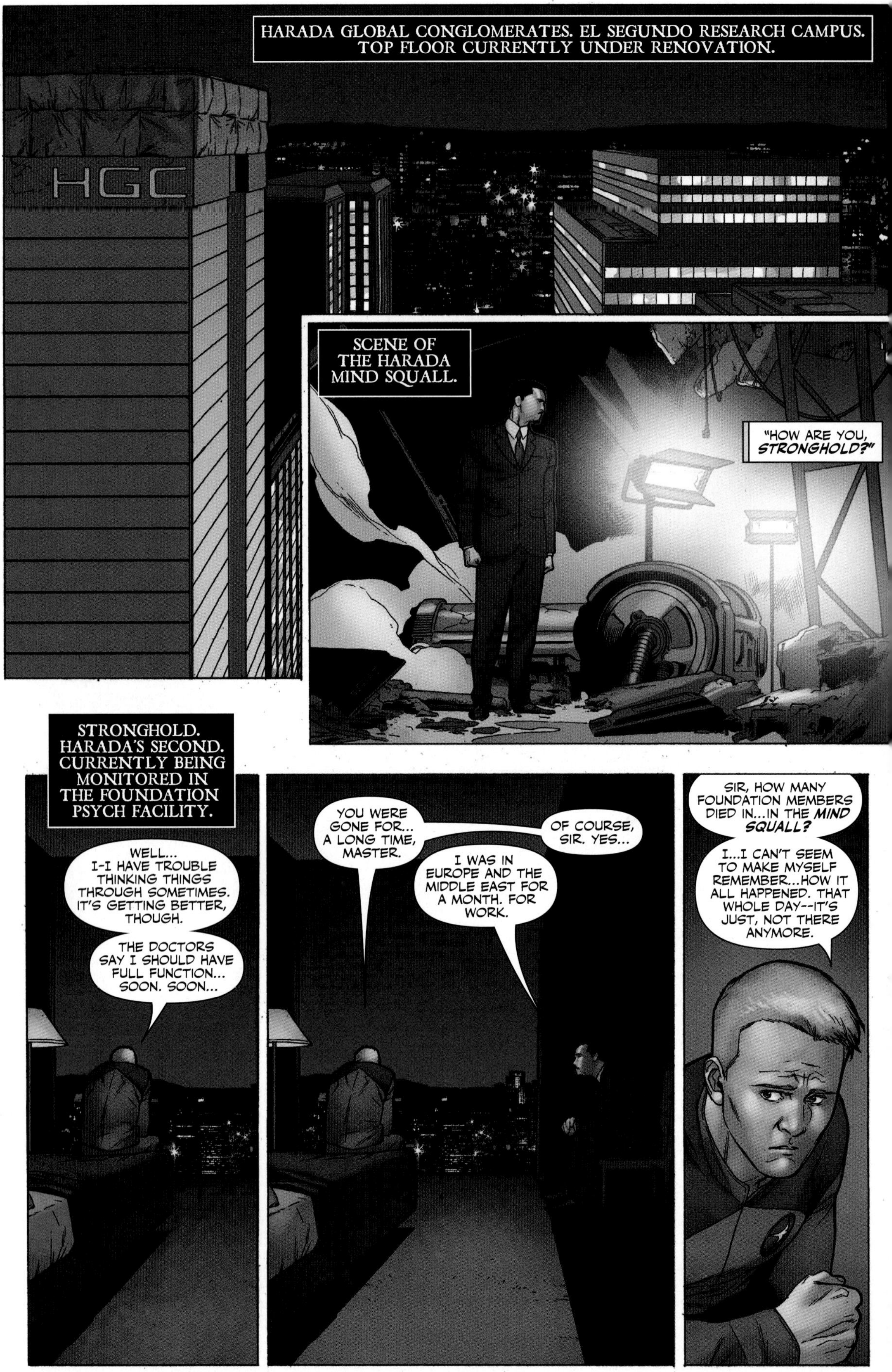
HARADA GLOBAL CONGLOMERATES. EL SEGUNDO RESEARCH CAMPUS. TOP FLOOR CURRENTLY UNDER RENOVATION.
HGC
SCENE OF THE HARADA MIND SQUALL.
"HOW ARE YOU, *STRONGHOLD?*"
STRONGHOLD. HARADA'S SECOND. CURRENTLY BEING MONITORED IN THE FOUNDATION PSYCH FACILITY.
WELL... I-I HAVE TROUBLE THINKING THINGS THROUGH SOMETIMES. IT'S GETTING BETTER, THOUGH.
THE DOCTORS SAY I SHOULD HAVE FULL FUNCTION... SOON. SOON...
YOU WERE GONE FOR... A LONG TIME, MASTER.
OF COURSE, SIR. YES...
I WAS IN EUROPE AND THE MIDDLE EAST FOR A MONTH. FOR WORK.
SIR, HOW MANY FOUNDATION MEMBERS DIED IN...IN THE *MIND SQUALL?*
I...I CAN'T SEEM TO MAKE MYSELF REMEMBER...HOW IT ALL HAPPENED. THAT WHOLE DAY--IT'S JUST, NOT THERE ANYMORE.

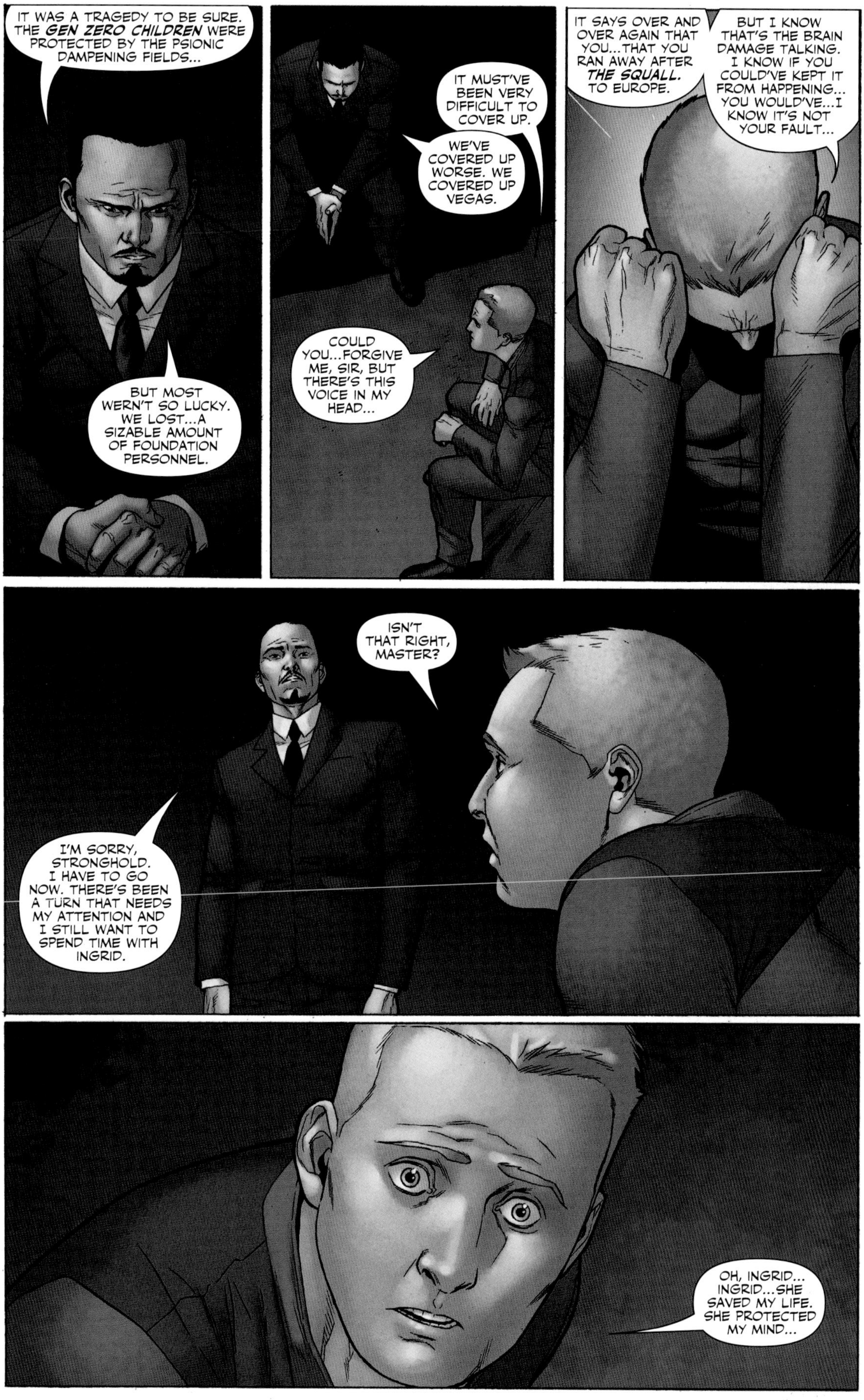
IT WAS A TRAGEDY TO BE SURE. THE GEN ZERO CHILDREN WERE PROTECTED BY THE PSIONIC DAMPENING FIELDS...
BUT MOST WERN'T SO LUCKY. WE LOST...A SIZABLE AMOUNT OF FOUNDATION PERSONNEL.
IT MUST'VE BEEN VERY DIFFICULT TO COVER UP.
WE'VE COVERED UP WORSE. WE COVERED UP VEGAS.
COULD YOU...FORGIVE ME, SIR, BUT THERE'S THIS VOICE IN MY HEAD...
IT SAYS OVER AND OVER AGAIN THAT YOU...THAT YOU RAN AWAY AFTER THE SQUALL. TO EUROPE.
BUT I KNOW THAT'S THE BRAIN DAMAGE TALKING. I KNOW IF YOU COULD'VE KEPT IT FROM HAPPENING... YOU WOULD'VE...I KNOW IT'S NOT YOUR FAULT...
ISN'T THAT RIGHT, MASTER?
I'M SORRY, STRONGHOLD. I HAVE TO GO NOW. THERE'S BEEN A TURN THAT NEEDS MY ATTENTION AND I STILL WANT TO SPEND TIME WITH INGRID.
OH, INGRID... INGRID...SHE SAVED MY LIFE. SHE PROTECTED MY MIND...

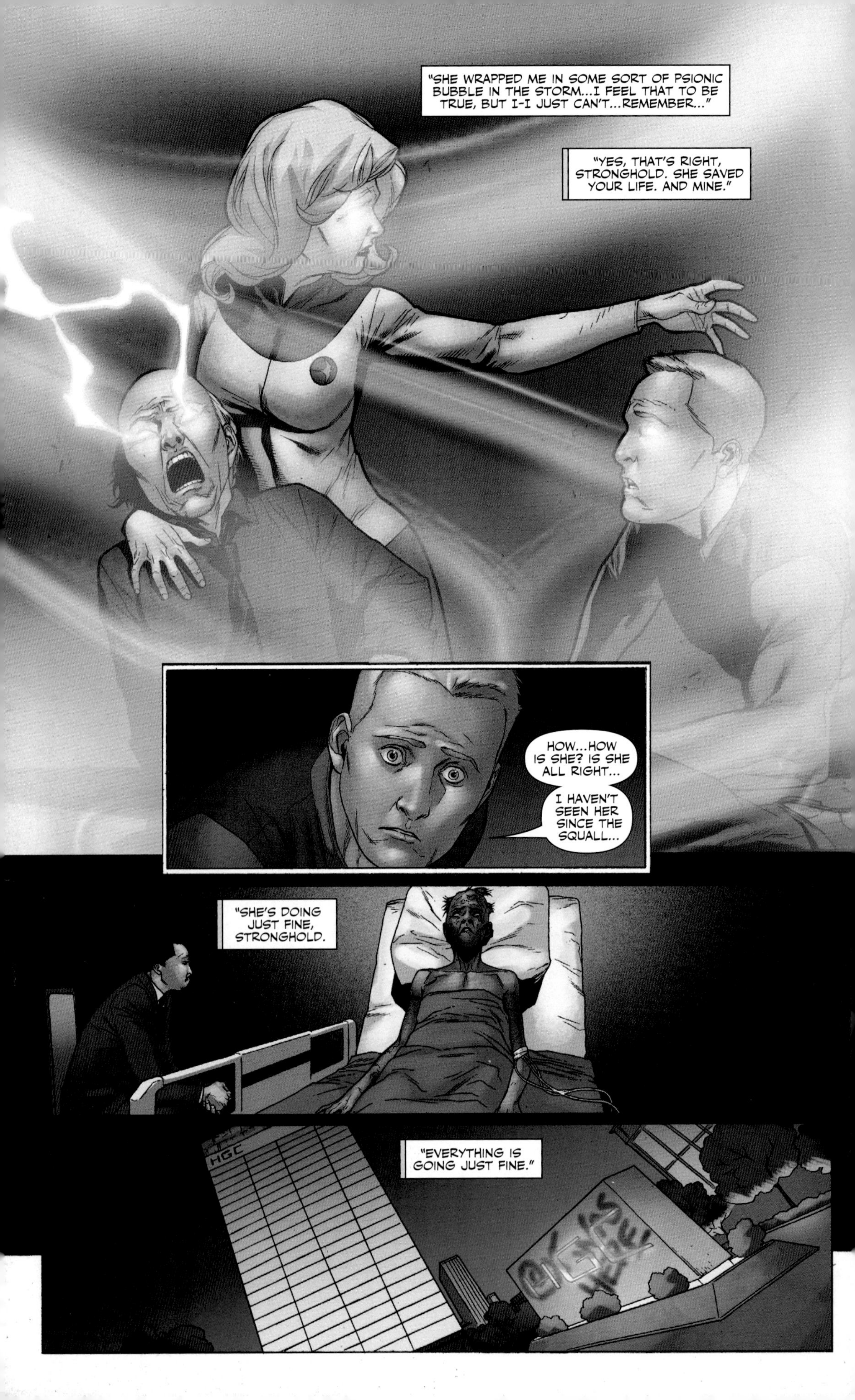
"SHE WRAPPED ME IN SOME SORT OF PSIONIC BUBBLE IN THE STORM...I FEEL THAT TO BE TRUE, BUT I-I JUST CAN'T...REMEMBER..."
"YES, THAT'S RIGHT, STRONGHOLD. SHE SAVED YOUR LIFE. AND MINE."
HOW...HOW IS SHE? IS SHE ALL RIGHT...
I HAVEN'T SEEN HER SINCE THE SQUALL...
"SHE'S DOING JUST FINE, STRONGHOLD.
HGC
"EVERYTHING IS GOING JUST FINE."

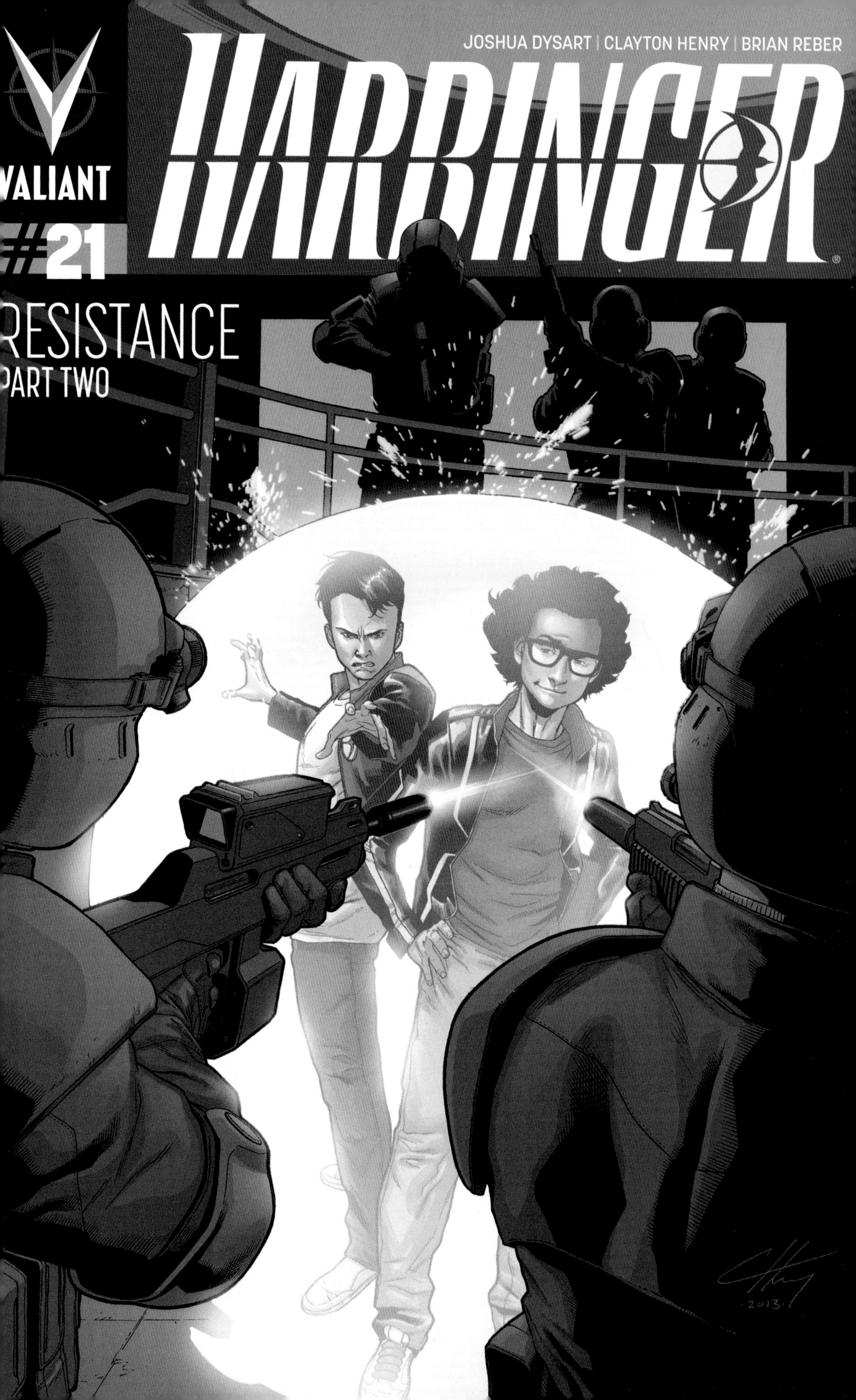
VALIANT
#21
JOSHUA DYSART | CLAYTON HENRY | BRIAN REBER
HARBINGER
RESISTANCE
PART TWO
2013

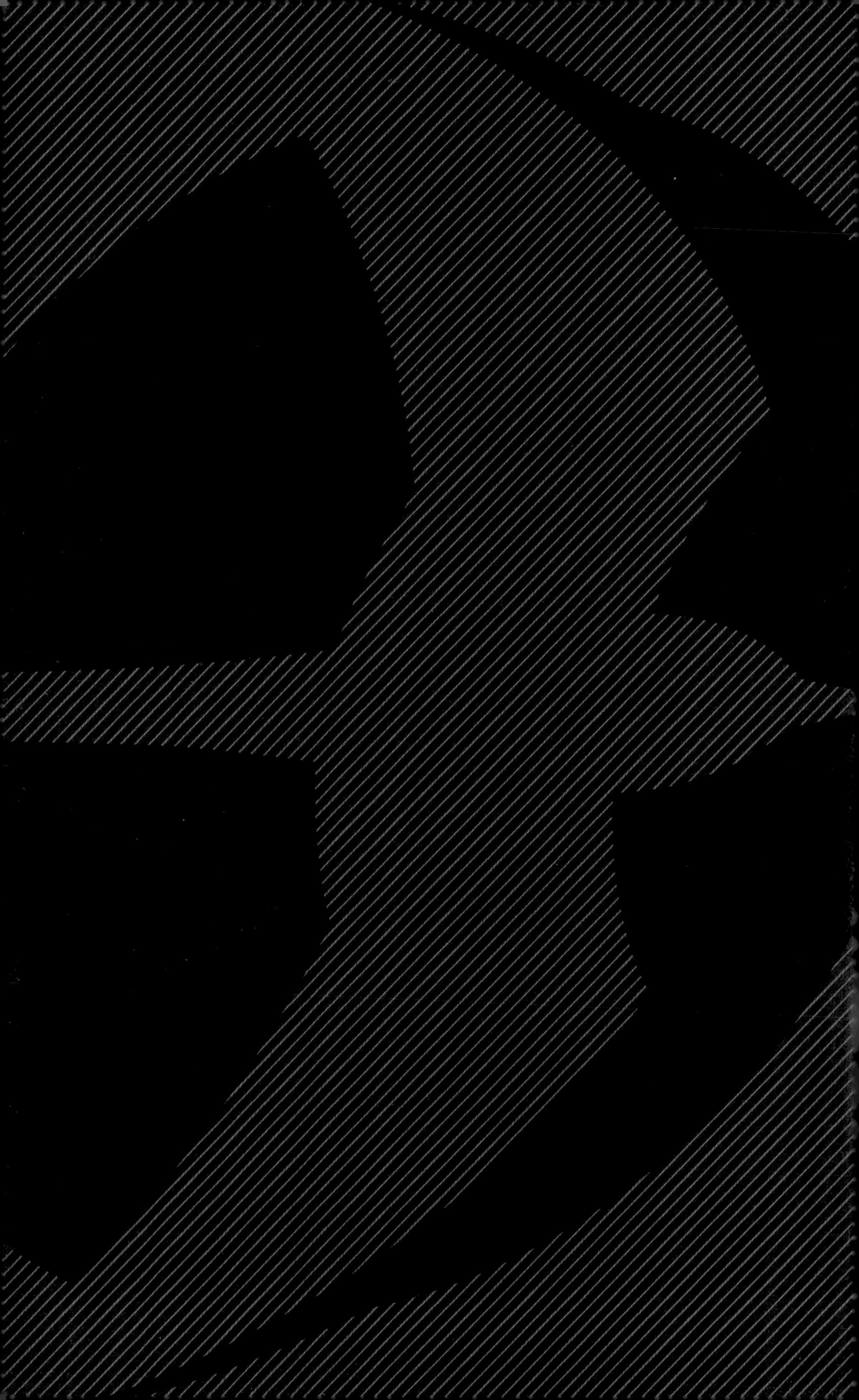

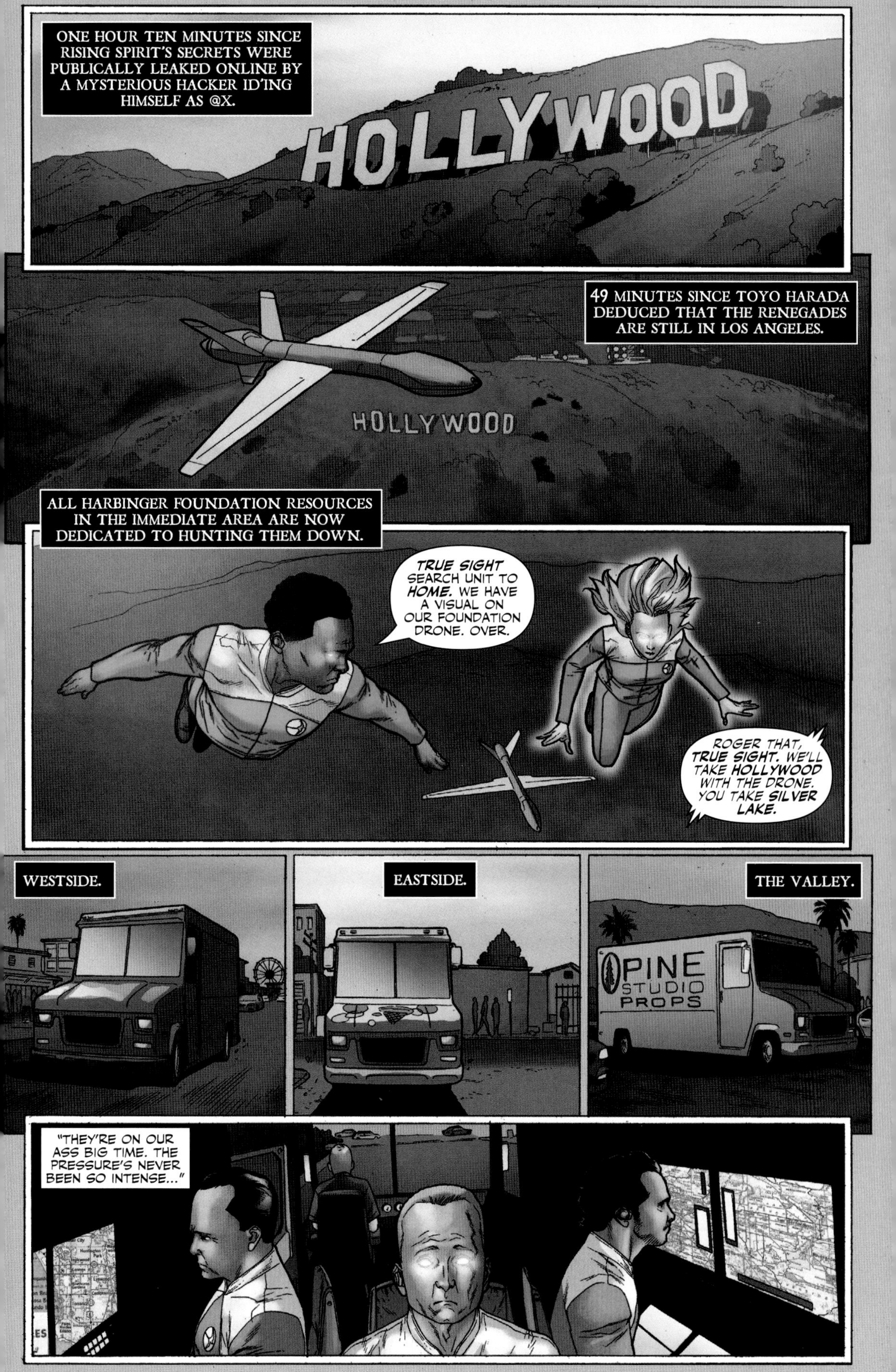
ONE HOUR TEN MINUTES SINCE RISING SPIRIT'S SECRETS WERE PUBLICALLY LEAKED ONLINE BY A MYSTERIOUS HACKER ID'ING HIMSELF AS @X.
HOLLYWOOD
49 MINUTES SINCE TOYO HARADA DEDUCED THAT THE RENEGADES ARE STILL IN LOS ANGELES.
HOLLYWOOD
ALL HARBINGER FOUNDATION RESOURCES IN THE IMMEDIATE AREA ARE NOW DEDICATED TO HUNTING THEM DOWN.
TRUE SIGHT SEARCH UNIT TO HOME. WE HAVE A VISUAL ON OUR FOUNDATION DRONE. OVER.
ROGER THAT, TRUE SIGHT. WE'LL TAKE HOLLYWOOD WITH THE DRONE. YOU TAKE SILVER LAKE.
WESTSIDE.
EASTSIDE.
THE VALLEY.
PINE STUDIO PROPS
"THEY'RE ON OUR ASS BIG TIME. THE PRESSURE'S NEVER BEEN SO INTENSE..."

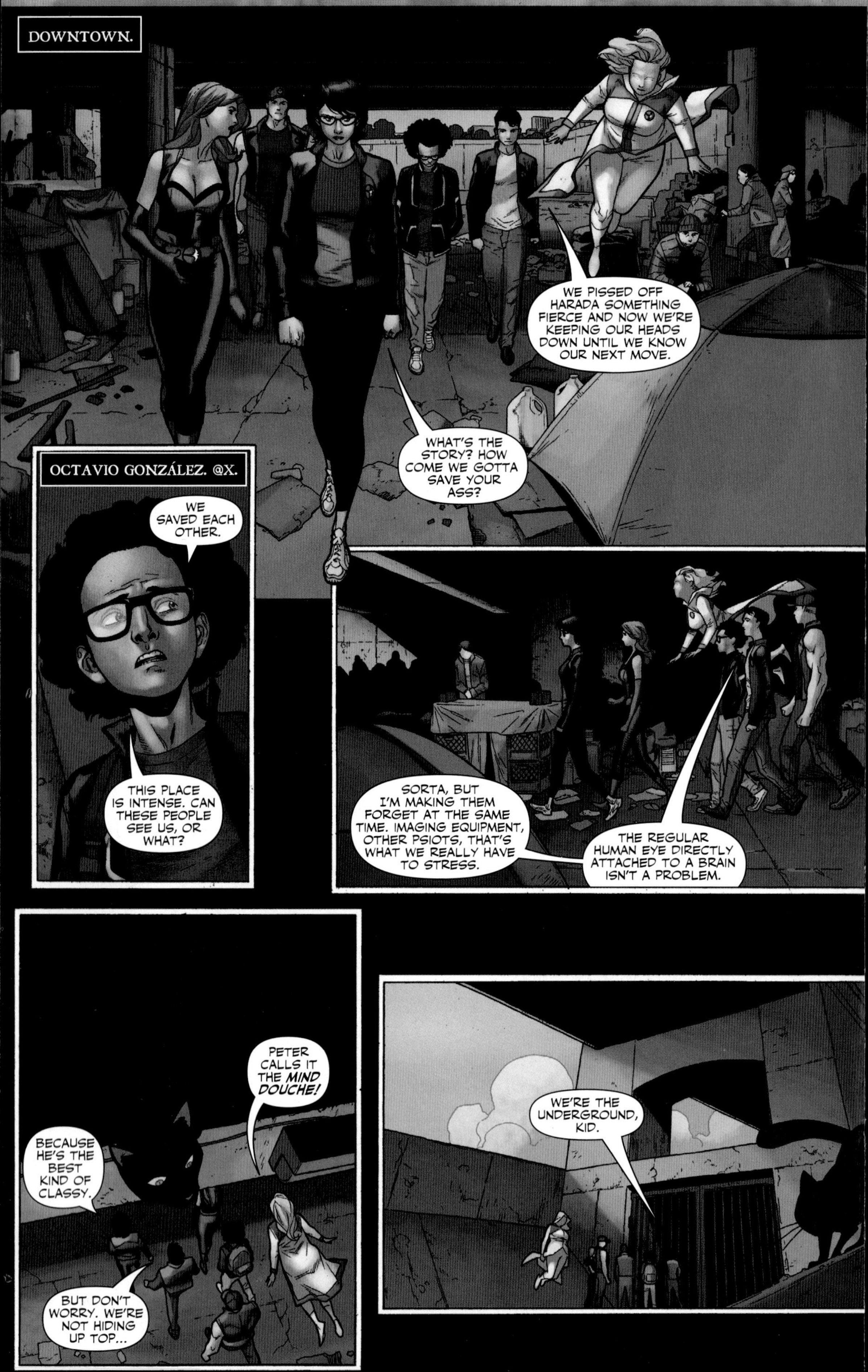
DOWNTOWN.
WE PISSED OFF HARADA SOMETHING FIERCE AND NOW WE'RE KEEPING OUR HEADS DOWN UNTIL WE KNOW OUR NEXT MOVE.
WHAT'S THE STORY? HOW COME WE GOTTA SAVE YOUR ASS?
OCTAVIO GONZÁLEZ. @X.
WE SAVED EACH OTHER.
THIS PLACE IS INTENSE. CAN THESE PEOPLE SEE US, OR WHAT?
THE REGULAR HUMAN EYE DIRECTLY ATTACHED TO A BRAIN ISN'T A PROBLEM.
SORTA, BUT I'M MAKING THEM FORGET AT THE SAME TIME. IMAGING EQUIPMENT, OTHER PSIOTS, THAT'S WHAT WE REALLY HAVE TO STRESS.
PETER CALLS IT THE *MIND DOUCHE!*
BECAUSE HE'S THE BEST KIND OF CLASSY.
BUT DON'T WORRY. WE'RE NOT HIDING UP TOP...
WE'RE THE UNDERGROUND, KID.

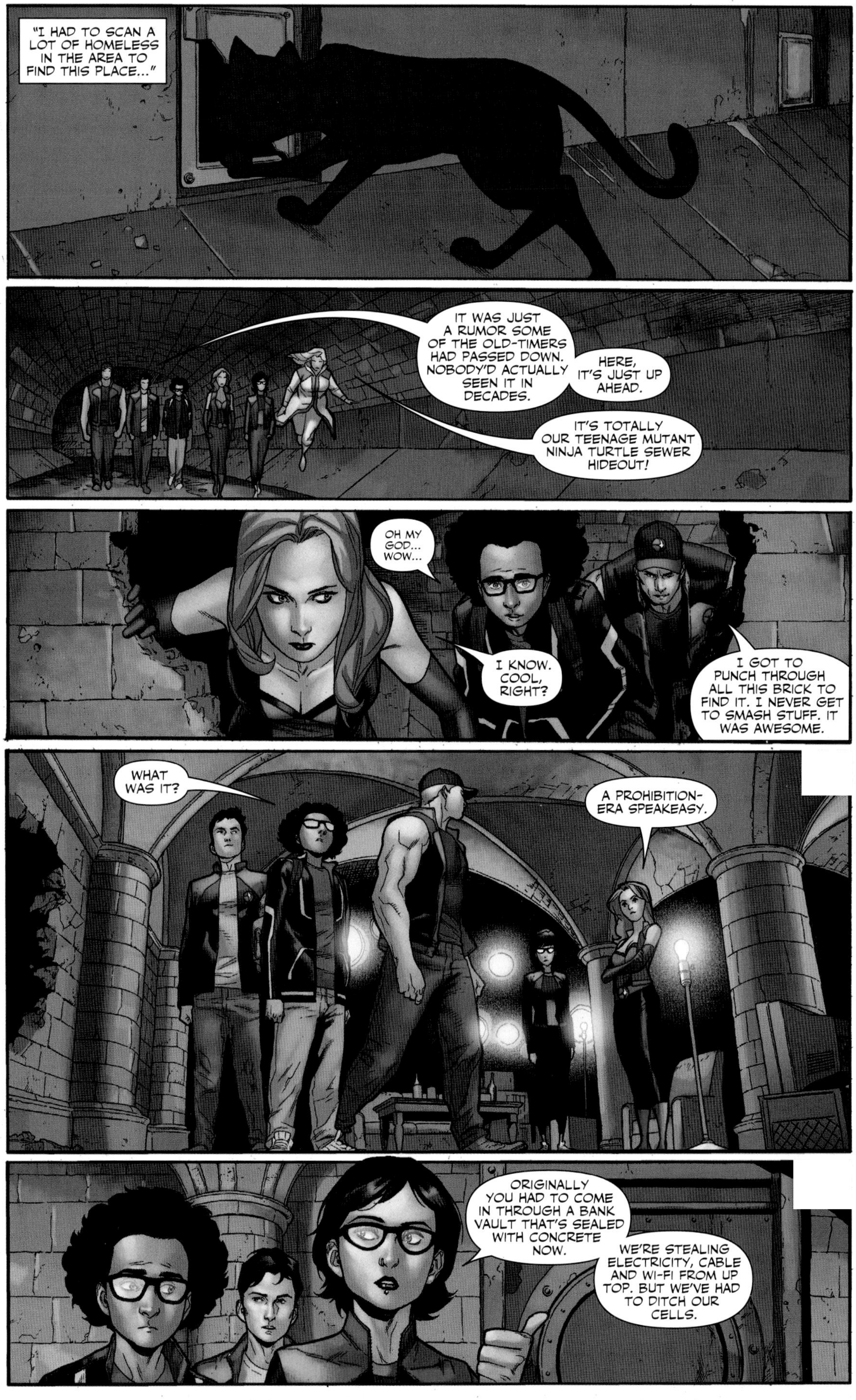
"I HAD TO SCAN A LOT OF HOMELESS IN THE AREA TO FIND THIS PLACE..."
IT WAS JUST A RUMOR SOME OF THE OLD-TIMERS HAD PASSED DOWN. NOBODY'D ACTUALLY SEEN IT IN DECADES.
HERE, IT'S JUST UP AHEAD.
IT'S TOTALLY OUR TEENAGE MUTANT NINJA TURTLE SEWER HIDEOUT!
OH MY GOD... WOW...
I KNOW. COOL, RIGHT?
I GOT TO PUNCH THROUGH ALL THIS BRICK TO FIND IT. I NEVER GET TO SMASH STUFF. IT WAS AWESOME.
WHAT WAS IT?
A PROHIBITION-ERA SPEAKEASY.
ORIGINALLY YOU HAD TO COME IN THROUGH A BANK VAULT THAT'S SEALED WITH CONCRETE NOW.
WE'RE STEALING ELECTRICITY, CABLE AND WI-FI FROM UP TOP. BUT WE'VE HAD TO DITCH OUR CELLS.

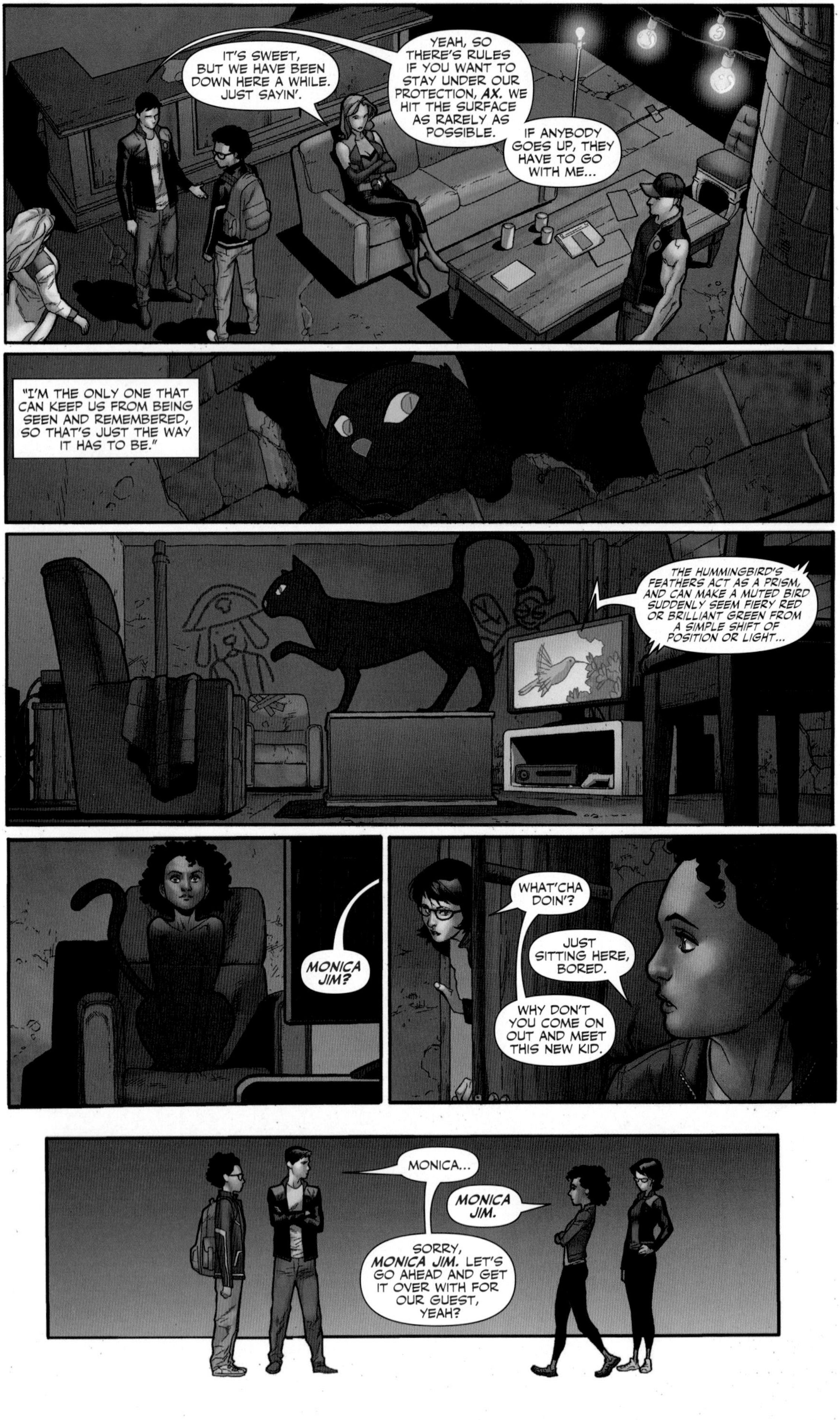

IT'S SWEET, BUT WE HAVE BEEN DOWN HERE A WHILE. JUST SAYIN'.
YEAH, SO THERE'S RULES IF YOU WANT TO STAY UNDER OUR PROTECTION, AX. WE HIT THE SURFACE AS RARELY AS POSSIBLE.
IF ANYBODY GOES UP, THEY HAVE TO GO WITH ME...
"I'M THE ONLY ONE THAT CAN KEEP US FROM BEING SEEN AND REMEMBERED, SO THAT'S JUST THE WAY IT HAS TO BE."
THE HUMMINGBIRD'S FEATHERS ACT AS A PRISM, AND CAN MAKE A MUTED BIRD SUDDENLY SEEM FIERY RED OR BRILLIANT GREEN FROM A SIMPLE SHIFT OF POSITION OR LIGHT...
MONICA JIM?
WHAT'CHA DOIN'?
JUST SITTING HERE, BORED.
WHY DON'T YOU COME ON OUT AND MEET THIS NEW KID.
MONICA...
MONICA JIM.
SORRY, MONICA JIM. LET'S GO AHEAD AND GET IT OVER WITH FOR OUR GUEST, YEAH?

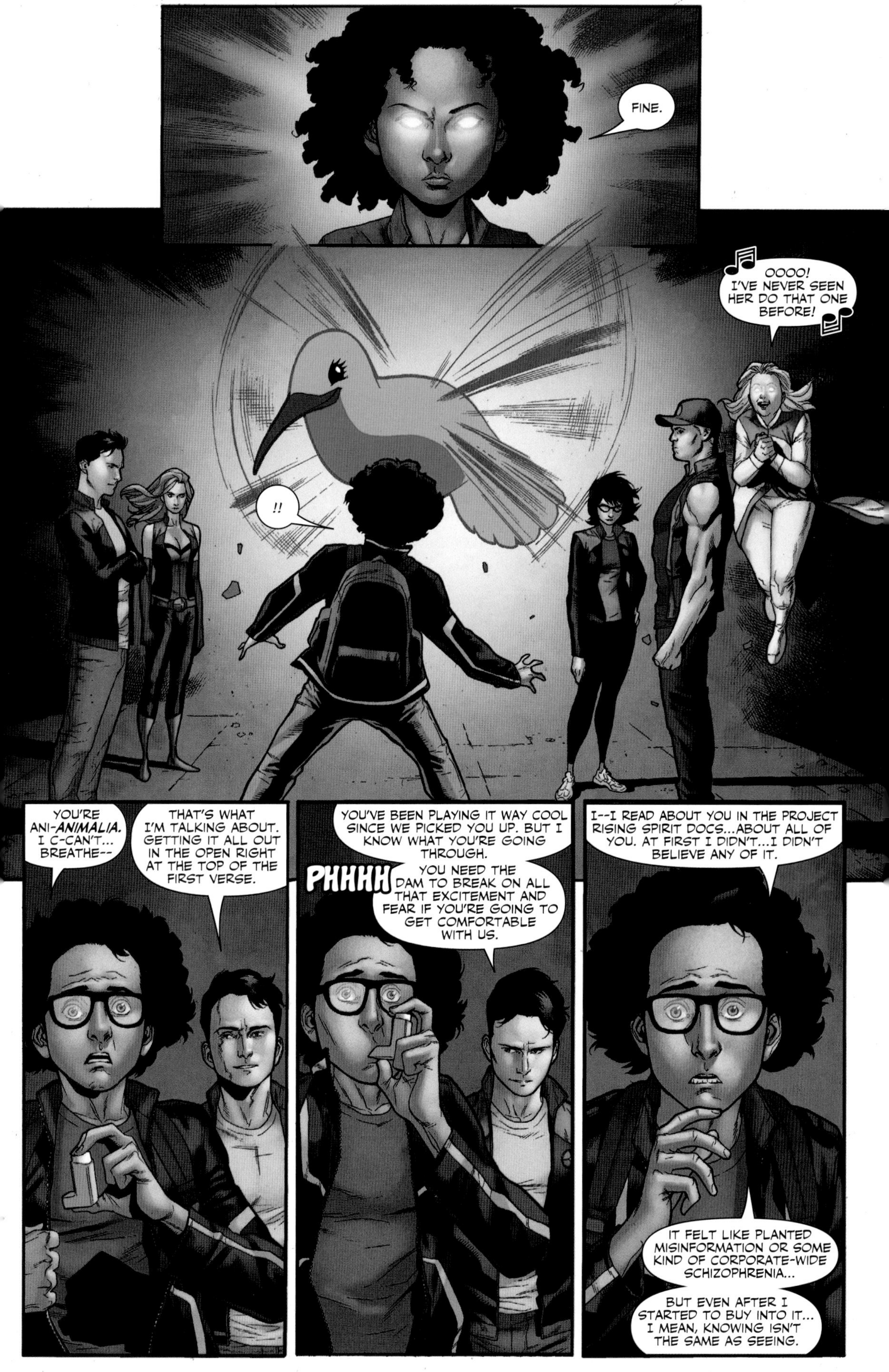

FINE.
OOOO! I'VE NEVER SEEN HER DO THAT ONE BEFORE!
!!
YOU'RE ANI-*ANIMALIA.* I C-CAN'T... BREATHE--
THAT'S WHAT I'M TALKING ABOUT. GETTING IT ALL OUT IN THE OPEN RIGHT AT THE TOP OF THE FIRST VERSE.
YOU'VE BEEN PLAYING IT WAY COOL SINCE WE PICKED YOU UP. BUT I KNOW WHAT YOU'RE GOING THROUGH.
PHHHH
YOU NEED THE DAM TO BREAK ON ALL THAT EXCITEMENT AND FEAR IF YOU'RE GOING TO GET COMFORTABLE WITH US.
I--I READ ABOUT YOU IN THE PROJECT RISING SPIRIT DOCS...ABOUT ALL OF YOU. AT FIRST I DIDN'T...I DIDN'T BELIEVE ANY OF IT.
IT FELT LIKE PLANTED MISINFORMATION OR SOME KIND OF CORPORATE-WIDE SCHIZOPHRENIA...
BUT EVEN AFTER I STARTED TO BUY INTO IT... I MEAN, KNOWING ISN'T THE SAME AS SEEING.

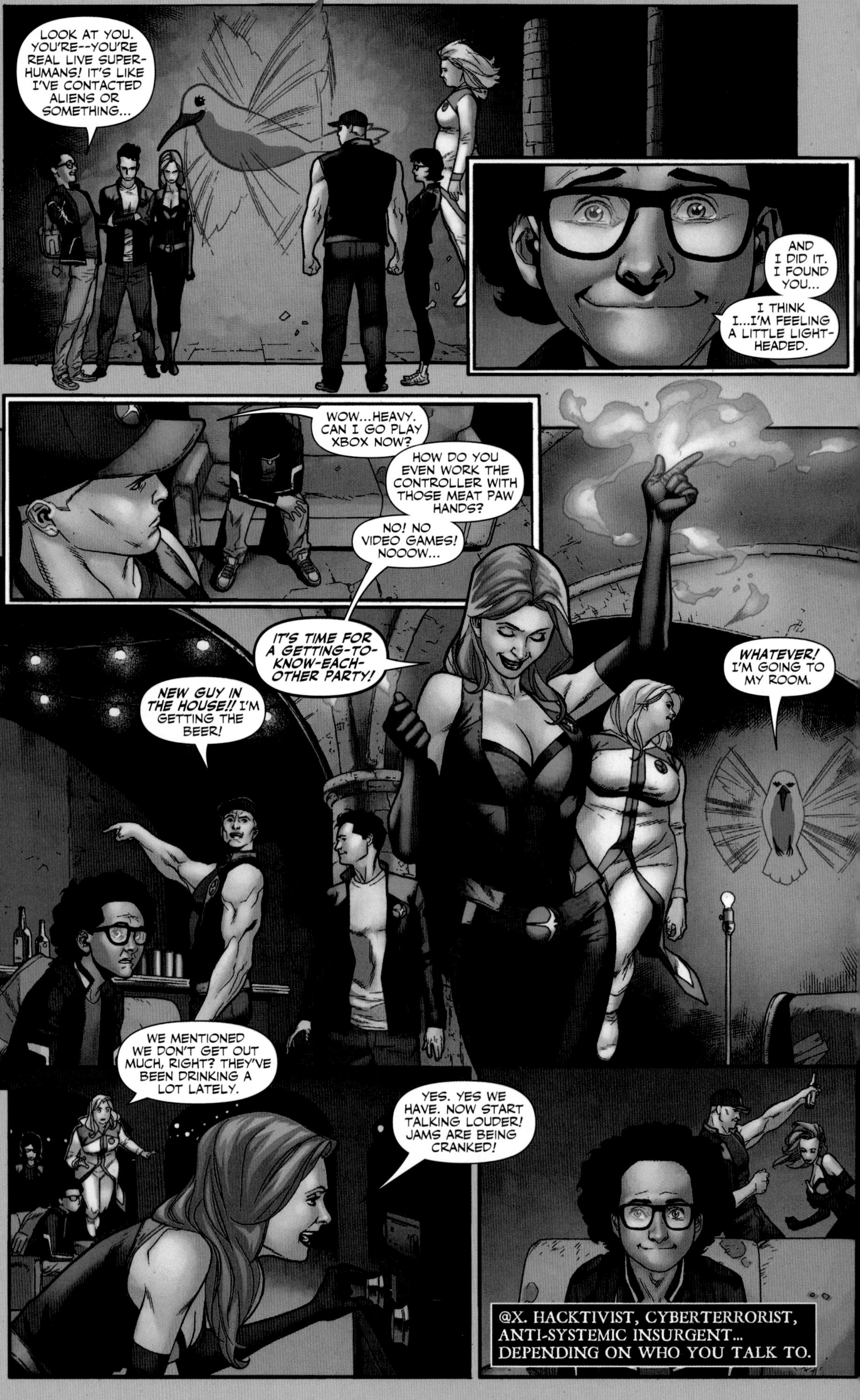
LOOK AT YOU. YOU'RE--YOU'RE REAL LIVE SUPER-HUMANS! IT'S LIKE I'VE CONTACTED ALIENS OR SOMETHING...
AND I DID IT. I FOUND YOU...
I THINK I...I'M FEELING A LITTLE LIGHT-HEADED.
WOW...HEAVY. CAN I GO PLAY XBOX NOW?
HOW DO YOU EVEN WORK THE CONTROLLER WITH THOSE MEAT PAW HANDS?
NO! NO VIDEO GAMES! NOOOW...
IT'S TIME FOR A GETTING-TO-KNOW-EACH-OTHER PARTY!
NEW GUY IN THE HOUSE!! I'M GETTING THE BEER!
WHATEVER! I'M GOING TO MY ROOM.
WE MENTIONED WE DON'T GET OUT MUCH, RIGHT? THEY'VE BEEN DRINKING A LOT LATELY.
YES. YES WE HAVE. NOW START TALKING LOUDER! JAMS ARE BEING CRANKED!
@X. HACKTIVIST, CYBERTERRORIST, ANTI-SYSTEMIC INSURGENT... DEPENDING ON WHO YOU TALK TO.

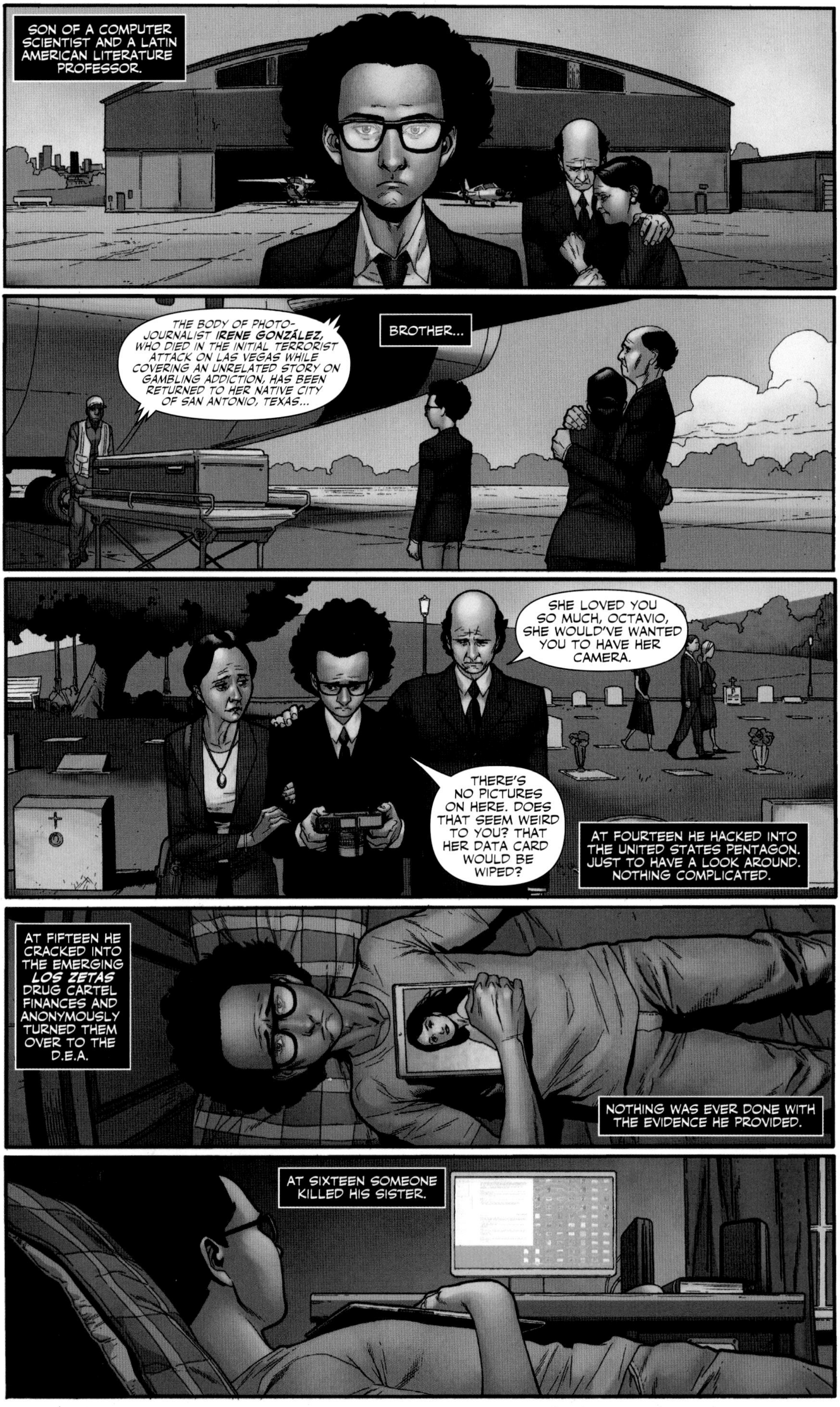
SON OF A COMPUTER SCIENTIST AND A LATIN AMERICAN LITERATURE PROFESSOR.
THE BODY OF PHOTO-JOURNALIST IRENE GONZÁLEZ, WHO DIED IN THE INITIAL TERRORIST ATTACK ON LAS VEGAS WHILE COVERING AN UNRELATED STORY ON GAMBLING ADDICTION, HAS BEEN RETURNED TO HER NATIVE CITY OF SAN ANTONIO, TEXAS...
BROTHER...
SHE LOVED YOU SO MUCH, OCTAVIO, SHE WOULD'VE WANTED YOU TO HAVE HER CAMERA.
THERE'S NO PICTURES ON HERE. DOES THAT SEEM WEIRD TO YOU? THAT HER DATA CARD WOULD BE WIPED?
AT FOURTEEN HE HACKED INTO THE UNITED STATES PENTAGON. JUST TO HAVE A LOOK AROUND. NOTHING COMPLICATED.
AT FIFTEEN HE CRACKED INTO THE EMERGING LOS ZETAS DRUG CARTEL FINANCES AND ANONYMOUSLY TURNED THEM OVER TO THE D.E.A.
NOTHING WAS EVER DONE WITH THE EVIDENCE HE PROVIDED.
AT SIXTEEN SOMEONE KILLED HIS SISTER.

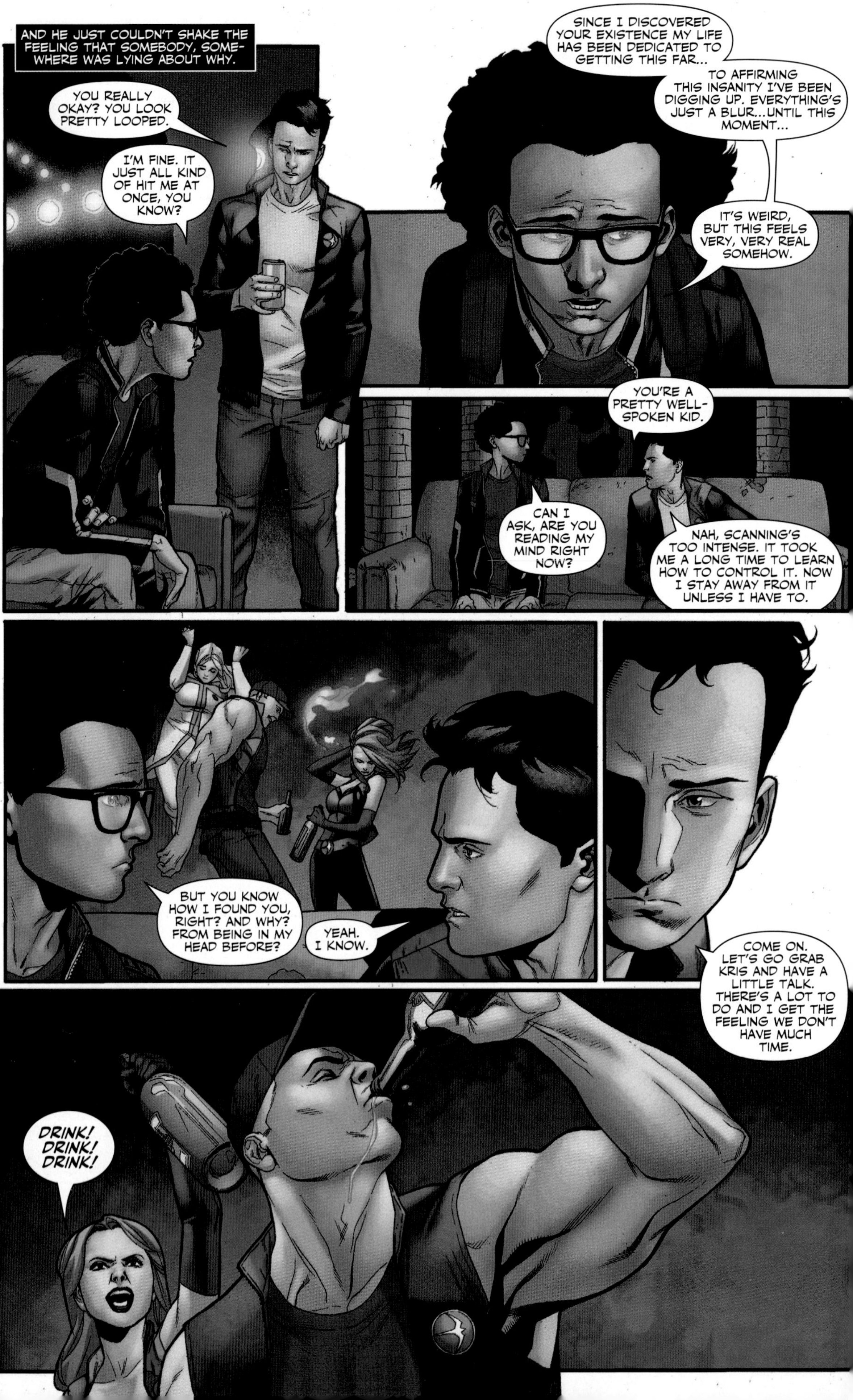
AND HE JUST COULDN'T SHAKE THE FEELING THAT SOMEBODY, SOME-WHERE WAS LYING ABOUT WHY.
YOU REALLY OKAY? YOU LOOK PRETTY LOOPED.
I'M FINE. IT JUST ALL KIND OF HIT ME AT ONCE, YOU KNOW?
SINCE I DISCOVERED YOUR EXISTENCE MY LIFE HAS BEEN DEDICATED TO GETTING THIS FAR...
TO AFFIRMING THIS INSANITY I'VE BEEN DIGGING UP. EVERYTHING'S JUST A BLUR...UNTIL THIS MOMENT...
IT'S WEIRD, BUT THIS FEELS VERY, VERY REAL SOMEHOW.
YOU'RE A PRETTY WELL-SPOKEN KID.
CAN I ASK, ARE YOU READING MY MIND RIGHT NOW?
NAH, SCANNING'S TOO INTENSE. IT TOOK ME A LONG TIME TO LEARN HOW TO CONTROL IT. NOW I STAY AWAY FROM IT UNLESS I HAVE TO.
BUT YOU KNOW HOW I FOUND YOU, RIGHT? AND WHY? FROM BEING IN MY HEAD BEFORE?
YEAH. I KNOW.
COME ON. LET'S GO GRAB KRIS AND HAVE A LITTLE TALK. THERE'S A LOT TO DO AND I GET THE FEELING WE DON'T HAVE MUCH TIME.
DRINK! DRINK! DRINK!

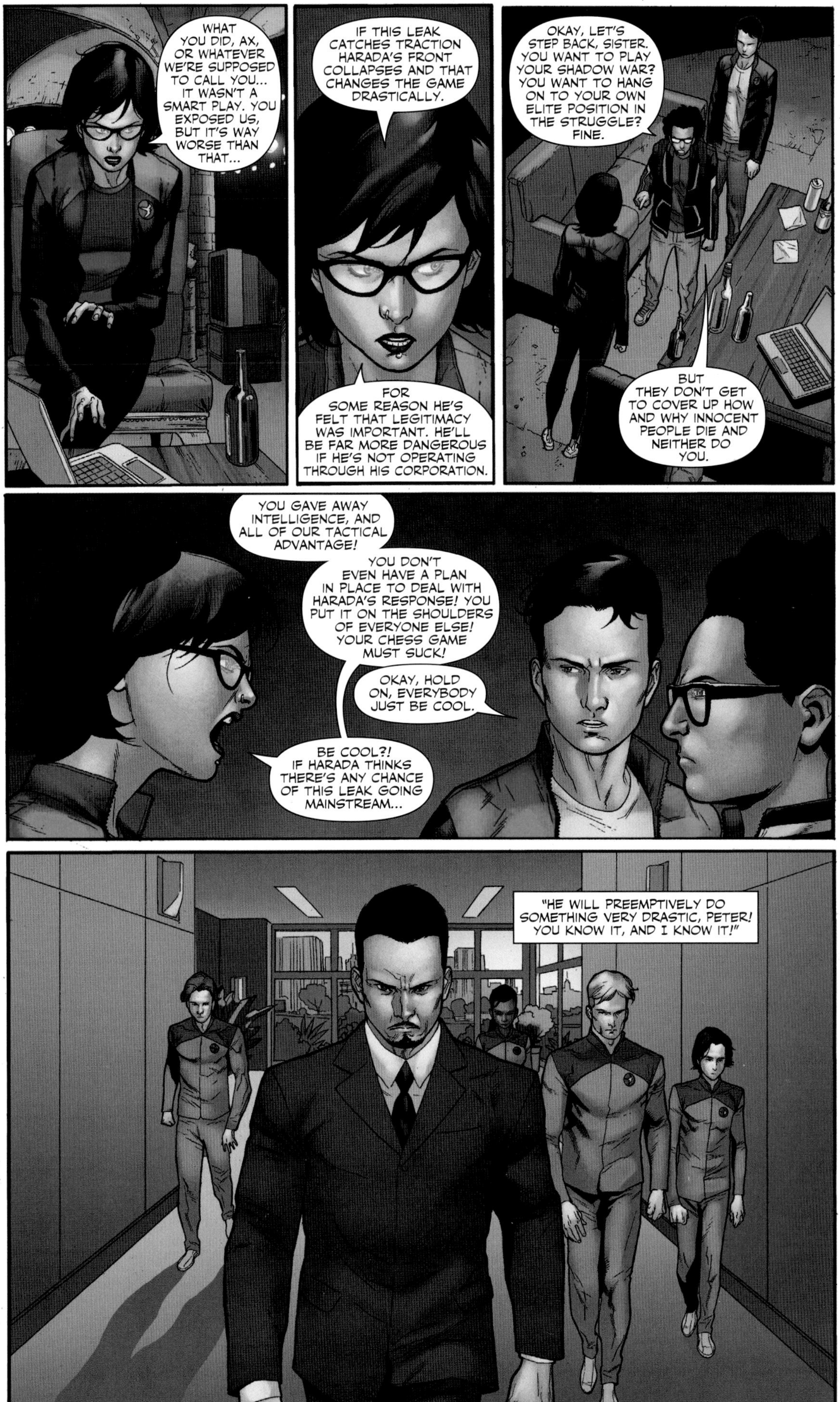
WHAT YOU DID, AX, OR WHATEVER WE'RE SUPPOSED TO CALL YOU... IT WASN'T A SMART PLAY. YOU EXPOSED US, BUT IT'S WAY WORSE THAN THAT...
IF THIS LEAK CATCHES TRACTION HARADA'S FRONT COLLAPSES AND THAT CHANGES THE GAME DRASTICALLY.
FOR SOME REASON HE'S FELT THAT LEGITIMACY WAS IMPORTANT. HE'LL BE FAR MORE DANGEROUS IF HE'S NOT OPERATING THROUGH HIS CORPORATION.
OKAY, LET'S STEP BACK, SISTER. YOU WANT TO PLAY YOUR SHADOW WAR? YOU WANT TO HANG ON TO YOUR OWN ELITE POSITION IN THE STRUGGLE? FINE.
BUT THEY DON'T GET TO COVER UP HOW AND WHY INNOCENT PEOPLE DIE AND NEITHER DO YOU.
YOU GAVE AWAY INTELLIGENCE, AND ALL OF OUR TACTICAL ADVANTAGE!
YOU DON'T EVEN HAVE A PLAN IN PLACE TO DEAL WITH HARADA'S RESPONSE! YOU PUT IT ON THE SHOULDERS OF EVERYONE ELSE! YOUR CHESS GAME MUST SUCK!
OKAY, HOLD ON, EVERYBODY JUST BE COOL.
BE COOL?! IF HARADA THINKS THERE'S ANY CHANCE OF THIS LEAK GOING MAINSTREAM...
"HE WILL PREEMPTIVELY DO SOMETHING VERY DRASTIC, PETER! YOU KNOW IT, AND I KNOW IT!"

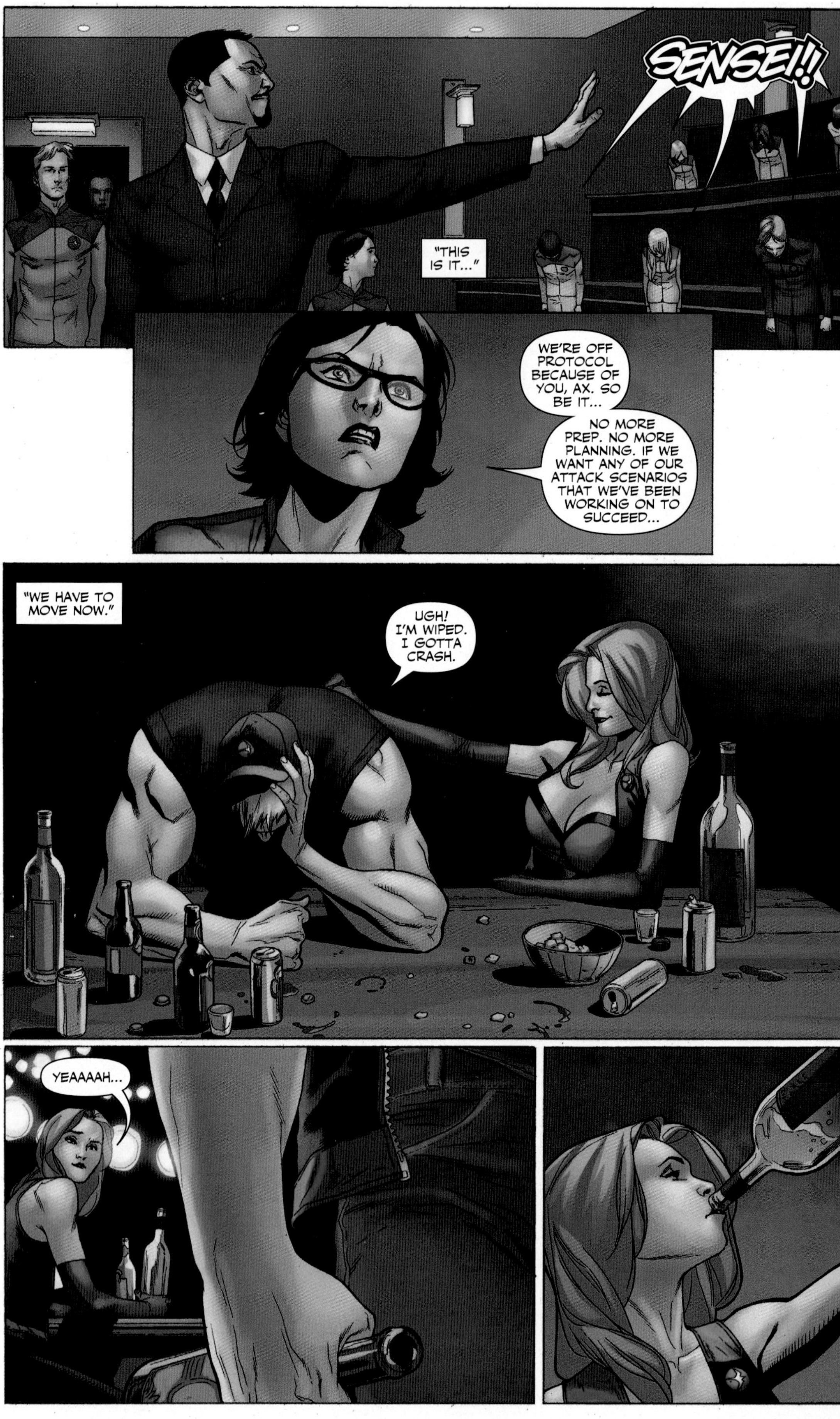
SENSEI!!
"THIS IS IT..."
WE'RE OFF PROTOCOL BECAUSE OF YOU, AX. SO BE IT...
NO MORE PREP. NO MORE PLANNING. IF WE WANT ANY OF OUR ATTACK SCENARIOS THAT WE'VE BEEN WORKING ON TO SUCCEED...
"WE HAVE TO MOVE NOW."
UGH! I'M WIPED. I GOTTA CRASH.
YEAAAAH...

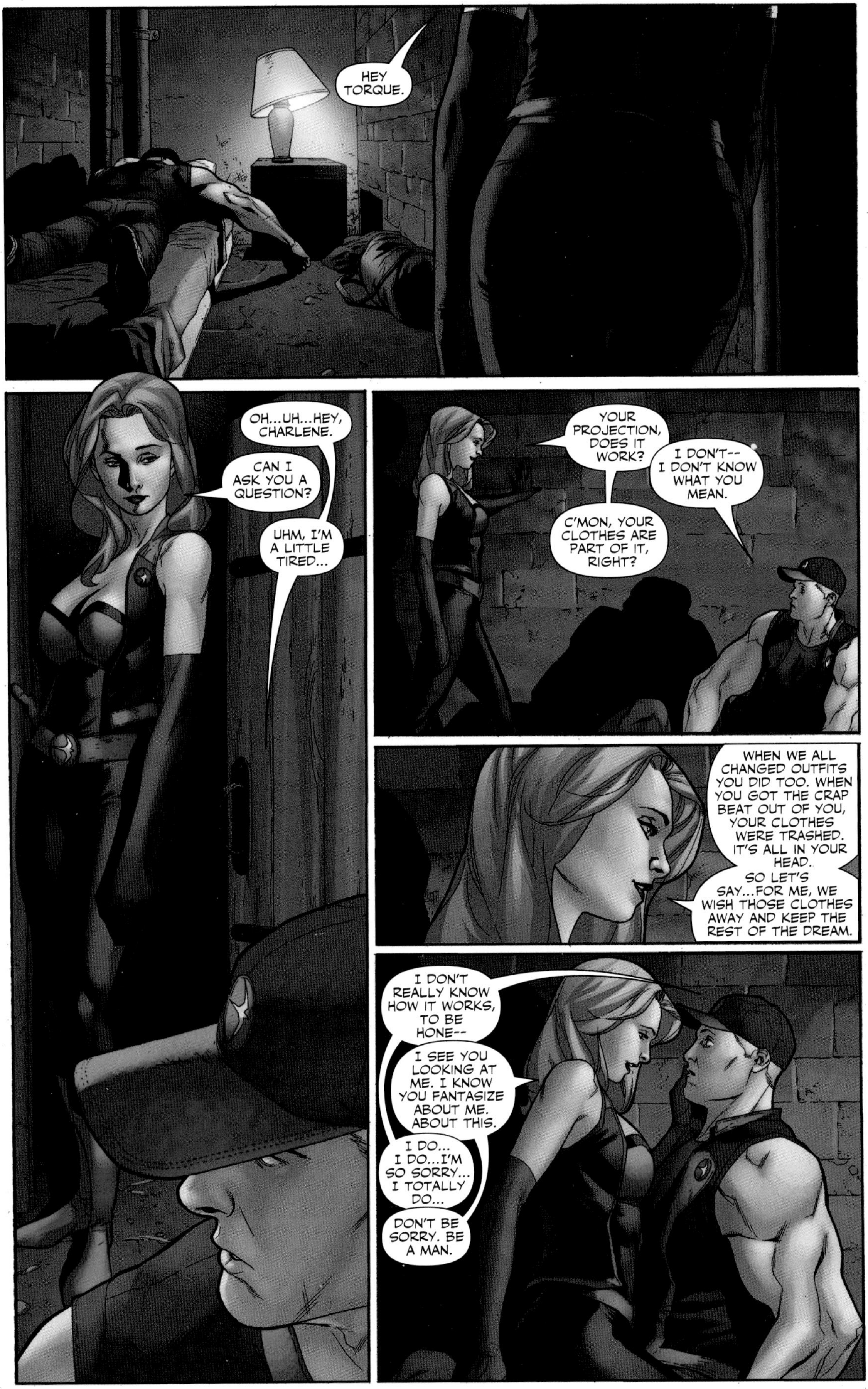
HEY TORQUE.
OH...UH...HEY, CHARLENE.
CAN I ASK YOU A QUESTION?
UHM, I'M A LITTLE TIRED...
YOUR PROJECTION, DOES IT WORK?
I DON'T-- I DON'T KNOW WHAT YOU MEAN.
C'MON, YOUR CLOTHES ARE PART OF IT, RIGHT?
WHEN WE ALL CHANGED OUTFITS YOU DID TOO. WHEN YOU GOT THE CRAP BEAT OUT OF YOU, YOUR CLOTHES WERE TRASHED. IT'S ALL IN YOUR HEAD.
SO LET'S SAY...FOR ME, WE WISH THOSE CLOTHES AWAY AND KEEP THE REST OF THE DREAM.
I DON'T REALLY KNOW HOW IT WORKS, TO BE HONE--
I SEE YOU LOOKING AT ME. I KNOW YOU FANTASIZE ABOUT ME. ABOUT THIS.
I DO... I DO...I'M SO SORRY... I TOTALLY DO...
DON'T BE SORRY. BE A MAN.

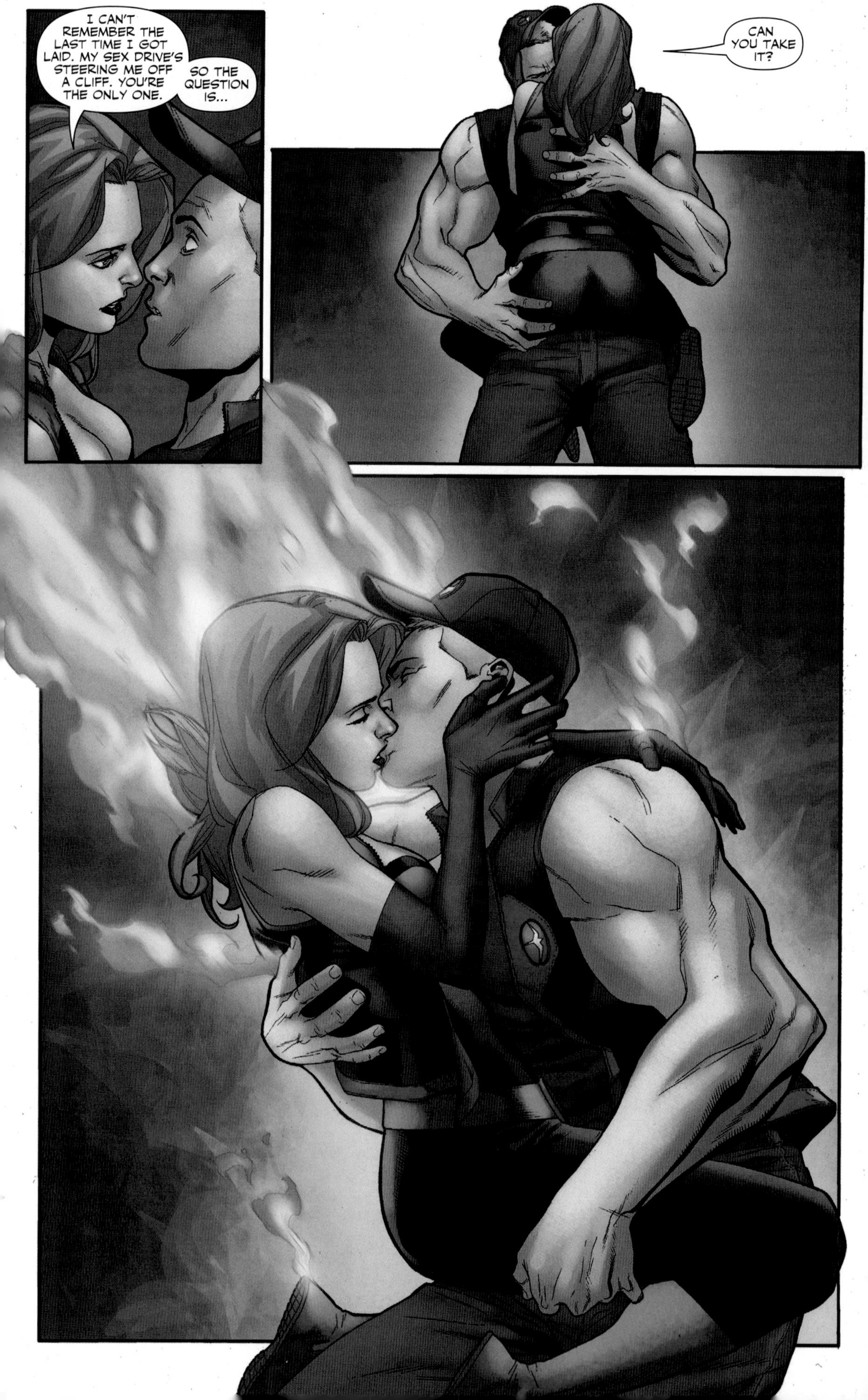
I CAN'T REMEMBER THE LAST TIME I GOT LAID. MY SEX DRIVE'S STEERING ME OFF A CLIFF. YOU'RE THE ONLY ONE.
SO THE QUESTION IS...
CAN YOU TAKE IT?

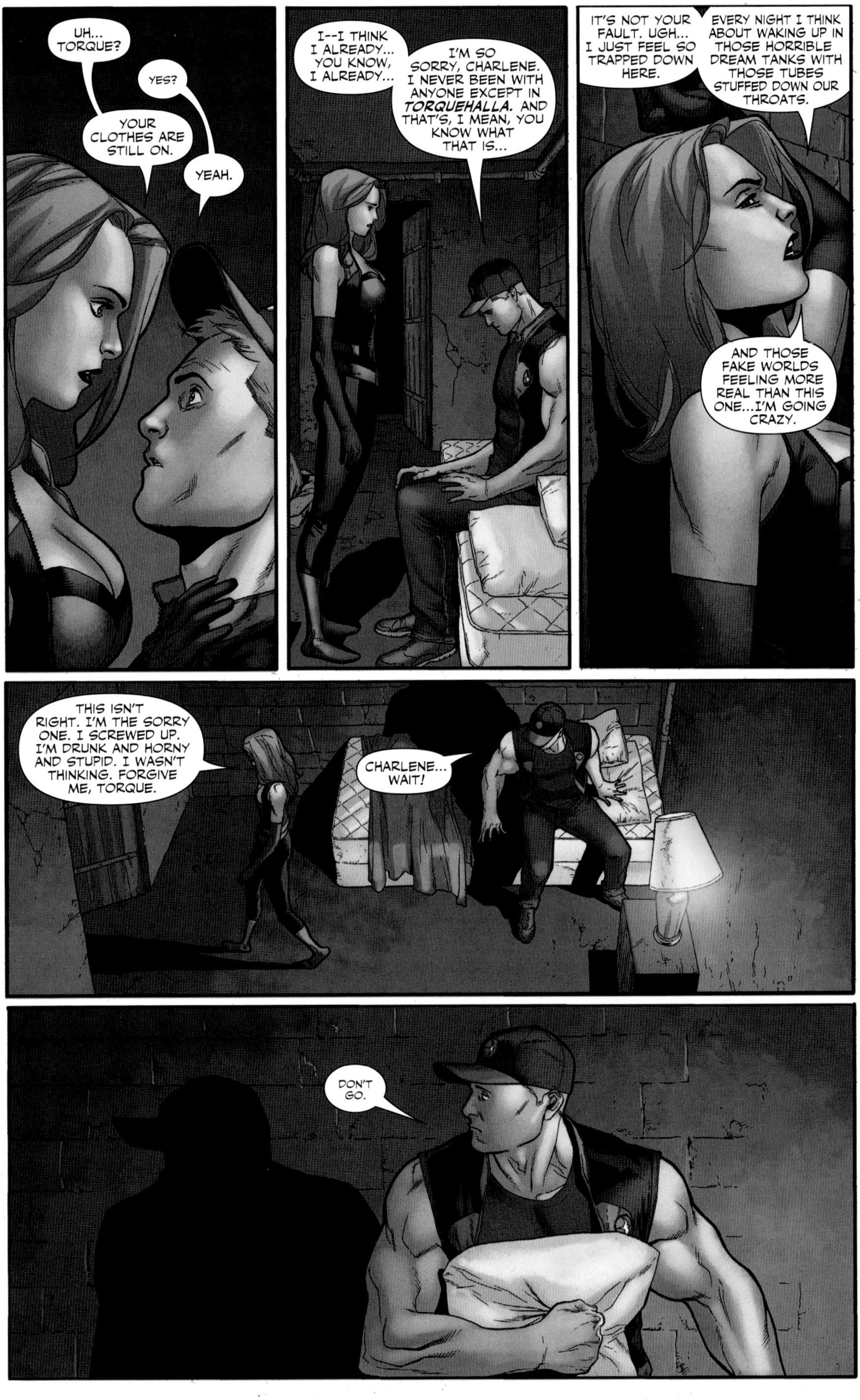
UH... TORQUE?
YES?
YOUR CLOTHES ARE STILL ON.
YEAH.
I--I THINK I ALREADY... YOU KNOW, I ALREADY...
I'M SO SORRY, CHARLENE. I NEVER BEEN WITH ANYONE EXCEPT IN TORQUEHALLA. AND THAT'S, I MEAN, YOU KNOW WHAT THAT IS...
IT'S NOT YOUR FAULT. UGH... I JUST FEEL SO TRAPPED DOWN HERE.
EVERY NIGHT I THINK ABOUT WAKING UP IN THOSE HORRIBLE DREAM TANKS WITH THOSE TUBES STUFFED DOWN OUR THROATS.
AND THOSE FAKE WORLDS FEELING MORE REAL THAN THIS ONE...I'M GOING CRAZY.
THIS ISN'T RIGHT. I'M THE SORRY ONE. I SCREWED UP. I'M DRUNK AND HORNY AND STUPID. I WASN'T THINKING. FORGIVE ME, TORQUE.
CHARLENE... WAIT!
DON'T GO.

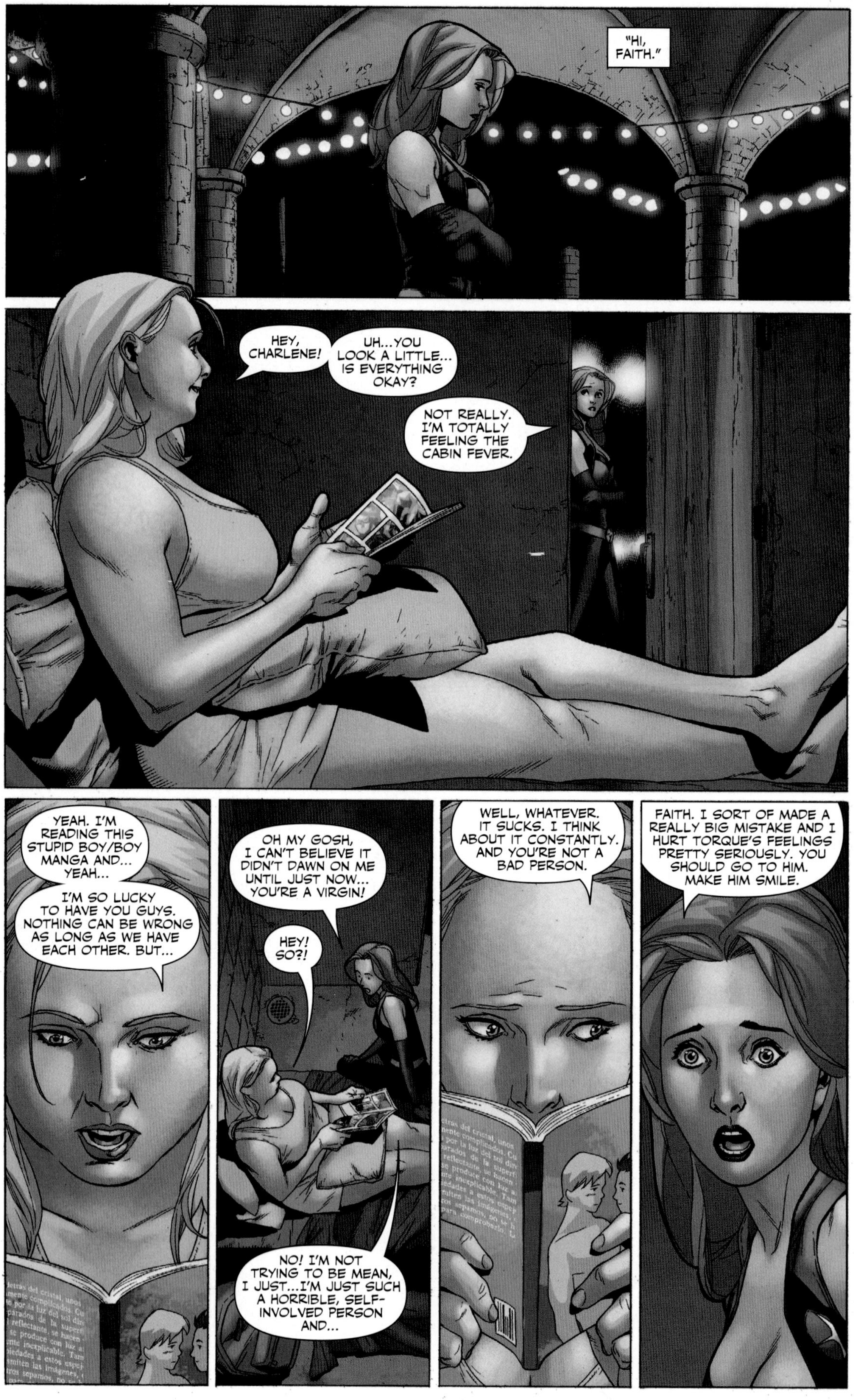
"HI, FAITH."
HEY, CHARLENE!
UH...YOU LOOK A LITTLE... IS EVERYTHING OKAY?
NOT REALLY. I'M TOTALLY FEELING THE CABIN FEVER.
YEAH. I'M READING THIS STUPID BOY/BOY MANGA AND... YEAH...
I'M SO LUCKY TO HAVE YOU GUYS. NOTHING CAN BE WRONG AS LONG AS WE HAVE EACH OTHER. BUT...
OH MY GOSH, I CAN'T BELIEVE IT DIDN'T DAWN ON ME UNTIL JUST NOW... YOU'RE A VIRGIN!
HEY! SO?!
NO! I'M NOT TRYING TO BE MEAN, I JUST...I'M JUST SUCH A HORRIBLE, SELF-INVOLVED PERSON AND...
WELL, WHATEVER. IT SUCKS. I THINK ABOUT IT CONSTANTLY. AND YOU'RE NOT A BAD PERSON.
FAITH. I SORT OF MADE A REALLY BIG MISTAKE AND I HURT TORQUE'S FEELINGS PRETTY SERIOUSLY. YOU SHOULD GO TO HIM. MAKE HIM SMILE.

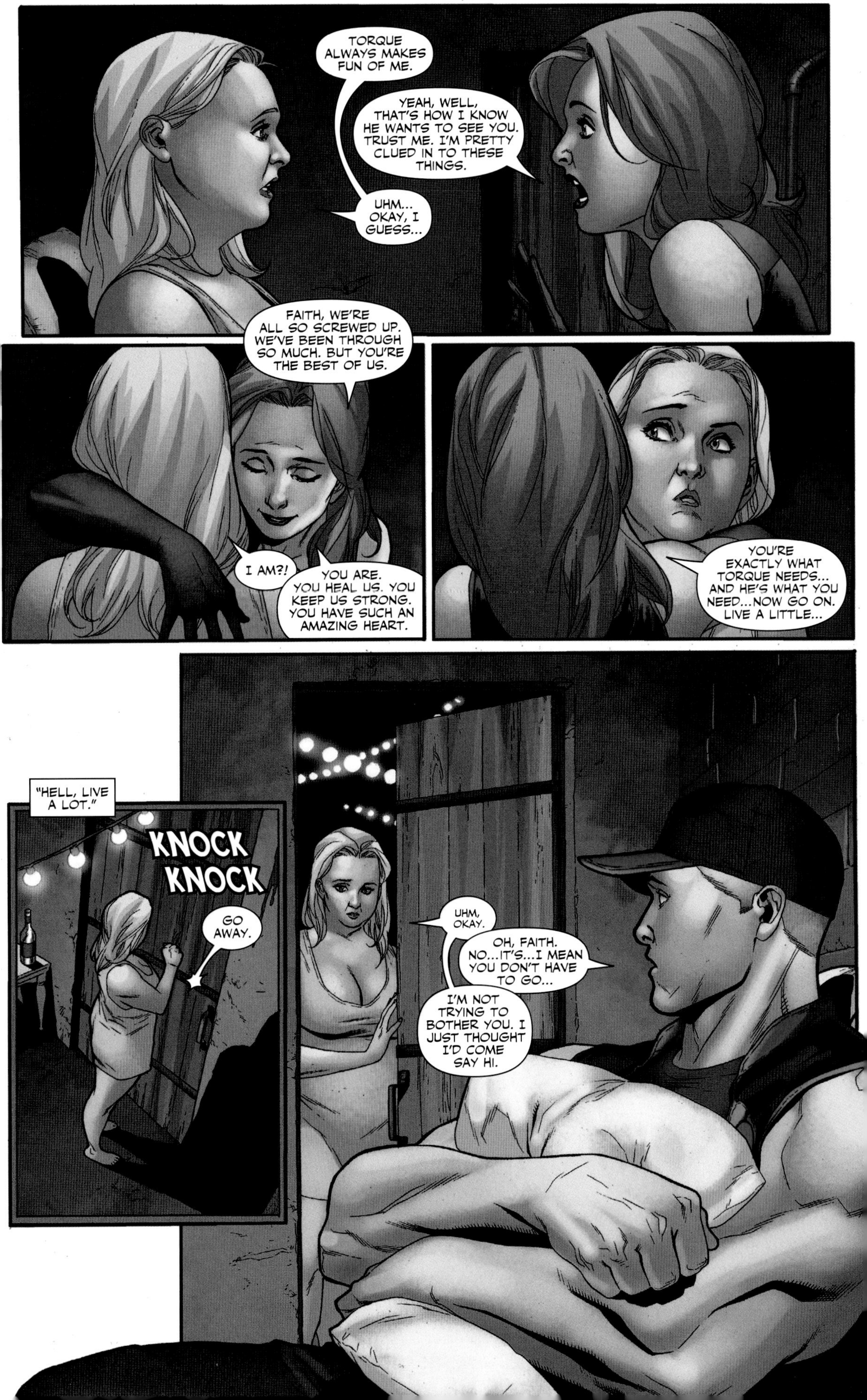
TORQUE ALWAYS MAKES FUN OF ME.
YEAH, WELL, THAT'S HOW I KNOW HE WANTS TO SEE YOU. TRUST ME. I'M PRETTY CLUED IN TO THESE THINGS.
UHM... OKAY, I GUESS...
FAITH, WE'RE ALL SO SCREWED UP. WE'VE BEEN THROUGH SO MUCH. BUT YOU'RE THE BEST OF US.
I AM?!
YOU ARE. YOU HEAL US. YOU KEEP US STRONG. YOU HAVE SUCH AN AMAZING HEART.
YOU'RE EXACTLY WHAT TORQUE NEEDS... AND HE'S WHAT YOU NEED...NOW GO ON. LIVE A LITTLE...
"HELL, LIVE A LOT."
KNOCK KNOCK
GO AWAY.
UHM, OKAY.
OH, FAITH. NO...IT'S...I MEAN YOU DON'T HAVE TO GO...
I'M NOT TRYING TO BOTHER YOU. I JUST THOUGHT I'D COME SAY HI.

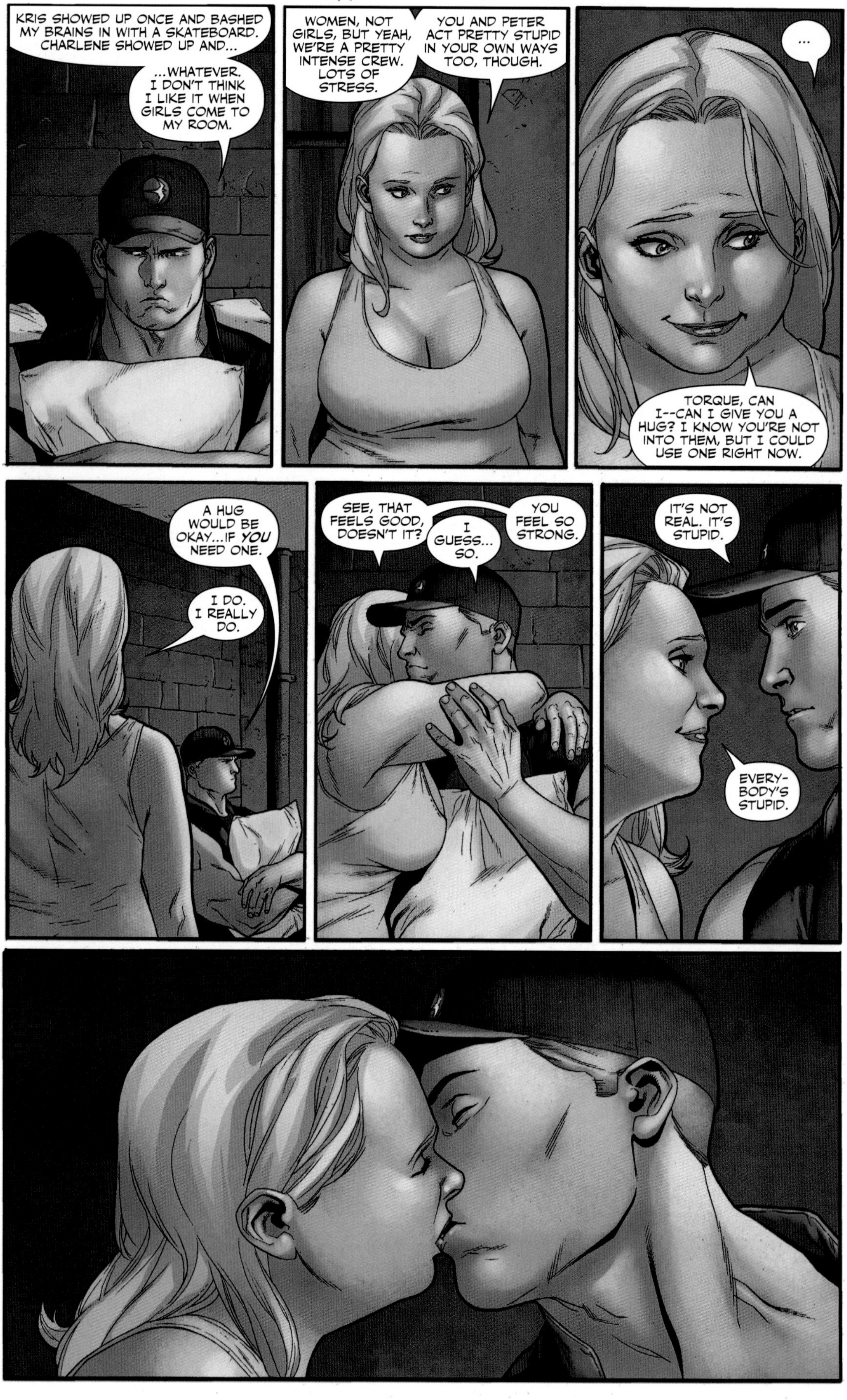
KRIS SHOWED UP ONCE AND BASHED MY BRAINS IN WITH A SKATEBOARD. CHARLENE SHOWED UP AND...
...WHATEVER. I DON'T THINK I LIKE IT WHEN GIRLS COME TO MY ROOM.
WOMEN, NOT GIRLS, BUT YEAH, WE'RE A PRETTY INTENSE CREW. LOTS OF STRESS.
YOU AND PETER ACT PRETTY STUPID IN YOUR OWN WAYS TOO, THOUGH.
...
TORQUE, CAN I--CAN I GIVE YOU A HUG? I KNOW YOU'RE NOT INTO THEM, BUT I COULD USE ONE RIGHT NOW.
A HUG WOULD BE OKAY...IF *YOU* NEED ONE.
I DO. I REALLY DO.
SEE, THAT FEELS GOOD, DOESN'T IT?
I GUESS... SO.
YOU FEEL SO STRONG.
IT'S NOT REAL. IT'S STUPID.
EVERY-BODY'S STUPID.

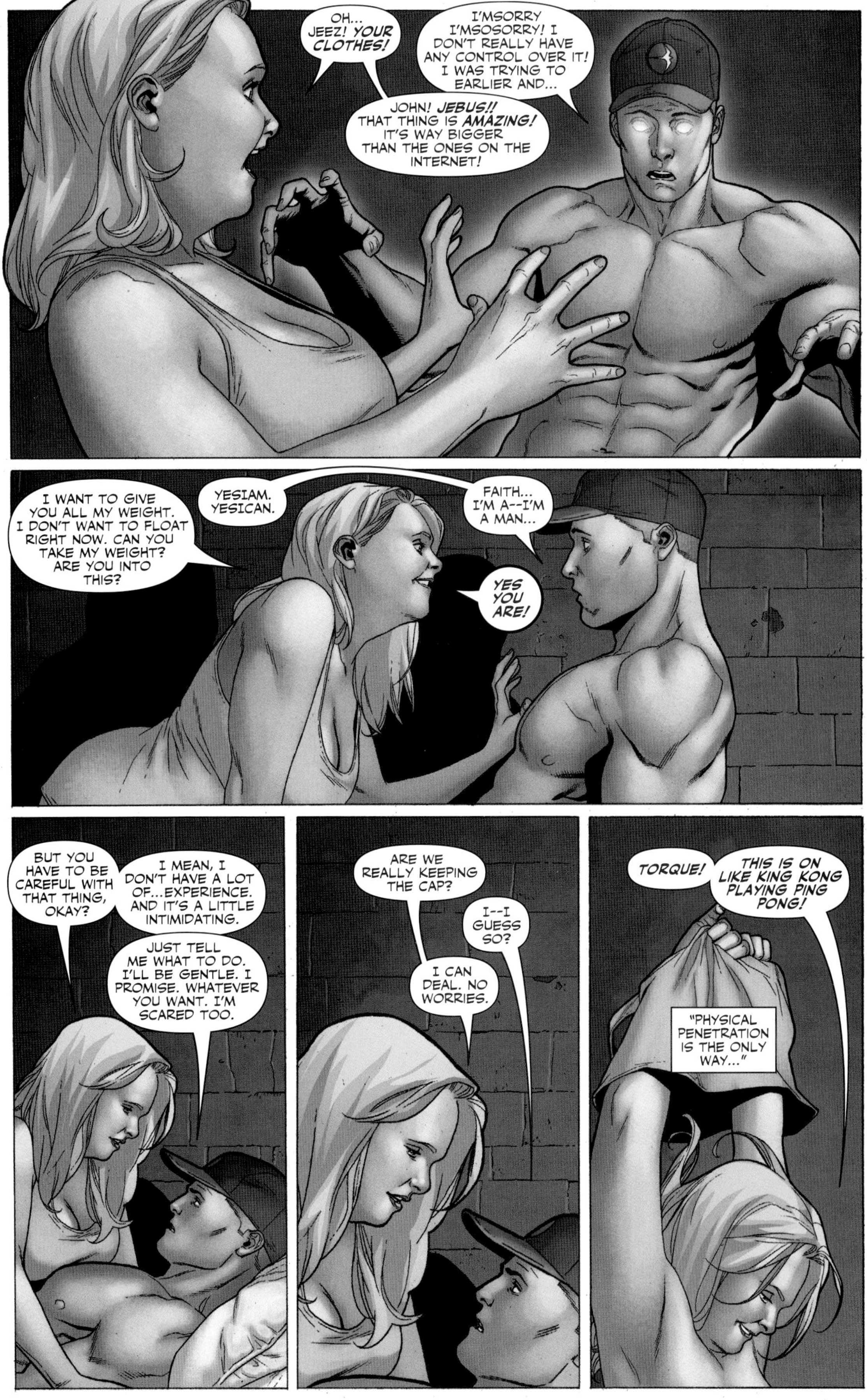

OH... JEEZ! *YOUR CLOTHES!*
I'MSORRY I'MSOSORRY! I DON'T REALLY HAVE ANY CONTROL OVER IT! I WAS TRYING TO EARLIER AND...
JOHN! *JEBUS!!* THAT THING IS *AMAZING!* IT'S WAY BIGGER THAN THE ONES ON THE INTERNET!
I WANT TO GIVE YOU ALL MY WEIGHT. I DON'T WANT TO FLOAT RIGHT NOW. CAN YOU TAKE MY WEIGHT? ARE YOU INTO THIS?
YESIAM. YESICAN.
FAITH... I'M A--I'M A MAN...
YES YOU ARE!
BUT YOU HAVE TO BE CAREFUL WITH THAT THING, OKAY?
I MEAN, I DON'T HAVE A LOT OF...EXPERIENCE. AND IT'S A LITTLE INTIMIDATING.
JUST TELL ME WHAT TO DO. I'LL BE GENTLE. I PROMISE. WHATEVER YOU WANT. I'M SCARED TOO.
ARE WE REALLY KEEPING THE CAP?
I--I GUESS SO?
I CAN DEAL. NO WORRIES.
TORQUE!
THIS IS ON LIKE KING KONG PLAYING PING PONG!
"PHYSICAL PENETRATION IS THE ONLY WAY..."

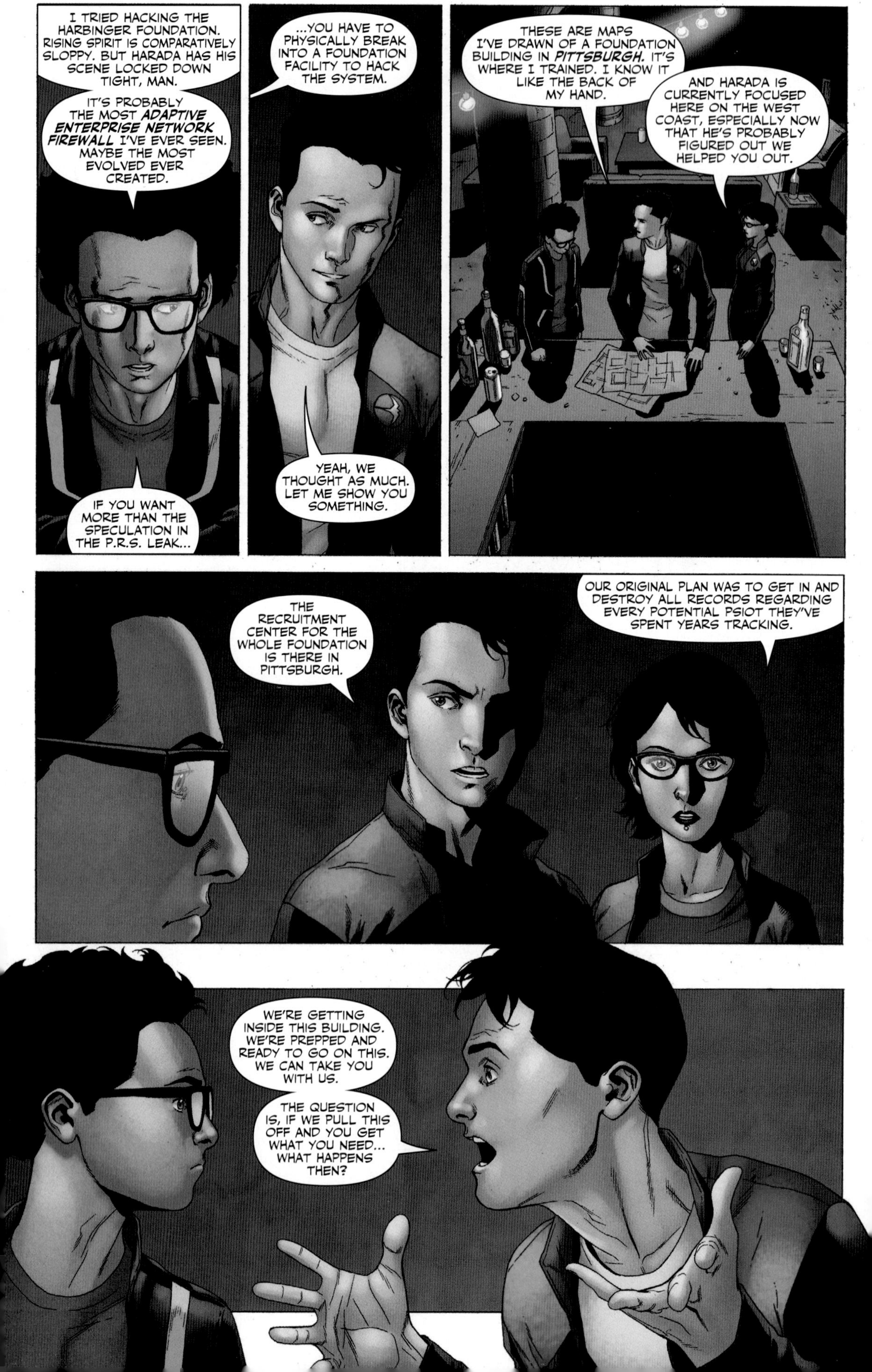
I TRIED HACKING THE HARBINGER FOUNDATION. RISING SPIRIT IS COMPARATIVELY SLOPPY. BUT HARADA HAS HIS SCENE LOCKED DOWN TIGHT, MAN.
IT'S PROBABLY THE MOST ADAPTIVE ENTERPRISE NETWORK FIREWALL I'VE EVER SEEN. MAYBE THE MOST EVOLVED EVER CREATED.
IF YOU WANT MORE THAN THE SPECULATION IN THE P.R.S. LEAK...
...YOU HAVE TO PHYSICALLY BREAK INTO A FOUNDATION FACILITY TO HACK THE SYSTEM.
YEAH, WE THOUGHT AS MUCH. LET ME SHOW YOU SOMETHING.
THESE ARE MAPS I'VE DRAWN OF A FOUNDATION BUILDING IN PITTSBURGH. IT'S WHERE I TRAINED. I KNOW IT LIKE THE BACK OF MY HAND.
AND HARADA IS CURRENTLY FOCUSED HERE ON THE WEST COAST, ESPECIALLY NOW THAT HE'S PROBABLY FIGURED OUT WE HELPED YOU OUT.
THE RECRUITMENT CENTER FOR THE WHOLE FOUNDATION IS THERE IN PITTSBURGH.
OUR ORIGINAL PLAN WAS TO GET IN AND DESTROY ALL RECORDS REGARDING EVERY POTENTIAL PSIOT THEY'VE SPENT YEARS TRACKING.
WE'RE GETTING INSIDE THIS BUILDING. WE'RE PREPPED AND READY TO GO ON THIS. WE CAN TAKE YOU WITH US.
THE QUESTION IS, IF WE PULL THIS OFF AND YOU GET WHAT YOU NEED... WHAT HAPPENS THEN?

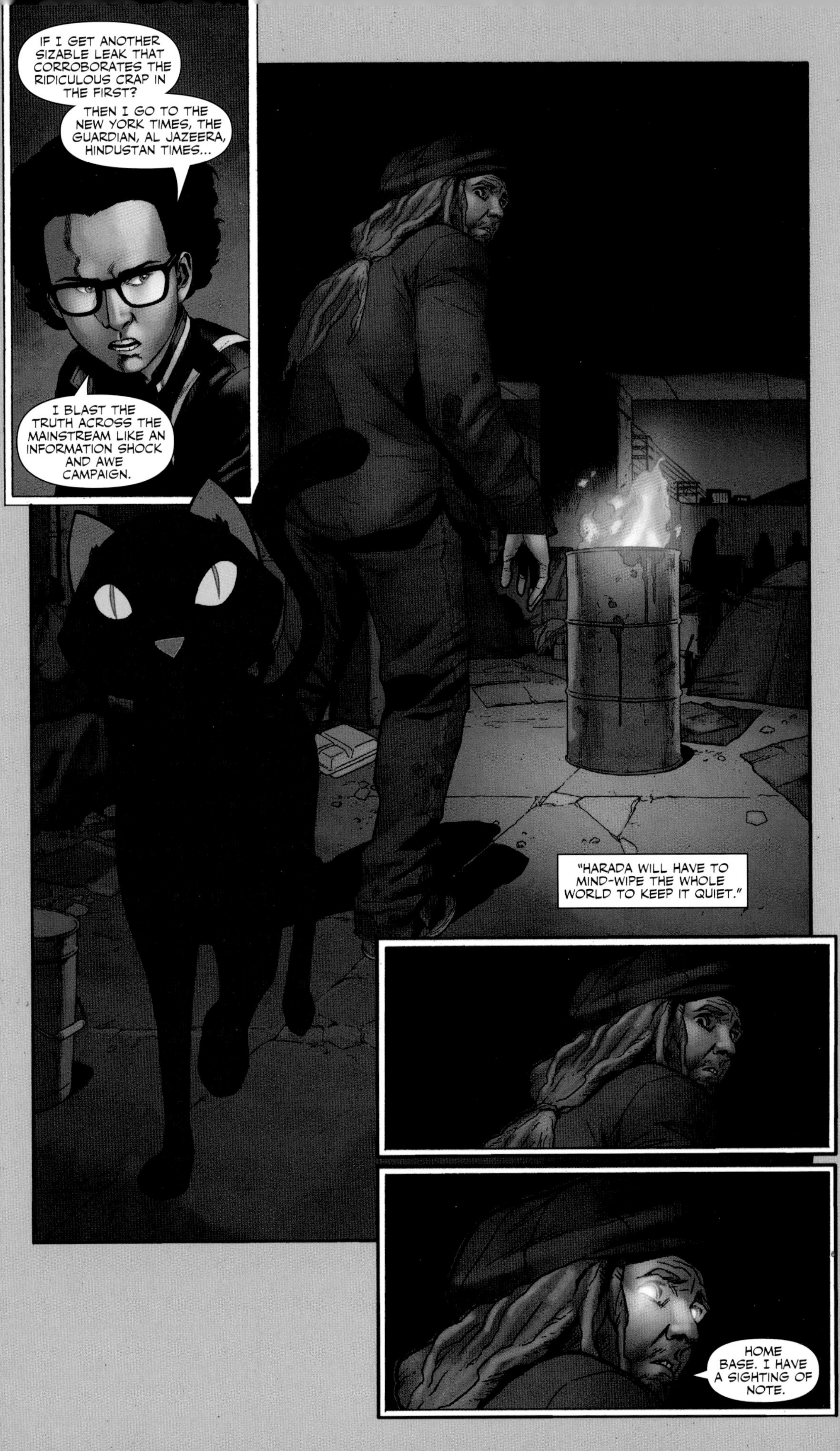
IF I GET ANOTHER SIZABLE LEAK THAT CORROBORATES THE RIDICULOUS CRAP IN THE FIRST?
THEN I GO TO THE NEW YORK TIMES, THE GUARDIAN, AL JAZEERA, HINDUSTAN TIMES...
I BLAST THE TRUTH ACROSS THE MAINSTREAM LIKE AN INFORMATION SHOCK AND AWE CAMPAIGN.
"HARADA WILL HAVE TO MIND-WIPE THE WHOLE WORLD TO KEEP IT QUIET."
HOME BASE. I HAVE A SIGHTING OF NOTE.

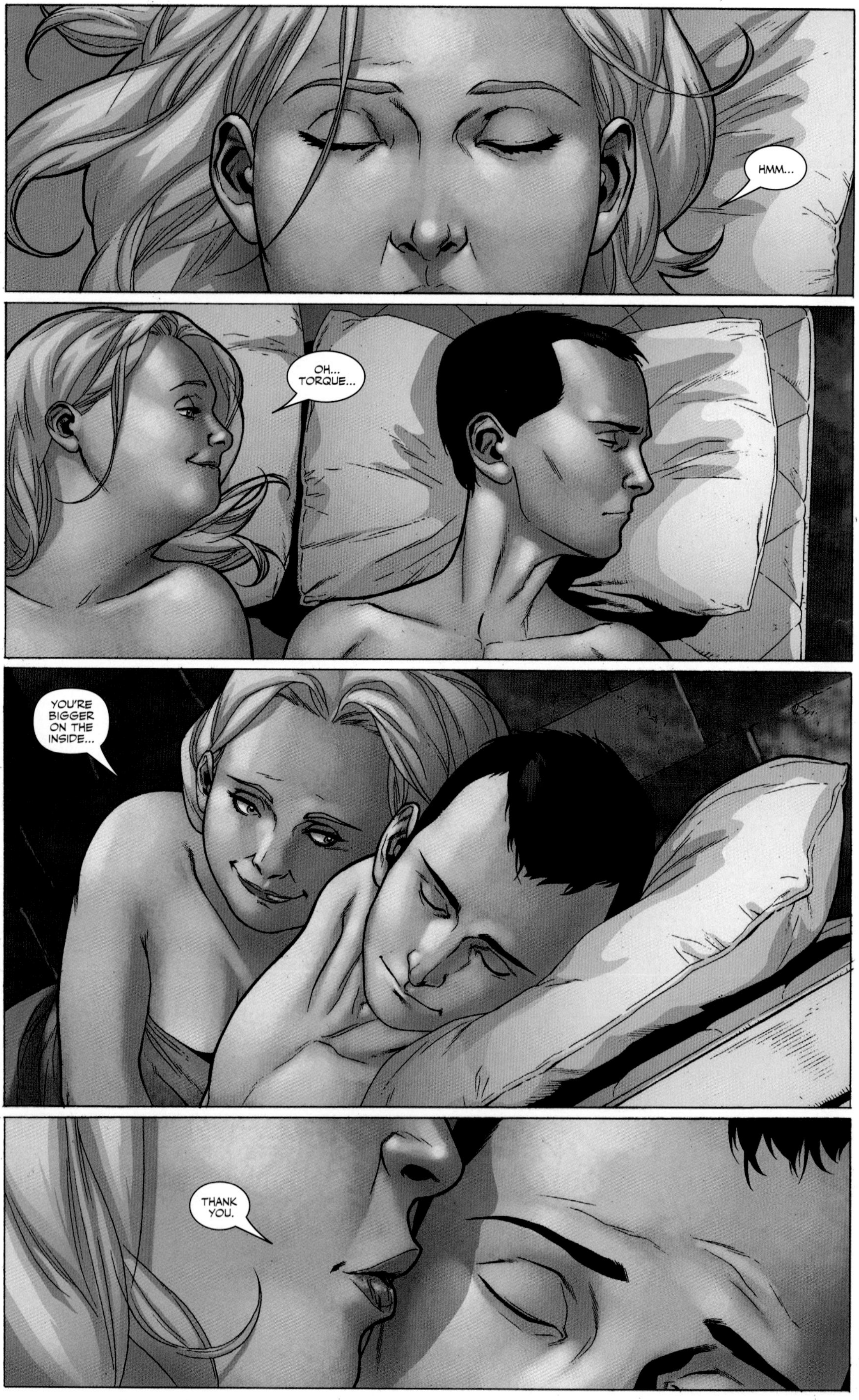
HMM...
OH... TORQUE...
YOU'RE BIGGER ON THE INSIDE...
THANK YOU.

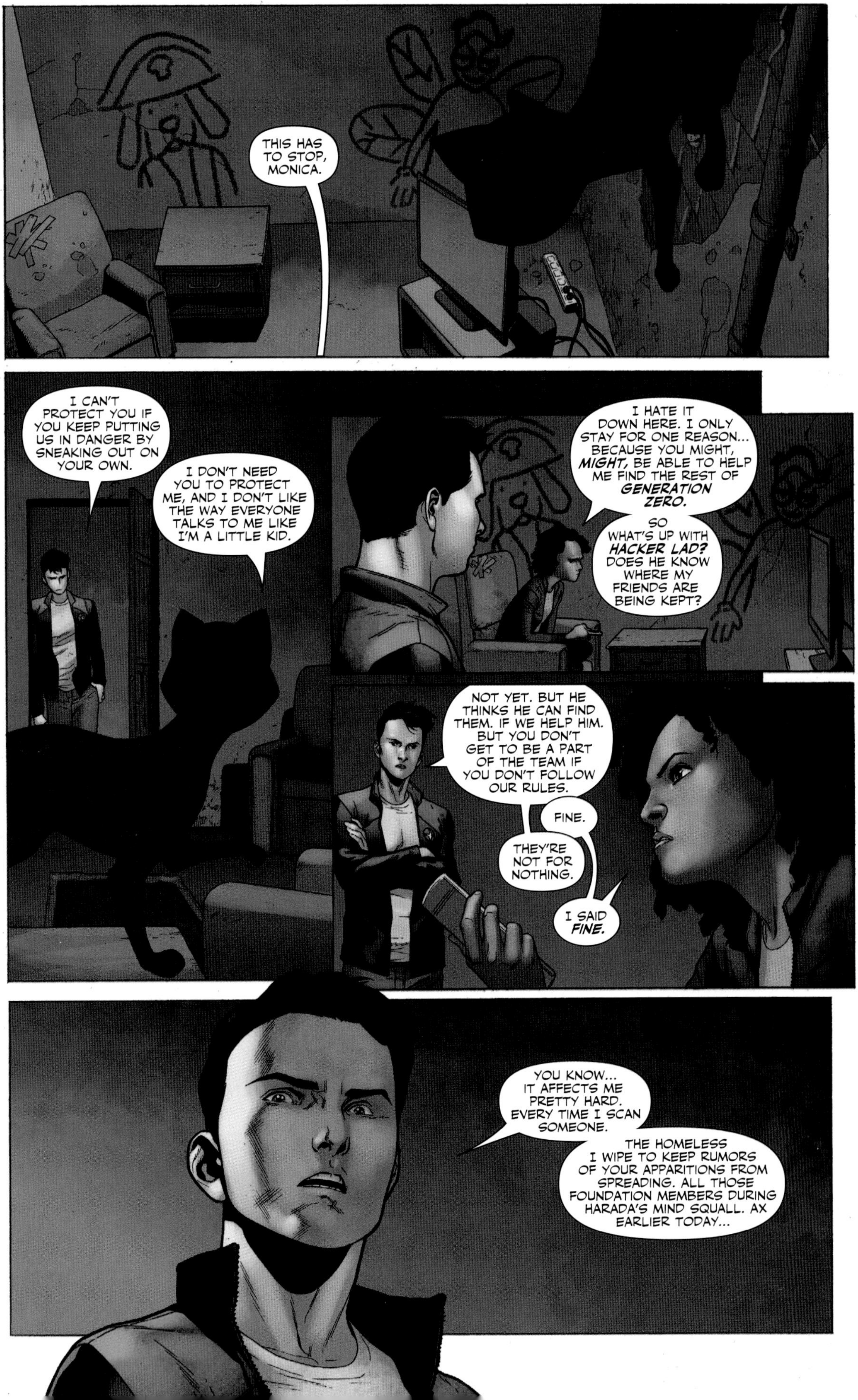
THIS HAS TO STOP, MONICA.
I CAN'T PROTECT YOU IF YOU KEEP PUTTING US IN DANGER BY SNEAKING OUT ON YOUR OWN.
I DON'T NEED YOU TO PROTECT ME, AND I DON'T LIKE THE WAY EVERYONE TALKS TO ME LIKE I'M A LITTLE KID.
I HATE IT DOWN HERE. I ONLY STAY FOR ONE REASON... BECAUSE YOU MIGHT, MIGHT, BE ABLE TO HELP ME FIND THE REST OF GENERATION ZERO.
SO WHAT'S UP WITH HACKER LAD? DOES HE KNOW WHERE MY FRIENDS ARE BEING KEPT?
NOT YET. BUT HE THINKS HE CAN FIND THEM. IF WE HELP HIM. BUT YOU DON'T GET TO BE A PART OF THE TEAM IF YOU DON'T FOLLOW OUR RULES.
FINE.
THEY'RE NOT FOR NOTHING.
I SAID FINE.
YOU KNOW... IT AFFECTS ME PRETTY HARD. EVERY TIME I SCAN SOMEONE.
THE HOMELESS I WIPE TO KEEP RUMORS OF YOUR APPARITIONS FROM SPREADING. ALL THOSE FOUNDATION MEMBERS DURING HARADA'S MIND SQUALL. AX EARLIER TODAY...

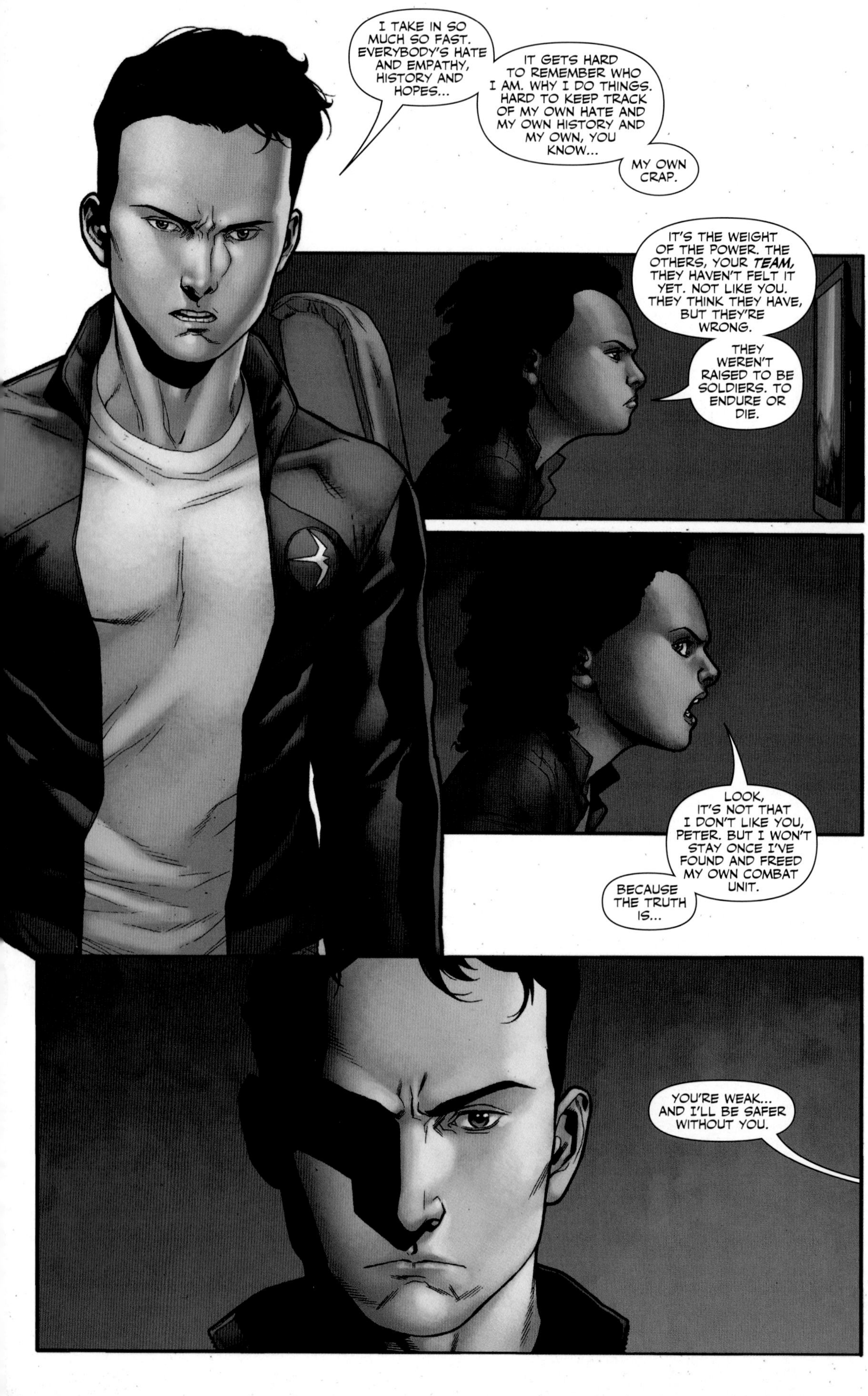
I TAKE IN SO MUCH SO FAST. EVERYBODY'S HATE AND EMPATHY, HISTORY AND HOPES...
IT GETS HARD TO REMEMBER WHO I AM. WHY I DO THINGS. HARD TO KEEP TRACK OF MY OWN HATE AND MY OWN HISTORY AND MY OWN, YOU KNOW...
MY OWN CRAP.
IT'S THE WEIGHT OF THE POWER. THE OTHERS, YOUR *TEAM,* THEY HAVEN'T FELT IT YET. NOT LIKE YOU. THEY THINK THEY HAVE, BUT THEY'RE WRONG.
THEY WEREN'T RAISED TO BE SOLDIERS. TO ENDURE OR DIE.
LOOK, IT'S NOT THAT I DON'T LIKE YOU, PETER. BUT I WON'T STAY ONCE I'VE FOUND AND FREED MY OWN COMBAT UNIT.
BECAUSE THE TRUTH IS...
YOU'RE WEAK... AND I'LL BE SAFER WITHOUT YOU.

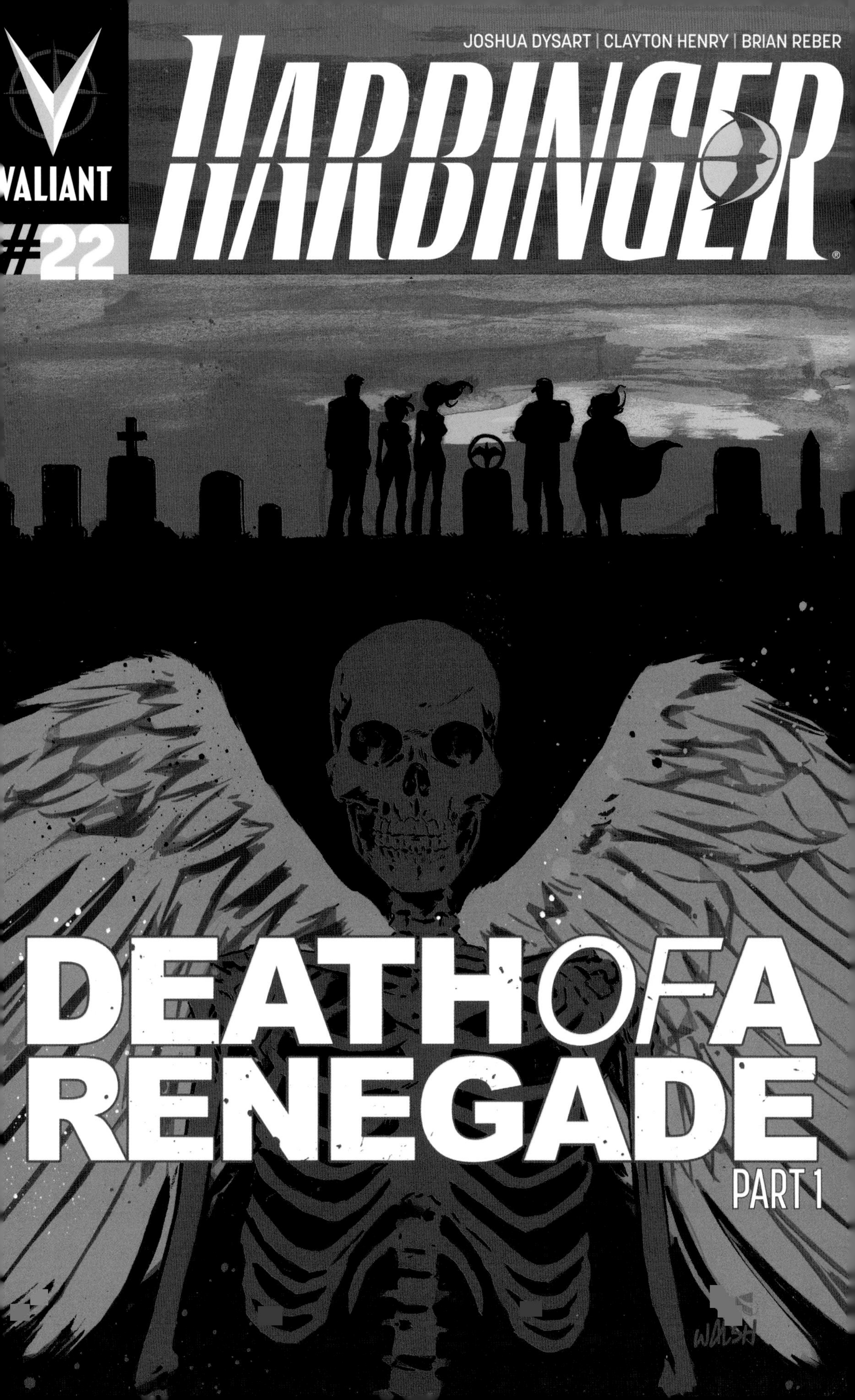
VALIANT
#22
JOSHUA DYSART | CLAYTON HENRY | BRIAN REBER
HARBINGER
DEATH OF A
RENEGADE
PART 1
WALSH

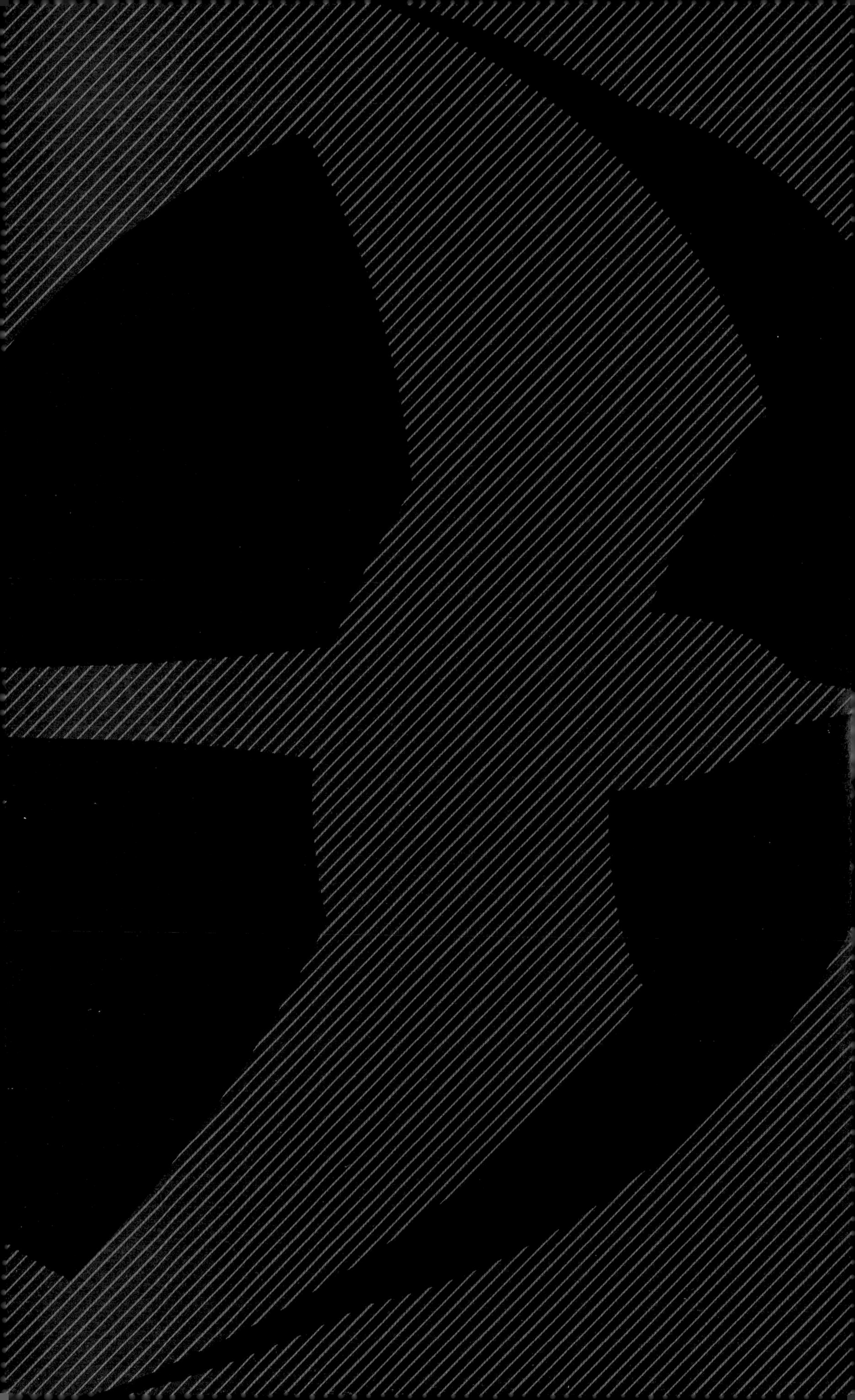

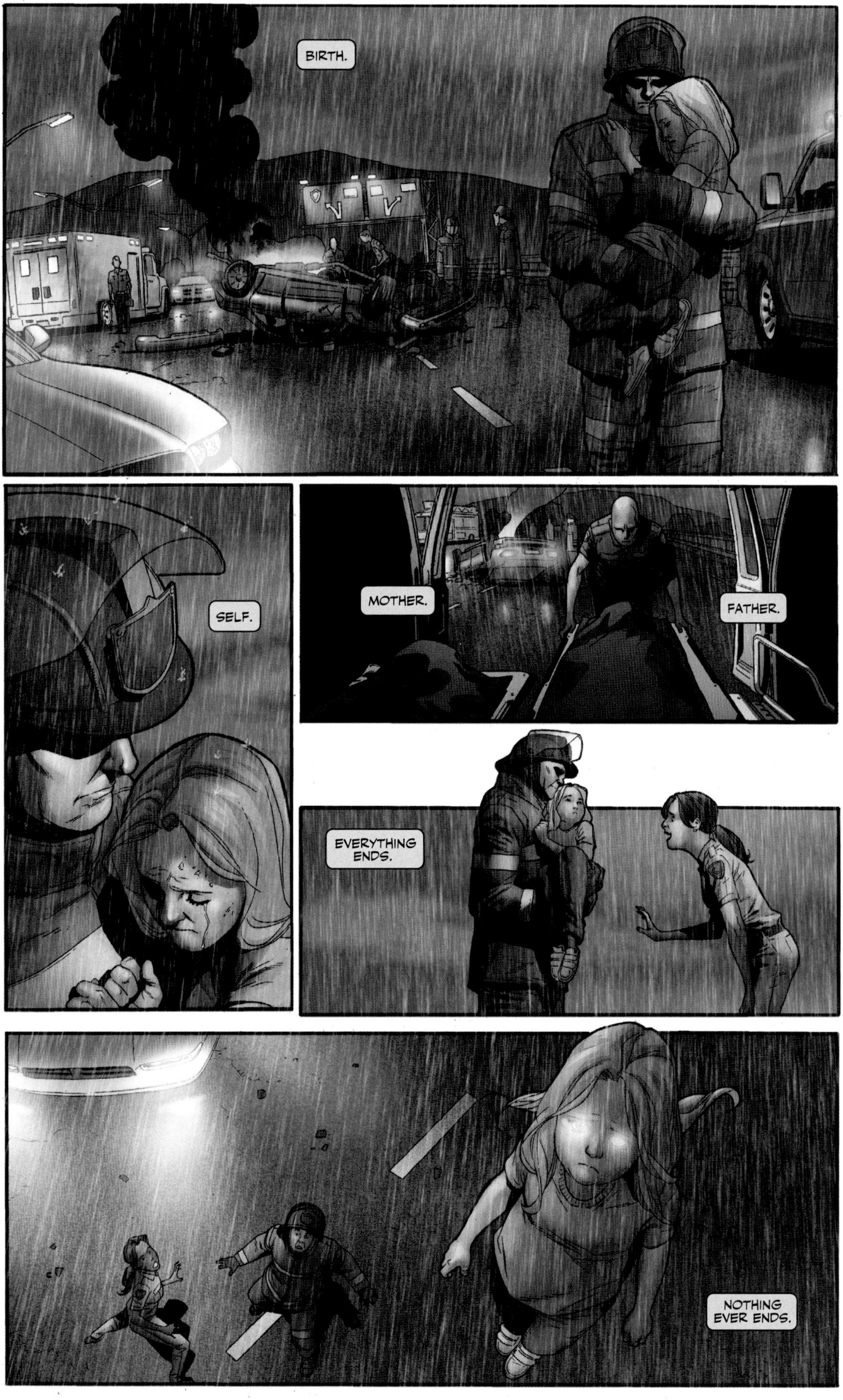
BIRTH.
SELF.
MOTHER.
FATHER.
EVERYTHING ENDS.
NOTHING EVER ENDS.

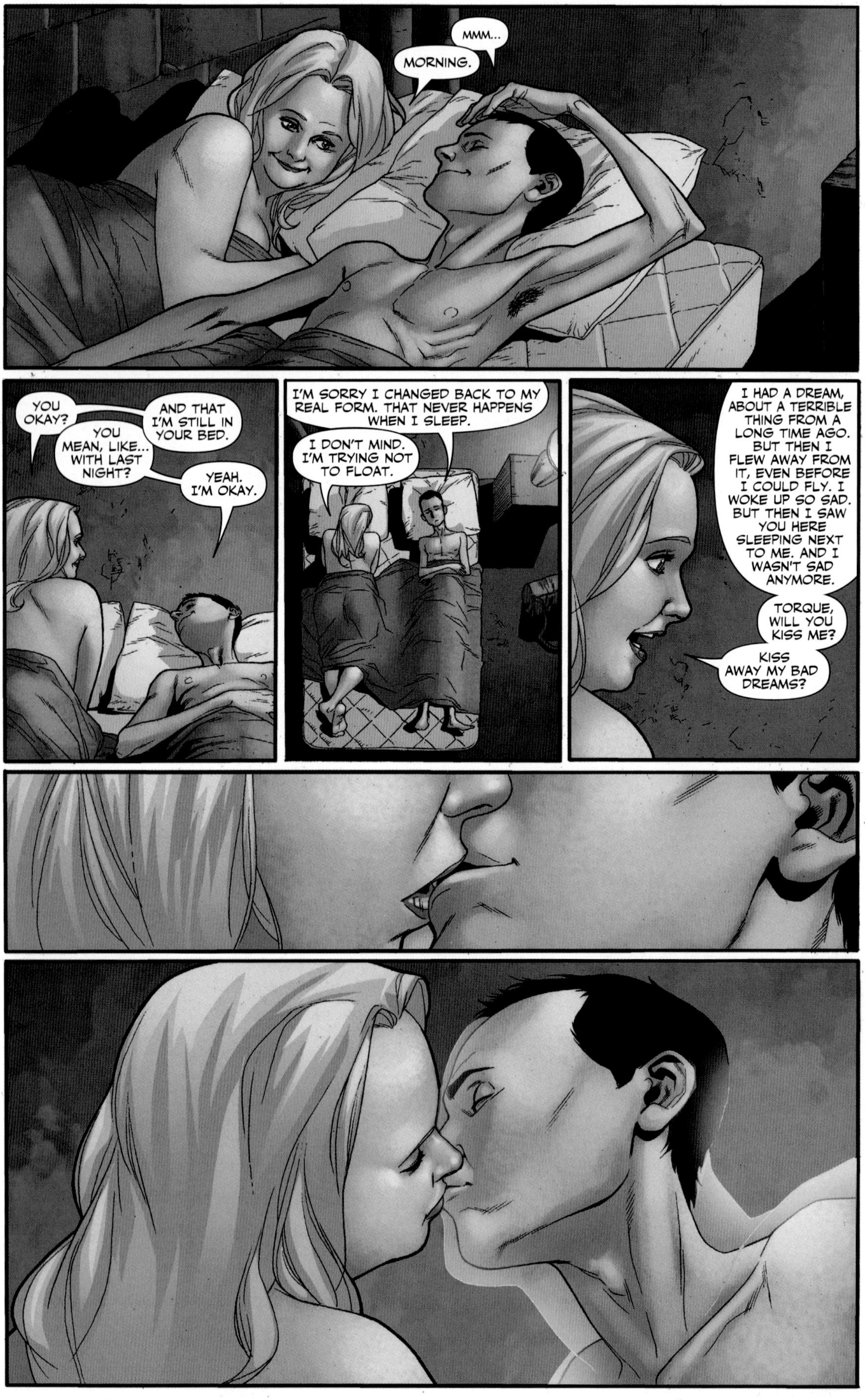
MMM...
MORNING.
YOU OKAY?
AND THAT I'M STILL IN YOUR BED.
YOU MEAN, LIKE... WITH LAST NIGHT?
YEAH. I'M OKAY.
I'M SORRY I CHANGED BACK TO MY REAL FORM. THAT NEVER HAPPENS WHEN I SLEEP.
I DON'T MIND. I'M TRYING NOT TO FLOAT.
I HAD A DREAM, ABOUT A TERRIBLE THING FROM A LONG TIME AGO. BUT THEN I FLEW AWAY FROM IT, EVEN BEFORE I COULD FLY. I WOKE UP SO SAD. BUT THEN I SAW YOU HERE SLEEPING NEXT TO ME. AND I WASN'T SAD ANYMORE.
TORQUE, WILL YOU KISS ME?
KISS AWAY MY BAD DREAMS?

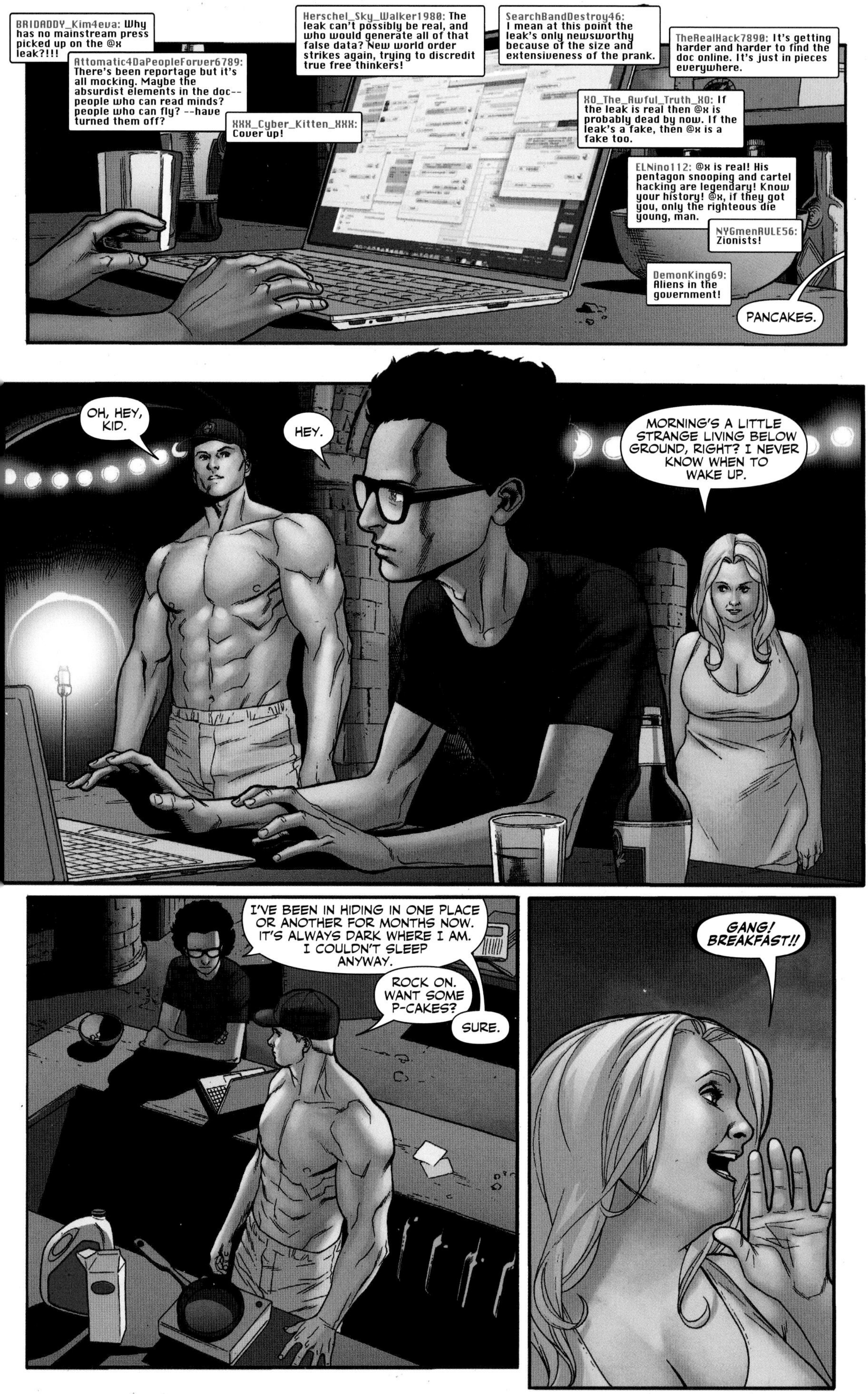

BRIDADDY_Kim4eva: Why has no mainstream press picked up on the @x leak?!!!
Attomatic4DaPeopleForver6789: There's been reportage but it's all mocking. Maybe the absurdist elements in the doc-- people who can read minds? people who can fly? --have turned them off?
XXX_Cyber_Kitten_XXX: Cover up!
Herschel_Sky_Walker1980: The leak can't possibly be real, and who would generate all of that false data? New world order strikes again, trying to discredit true free thinkers!
SearchBandDestroy46: I mean at this point the leak's only newsworthy because of the size and extensiveness of the prank.
TheRealHack7890: It's getting harder and harder to find the doc online. It's just in pieces everywhere.
XO_The_Awful_Truth_XO: If the leak is real then @x is probably dead by now. If the leak's a fake, then @x is a fake too.
ELNino112: @x is real! His pentagon snooping and cartel hacking are legendary! Know your history! @x, if they got you, only the righteous die young, man.
NYGmenRULE56: Zionists!
DemonKing69: Aliens in the government!
PANCAKES.
OH, HEY, KID.
HEY.
MORNING'S A LITTLE STRANGE LIVING BELOW GROUND, RIGHT? I NEVER KNOW WHEN TO WAKE UP.
I'VE BEEN IN HIDING IN ONE PLACE OR ANOTHER FOR MONTHS NOW. IT'S ALWAYS DARK WHERE I AM. I COULDN'T SLEEP ANYWAY.
ROCK ON. WANT SOME P-CAKES?
SURE.
GANG! BREAKFAST!!

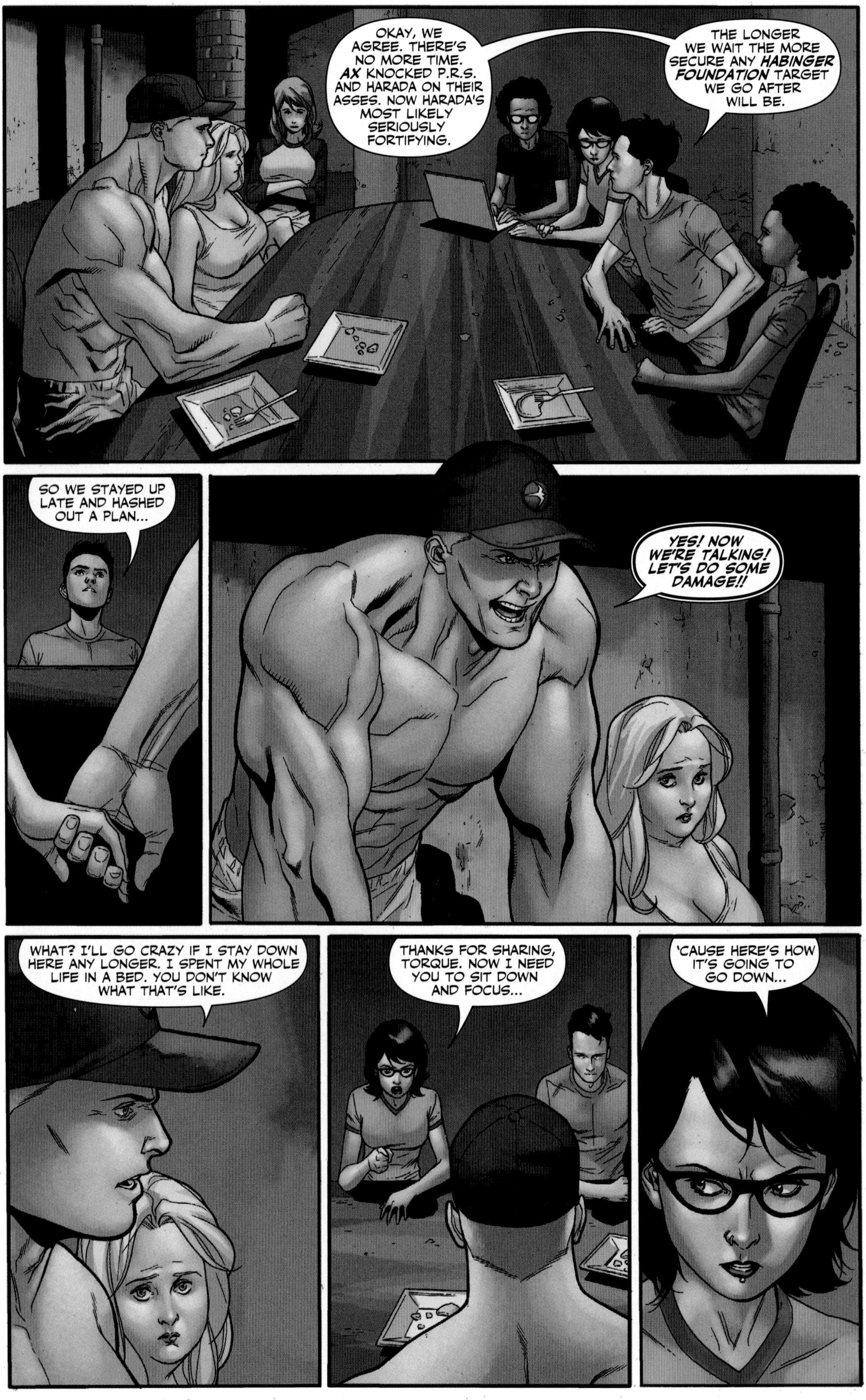
OKAY, WE AGREE. THERE'S NO MORE TIME. AX KNOCKED P.R.S. AND HARADA ON THEIR ASSES. NOW HARADA'S MOST LIKELY SERIOUSLY FORTIFYING.
THE LONGER WE WAIT THE MORE SECURE ANY HABINGER FOUNDATION TARGET WE GO AFTER WILL BE.
SO WE STAYED UP LATE AND HASHED OUT A PLAN...
YES! NOW WE'RE TALKING! LET'S DO SOME DAMAGE!!
WHAT? I'LL GO CRAZY IF I STAY DOWN HERE ANY LONGER. I SPENT MY WHOLE LIFE IN A BED. YOU DON'T KNOW WHAT THAT'S LIKE.
THANKS FOR SHARING, TORQUE. NOW I NEED YOU TO SIT DOWN AND FOCUS...
'CAUSE HERE'S HOW IT'S GOING TO GO DOWN...

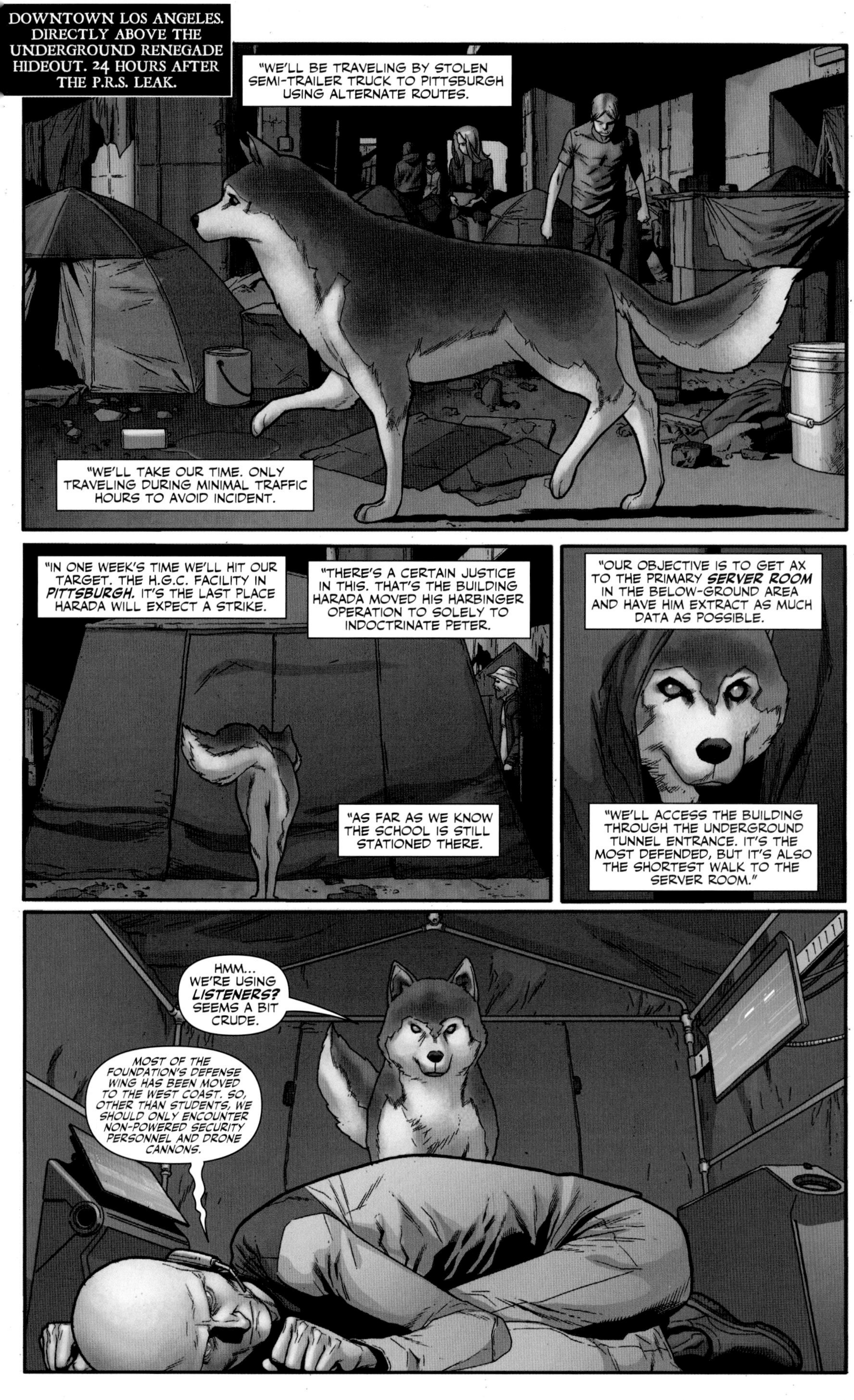
DOWNTOWN LOS ANGELES. DIRECTLY ABOVE THE UNDERGROUND RENEGADE HIDEOUT. 24 HOURS AFTER THE P.R.S. LEAK.
"WE'LL BE TRAVELING BY STOLEN SEMI-TRAILER TRUCK TO PITTSBURGH USING ALTERNATE ROUTES.
"WE'LL TAKE OUR TIME. ONLY TRAVELING DURING MINIMAL TRAFFIC HOURS TO AVOID INCIDENT.
"IN ONE WEEK'S TIME WE'LL HIT OUR TARGET. THE H.G.C. FACILITY IN PITTSBURGH. IT'S THE LAST PLACE HARADA WILL EXPECT A STRIKE.
"THERE'S A CERTAIN JUSTICE IN THIS. THAT'S THE BUILDING HARADA MOVED HIS HARBINGER OPERATION TO SOLELY TO INDOCTRINATE PETER.
"AS FAR AS WE KNOW THE SCHOOL IS STILL STATIONED THERE.
"OUR OBJECTIVE IS TO GET AX TO THE PRIMARY SERVER ROOM IN THE BELOW-GROUND AREA AND HAVE HIM EXTRACT AS MUCH DATA AS POSSIBLE.
"WE'LL ACCESS THE BUILDING THROUGH THE UNDERGROUND TUNNEL ENTRANCE. IT'S THE MOST DEFENDED, BUT IT'S ALSO THE SHORTEST WALK TO THE SERVER ROOM."
HMM... WE'RE USING LISTENERS? SEEMS A BIT CRUDE.
MOST OF THE FOUNDATION'S DEFENSE WING HAS BEEN MOVED TO THE WEST COAST. SO, OTHER THAN STUDENTS, WE SHOULD ONLY ENCOUNTER NON-POWERED SECURITY PERSONNEL AND DRONE CANNONS.

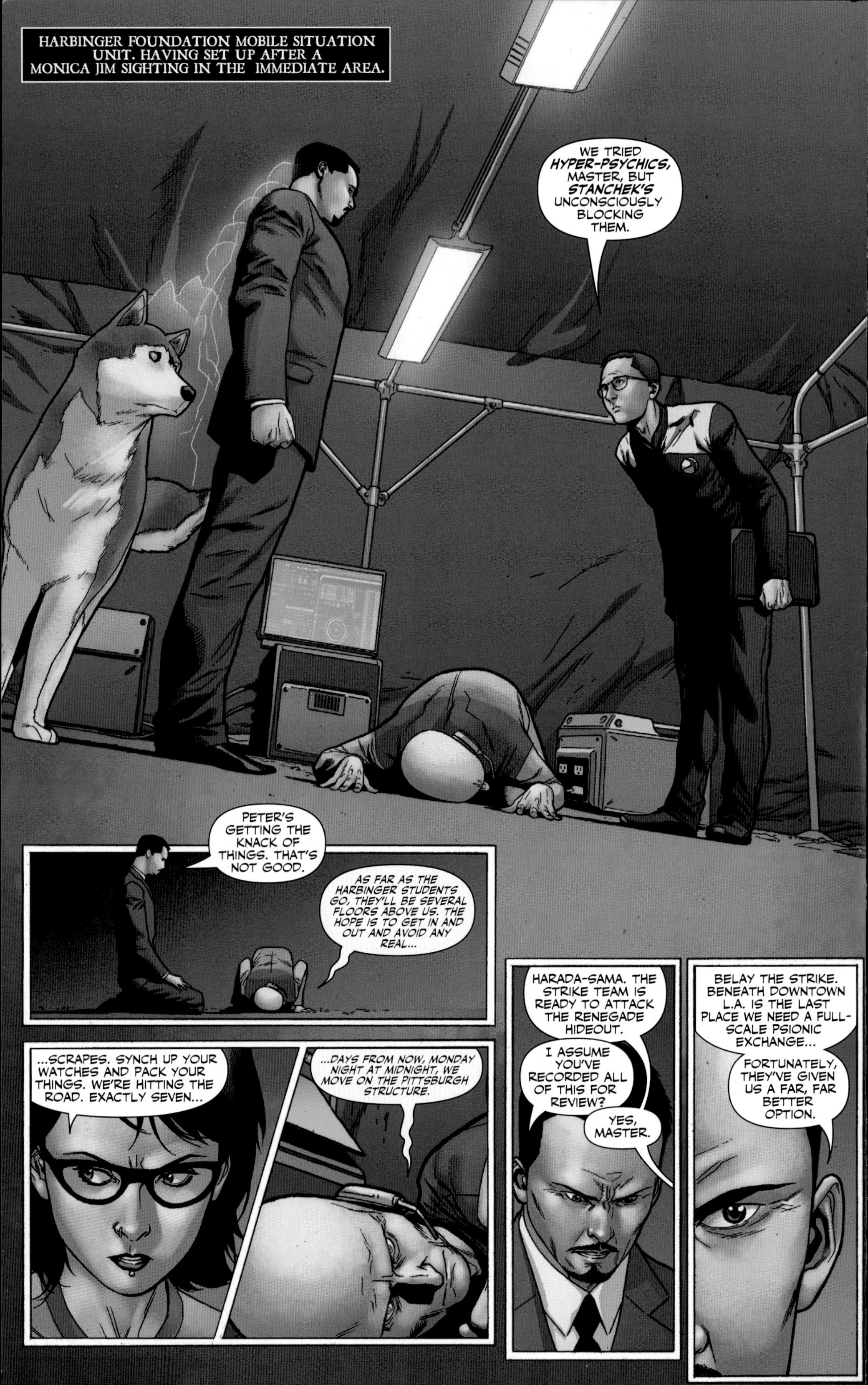
HARBINGER FOUNDATION MOBILE SITUATION UNIT. HAVING SET UP AFTER A MONICA JIM SIGHTING IN THE IMMEDIATE AREA.
WE TRIED HYPER-PSYCHICS, MASTER, BUT STANCHEK'S UNCONSCIOUSLY BLOCKING THEM.
PETER'S GETTING THE KNACK OF THINGS. THAT'S NOT GOOD.
AS FAR AS THE HARBINGER STUDENTS GO, THEY'LL BE SEVERAL FLOORS ABOVE US. THE HOPE IS TO GET IN AND OUT AND AVOID ANY REAL...
...SCRAPES. SYNCH UP YOUR WATCHES AND PACK YOUR THINGS. WE'RE HITTING THE ROAD. EXACTLY SEVEN...
...DAYS FROM NOW, MONDAY NIGHT AT MIDNIGHT, WE MOVE ON THE PITTSBURGH STRUCTURE.
HARADA-SAMA. THE STRIKE TEAM IS READY TO ATTACK THE RENEGADE HIDEOUT.
I ASSUME YOU'VE RECORDED ALL OF THIS FOR REVIEW?
YES, MASTER.
BELAY THE STRIKE. BENEATH DOWNTOWN L.A. IS THE LAST PLACE WE NEED A FULL-SCALE PSIONIC EXCHANGE...
FORTUNATELY, THEY'VE GIVEN US A FAR, FAR BETTER OPTION.

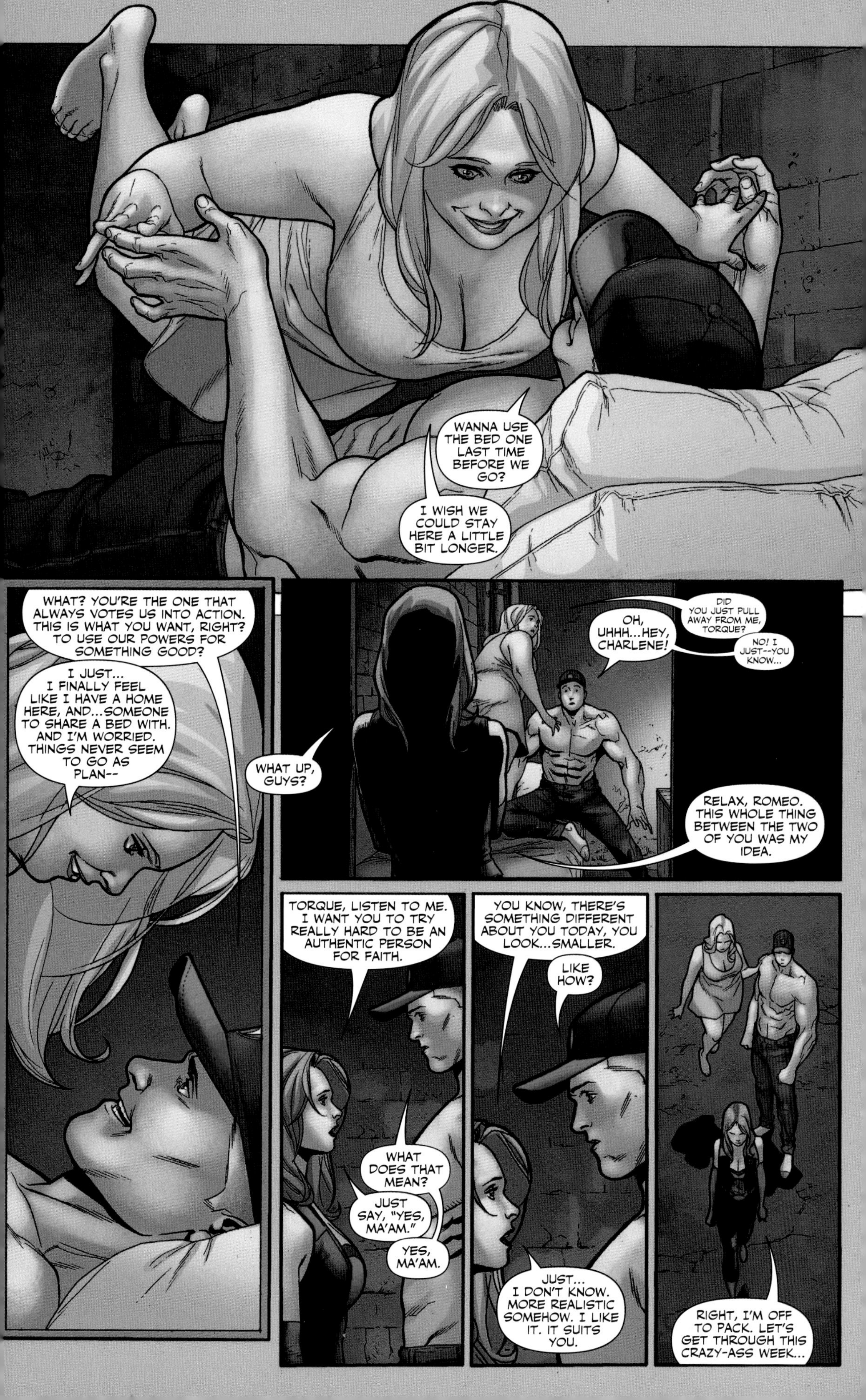
WANNA USE THE BED ONE LAST TIME BEFORE WE GO?
I WISH WE COULD STAY HERE A LITTLE BIT LONGER.
WHAT? YOU'RE THE ONE THAT ALWAYS VOTES US INTO ACTION. THIS IS WHAT YOU WANT, RIGHT? TO USE OUR POWERS FOR SOMETHING GOOD?
I JUST... I FINALLY FEEL LIKE I HAVE A HOME HERE, AND...SOMEONE TO SHARE A BED WITH. AND I'M WORRIED. THINGS NEVER SEEM TO GO AS PLAN--
WHAT UP, GUYS?
OH, UHHH...HEY, CHARLENE!
DID YOU JUST PULL AWAY FROM ME, TORQUE?
NO! I JUST--YOU KNOW...
RELAX, ROMEO. THIS WHOLE THING BETWEEN THE TWO OF YOU WAS MY IDEA.
TORQUE, LISTEN TO ME. I WANT YOU TO TRY REALLY HARD TO BE AN AUTHENTIC PERSON FOR FAITH.
WHAT DOES THAT MEAN?
JUST SAY, "YES, MA'AM."
YES, MA'AM.
YOU KNOW, THERE'S SOMETHING DIFFERENT ABOUT YOU TODAY, YOU LOOK...SMALLER.
LIKE HOW?
JUST... I DON'T KNOW. MORE REALISTIC SOMEHOW. I LIKE IT. IT SUITS YOU.
RIGHT, I'M OFF TO PACK. LET'S GET THROUGH THIS CRAZY-ASS WEEK...

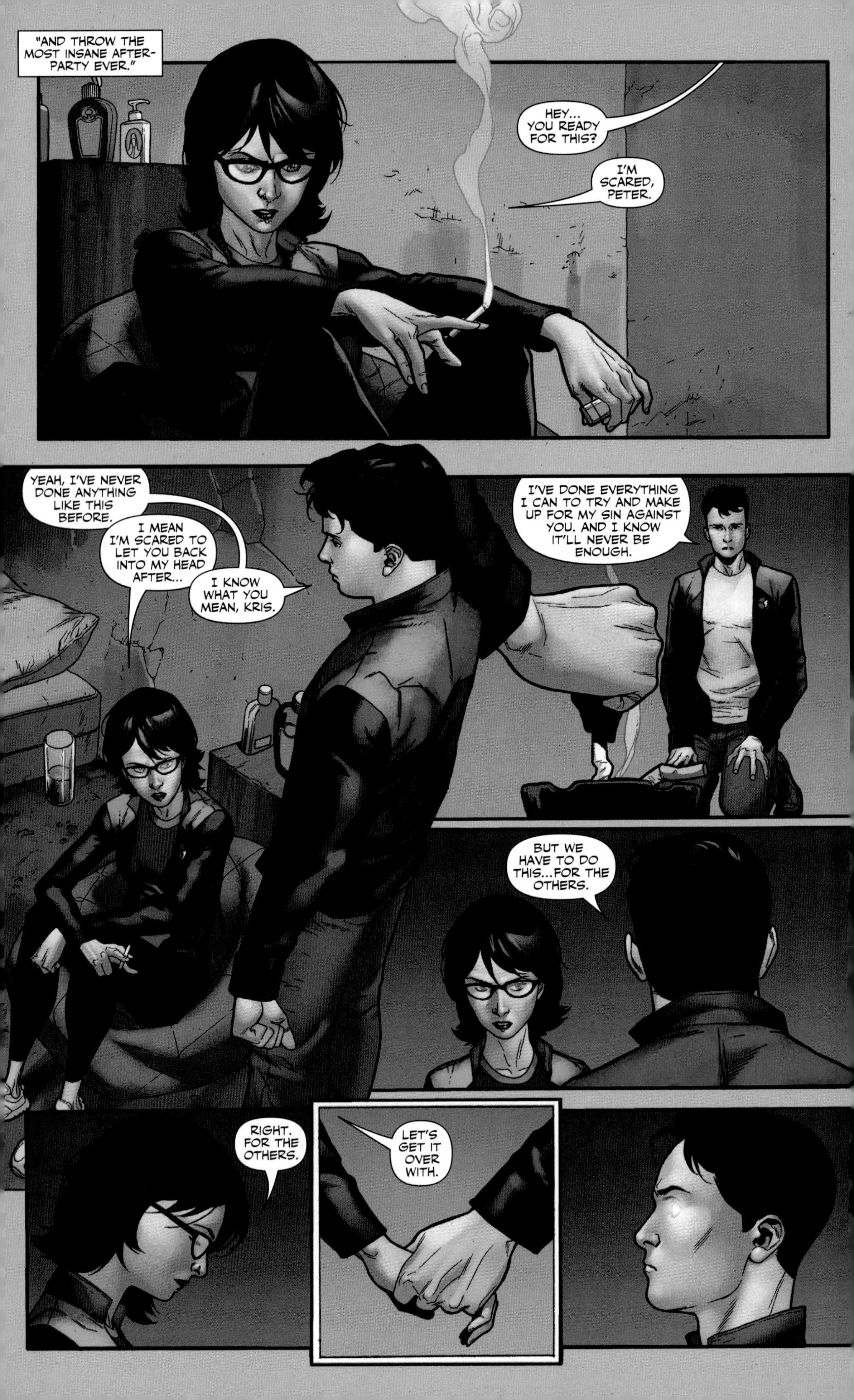
"AND THROW THE MOST INSANE AFTER-PARTY EVER."
HEY... YOU READY FOR THIS?
I'M SCARED, PETER.
YEAH, I'VE NEVER DONE ANYTHING LIKE THIS BEFORE.
I MEAN I'M SCARED TO LET YOU BACK INTO MY HEAD AFTER...
I KNOW WHAT YOU MEAN, KRIS.
I'VE DONE EVERYTHING I CAN TO TRY AND MAKE UP FOR MY SIN AGAINST YOU. AND I KNOW IT'LL NEVER BE ENOUGH.
BUT WE HAVE TO DO THIS...FOR THE OTHERS.
RIGHT. FOR THE OTHERS.
LET'S GET IT OVER WITH.

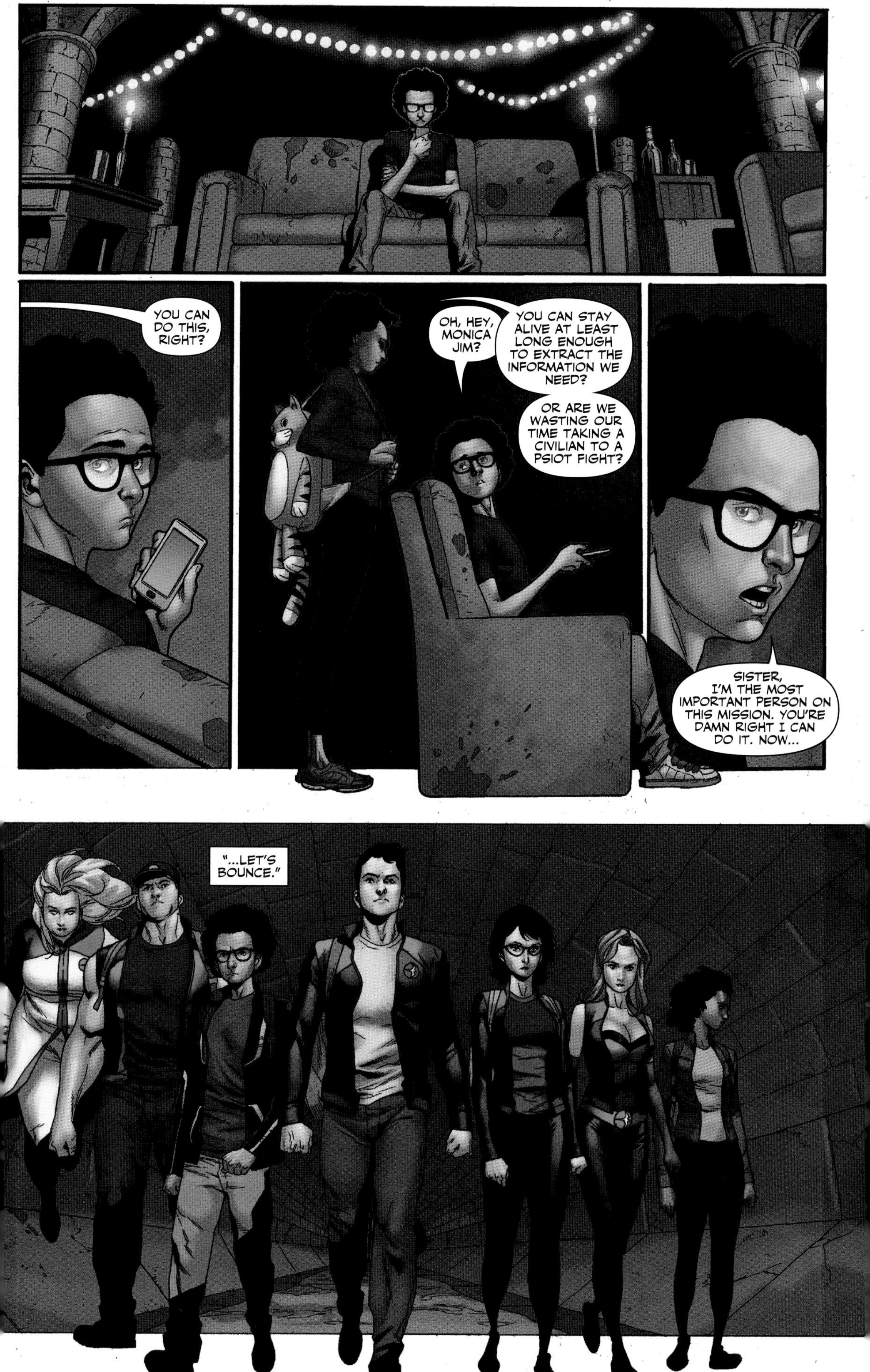
YOU CAN DO THIS, RIGHT?
OH, HEY, MONICA JIM?
YOU CAN STAY ALIVE AT LEAST LONG ENOUGH TO EXTRACT THE INFORMATION WE NEED?
OR ARE WE WASTING OUR TIME TAKING A CIVILIAN TO A PSIOT FIGHT?
SISTER, I'M THE MOST IMPORTANT PERSON ON THIS MISSION. YOU'RE DAMN RIGHT I CAN DO IT. NOW...
"...LET'S BOUNCE."

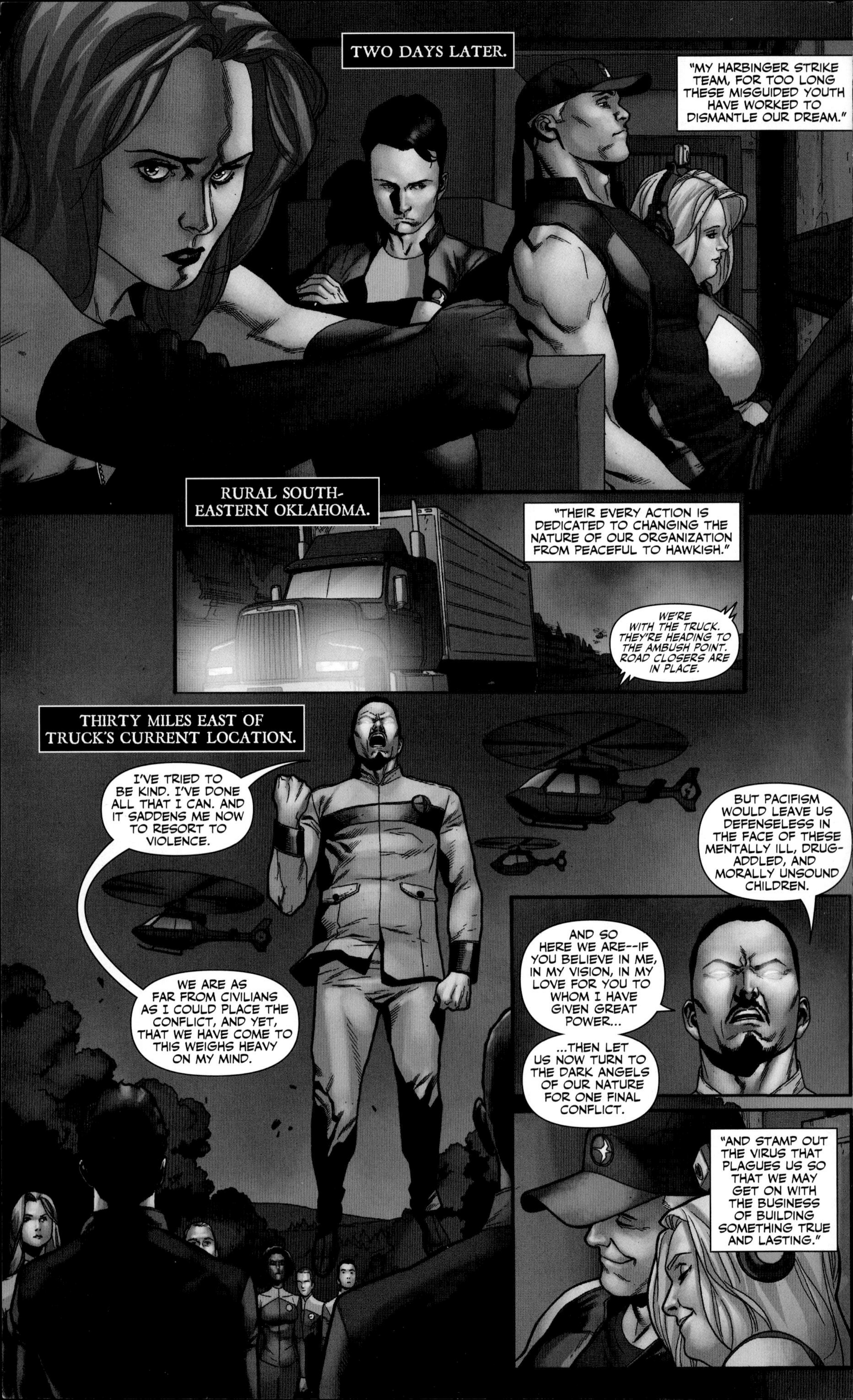

TWO DAYS LATER.
"MY HARBINGER STRIKE TEAM, FOR TOO LONG THESE MISGUIDED YOUTH HAVE WORKED TO DISMANTLE OUR DREAM."
RURAL SOUTH-EASTERN OKLAHOMA.
"THEIR EVERY ACTION IS DEDICATED TO CHANGING THE NATURE OF OUR ORGANIZATION FROM PEACEFUL TO HAWKISH."
WE'RE WITH THE TRUCK. THEY'RE HEADING TO THE AMBUSH POINT. ROAD CLOSERS ARE IN PLACE.
THIRTY MILES EAST OF TRUCK'S CURRENT LOCATION.
I'VE TRIED TO BE KIND. I'VE DONE ALL THAT I CAN. AND IT SADDENS ME NOW TO RESORT TO VIOLENCE.
WE ARE AS FAR FROM CIVILIANS AS I COULD PLACE THE CONFLICT, AND YET, THAT WE HAVE COME TO THIS WEIGHS HEAVY ON MY MIND.
BUT PACIFISM WOULD LEAVE US DEFENSELESS IN THE FACE OF THESE MENTALLY ILL, DRUG-ADDLED, AND MORALLY UNSOUND CHILDREN.
AND SO HERE WE ARE--IF YOU BELIEVE IN ME, IN MY VISION, IN MY LOVE FOR YOU TO WHOM I HAVE GIVEN GREAT POWER...
...THEN LET US NOW TURN TO THE DARK ANGELS OF OUR NATURE FOR ONE FINAL CONFLICT.
"AND STAMP OUT THE VIRUS THAT PLAGUES US SO THAT WE MAY GET ON WITH THE BUSINESS OF BUILDING SOMETHING TRUE AND LASTING."

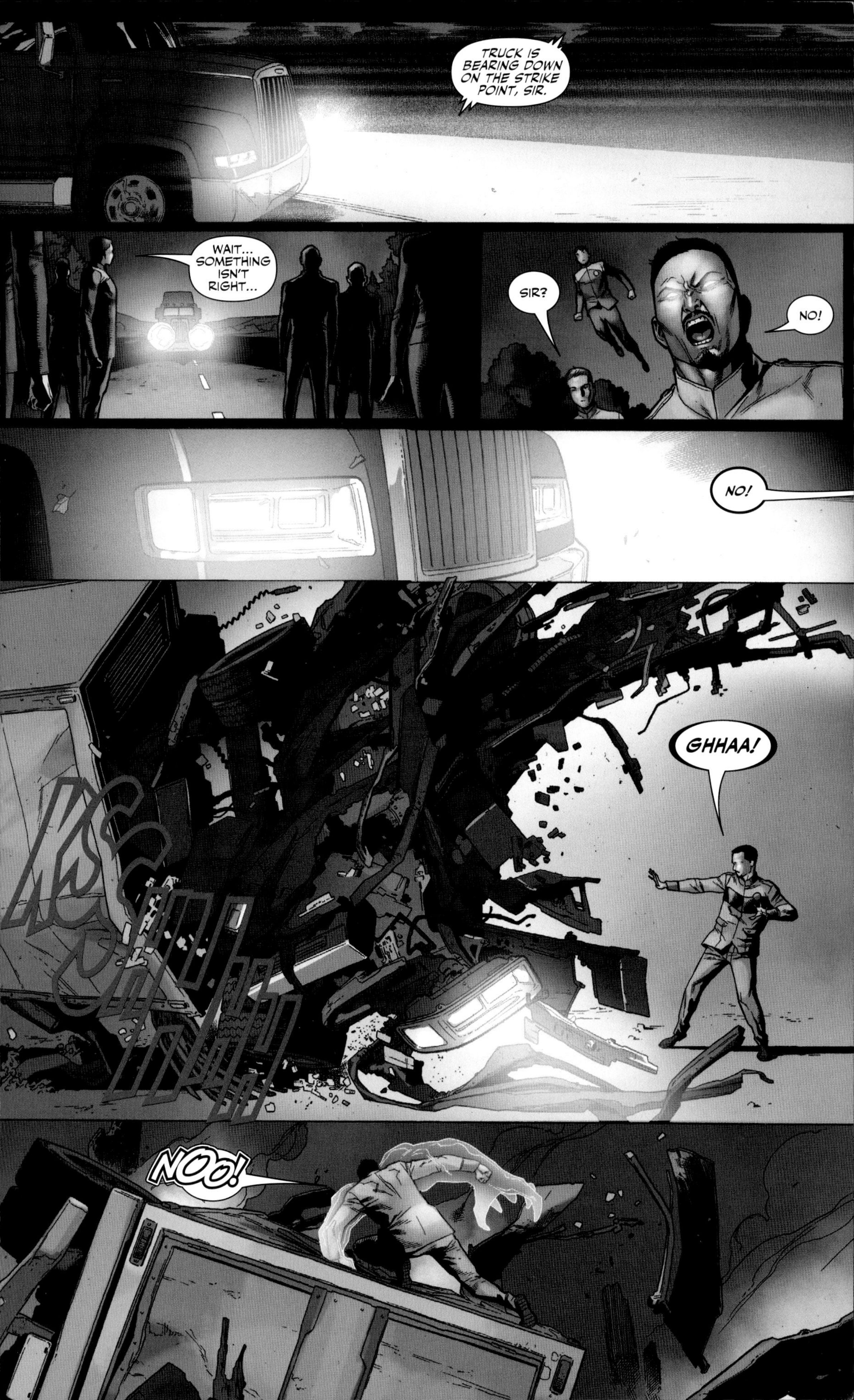
TRUCK IS BEARING DOWN ON THE STRIKE POINT, SIR.
WAIT... SOMETHING ISN'T RIGHT...
SIR?
NO!
NO!
GHHAA!
NOO!

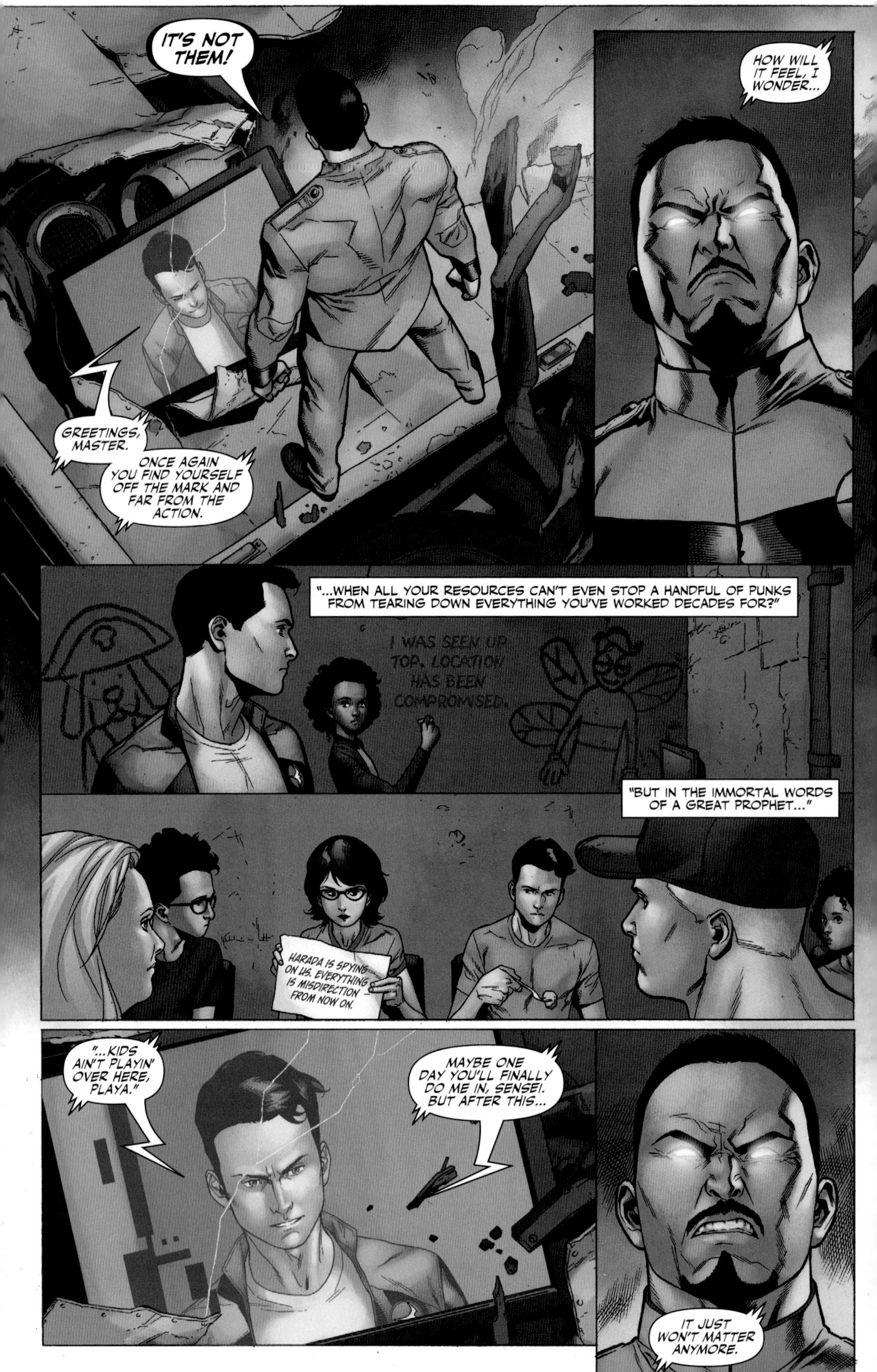
IT'S NOT THEM!
GREETINGS, MASTER.
ONCE AGAIN YOU FIND YOURSELF OFF THE MARK AND FAR FROM THE ACTION.
HOW WILL IT FEEL, I WONDER...
"...WHEN ALL YOUR RESOURCES CAN'T EVEN STOP A HANDFUL OF PUNKS FROM TEARING DOWN EVERYTHING YOU'VE WORKED DECADES FOR?"
I WAS SEEN UP TOP. LOCATION HAS BEEN COMPROMISED.
"BUT IN THE IMMORTAL WORDS OF A GREAT PROPHET..."
HARADA IS SPYING ON US. EVERYTHING IS MISDIRECTION FROM NOW ON.
"...KIDS AIN'T PLAYIN' OVER HERE, PLAYA."
MAYBE ONE DAY YOU'LL FINALLY DO ME IN, SENSEI. BUT AFTER THIS...
IT JUST WON'T MATTER ANYMORE.

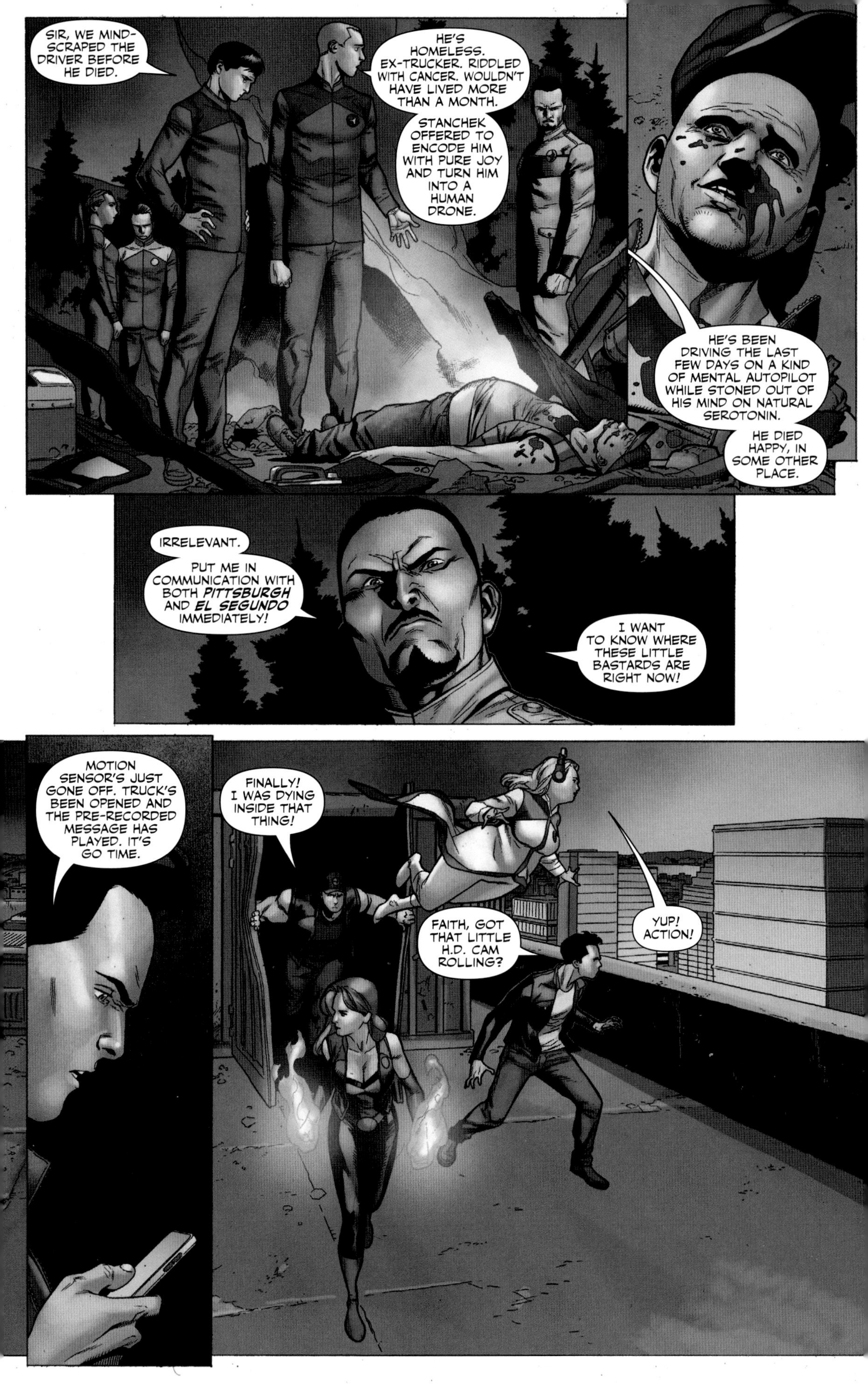
SIR, WE MIND-SCRAPED THE DRIVER BEFORE HE DIED.
HE'S HOMELESS. EX-TRUCKER. RIDDLED WITH CANCER. WOULDN'T HAVE LIVED MORE THAN A MONTH.
STANCHEK OFFERED TO ENCODE HIM WITH PURE JOY AND TURN HIM INTO A HUMAN DRONE.
HE'S BEEN DRIVING THE LAST FEW DAYS ON A KIND OF MENTAL AUTOPILOT WHILE STONED OUT OF HIS MIND ON NATURAL SEROTONIN.
HE DIED HAPPY, IN SOME OTHER PLACE.
IRRELEVANT.
PUT ME IN COMMUNICATION WITH BOTH *PITTSBURGH* AND *EL SEGUNDO* IMMEDIATELY!
I WANT TO KNOW WHERE THESE LITTLE BASTARDS ARE RIGHT NOW!
MOTION SENSOR'S JUST GONE OFF. TRUCK'S BEEN OPENED AND THE PRE-RECORDED MESSAGE HAS PLAYED. IT'S GO TIME.
FINALLY! I WAS DYING INSIDE THAT THING!
YUP! ACTION!
FAITH, GOT THAT LITTLE H.D. CAM ROLLING?

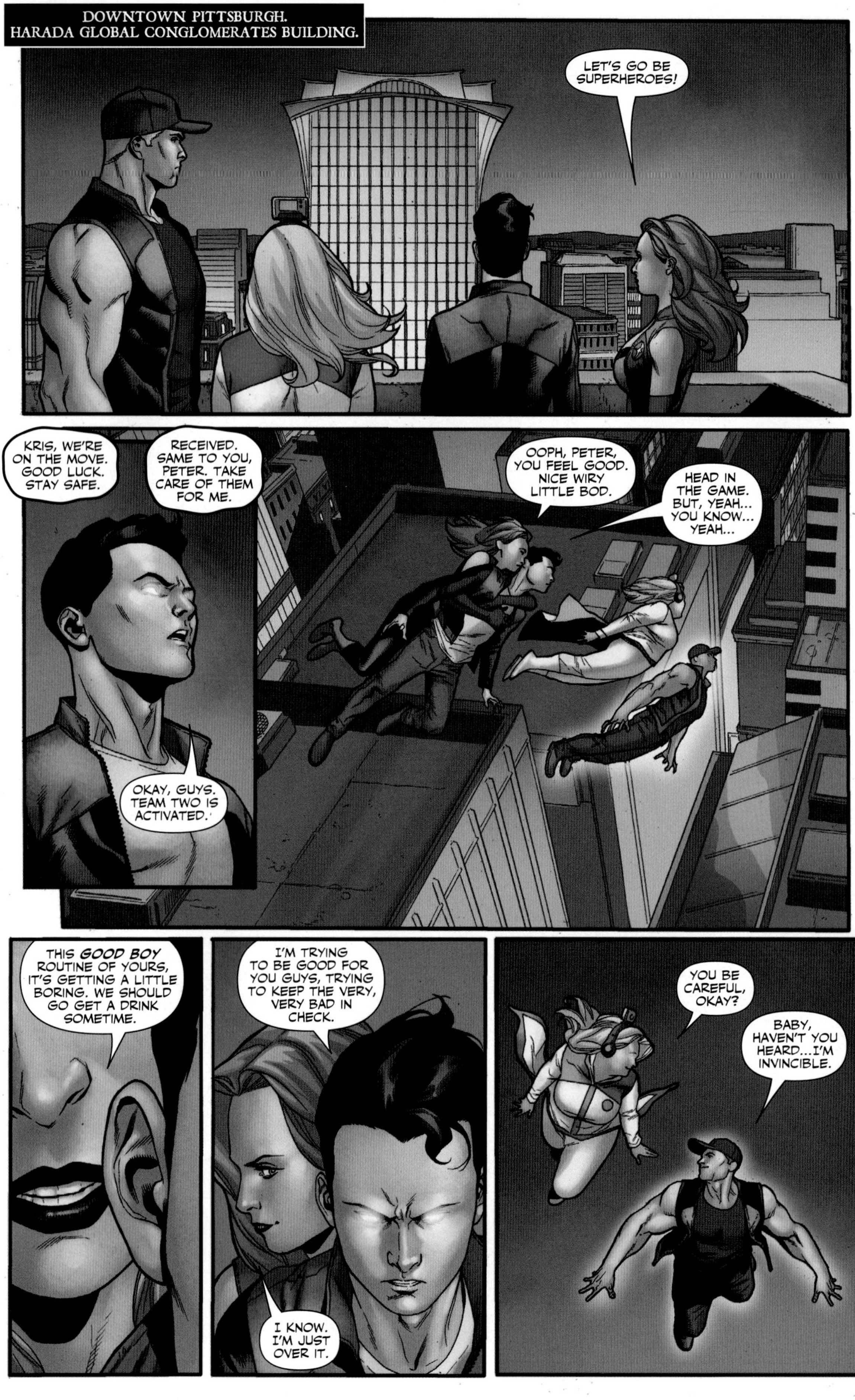
DOWNTOWN PITTSBURGH.
HARADA GLOBAL CONGLOMERATES BUILDING.
LET'S GO BE SUPERHEROES!
KRIS, WE'RE ON THE MOVE. GOOD LUCK. STAY SAFE.
RECEIVED. SAME TO YOU, PETER. TAKE CARE OF THEM FOR ME.
OKAY, GUYS. TEAM TWO IS ACTIVATED.
OOPH, PETER, YOU FEEL GOOD. NICE WIRY LITTLE BOD.
HEAD IN THE GAME. BUT, YEAH... YOU KNOW... YEAH...
THIS GOOD BOY ROUTINE OF YOURS, IT'S GETTING A LITTLE BORING. WE SHOULD GO GET A DRINK SOMETIME.
I'M TRYING TO BE GOOD FOR YOU GUYS, TRYING TO KEEP THE VERY, VERY BAD IN CHECK.
I KNOW. I'M JUST OVER IT.
YOU BE CAREFUL, OKAY?
BABY, HAVEN'T YOU HEARD...I'M INVINCIBLE.

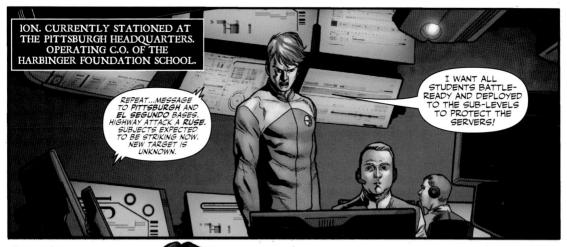

ION. CURRENTLY STATIONED AT THE PITTSBURGH HEADQUARTERS. OPERATING C.O. OF THE HARBINGER FOUNDATION SCHOOL.

REPEAT...MESSAGE TO PITTSBURGH AND EL SEGUNDO BASES. HIGHWAY ATTACK A RUSE. SUBJECTS EXPECTED TO BE STRIKING NOW. NEW TARGET IS UNKNOWN.

I WANT ALL STUDENTS BATTLE-READY AND DEPLOYED TO THE SUB-LEVELS TO PROTECT THE SERVERS!

THIS BUILDING IS NOW ON COMBAT ALERT!

EVERYONE TO THE SUB-LEVEL! LET'S GO!

DARPAN. SPECIAL PERSONAL WARD OF TOYO HARADA.

LET'S LET OURSELVES IN, SHALL WE?

HERE WE GO, TORQUE!

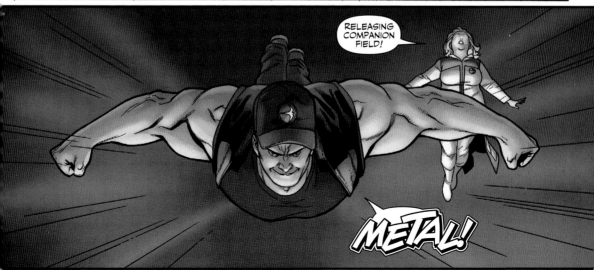

RELEASING COMPANION FIELD!

METAL!

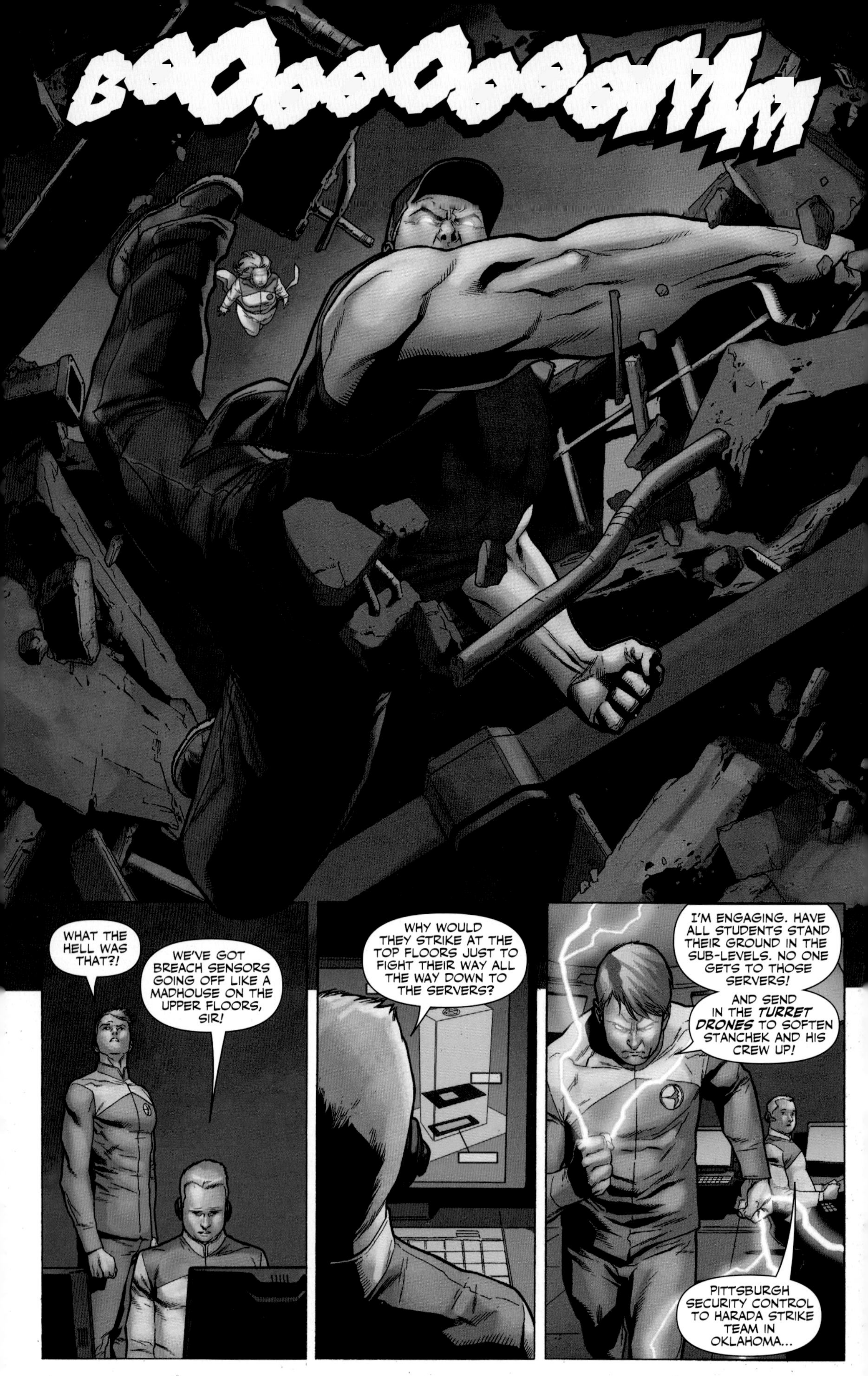
BOOOOOOOOOMM
WHAT THE HELL WAS THAT?!
WE'VE GOT BREACH SENSORS GOING OFF LIKE A MADHOUSE ON THE UPPER FLOORS, SIR!
WHY WOULD THEY STRIKE AT THE TOP FLOORS JUST TO FIGHT THEIR WAY ALL THE WAY DOWN TO THE SERVERS?
I'M ENGAGING. HAVE ALL STUDENTS STAND THEIR GROUND IN THE SUB-LEVELS. NO ONE GETS TO THOSE SERVERS!
AND SEND IN THE TURRET DRONES TO SOFTEN STANCHEK AND HIS CREW UP!
PITTSBURGH SECURITY CONTROL TO HARADA STRIKE TEAM IN OKLAHOMA...

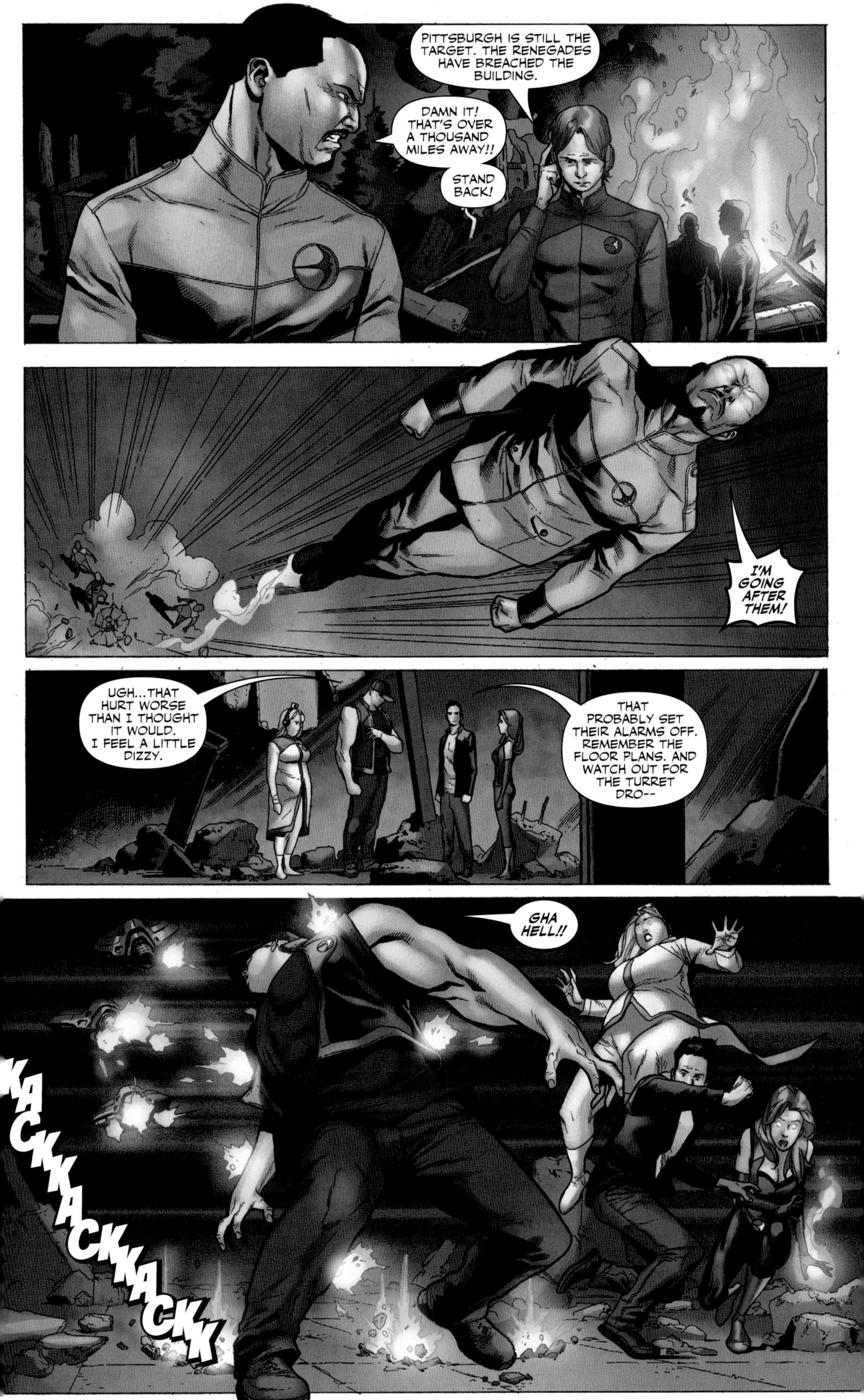
PITTSBURGH IS STILL THE TARGET. THE RENEGADES HAVE BREACHED THE BUILDING.
DAMN IT! THAT'S OVER A THOUSAND MILES AWAY!!
STAND BACK!
I'M GOING AFTER THEM!
UGH...THAT HURT WORSE THAN I THOUGHT IT WOULD. I FEEL A LITTLE DIZZY.
THAT PROBABLY SET THEIR ALARMS OFF. REMEMBER THE FLOOR PLANS. AND WATCH OUT FOR THE TURRET DRO--
GHA HELL!!
KACKKACKKACKK

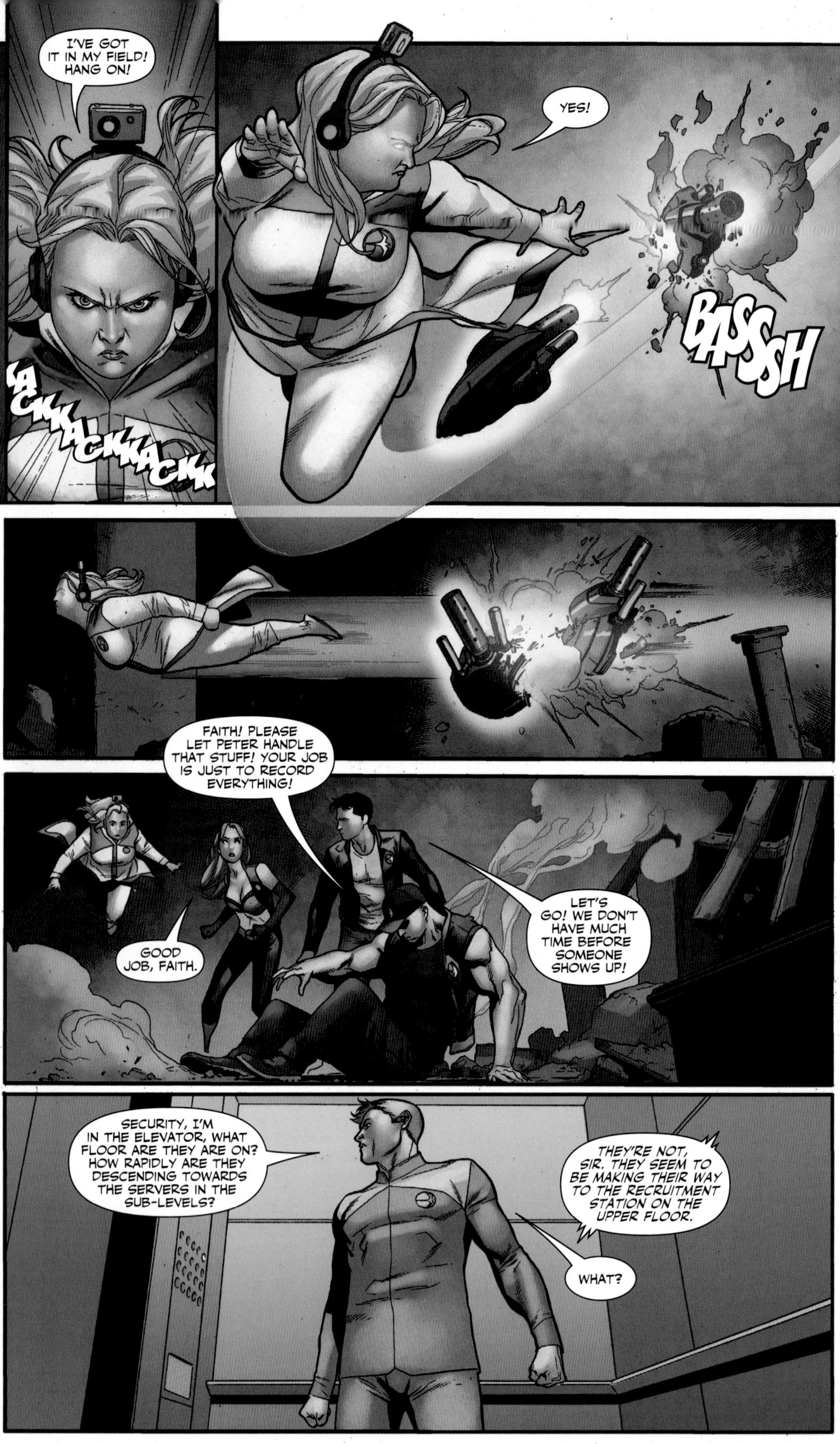
I'VE GOT IT IN MY FIELD! HANG ON!
KACKKACKKACKK
YES!
BASSSH
FAITH! PLEASE LET PETER HANDLE THAT STUFF! YOUR JOB IS JUST TO RECORD EVERYTHING!
GOOD JOB, FAITH.
LET'S GO! WE DON'T HAVE MUCH TIME BEFORE SOMEONE SHOWS UP!
SECURITY, I'M IN THE ELEVATOR, WHAT FLOOR ARE THEY ARE ON? HOW RAPIDLY ARE THEY DESCENDING TOWARDS THE SERVERS IN THE SUB-LEVELS?
THEY'RE NOT, SIR. THEY SEEM TO BE MAKING THEIR WAY TO THE RECRUITMENT STATION ON THE UPPER FLOOR.
WHAT?

HERE WE ARE! YOU KNOW WHAT TO DO.

CHARLENE, LAY DOWN A BARRIER OF FIRE ALL OVER THIS FLOOR TO SLOW DOWN ANY PSIOTS WHO MIGHT BE COMING AFTER US.

GOT IT!

TORQUE, RUN SAFETY FOR CHARLENE.

ON IT.

ABRACADABRA MOTHERF—

FWOOOOM

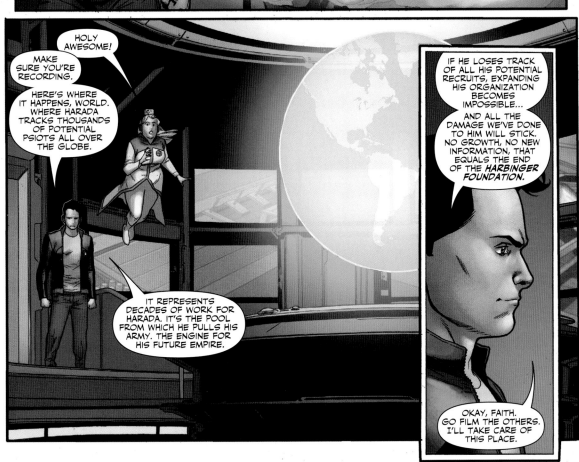

HOLY AWESOME!

MAKE SURE YOU'RE RECORDING.

HERE'S WHERE IT HAPPENS, WORLD. WHERE HARADA TRACKS THOUSANDS OF POTENTIAL PSIOTS ALL OVER THE GLOBE.

IT REPRESENTS DECADES OF WORK FOR HARADA. IT'S THE POOL FROM WHICH HE PULLS HIS ARMY. THE ENGINE FOR HIS FUTURE EMPIRE.

IF HE LOSES TRACK OF ALL HIS POTENTIAL RECRUITS, EXPANDING HIS ORGANIZATION BECOMES IMPOSSIBLE...

AND ALL THE DAMAGE WE'VE DONE TO HIM WILL STICK. NO GROWTH, NO NEW INFORMATION, THAT EQUALS THE END OF THE HARBINGER FOUNDATION.

OKAY, FAITH. GO FILM THE OTHERS. I'LL TAKE CARE OF THIS PLACE.

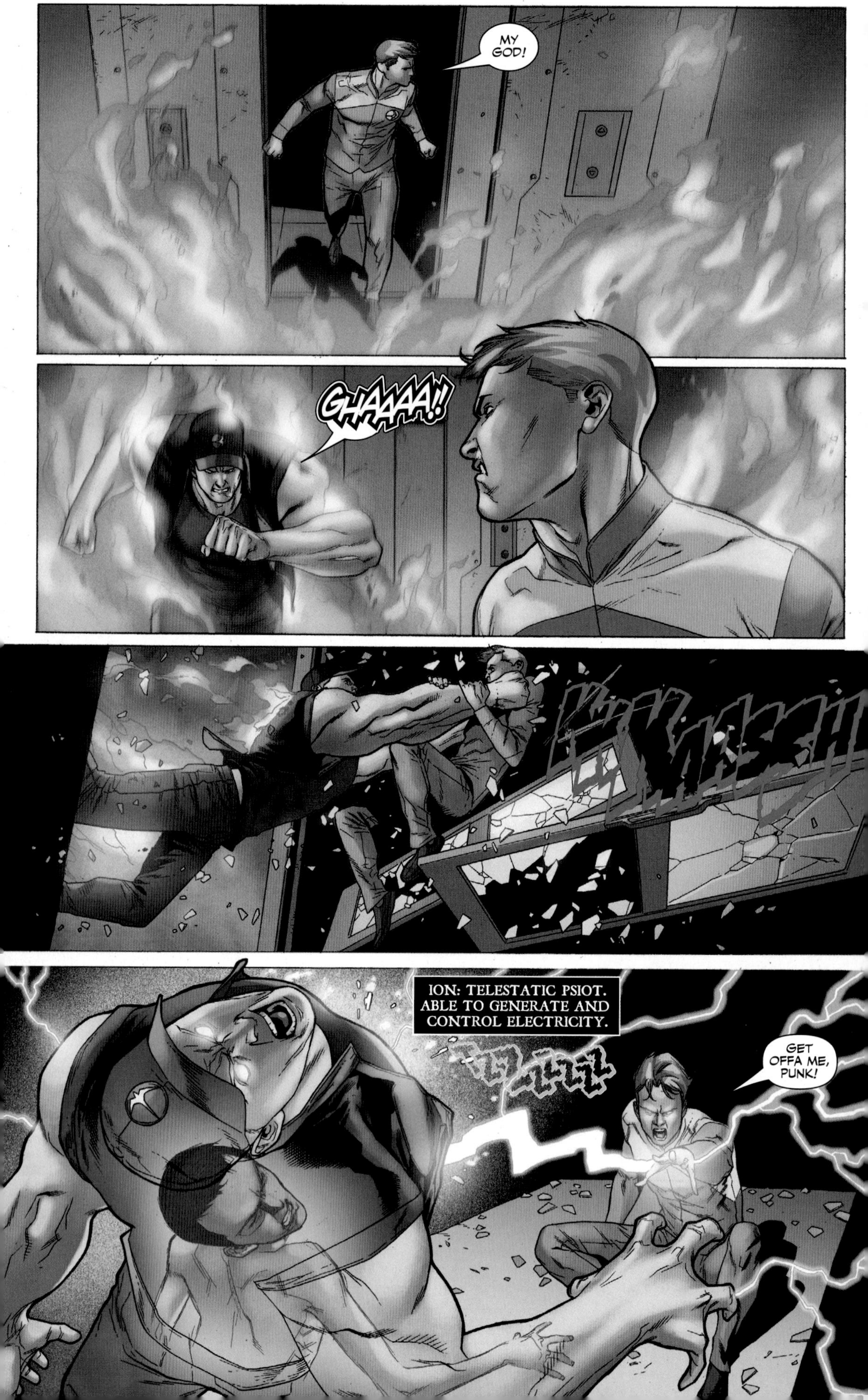
MY GOD!
GHAAAA!!
ION: TELESTATIC PSIOT. ABLE TO GENERATE AND CONTROL ELECTRICITY.
GET OFFA ME, PUNK!

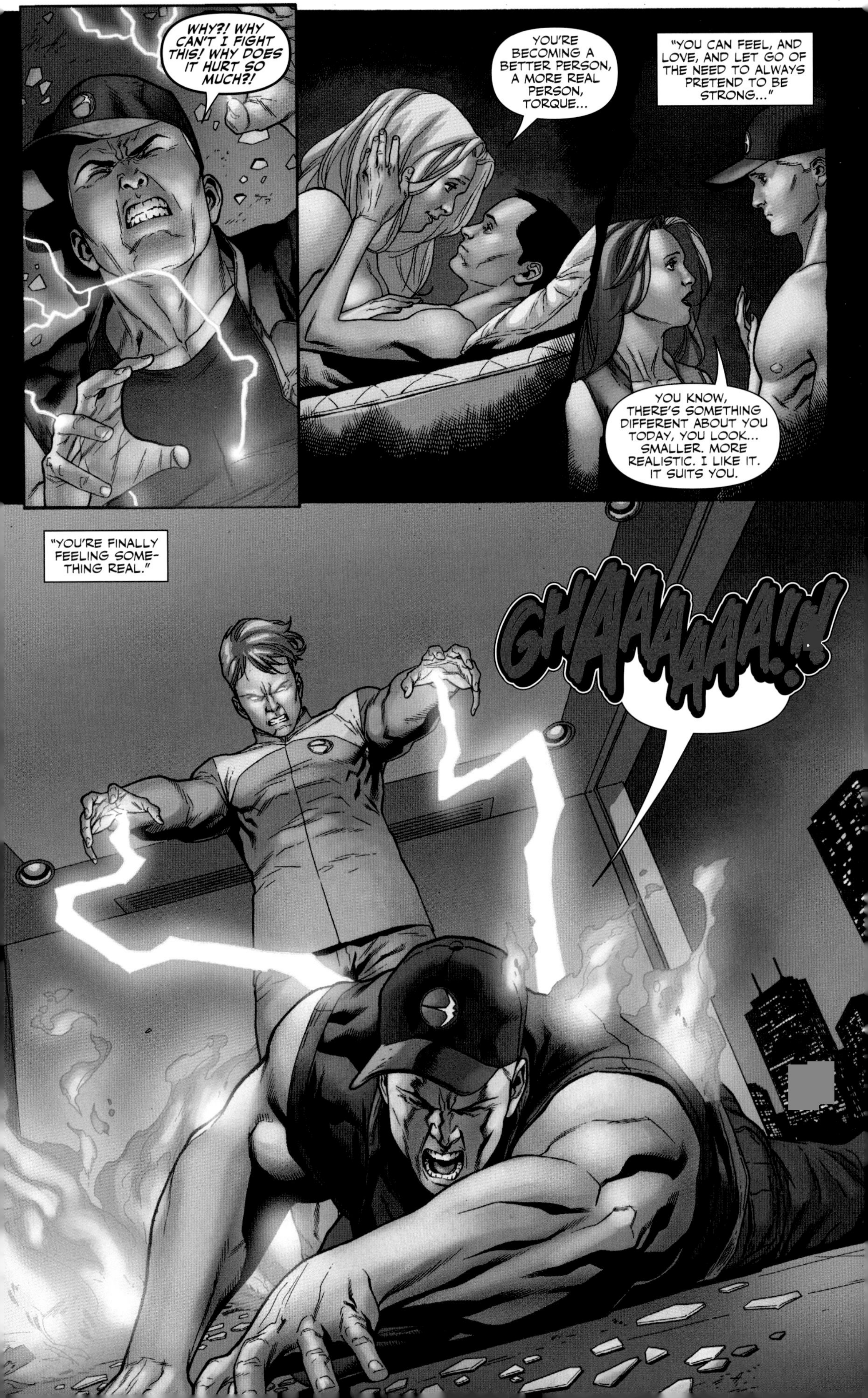
WHY?! WHY CAN'T I FIGHT THIS! WHY DOES IT HURT SO MUCH?!
YOU'RE BECOMING A BETTER PERSON, A MORE REAL PERSON, TORQUE...
"YOU CAN FEEL, AND LOVE, AND LET GO OF THE NEED TO ALWAYS PRETEND TO BE STRONG..."
YOU KNOW, THERE'S SOMETHING DIFFERENT ABOUT YOU TODAY, YOU LOOK... SMALLER. MORE REALISTIC. I LIKE IT. IT SUITS YOU.
"YOU'RE FINALLY FEELING SOMETHING REAL."
GHAAAAAAA!!!

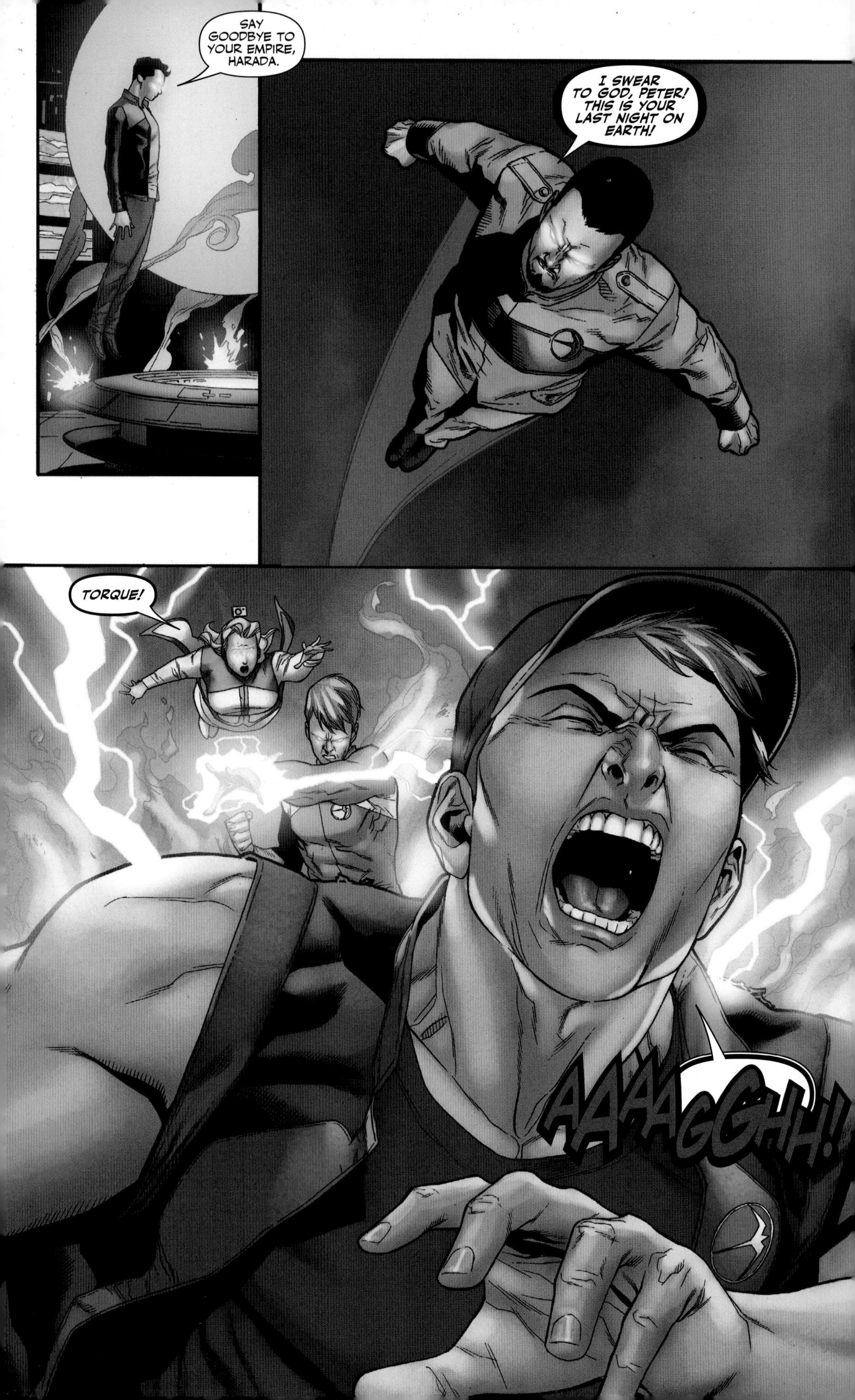
SAY GOODBYE TO YOUR EMPIRE, HARADA.
I SWEAR TO GOD, PETER! THIS IS YOUR LAST NIGHT ON EARTH!
TORQUE!
AAAAGGHH!

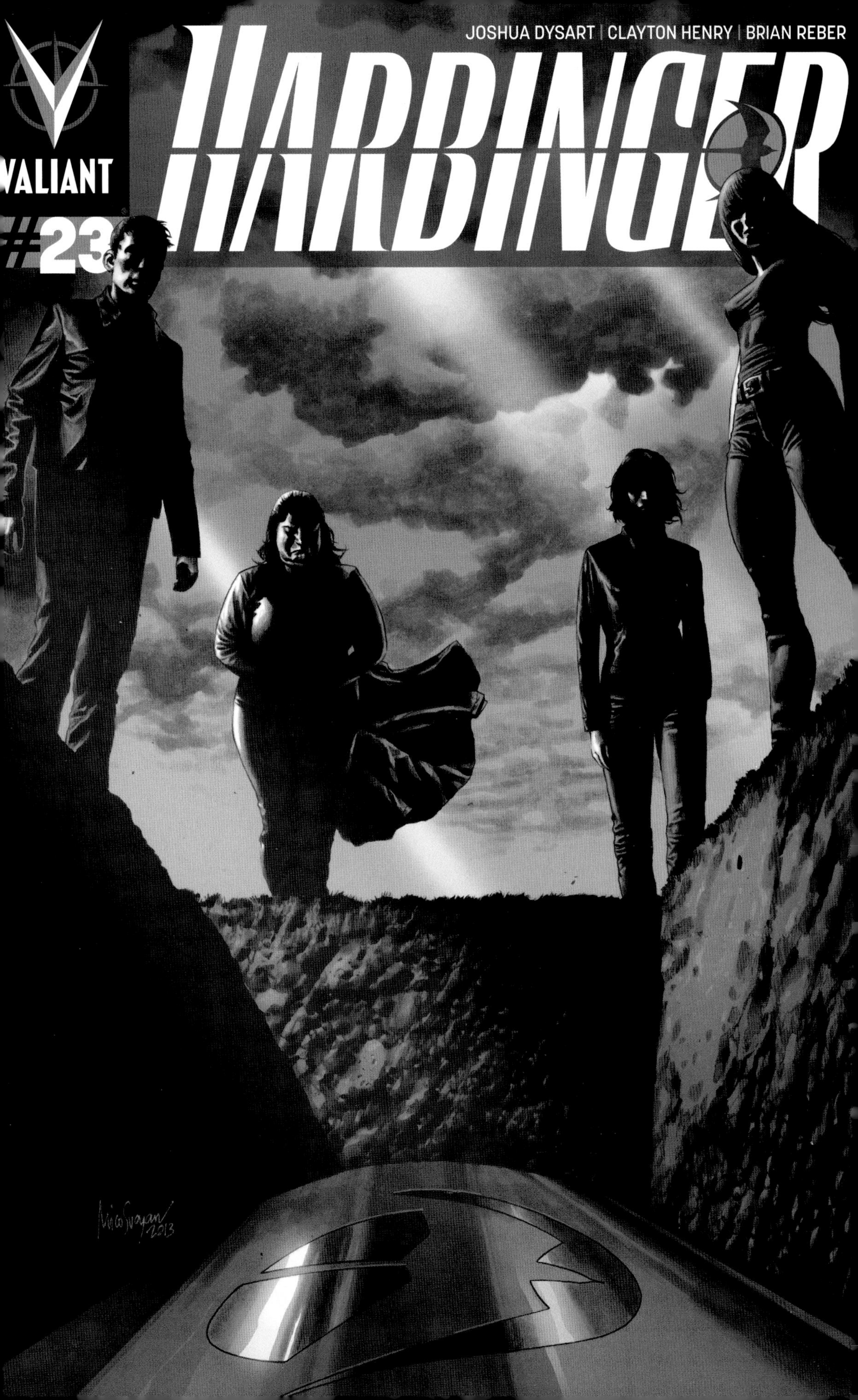
VALIANT
#23
JOSHUA DYSART | CLAYTON HENRY | BRIAN REBER
HARBINGER

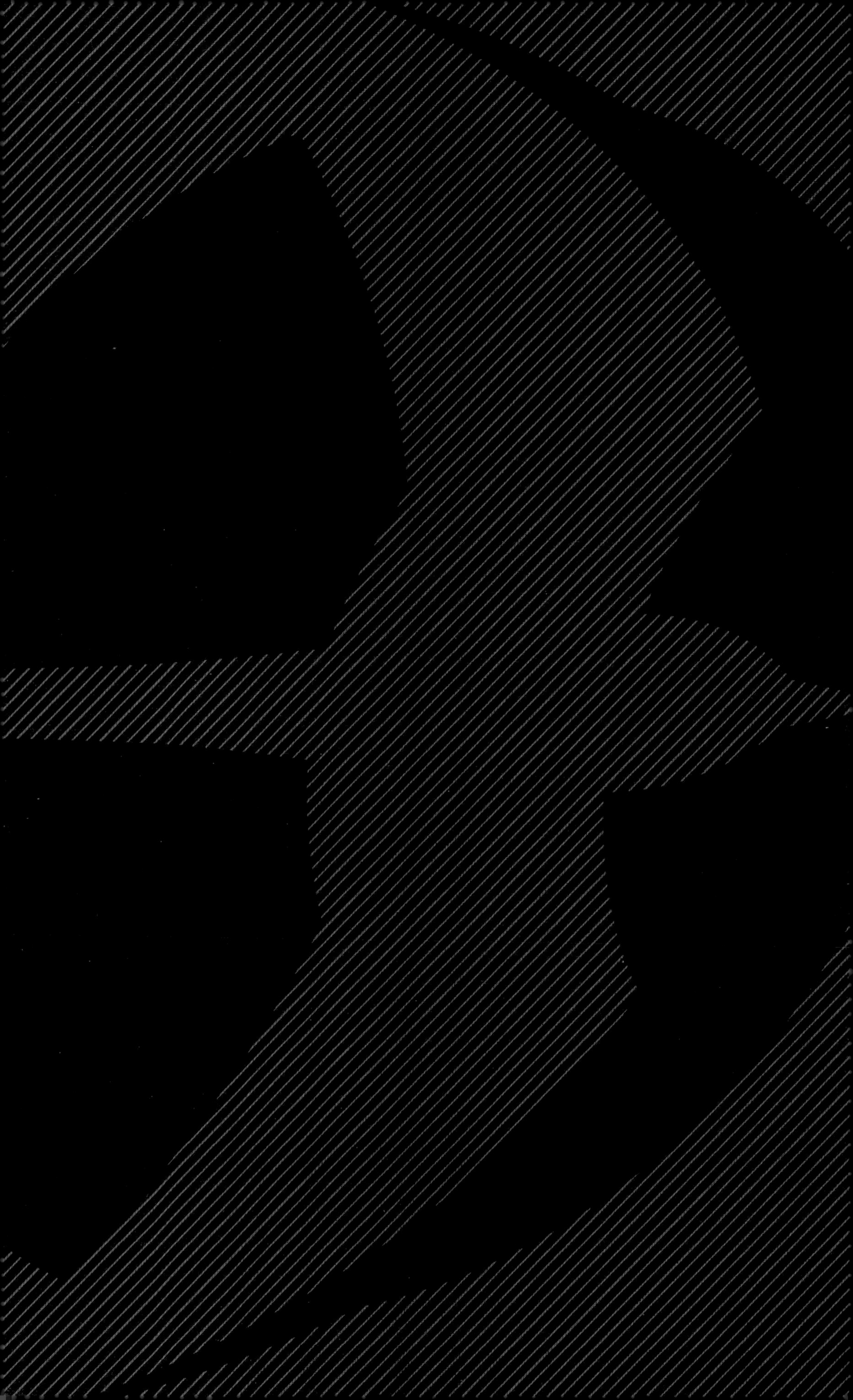

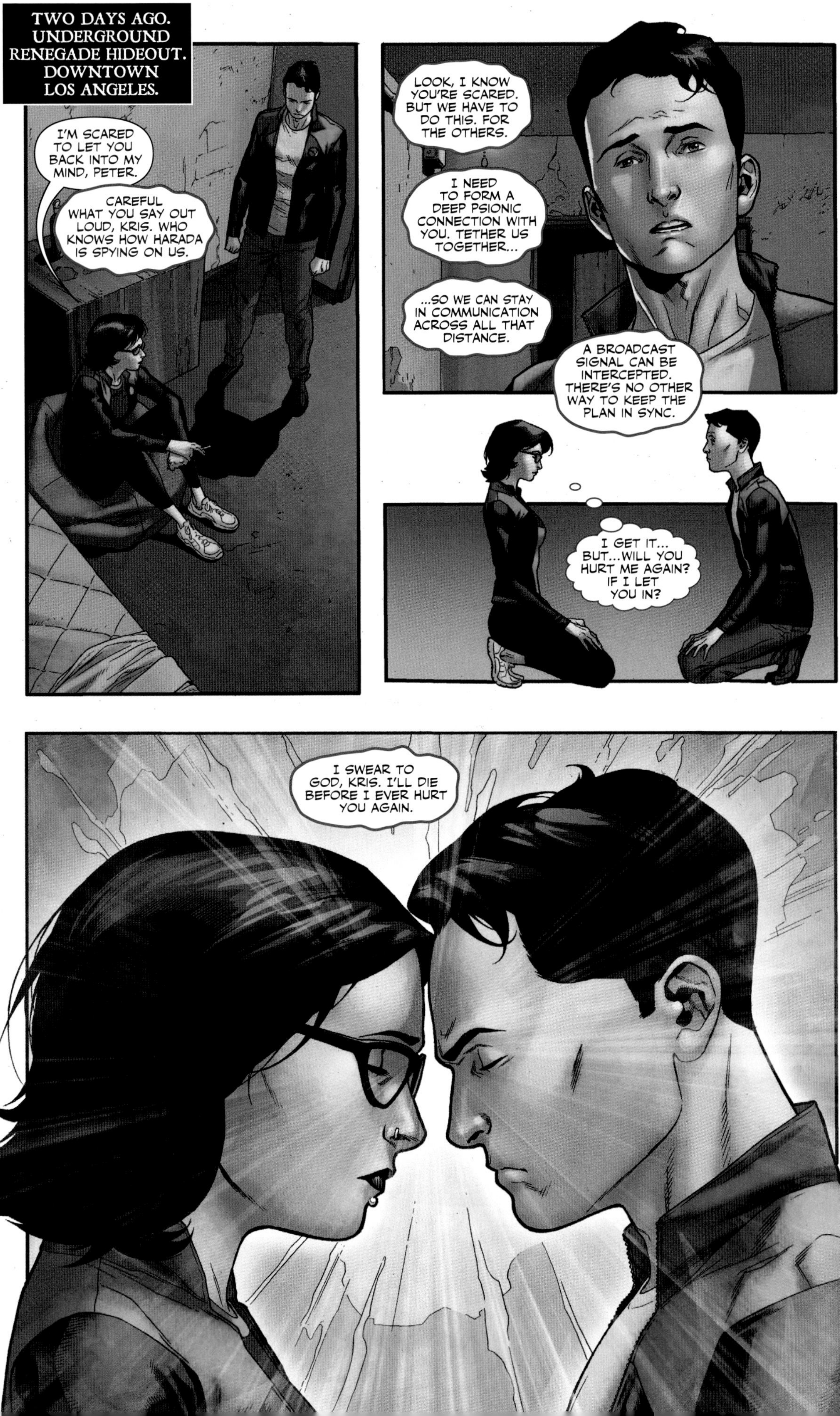
TWO DAYS AGO. UNDERGROUND RENEGADE HIDEOUT. DOWNTOWN LOS ANGELES.
I'M SCARED TO LET YOU BACK INTO MY MIND, PETER.
CAREFUL WHAT YOU SAY OUT LOUD, KRIS. WHO KNOWS HOW HARADA IS SPYING ON US.
LOOK, I KNOW YOU'RE SCARED. BUT WE HAVE TO DO THIS. FOR THE OTHERS.
I NEED TO FORM A DEEP PSIONIC CONNECTION WITH YOU. TETHER US TOGETHER...
...SO WE CAN STAY IN COMMUNICATION ACROSS ALL THAT DISTANCE.
A BROADCAST SIGNAL CAN BE INTERCEPTED. THERE'S NO OTHER WAY TO KEEP THE PLAN IN SYNC.
I GET IT... BUT...WILL YOU HURT ME AGAIN? IF I LET YOU IN?
I SWEAR TO GOD, KRIS. I'LL DIE BEFORE I EVER HURT YOU AGAIN.

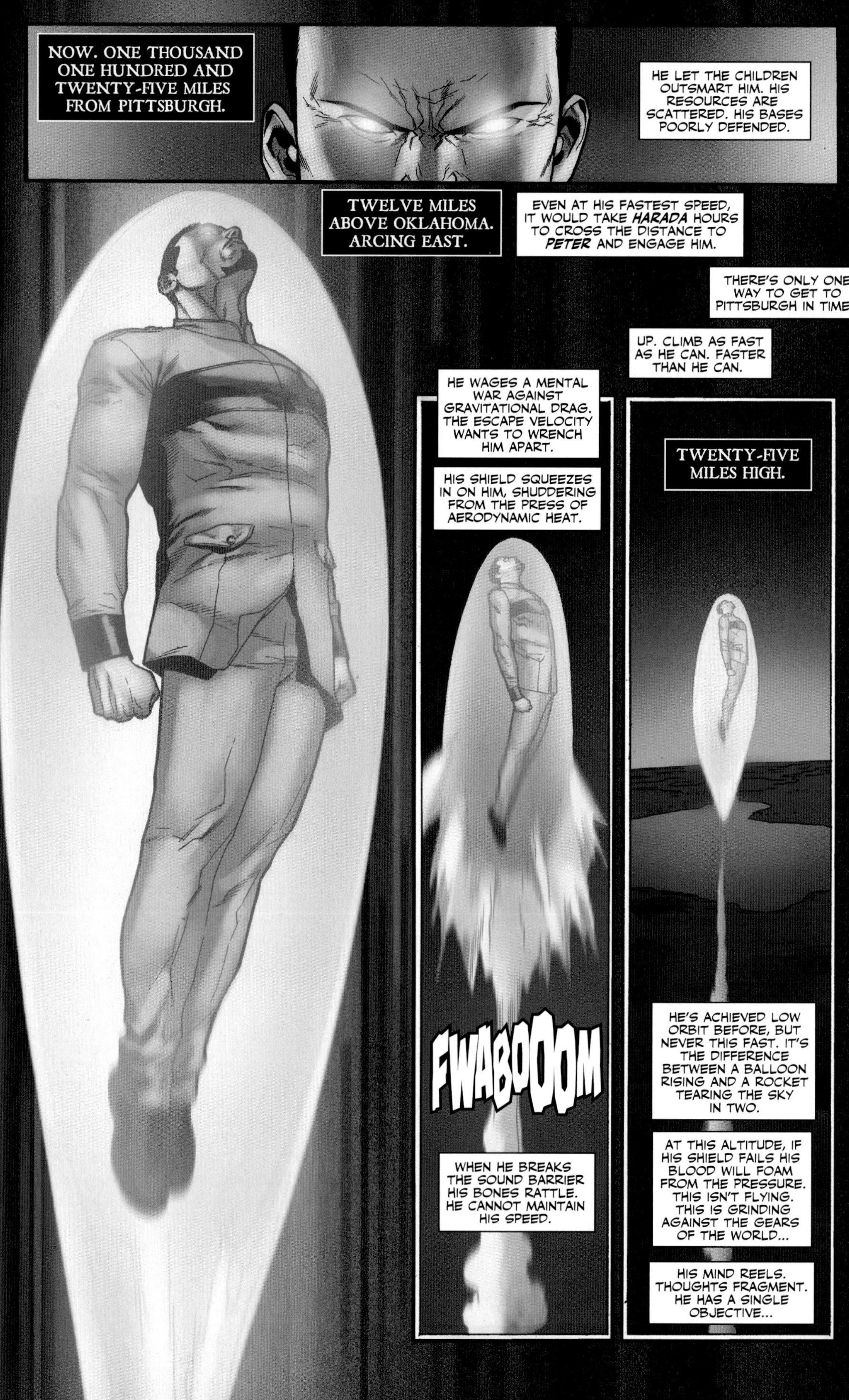
NOW. ONE THOUSAND ONE HUNDRED AND TWENTY-FIVE MILES FROM PITTSBURGH.
HE LET THE CHILDREN OUTSMART HIM. HIS RESOURCES ARE SCATTERED. HIS BASES POORLY DEFENDED.
TWELVE MILES ABOVE OKLAHOMA. ARCING EAST.
EVEN AT HIS FASTEST SPEED, IT WOULD TAKE HARADA HOURS TO CROSS THE DISTANCE TO PETER AND ENGAGE HIM.
THERE'S ONLY ONE WAY TO GET TO PITTSBURGH IN TIME.
UP. CLIMB AS FAST AS HE CAN. FASTER THAN HE CAN.
HE WAGES A MENTAL WAR AGAINST GRAVITATIONAL DRAG. THE ESCAPE VELOCITY WANTS TO WRENCH HIM APART.
HIS SHIELD SQUEEZES IN ON HIM, SHUDDERING FROM THE PRESS OF AERODYNAMIC HEAT.
FWABOOOM
WHEN HE BREAKS THE SOUND BARRIER HIS BONES RATTLE. HE CANNOT MAINTAIN HIS SPEED.
TWENTY-FIVE MILES HIGH.
HE'S ACHIEVED LOW ORBIT BEFORE, BUT NEVER THIS FAST. IT'S THE DIFFERENCE BETWEEN A BALLOON RISING AND A ROCKET TEARING THE SKY IN TWO.
AT THIS ALTITUDE, IF HIS SHIELD FAILS HIS BLOOD WILL FOAM FROM THE PRESSURE. THIS ISN'T FLYING. THIS IS GRINDING AGAINST THE GEARS OF THE WORLD...
HIS MIND REELS. THOUGHTS FRAGMENT. HE HAS A SINGLE OBJECTIVE...

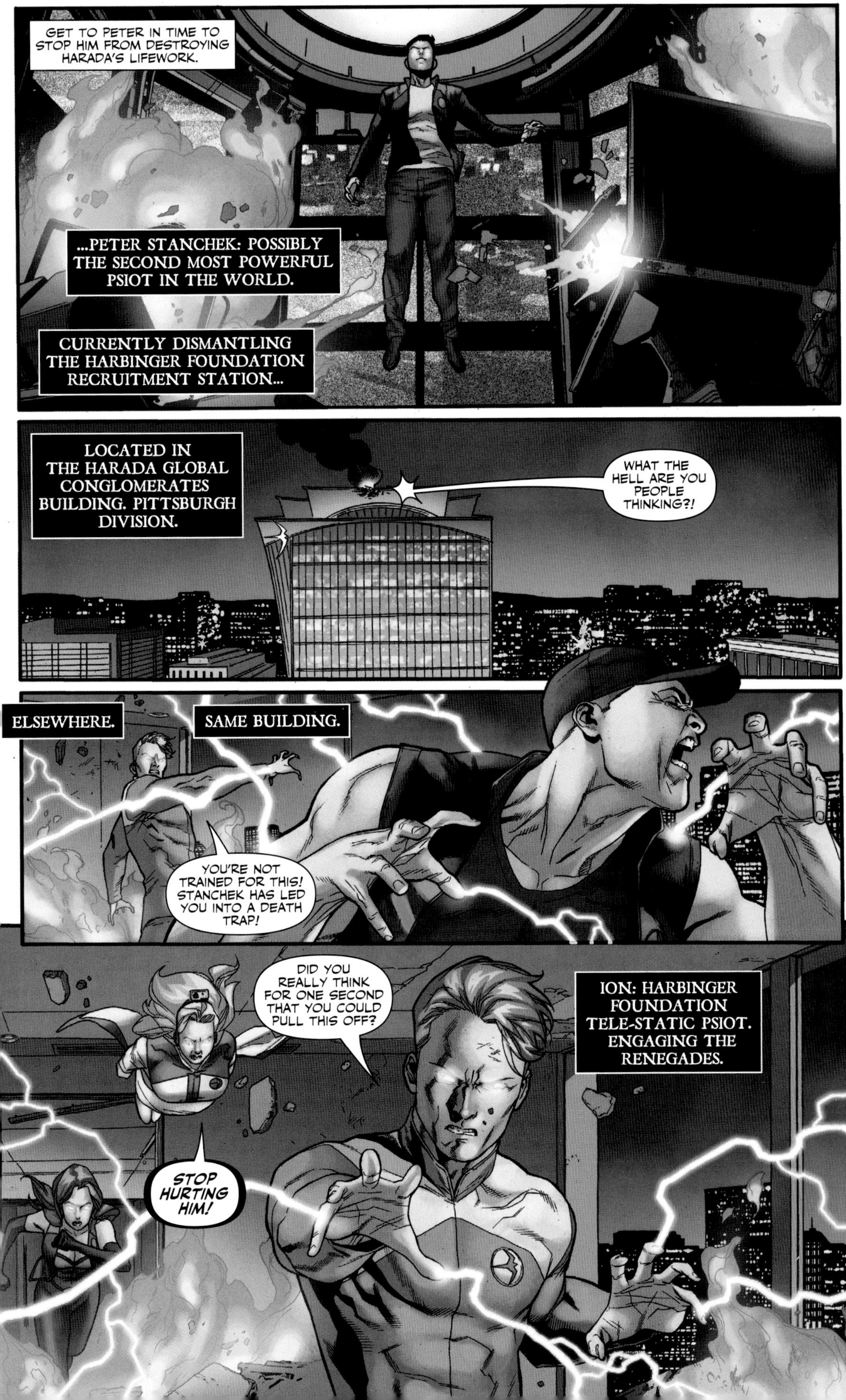
GET TO PETER IN TIME TO STOP HIM FROM DESTROYING HARADA'S LIFEWORK.
...PETER STANCHEK: POSSIBLY THE SECOND MOST POWERFUL PSIOT IN THE WORLD.
CURRENTLY DISMANTLING THE HARBINGER FOUNDATION RECRUITMENT STATION...
LOCATED IN THE HARADA GLOBAL CONGLOMERATES BUILDING. PITTSBURGH DIVISION.
WHAT THE HELL ARE YOU PEOPLE THINKING?!
ELSEWHERE.
SAME BUILDING.
YOU'RE NOT TRAINED FOR THIS! STANCHEK HAS LED YOU INTO A DEATH TRAP!
DID YOU REALLY THINK FOR ONE SECOND THAT YOU COULD PULL THIS OFF?
ION: HARBINGER FOUNDATION TELE-STATIC PSIOT. ENGAGING THE RENEGADES.
STOP HURTING HIM!

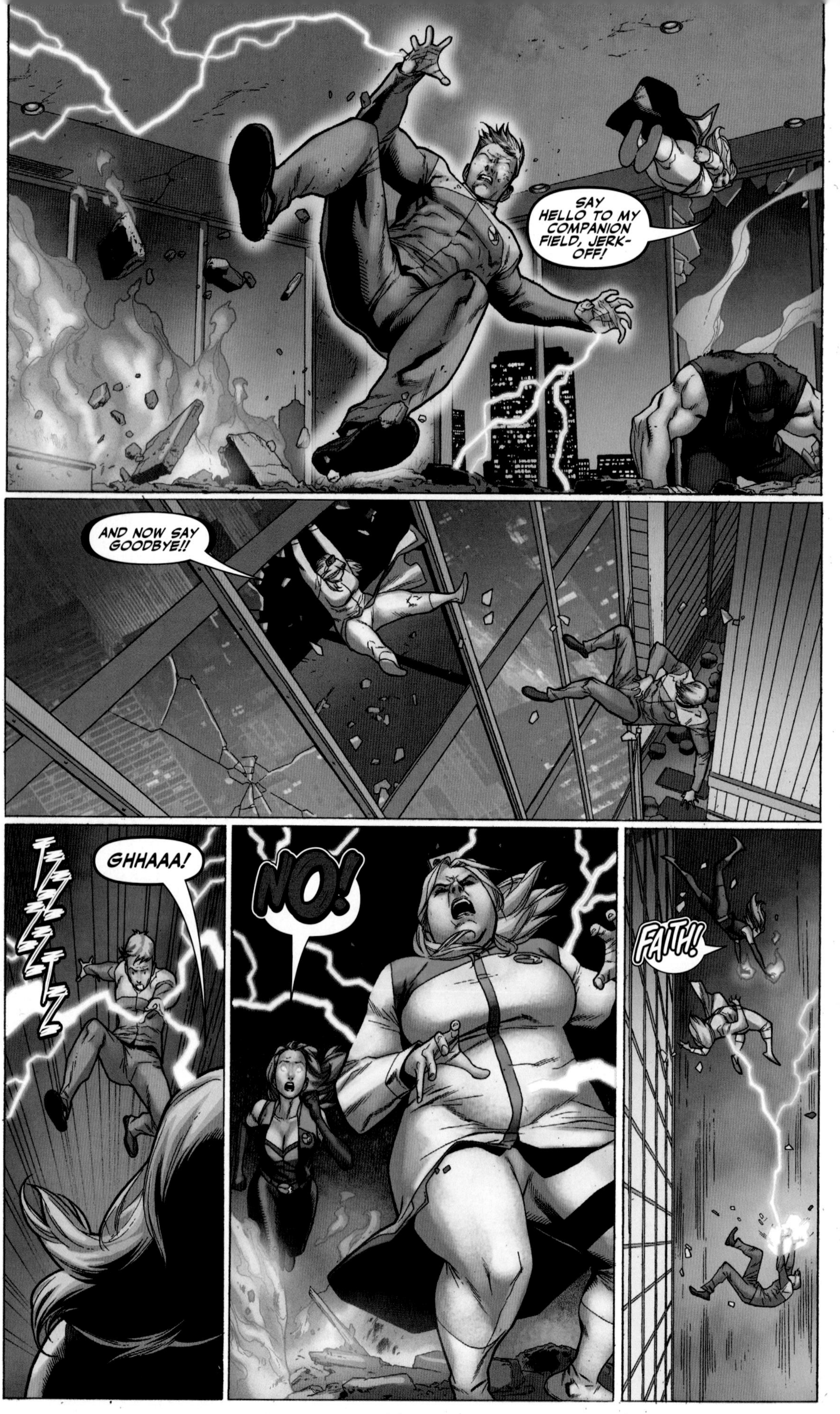
SAY HELLO TO MY COMPANION FIELD, JERK-OFF!
AND NOW SAY GOODBYE!!
GHHAAA!
NO!
FAITH!

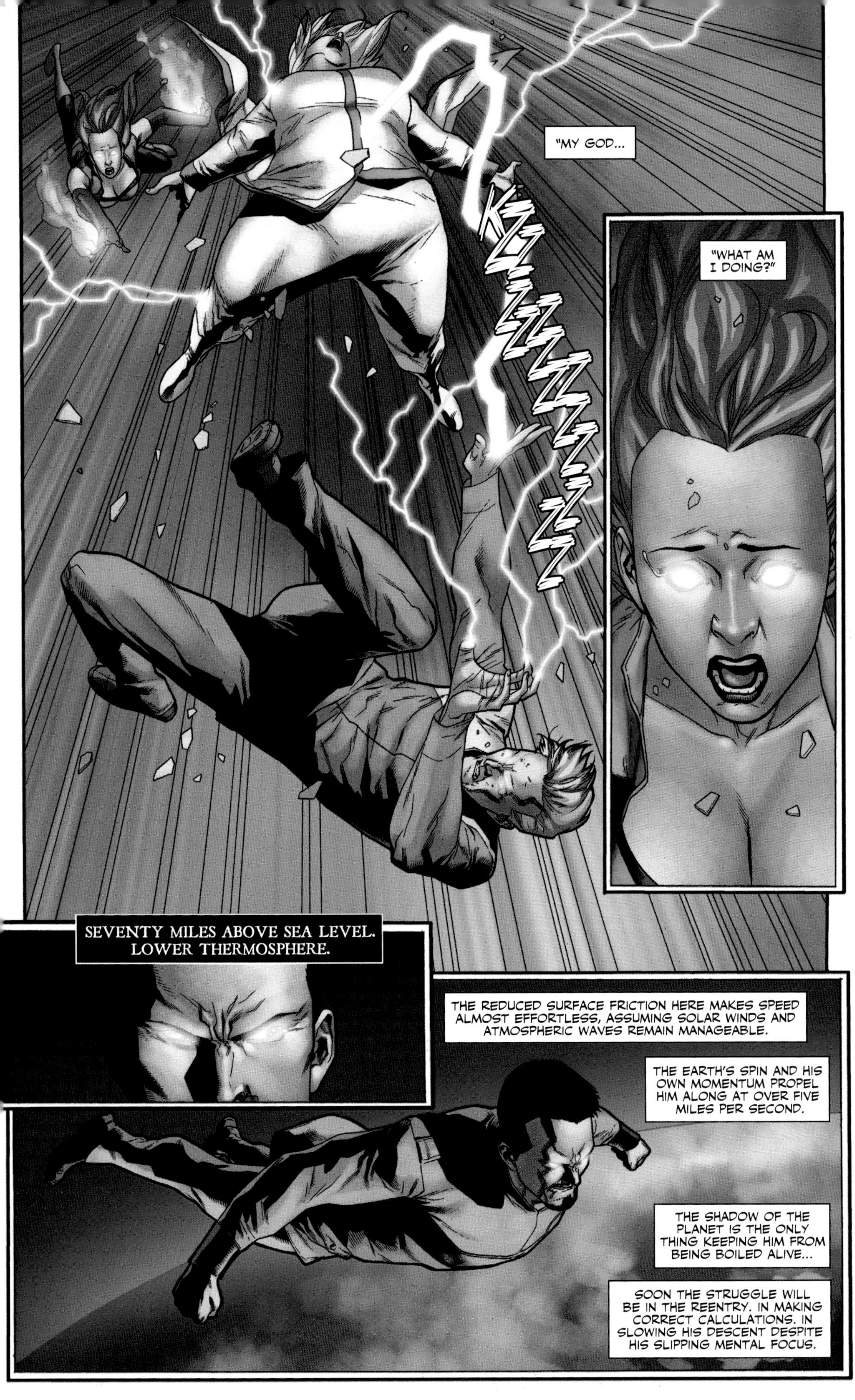
"MY GOD...
KZZZZZZZZZZZZZ
"WHAT AM I DOING?"
SEVENTY MILES ABOVE SEA LEVEL. LOWER THERMOSPHERE.
THE REDUCED SURFACE FRICTION HERE MAKES SPEED ALMOST EFFORTLESS, ASSUMING SOLAR WINDS AND ATMOSPHERIC WAVES REMAIN MANAGEABLE.
THE EARTH'S SPIN AND HIS OWN MOMENTUM PROPEL HIM ALONG AT OVER FIVE MILES PER SECOND.
THE SHADOW OF THE PLANET IS THE ONLY THING KEEPING HIM FROM BEING BOILED ALIVE...
SOON THE STRUGGLE WILL BE IN THE REENTRY. IN MAKING CORRECT CALCULATIONS. IN SLOWING HIS DESCENT DESPITE HIS SLIPPING MENTAL FOCUS.

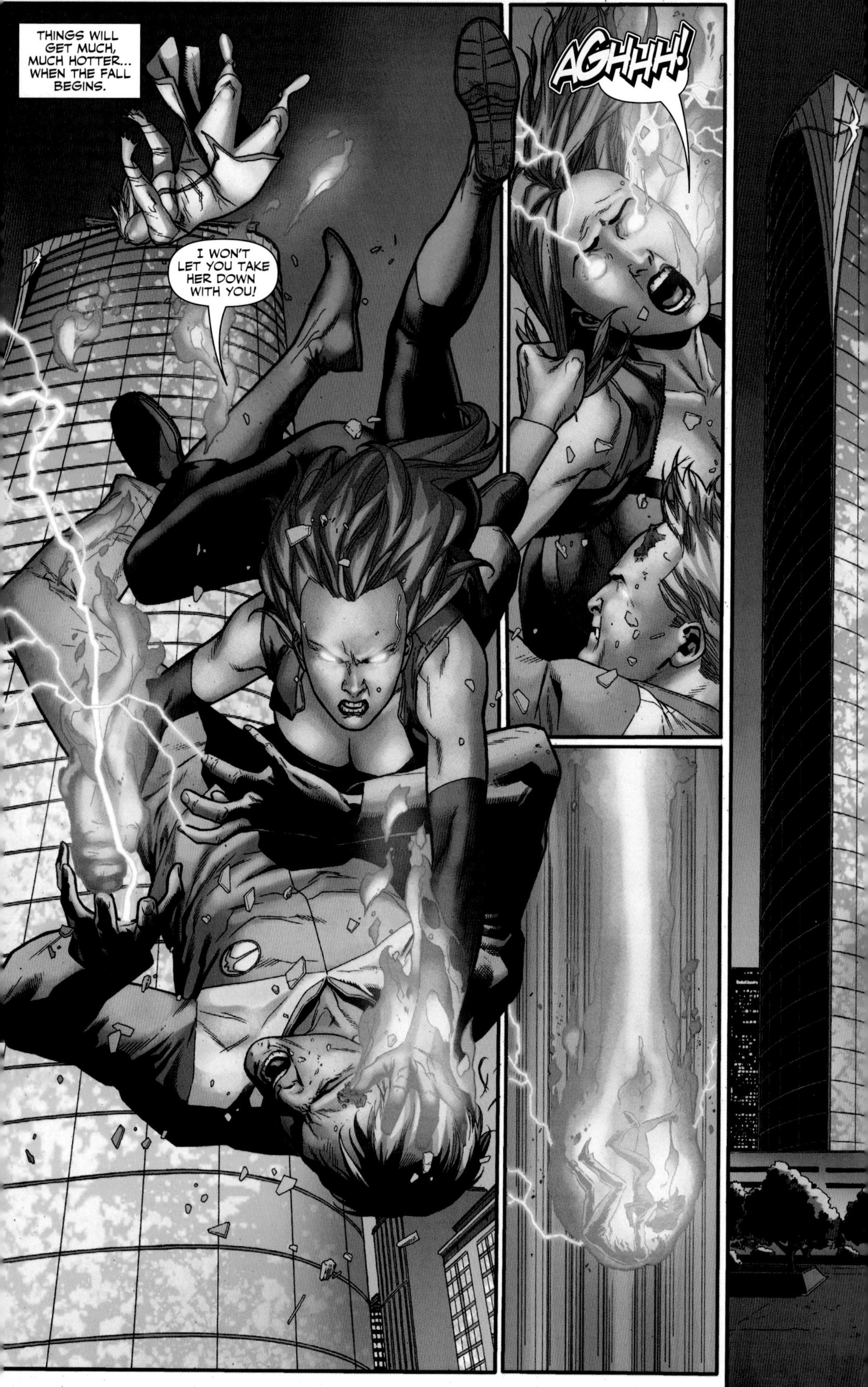
THINGS WILL GET MUCH, MUCH HOTTER... WHEN THE FALL BEGINS.
I WON'T LET YOU TAKE HER DOWN WITH YOU!
AGHHH!

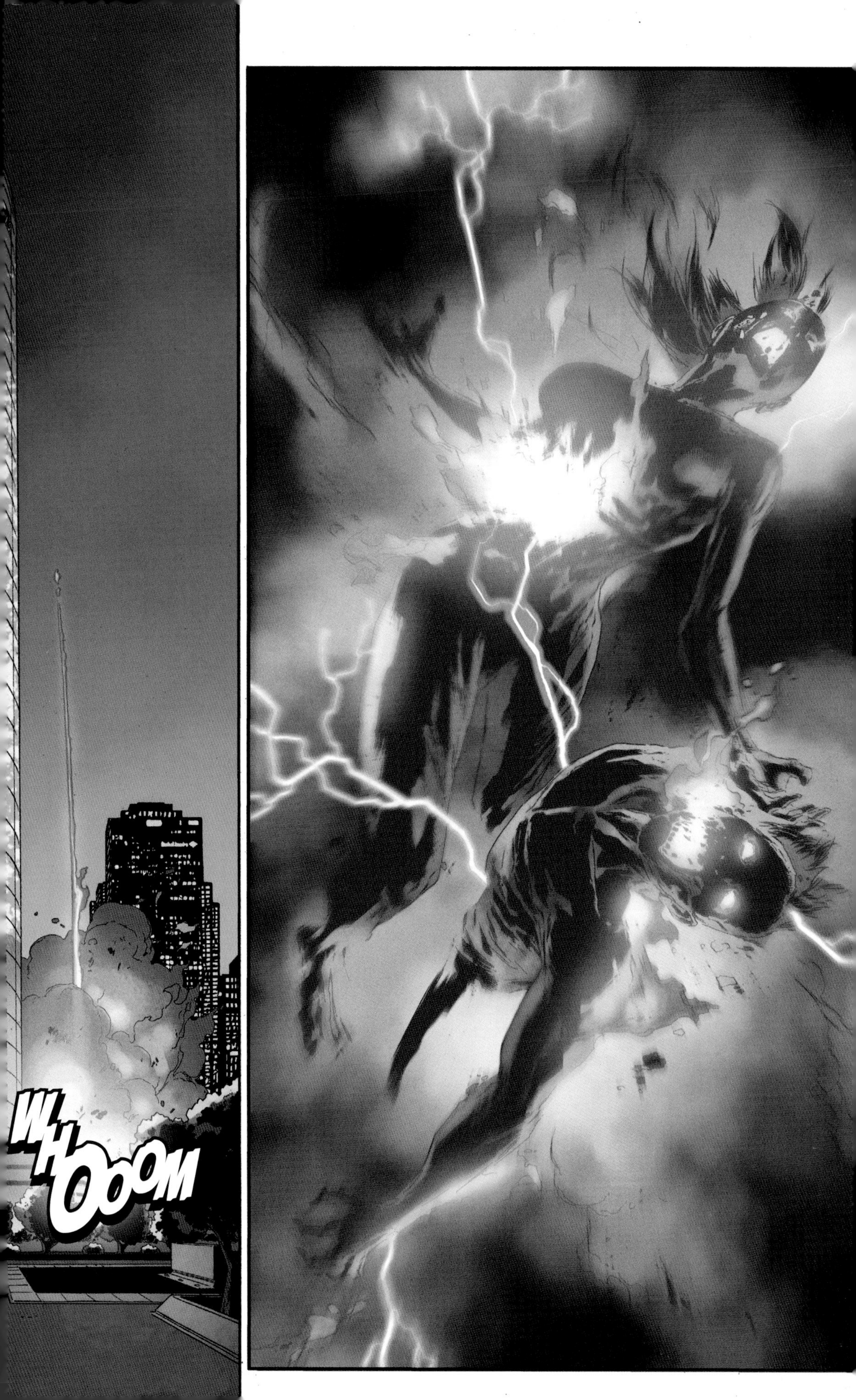
WHOOOM

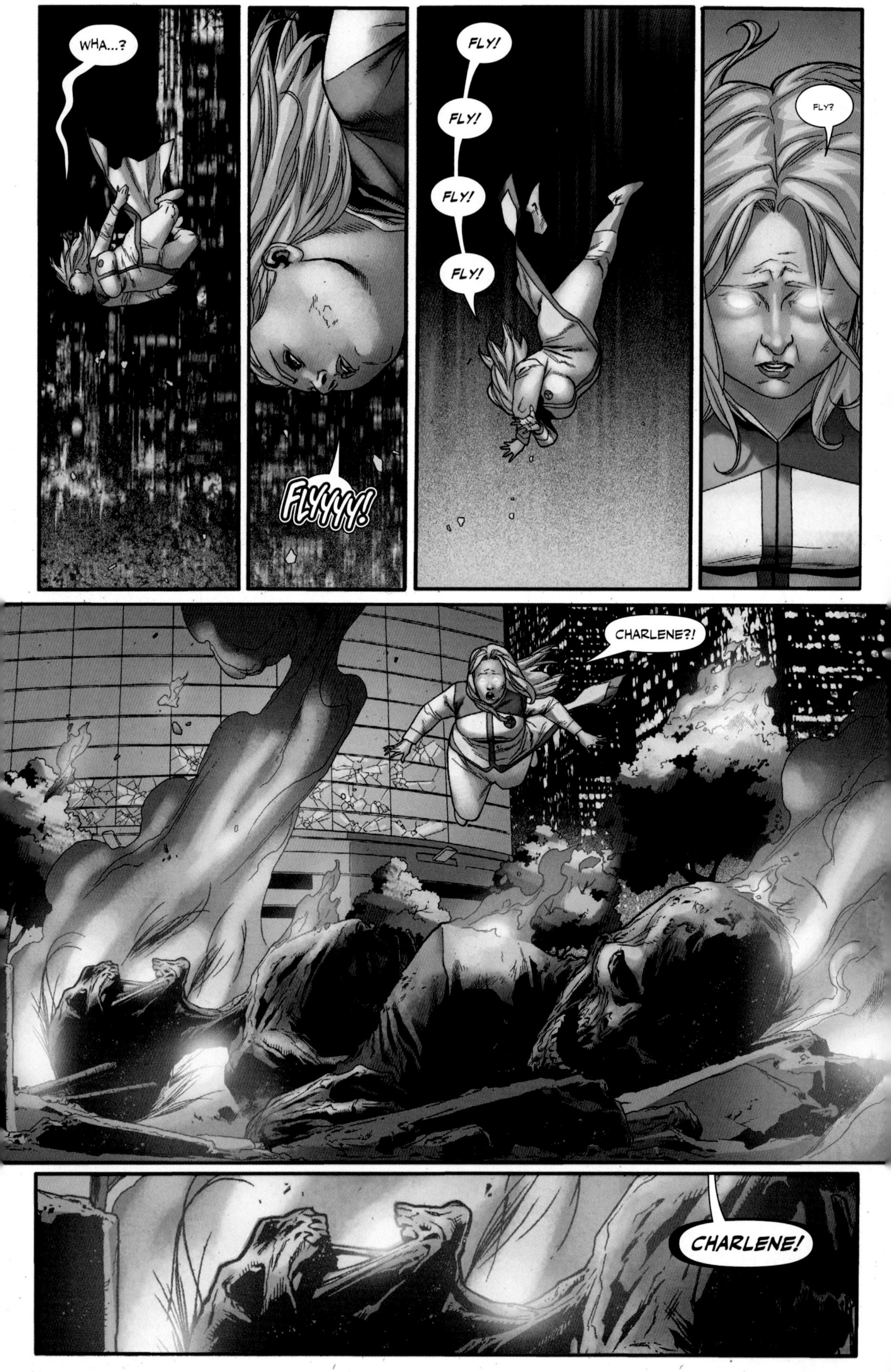
WHA...?
FLYYYY!
FLY!
FLY!
FLY!
FLY!
FLY?
CHARLENE?!
CHARLENE!

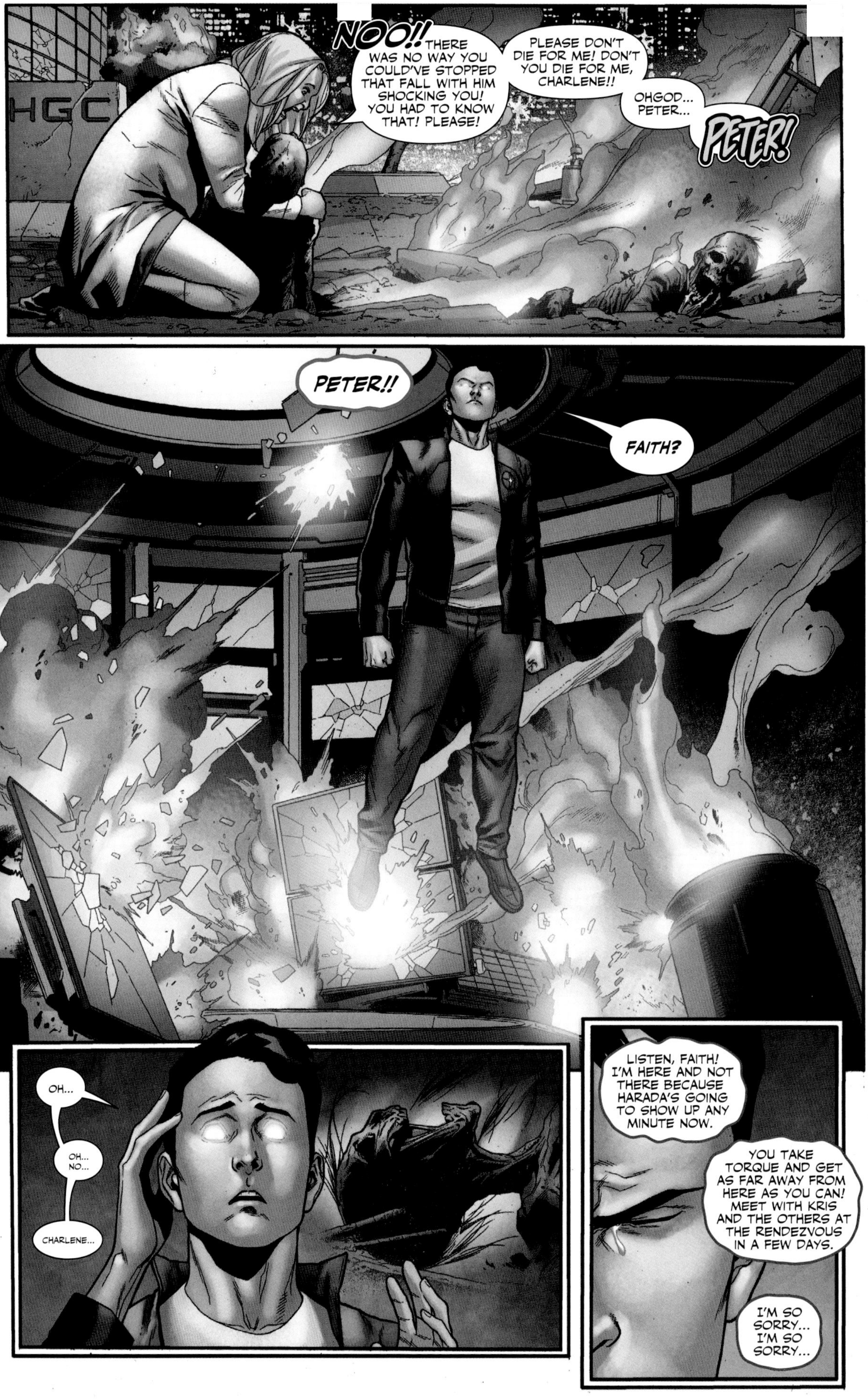
NOO!!
THERE WAS NO WAY YOU COULD'VE STOPPED THAT FALL WITH HIM SHOCKING YOU! YOU HAD TO KNOW THAT! PLEASE!
PLEASE DON'T DIE FOR ME! DON'T YOU DIE FOR ME, CHARLENE!!
OHGOD... PETER...
PETER!
PETER!!
FAITH?
OH...
OH... NO...
CHARLENE...
LISTEN, FAITH! I'M HERE AND NOT THERE BECAUSE HARADA'S GOING TO SHOW UP ANY MINUTE NOW.
YOU TAKE TORQUE AND GET AS FAR AWAY FROM HERE AS YOU CAN! MEET WITH KRIS AND THE OTHERS AT THE RENDEZVOUS IN A FEW DAYS.
I'M SO SORRY... I'M SO SORRY...

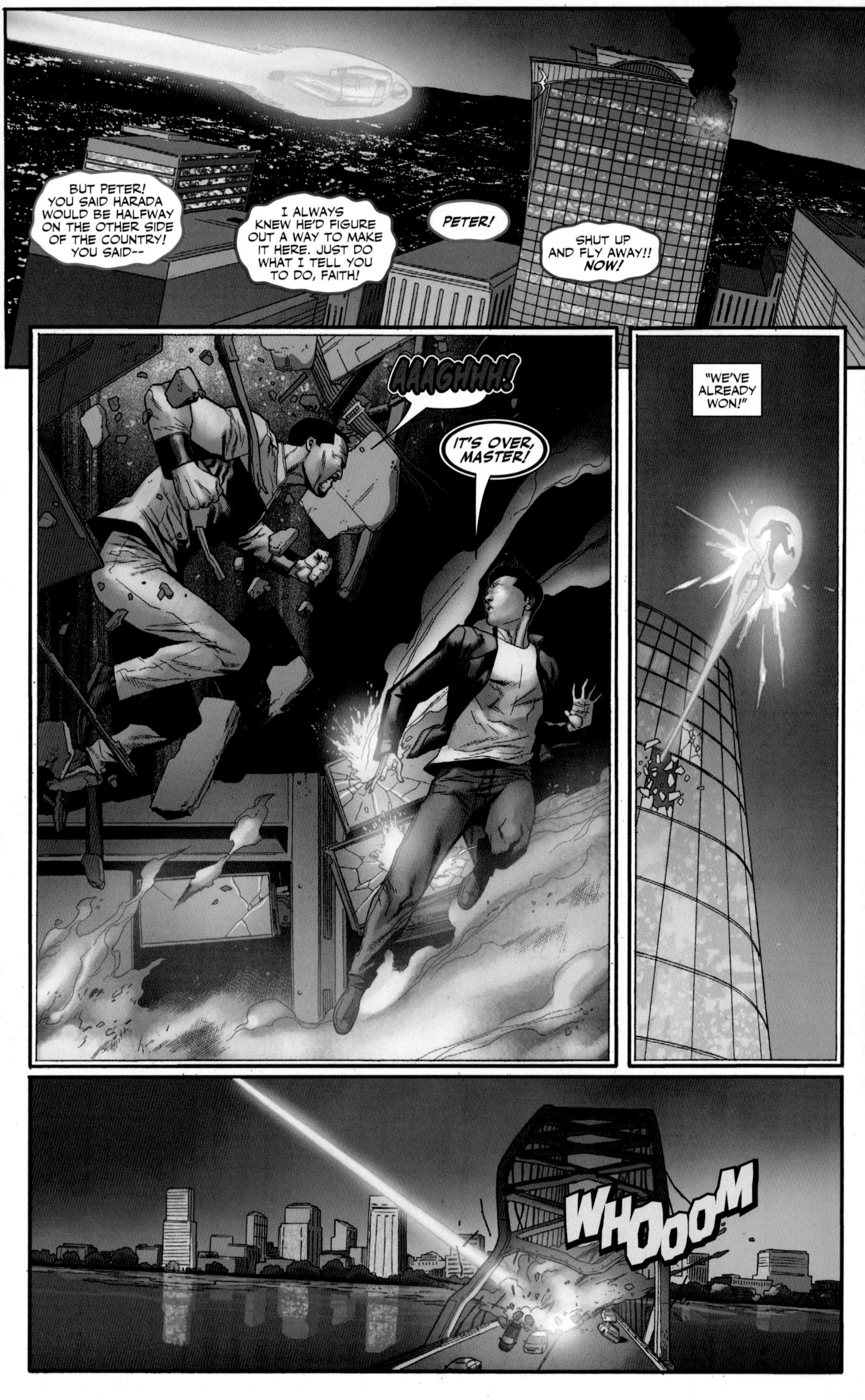
BUT PETER! YOU SAID HARADA WOULD BE HALFWAY ON THE OTHER SIDE OF THE COUNTRY! YOU SAID--
I ALWAYS KNEW HE'D FIGURE OUT A WAY TO MAKE IT HERE. JUST DO WHAT I TELL YOU TO DO, FAITH!
PETER!
SHUT UP AND FLY AWAY!! NOW!
AAAGHHH!
IT'S OVER, MASTER!
"WE'VE ALREADY WON!"
WHOOOOM

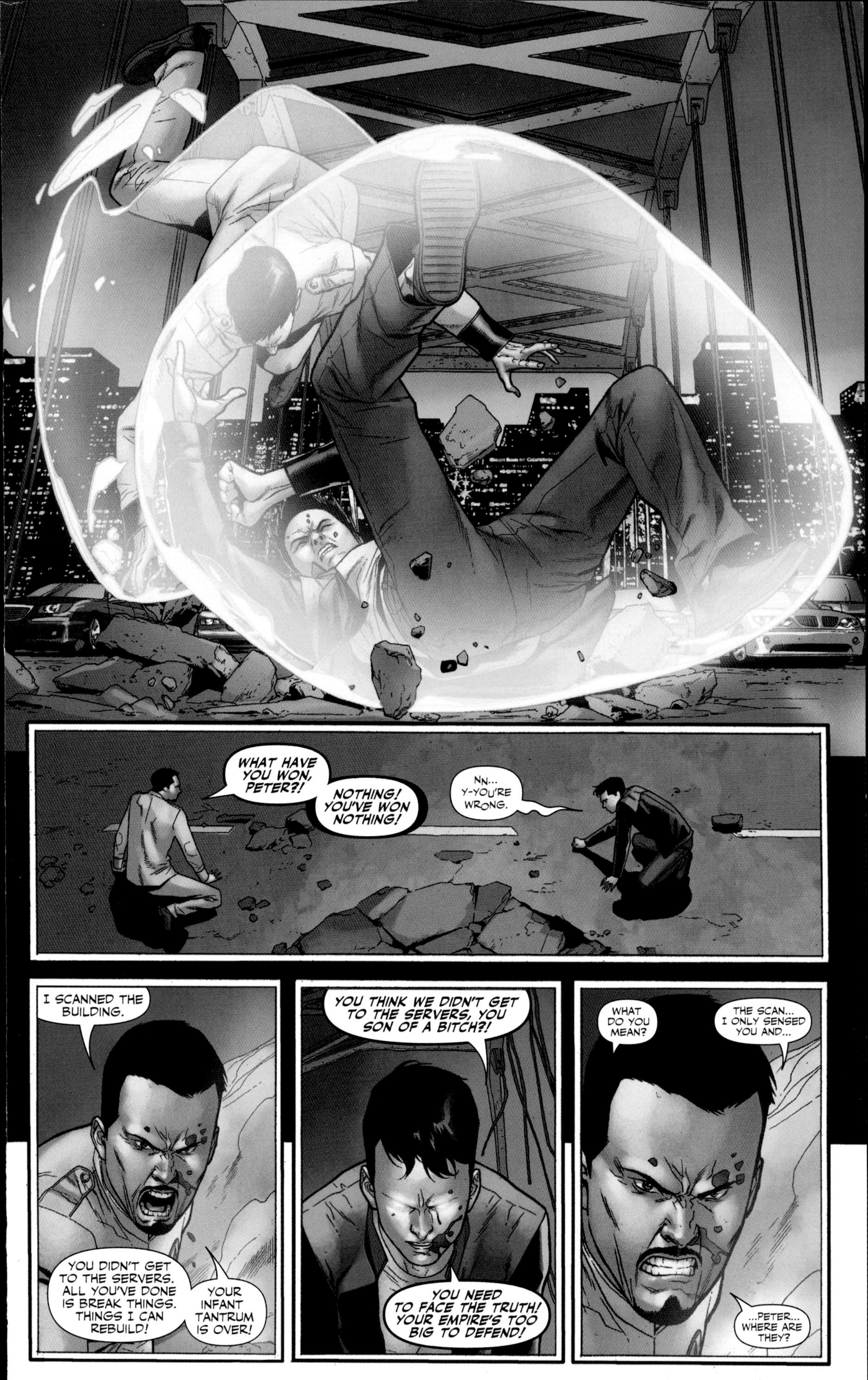
WHAT HAVE YOU WON, PETER?!
NOTHING! YOU'VE WON NOTHING!
NN... Y-YOU'RE WRONG.
I SCANNED THE BUILDING.
YOU DIDN'T GET TO THE SERVERS. ALL YOU'VE DONE IS BREAK THINGS. THINGS I CAN REBUILD!
YOUR INFANT TANTRUM IS OVER!
YOU THINK WE DIDN'T GET TO THE SERVERS, YOU SON OF A BITCH?!
YOU NEED TO FACE THE TRUTH! YOUR EMPIRE'S TOO BIG TO DEFEND!
WHAT DO YOU MEAN?
THE SCAN... I ONLY SENSED YOU AND...
...PETER... WHERE ARE THEY?

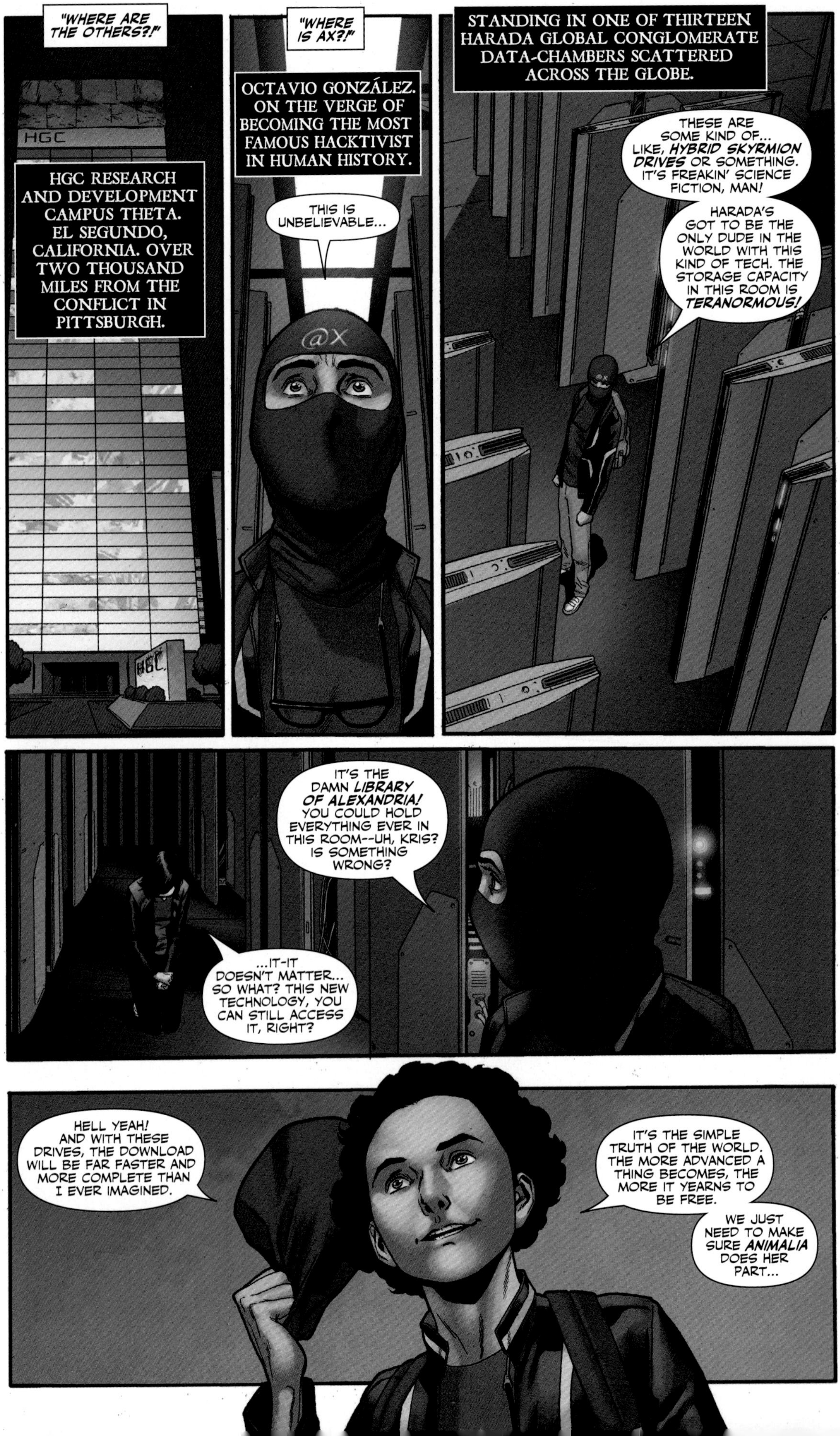
"WHERE ARE THE OTHERS?!"
HGC
HGC RESEARCH AND DEVELOPMENT CAMPUS THETA. EL SEGUNDO, CALIFORNIA. OVER TWO THOUSAND MILES FROM THE CONFLICT IN PITTSBURGH.
"WHERE IS AX?!"
OCTAVIO GONZÁLEZ. ON THE VERGE OF BECOMING THE MOST FAMOUS HACKTIVIST IN HUMAN HISTORY.
THIS IS UNBELIEVABLE...
@X
STANDING IN ONE OF THIRTEEN HARADA GLOBAL CONGLOMERATE DATA-CHAMBERS SCATTERED ACROSS THE GLOBE.
THESE ARE SOME KIND OF... LIKE, HYBRID SKYRMION DRIVES OR SOMETHING. IT'S FREAKIN' SCIENCE FICTION, MAN!
HARADA'S GOT TO BE THE ONLY DUDE IN THE WORLD WITH THIS KIND OF TECH. THE STORAGE CAPACITY IN THIS ROOM IS TERANORMOUS!
IT'S THE DAMN LIBRARY OF ALEXANDRIA! YOU COULD HOLD EVERYTHING EVER IN THIS ROOM--UH, KRIS? IS SOMETHING WRONG?
...IT-IT DOESN'T MATTER... SO WHAT? THIS NEW TECHNOLOGY, YOU CAN STILL ACCESS IT, RIGHT?
HELL YEAH! AND WITH THESE DRIVES, THE DOWNLOAD WILL BE FAR FASTER AND MORE COMPLETE THAN I EVER IMAGINED.
IT'S THE SIMPLE TRUTH OF THE WORLD. THE MORE ADVANCED A THING BECOMES, THE MORE IT YEARNS TO BE FREE.
WE JUST NEED TO MAKE SURE ANIMALIA DOES HER PART...

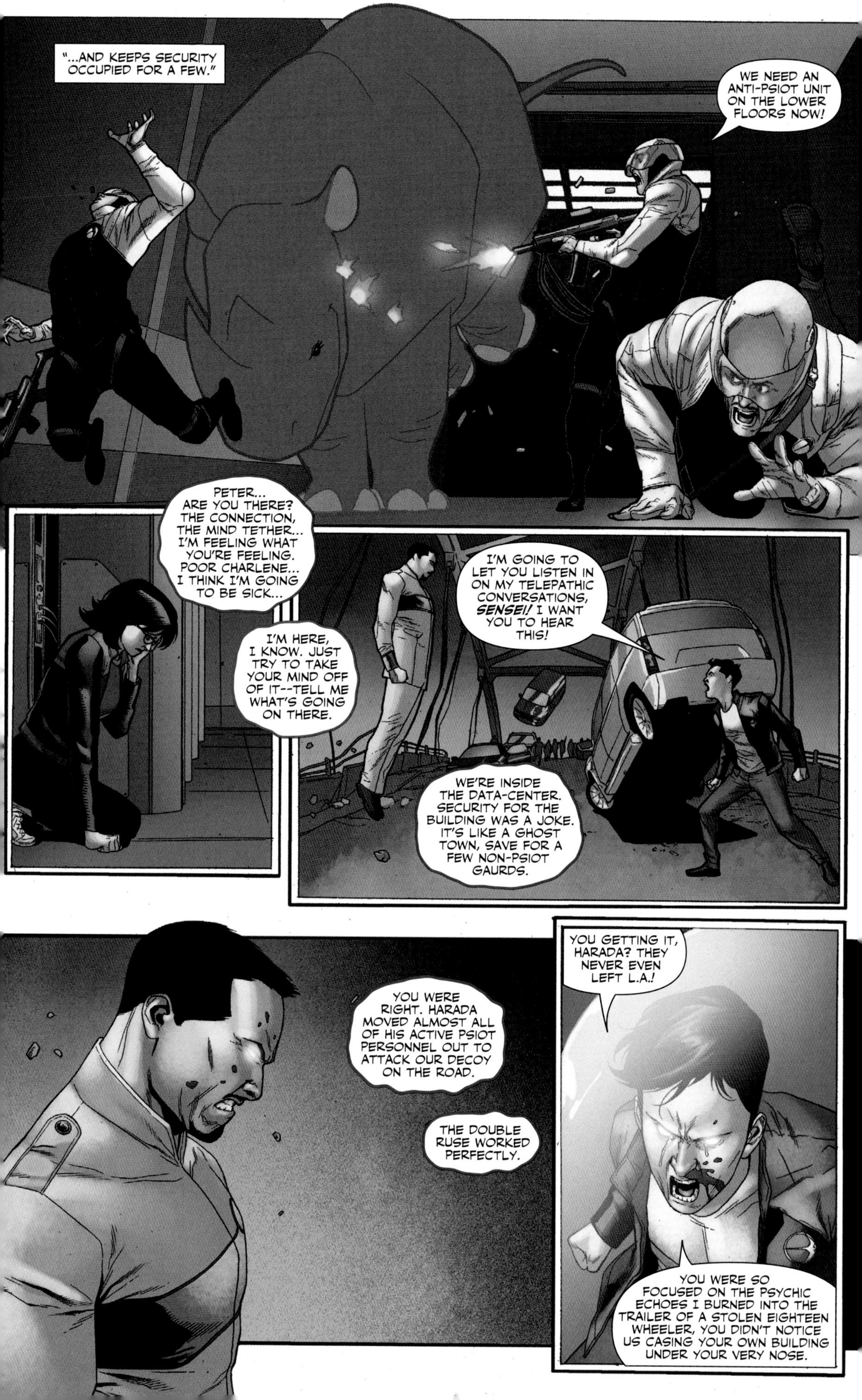
"...AND KEEPS SECURITY OCCUPIED FOR A FEW."
WE NEED AN ANTI-PSIOT UNIT ON THE LOWER FLOORS NOW!
PETER... ARE YOU THERE? THE CONNECTION, THE MIND TETHER... I'M FEELING WHAT YOU'RE FEELING. POOR CHARLENE... I THINK I'M GOING TO BE SICK...
I'M HERE, I KNOW. JUST TRY TO TAKE YOUR MIND OFF OF IT--TELL ME WHAT'S GOING ON THERE.
I'M GOING TO LET YOU LISTEN IN ON MY TELEPATHIC CONVERSATIONS, SENSEI! I WANT YOU TO HEAR THIS!
WE'RE INSIDE THE DATA-CENTER. SECURITY FOR THE BUILDING WAS A JOKE. IT'S LIKE A GHOST TOWN, SAVE FOR A FEW NON-PSIOT GAURDS.
YOU WERE RIGHT. HARADA MOVED ALMOST ALL OF HIS ACTIVE PSIOT PERSONNEL OUT TO ATTACK OUR DECOY ON THE ROAD.
THE DOUBLE RUSE WORKED PERFECTLY.
YOU GETTING IT, HARADA? THEY NEVER EVEN LEFT L.A.!
YOU WERE SO FOCUSED ON THE PSYCHIC ECHOES I BURNED INTO THE TRAILER OF A STOLEN EIGHTEEN WHEELER, YOU DIDN'T NOTICE US CASING YOUR OWN BUILDING UNDER YOUR VERY NOSE.

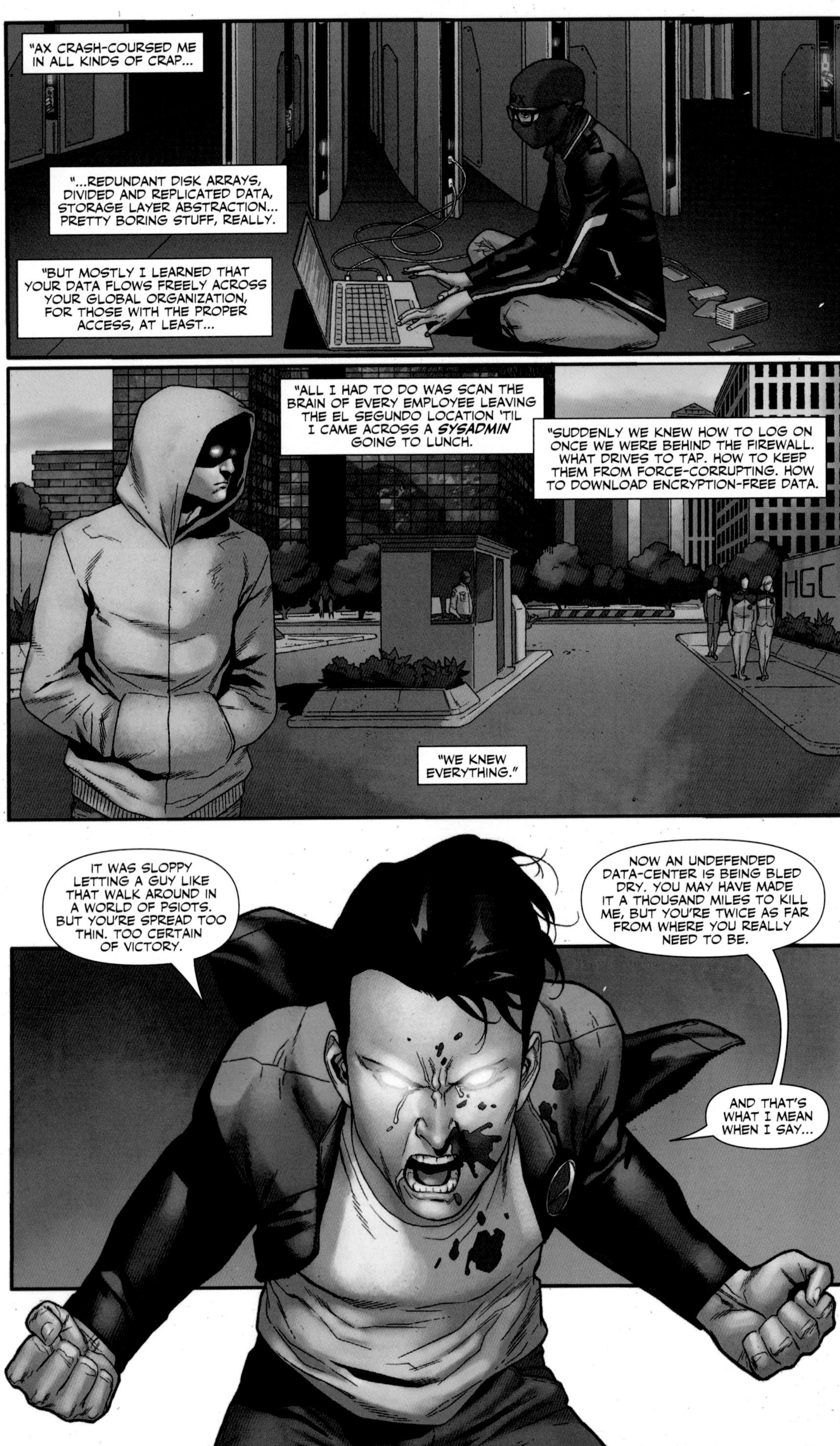

"AX CRASH-COURSED ME IN ALL KINDS OF CRAP...
"...REDUNDANT DISK ARRAYS, DIVIDED AND REPLICATED DATA, STORAGE LAYER ABSTRACTION... PRETTY BORING STUFF, REALLY.
"BUT MOSTLY I LEARNED THAT YOUR DATA FLOWS FREELY ACROSS YOUR GLOBAL ORGANIZATION, FOR THOSE WITH THE PROPER ACCESS, AT LEAST...
"ALL I HAD TO DO WAS SCAN THE BRAIN OF EVERY EMPLOYEE LEAVING THE EL SEGUNDO LOCATION 'TIL I CAME ACROSS A *SYSADMIN* GOING TO LUNCH.
"SUDDENLY WE KNEW HOW TO LOG ON ONCE WE WERE BEHIND THE FIREWALL. WHAT DRIVES TO TAP. HOW TO KEEP THEM FROM FORCE-CORRUPTING. HOW TO DOWNLOAD ENCRYPTION-FREE DATA.
HGC
"WE KNEW EVERYTHING."
IT WAS SLOPPY LETTING A GUY LIKE THAT WALK AROUND IN A WORLD OF PSIOTS. BUT YOU'RE SPREAD TOO THIN. TOO CERTAIN OF VICTORY.
NOW AN UNDEFENDED DATA-CENTER IS BEING BLED DRY. YOU MAY HAVE MADE IT A THOUSAND MILES TO KILL ME, BUT YOU'RE TWICE AS FAR FROM WHERE YOU REALLY NEED TO BE.
AND THAT'S WHAT I MEAN WHEN I SAY...

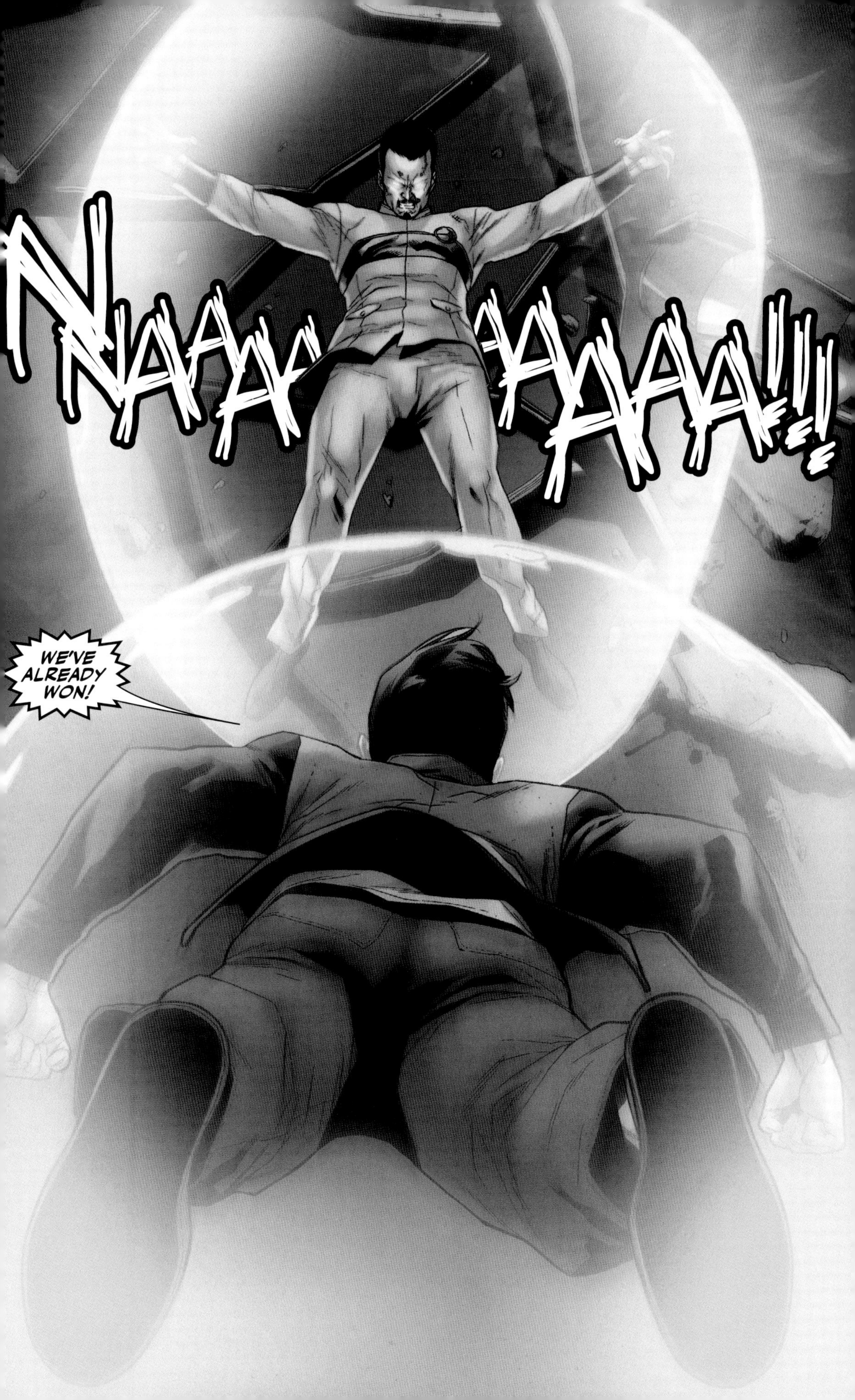
NAAAAAAAAAA!!!
WE'VE ALREADY WON!

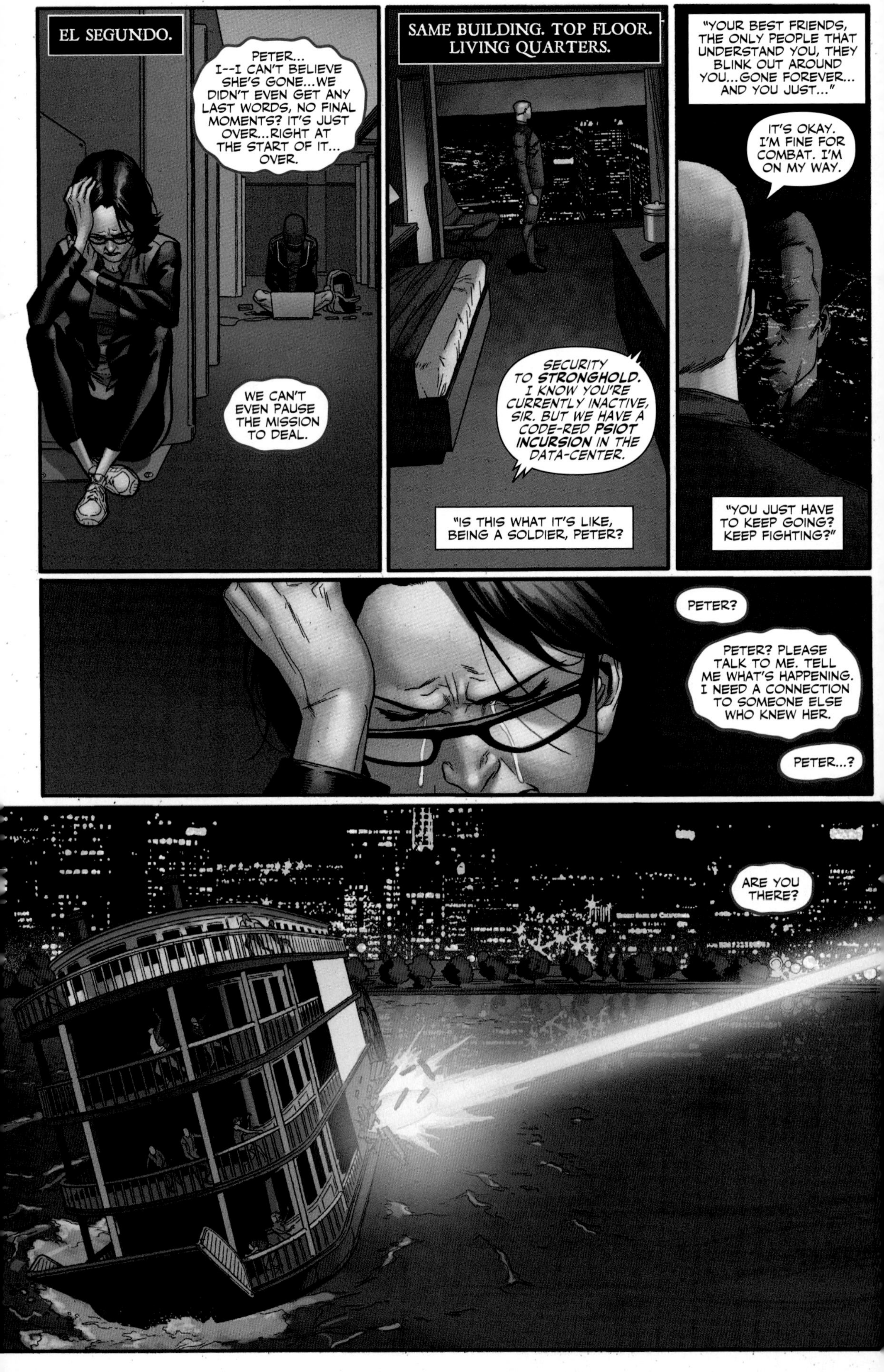
EL SEGUNDO.
PETER... I--I CAN'T BELIEVE SHE'S GONE...WE DIDN'T EVEN GET ANY LAST WORDS, NO FINAL MOMENTS? IT'S JUST OVER...RIGHT AT THE START OF IT... OVER.
WE CAN'T EVEN PAUSE THE MISSION TO DEAL.
SAME BUILDING. TOP FLOOR. LIVING QUARTERS.
SECURITY TO STRONGHOLD. I KNOW YOU'RE CURRENTLY INACTIVE, SIR. BUT WE HAVE A CODE-RED PSIOT INCURSION IN THE DATA-CENTER.
"IS THIS WHAT IT'S LIKE, BEING A SOLDIER, PETER?
"YOUR BEST FRIENDS, THE ONLY PEOPLE THAT UNDERSTAND YOU, THEY BLINK OUT AROUND YOU...GONE FOREVER... AND YOU JUST..."
IT'S OKAY. I'M FINE FOR COMBAT. I'M ON MY WAY.
"YOU JUST HAVE TO KEEP GOING? KEEP FIGHTING?"
PETER?
PETER? PLEASE TALK TO ME. TELL ME WHAT'S HAPPENING. I NEED A CONNECTION TO SOMEONE ELSE WHO KNEW HER.
PETER...?
ARE YOU THERE?

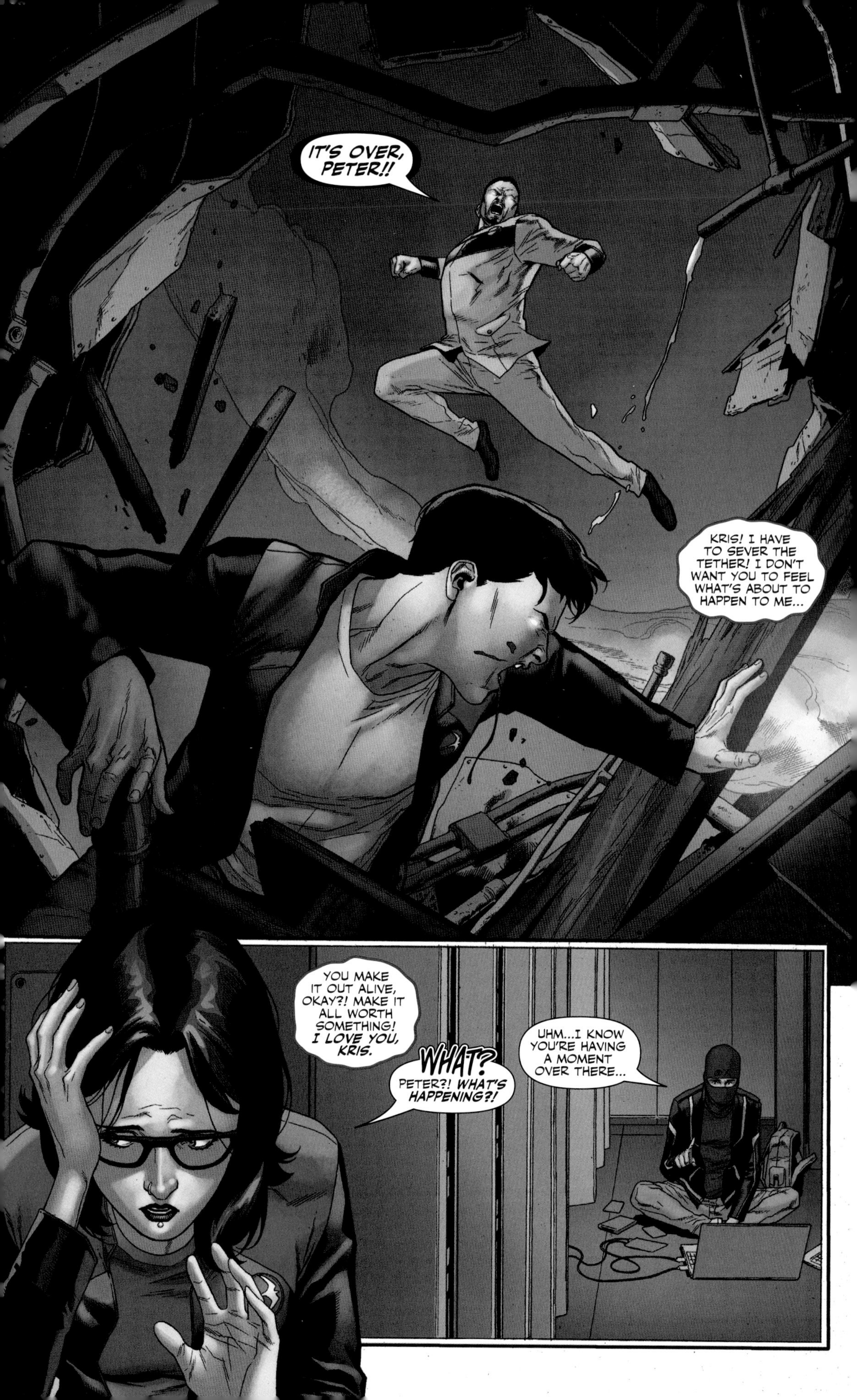
IT'S OVER, PETER!!
KRIS! I HAVE TO SEVER THE TETHER! I DON'T WANT YOU TO FEEL WHAT'S ABOUT TO HAPPEN TO ME...
YOU MAKE IT OUT ALIVE, OKAY?! MAKE IT ALL WORTH SOMETHING! I LOVE YOU, KRIS.
WHAT?
PETER?! WHAT'S HAPPENING?!
UHM...I KNOW YOU'RE HAVING A MOMENT OVER THERE...

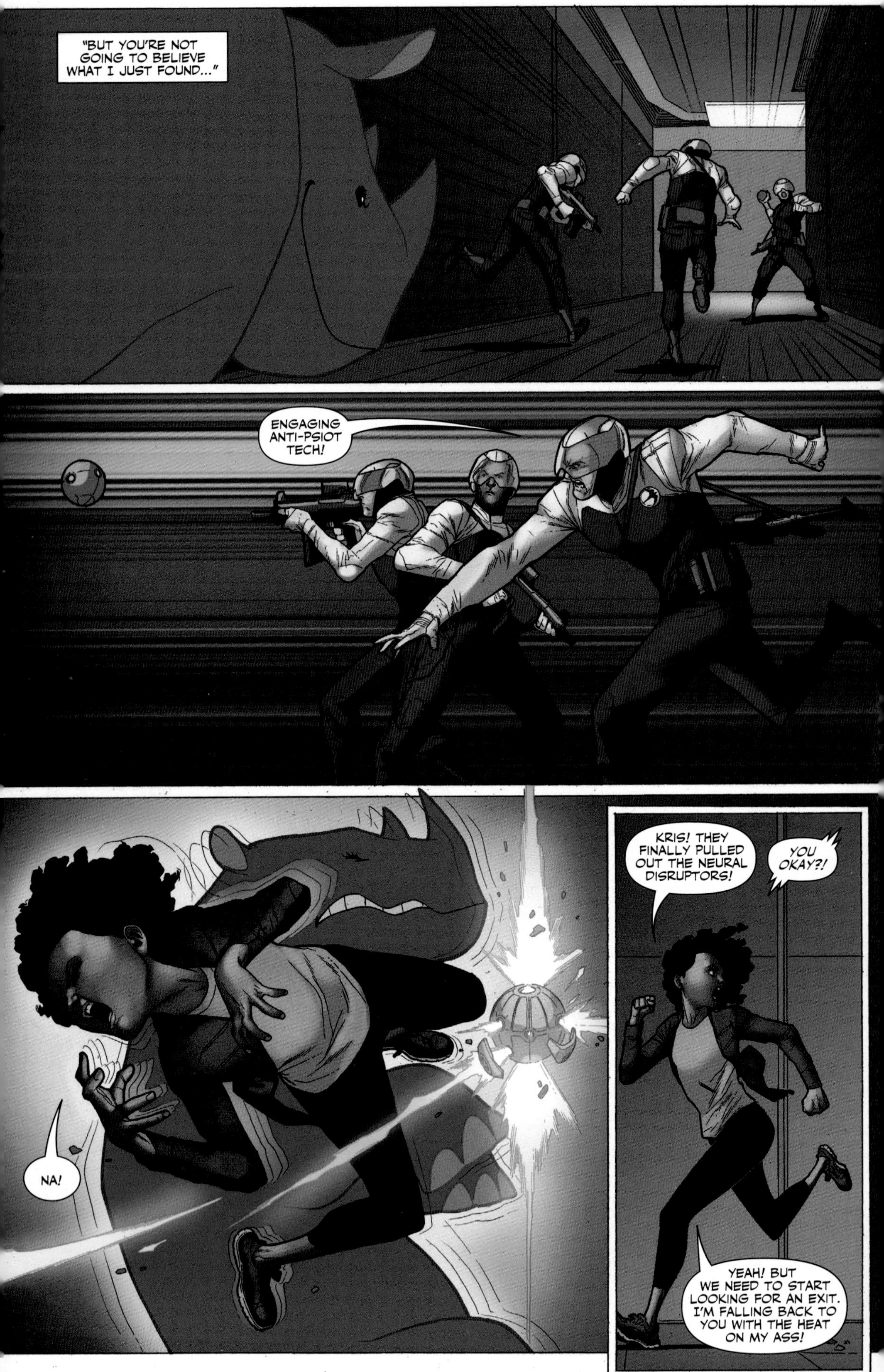
"BUT YOU'RE NOT GOING TO BELIEVE WHAT I JUST FOUND..."
ENGAGING ANTI-PSIOT TECH!
NA!
KRIS! THEY FINALLY PULLED OUT THE NEURAL DISRUPTORS!
YOU OKAY?!
YEAH! BUT WE NEED TO START LOOKING FOR AN EXIT. I'M FALLING BACK TO YOU WITH THE HEAT ON MY ASS!

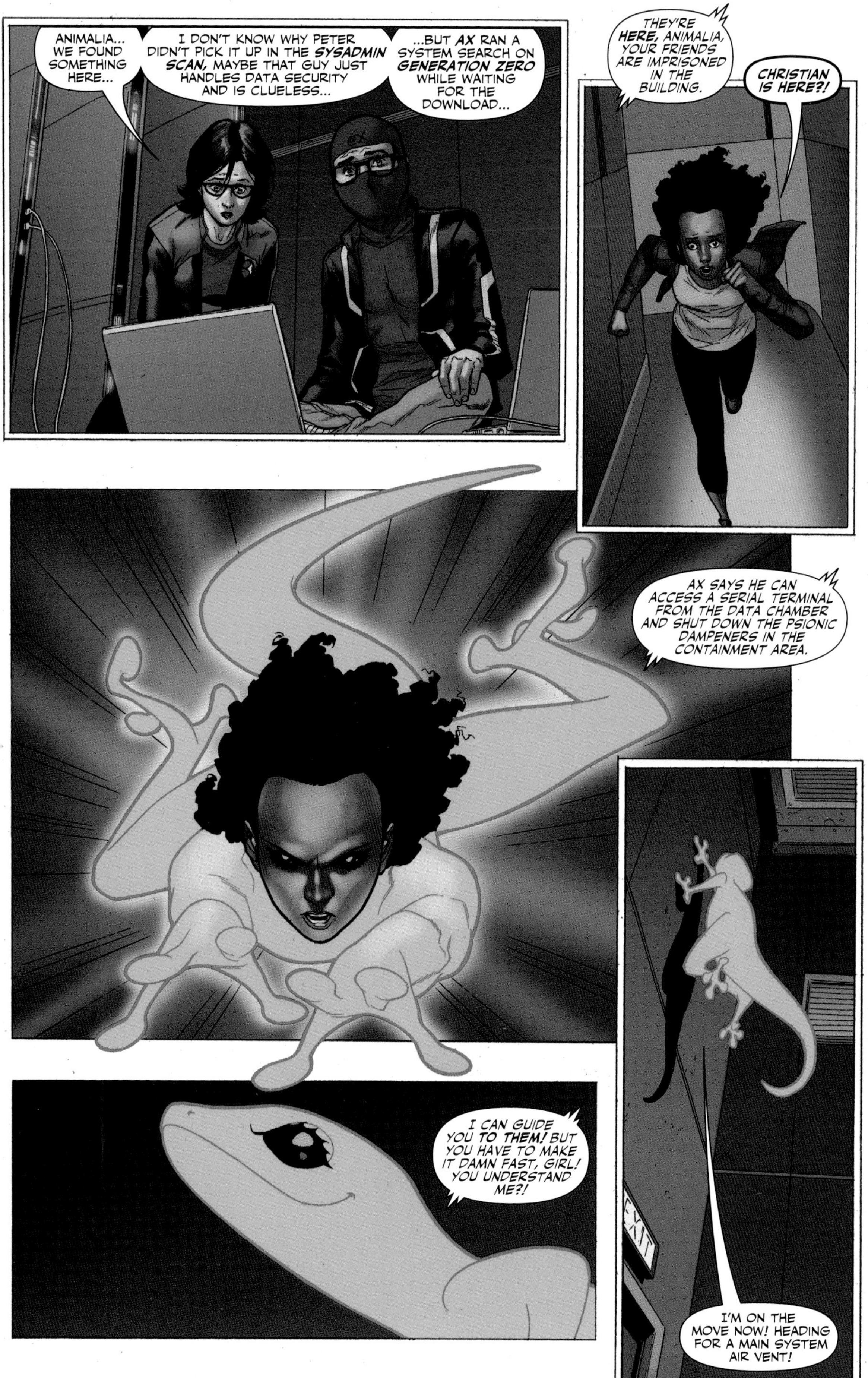

ANIMALIA... WE FOUND SOMETHING HERE...
I DON'T KNOW WHY PETER DIDN'T PICK IT UP IN THE **SYSADMIN SCAN,** MAYBE THAT GUY JUST HANDLES DATA SECURITY AND IS CLUELESS...
...BUT **AX** RAN A SYSTEM SEARCH ON **GENERATION ZERO** WHILE WAITING FOR THE DOWNLOAD...
THEY'RE **HERE,** ANIMALIA, YOUR FRIENDS ARE IMPRISONED IN THE BUILDING.
CHRISTIAN IS HERE?!
AX SAYS HE CAN ACCESS A SERIAL TERMINAL FROM THE DATA CHAMBER AND SHUT DOWN THE PSIONIC DAMPENERS IN THE CONTAINMENT AREA.
I CAN GUIDE YOU **TO THEM!** BUT YOU HAVE TO MAKE IT DAMN FAST, GIRL! YOU UNDERSTAND ME?!
I'M ON THE MOVE NOW! HEADING FOR A MAIN SYSTEM AIR VENT!

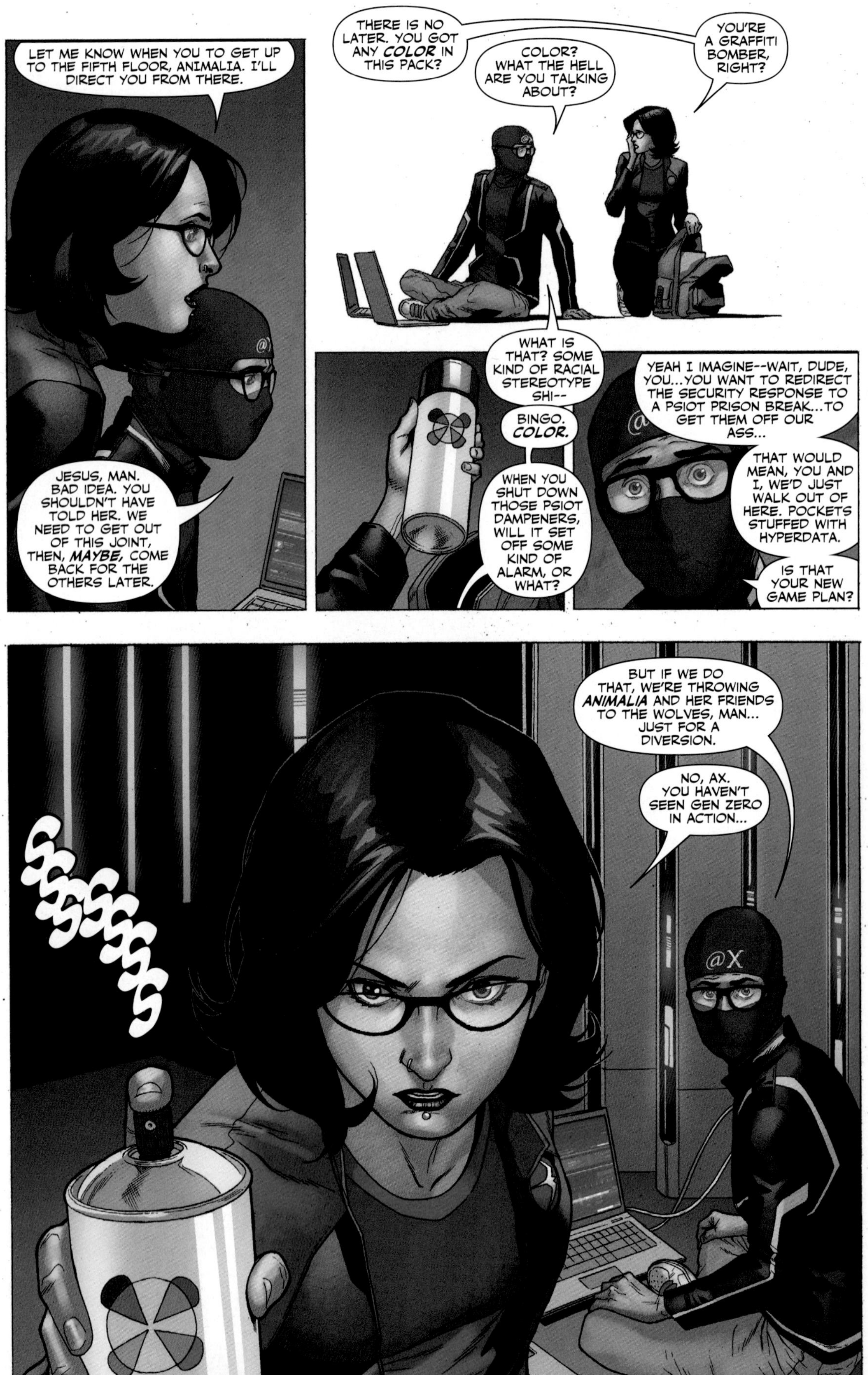

LET ME KNOW WHEN YOU TO GET UP TO THE FIFTH FLOOR, ANIMALIA. I'LL DIRECT YOU FROM THERE.
JESUS, MAN. BAD IDEA. YOU SHOULDN'T HAVE TOLD HER. WE NEED TO GET OUT OF THIS JOINT, THEN, *MAYBE,* COME BACK FOR THE OTHERS LATER.
THERE IS NO LATER. YOU GOT ANY *COLOR* IN THIS PACK?
COLOR? WHAT THE HELL ARE YOU TALKING ABOUT?
YOU'RE A GRAFFITI BOMBER, RIGHT?
WHAT IS THAT? SOME KIND OF RACIAL STEREOTYPE SHI--
BINGO. *COLOR.*
WHEN YOU SHUT DOWN THOSE PSIOT DAMPENERS, WILL IT SET OFF SOME KIND OF ALARM, OR WHAT?
YEAH I IMAGINE--WAIT, DUDE, YOU...YOU WANT TO REDIRECT THE SECURITY RESPONSE TO A PSIOT PRISON BREAK...TO GET THEM OFF OUR ASS...
THAT WOULD MEAN, YOU AND I, WE'D JUST WALK OUT OF HERE. POCKETS STUFFED WITH HYPERDATA.
IS THAT YOUR NEW GAME PLAN?
SSSSSSS
BUT IF WE DO THAT, WE'RE THROWING *ANIMALIA* AND HER FRIENDS TO THE WOLVES, MAN... JUST FOR A DIVERSION.
NO, AX. YOU HAVEN'T SEEN GEN ZERO IN ACTION...
@X

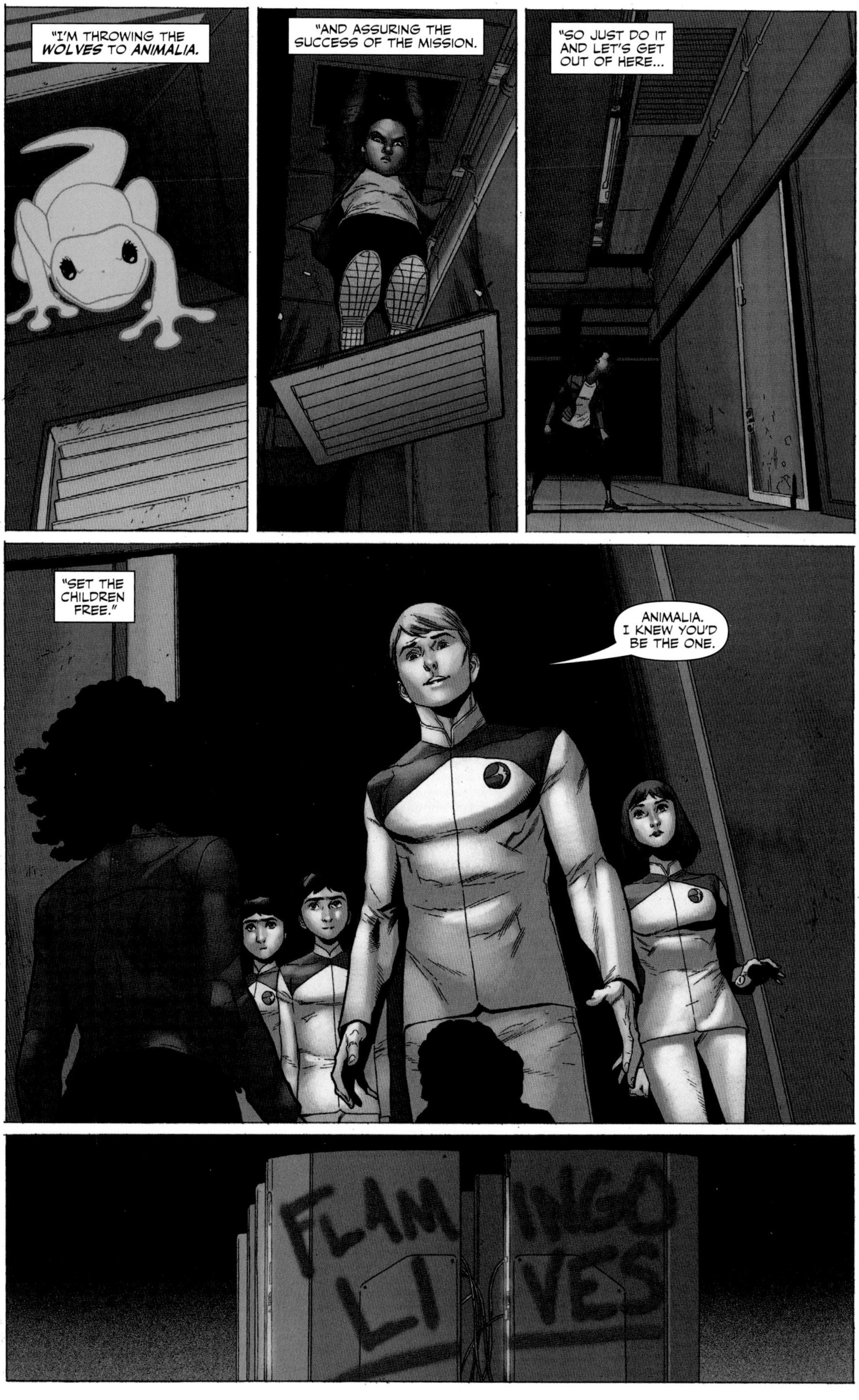
"I'M THROWING THE WOLVES TO ANIMALIA.
"AND ASSURING THE SUCCESS OF THE MISSION.
"SO JUST DO IT AND LET'S GET OUT OF HERE...
"SET THE CHILDREN FREE."
ANIMALIA. I KNEW YOU'D BE THE ONE.
FLAMINGO LIVES

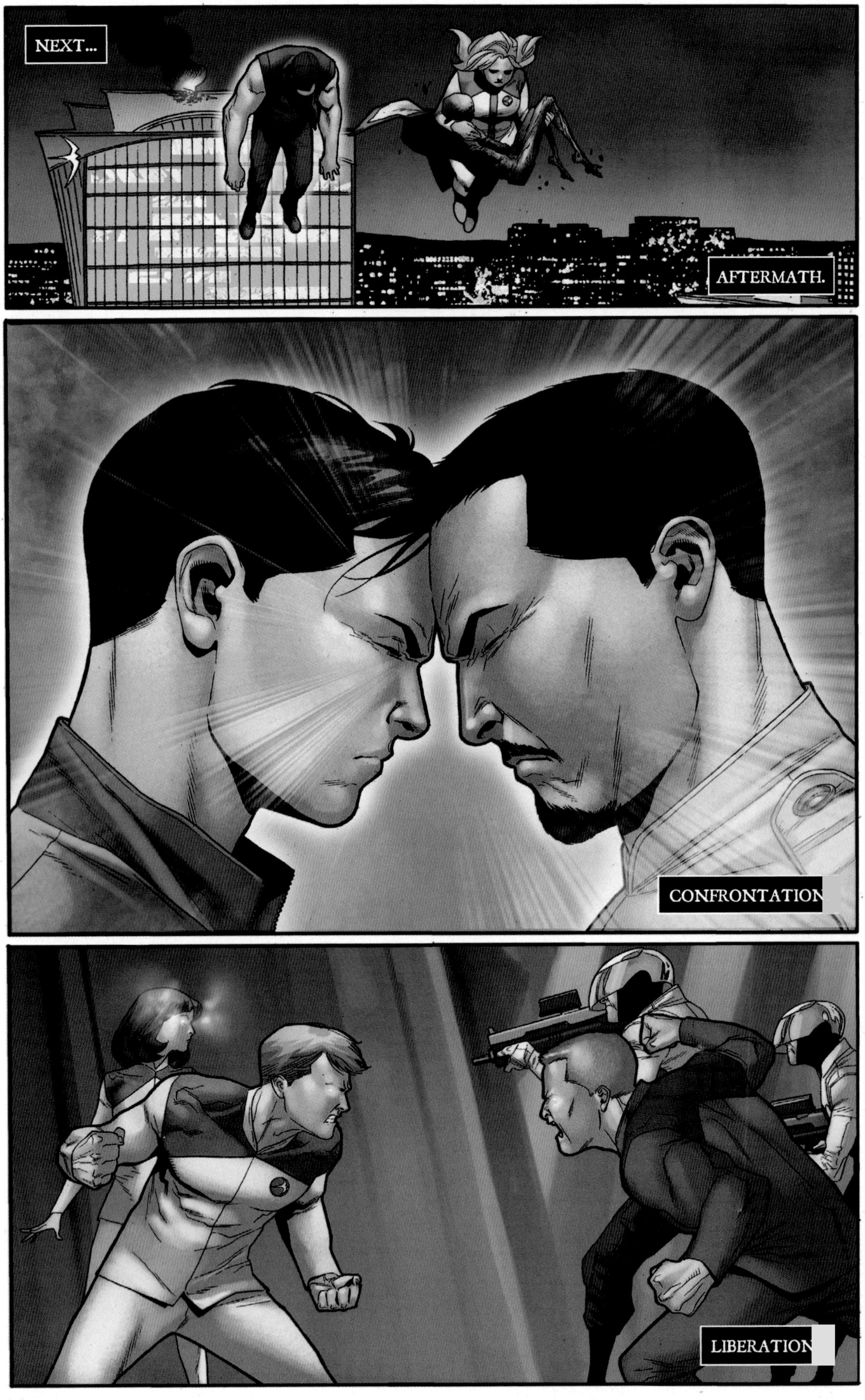
NEXT...
AFTERMATH.
CONFRONTATION
LIBERATION

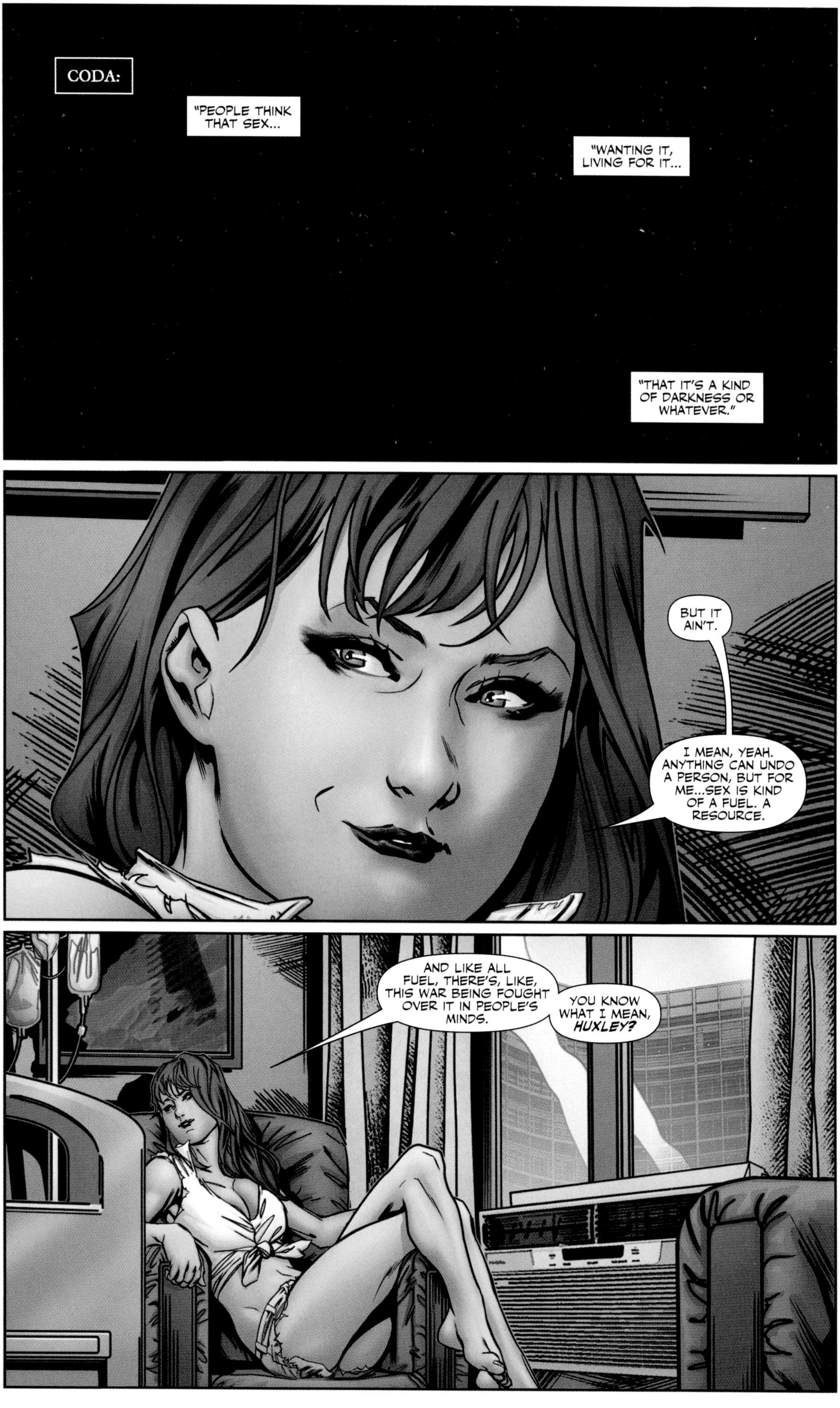
CODA:
"PEOPLE THINK THAT SEX...
"WANTING IT, LIVING FOR IT...
"THAT IT'S A KIND OF DARKNESS OR WHATEVER."
BUT IT AIN'T.
I MEAN, YEAH. ANYTHING CAN UNDO A PERSON, BUT FOR ME...SEX IS KIND OF A FUEL. A RESOURCE.
AND LIKE ALL FUEL, THERE'S, LIKE, THIS WAR BEING FOUGHT OVER IT IN PEOPLE'S MINDS.
YOU KNOW WHAT I MEAN, ***HUXLEY?***

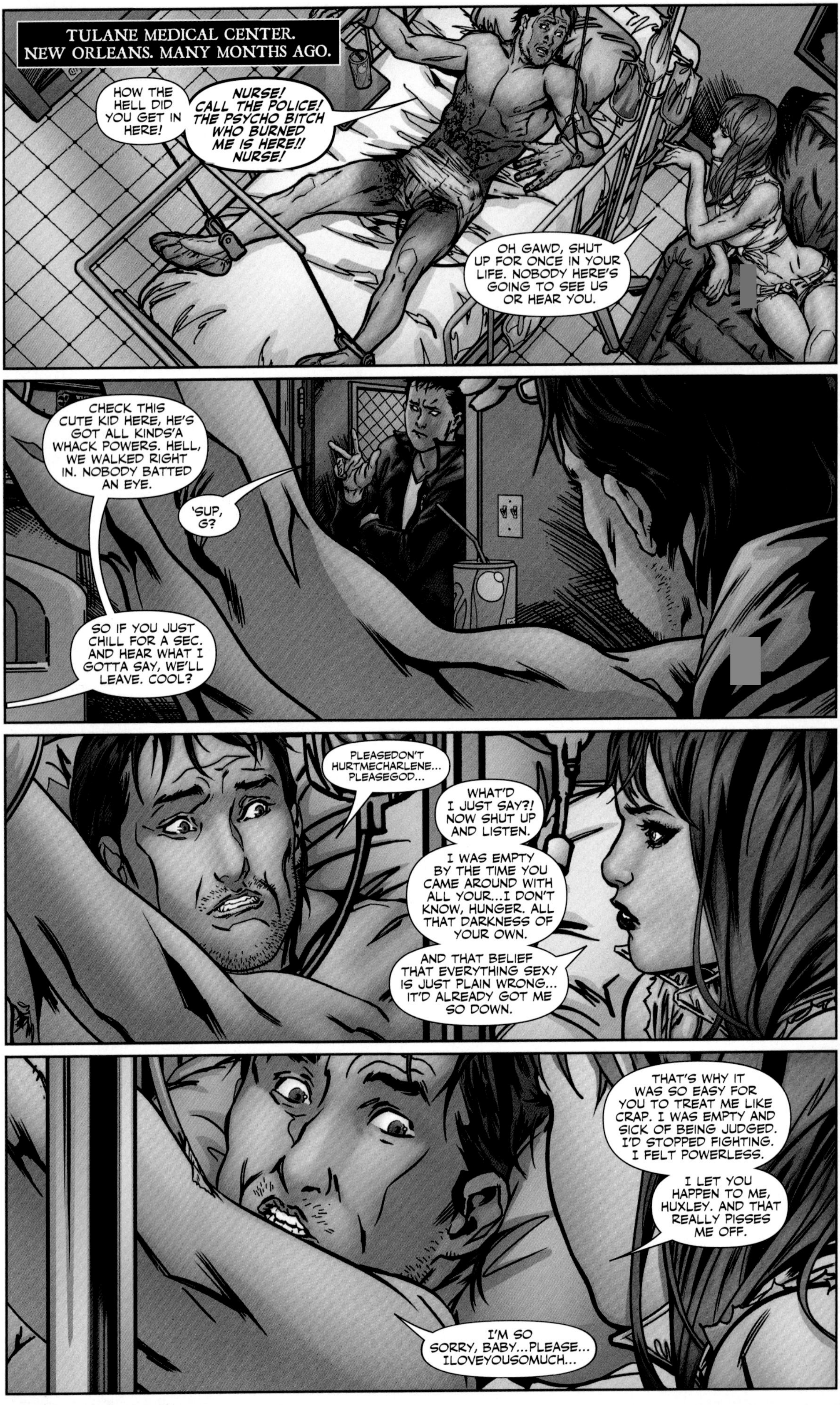
TULANE MEDICAL CENTER. NEW ORLEANS. MANY MONTHS AGO.
HOW THE HELL DID YOU GET IN HERE!
NURSE! CALL THE POLICE! THE PSYCHO BITCH WHO BURNED ME IS HERE!! NURSE!
OH GAWD, SHUT UP FOR ONCE IN YOUR LIFE. NOBODY HERE'S GOING TO SEE US OR HEAR YOU.
CHECK THIS CUTE KID HERE, HE'S GOT ALL KINDS'A WHACK POWERS. HELL, WE WALKED RIGHT IN. NOBODY BATTED AN EYE.
'SUP, G?
SO IF YOU JUST CHILL FOR A SEC. AND HEAR WHAT I GOTTA SAY, WE'LL LEAVE. COOL?
PLEASEDON'T HURTMECHARLENE... PLEASEGOD...
WHAT'D I JUST SAY?! NOW SHUT UP AND LISTEN.
I WAS EMPTY BY THE TIME YOU CAME AROUND WITH ALL YOUR...I DON'T KNOW, HUNGER. ALL THAT DARKNESS OF YOUR OWN.
AND THAT BELIEF THAT EVERYTHING SEXY IS JUST PLAIN WRONG... IT'D ALREADY GOT ME SO DOWN.
THAT'S WHY IT WAS SO EASY FOR YOU TO TREAT ME LIKE CRAP. I WAS EMPTY AND SICK OF BEING JUDGED. I'D STOPPED FIGHTING. I FELT POWERLESS.
I LET YOU HAPPEN TO ME, HUXLEY. AND THAT REALLY PISSES ME OFF.
I'M SO SORRY, BABY...PLEASE... ILOVEYOUSOMUCH...

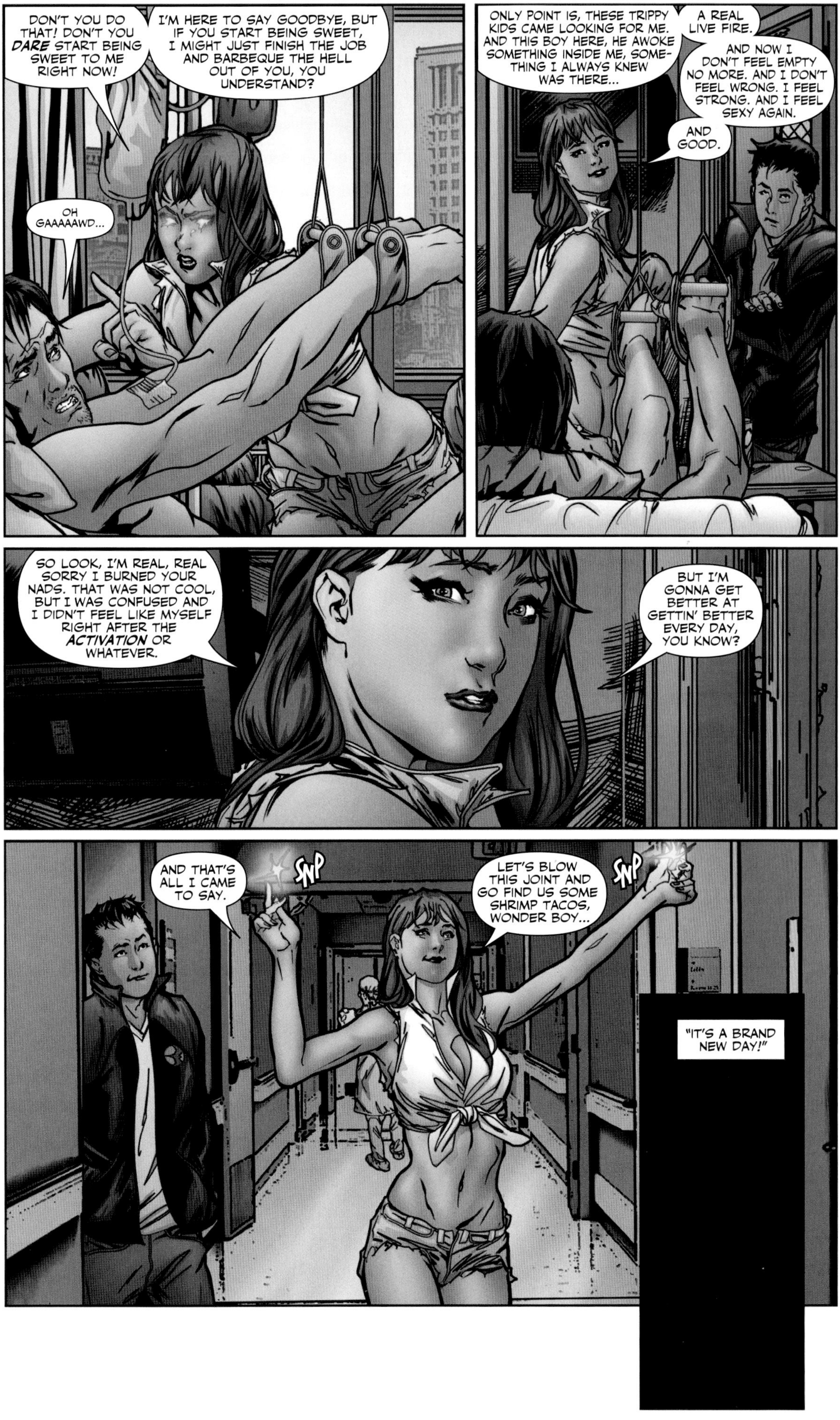

DON'T YOU DO THAT! DON'T YOU DARE START BEING SWEET TO ME RIGHT NOW!
I'M HERE TO SAY GOODBYE, BUT IF YOU START BEING SWEET, I MIGHT JUST FINISH THE JOB AND BARBEQUE THE HELL OUT OF YOU, YOU UNDERSTAND?
OH GAAAAAWD...
ONLY POINT IS, THESE TRIPPY KIDS CAME LOOKING FOR ME. AND THIS BOY HERE, HE AWOKE SOMETHING INSIDE ME, SOMETHING I ALWAYS KNEW WAS THERE...
A REAL LIVE FIRE.
AND NOW I DON'T FEEL EMPTY NO MORE. AND I DON'T FEEL WRONG. I FEEL STRONG. AND I FEEL SEXY AGAIN.
AND GOOD.
SO LOOK, I'M REAL, REAL SORRY I BURNED YOUR NADS. THAT WAS NOT COOL, BUT I WAS CONFUSED AND I DIDN'T FEEL LIKE MYSELF RIGHT AFTER THE ACTIVATION OR WHATEVER.
BUT I'M GONNA GET BETTER AT GETTIN' BETTER EVERY DAY, YOU KNOW?
AND THAT'S ALL I CAME TO SAY.
SNP
LET'S BLOW THIS JOINT AND GO FIND US SOME SHRIMP TACOS, WONDER BOY...
SNP
"IT'S A BRAND NEW DAY!"

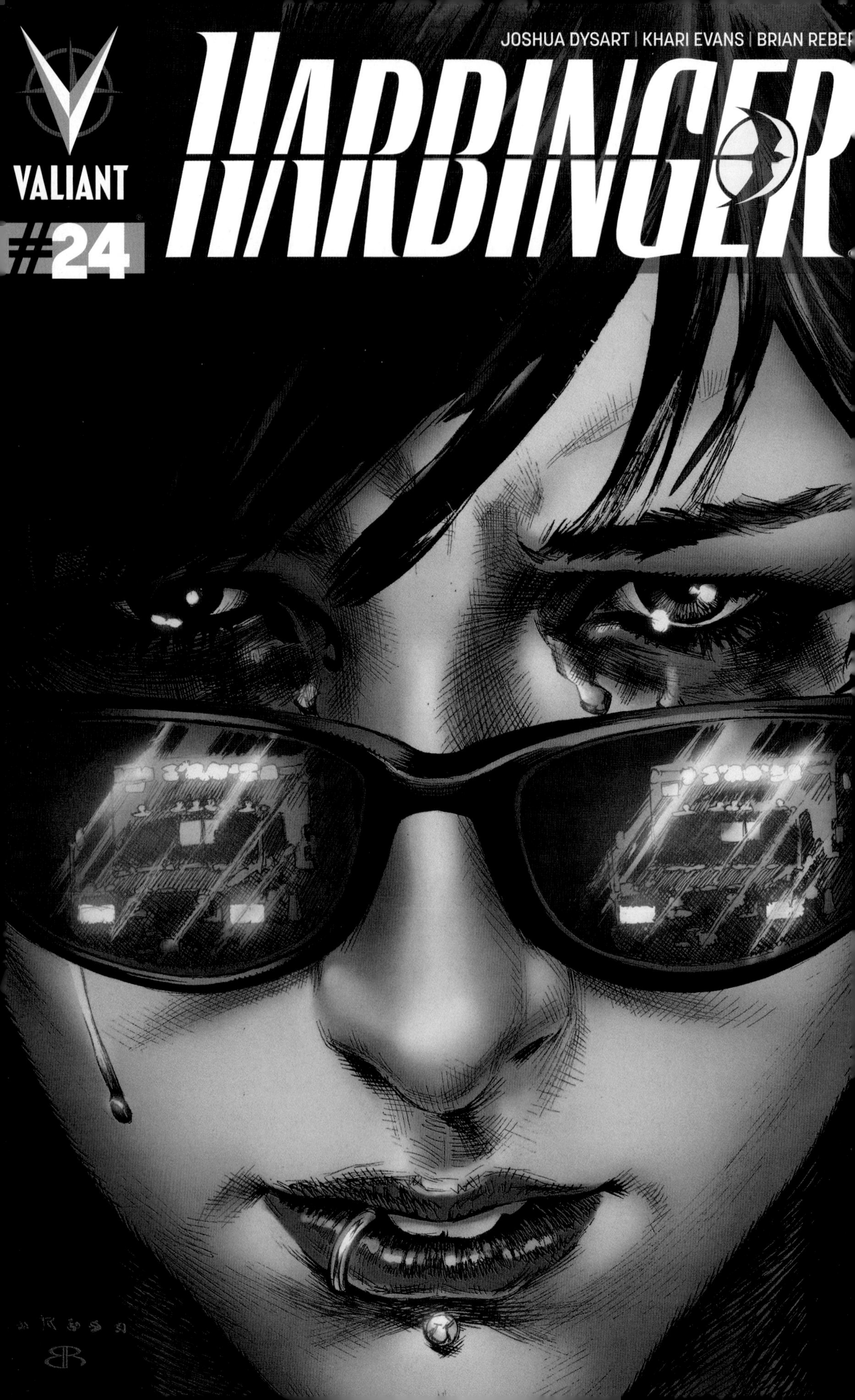
VALIANT
#24
JOSHUA DYSART | KHARI EVANS | BRIAN REBER
HARBINGER

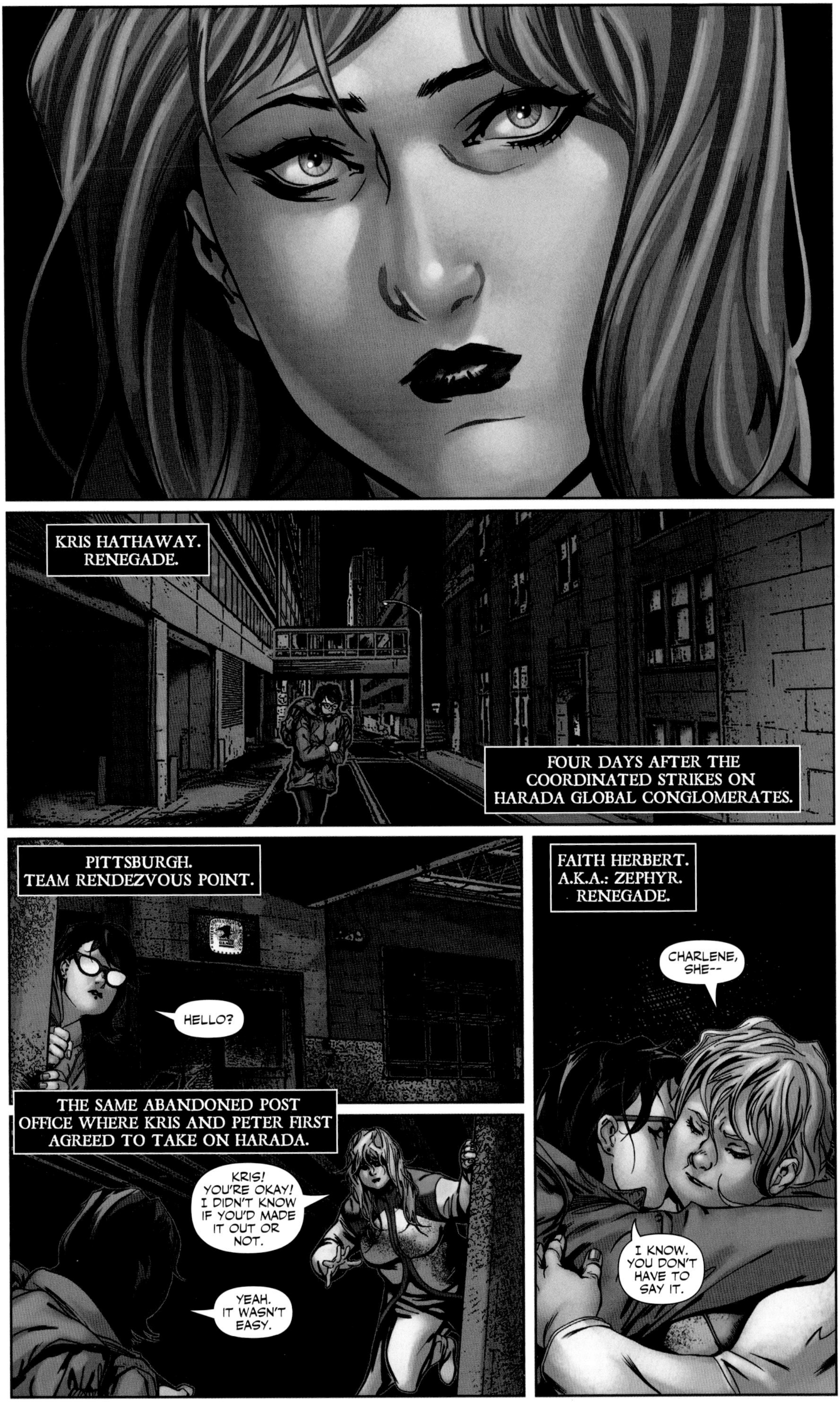
KRIS HATHAWAY.
RENEGADE.
FOUR DAYS AFTER THE COORDINATED STRIKES ON HARADA GLOBAL CONGLOMERATES.
PITTSBURGH.
TEAM RENDEZVOUS POINT.
HELLO?
THE SAME ABANDONED POST OFFICE WHERE KRIS AND PETER FIRST AGREED TO TAKE ON HARADA.
KRIS! YOU'RE OKAY! I DIDN'T KNOW IF YOU'D MADE IT OUT OR NOT.
YEAH. IT WASN'T EASY.
FAITH HERBERT.
A.K.A.: ZEPHYR.
RENEGADE.
CHARLENE, SHE--
I KNOW. YOU DON'T HAVE TO SAY IT.

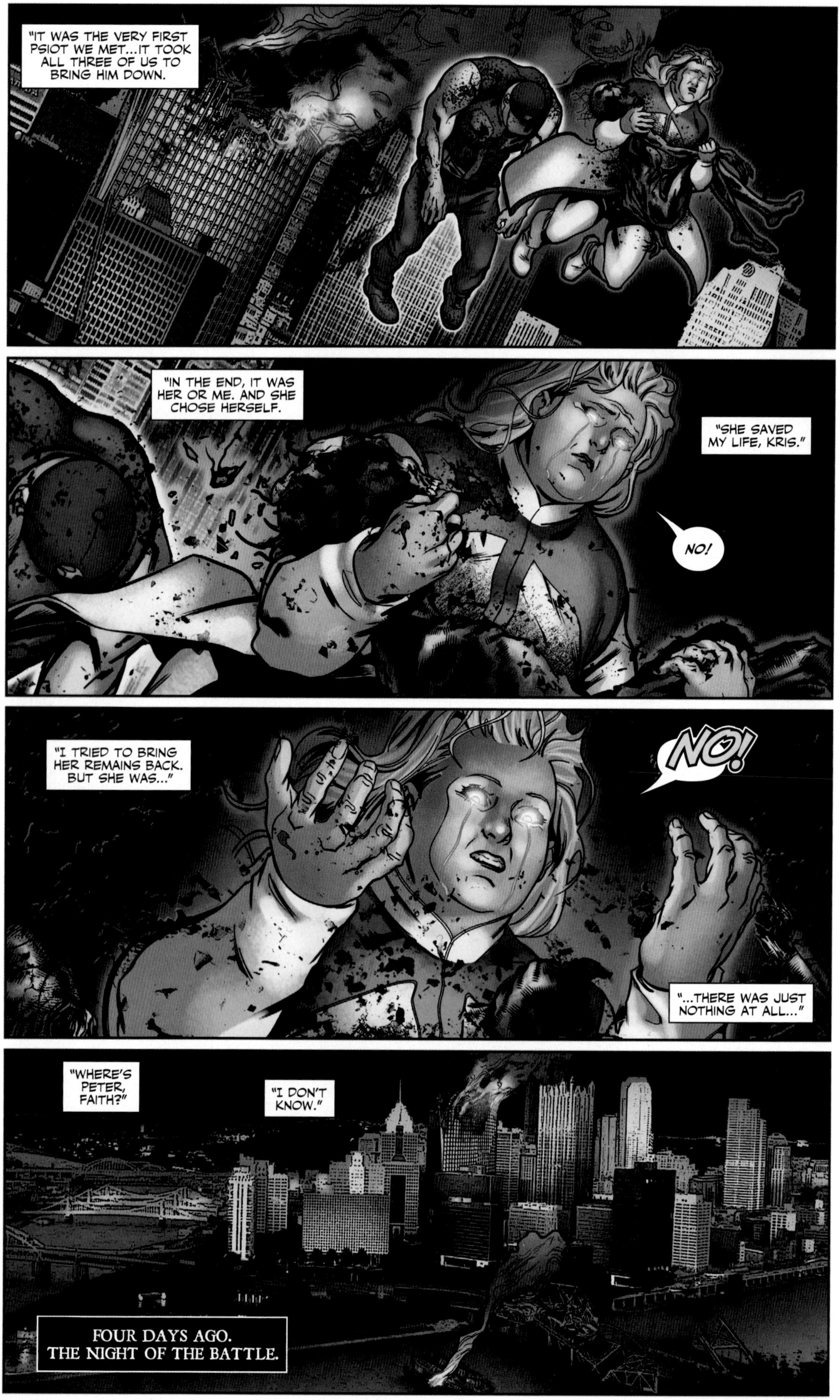
"IT WAS THE VERY FIRST PSIOT WE MET...IT TOOK ALL THREE OF US TO BRING HIM DOWN.
"IN THE END, IT WAS HER OR ME. AND SHE CHOSE HERSELF.
"SHE SAVED MY LIFE, KRIS."
NO!
"I TRIED TO BRING HER REMAINS BACK. BUT SHE WAS..."
NO!
"...THERE WAS JUST NOTHING AT ALL..."
"WHERE'S PETER, FAITH?"
"I DON'T KNOW."
FOUR DAYS AGO.
THE NIGHT OF THE BATTLE.

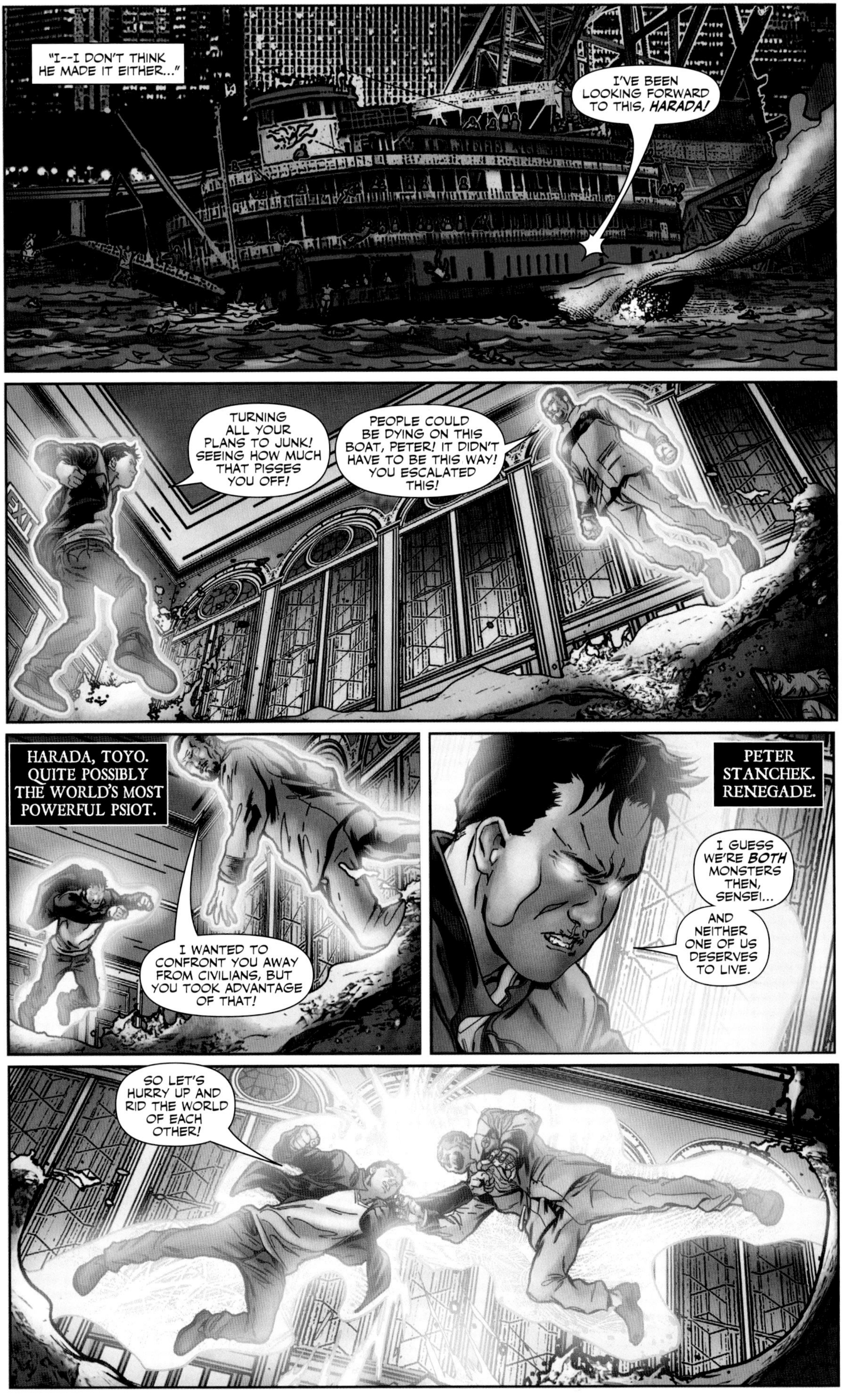
"I--I DON'T THINK HE MADE IT EITHER..."
I'VE BEEN LOOKING FORWARD TO THIS, *HARADA!*
TURNING ALL YOUR PLANS TO JUNK! SEEING HOW MUCH THAT PISSES YOU OFF!
PEOPLE COULD BE DYING ON THIS BOAT, PETER! IT DIDN'T HAVE TO BE THIS WAY! YOU ESCALATED THIS!
HARADA, TOYO. QUITE POSSIBLY THE WORLD'S MOST POWERFUL PSIOT.
I WANTED TO CONFRONT YOU AWAY FROM CIVILIANS, BUT YOU TOOK ADVANTAGE OF THAT!
PETER STANCHEK. RENEGADE.
I GUESS WE'RE *BOTH* MONSTERS THEN, SENSEI...
AND NEITHER ONE OF US DESERVES TO LIVE.
SO LET'S HURRY UP AND RID THE WORLD OF EACH OTHER!

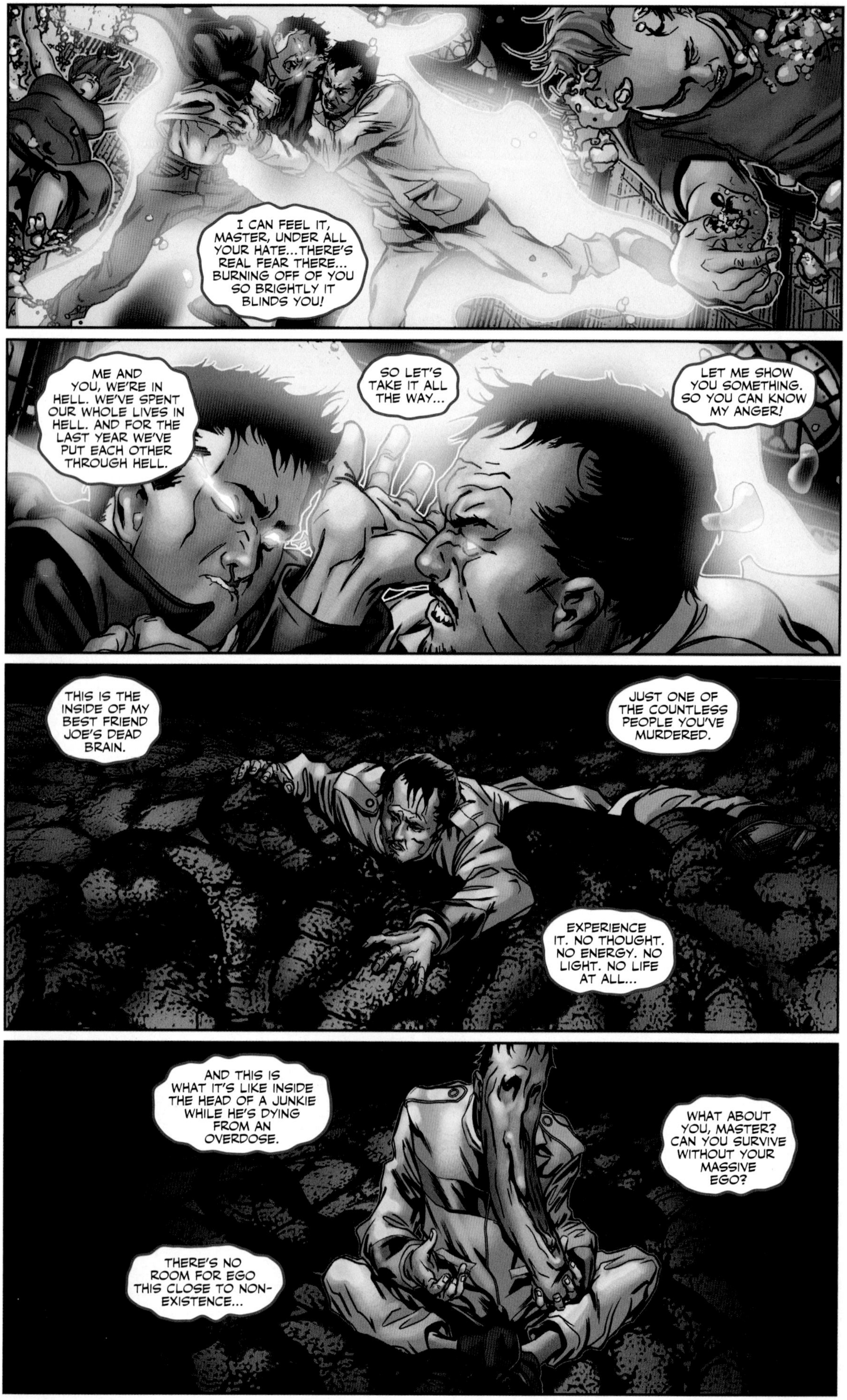
I CAN FEEL IT, MASTER, UNDER ALL YOUR HATE...THERE'S REAL FEAR THERE... BURNING OFF OF YOU SO BRIGHTLY IT BLINDS YOU!
ME AND YOU, WE'RE IN HELL. WE'VE SPENT OUR WHOLE LIVES IN HELL. AND FOR THE LAST YEAR WE'VE PUT EACH OTHER THROUGH HELL.
SO LET'S TAKE IT ALL THE WAY...
LET ME SHOW YOU SOMETHING. SO YOU CAN KNOW MY ANGER!
THIS IS THE INSIDE OF MY BEST FRIEND JOE'S DEAD BRAIN.
JUST ONE OF THE COUNTLESS PEOPLE YOU'VE MURDERED.
EXPERIENCE IT. NO THOUGHT. NO ENERGY. NO LIGHT. NO LIFE AT ALL...
AND THIS IS WHAT IT'S LIKE INSIDE THE HEAD OF A JUNKIE WHILE HE'S DYING FROM AN OVERDOSE.
WHAT ABOUT YOU, MASTER? CAN YOU SURVIVE WITHOUT YOUR MASSIVE EGO?
THERE'S NO ROOM FOR EGO THIS CLOSE TO NON-EXISTENCE...

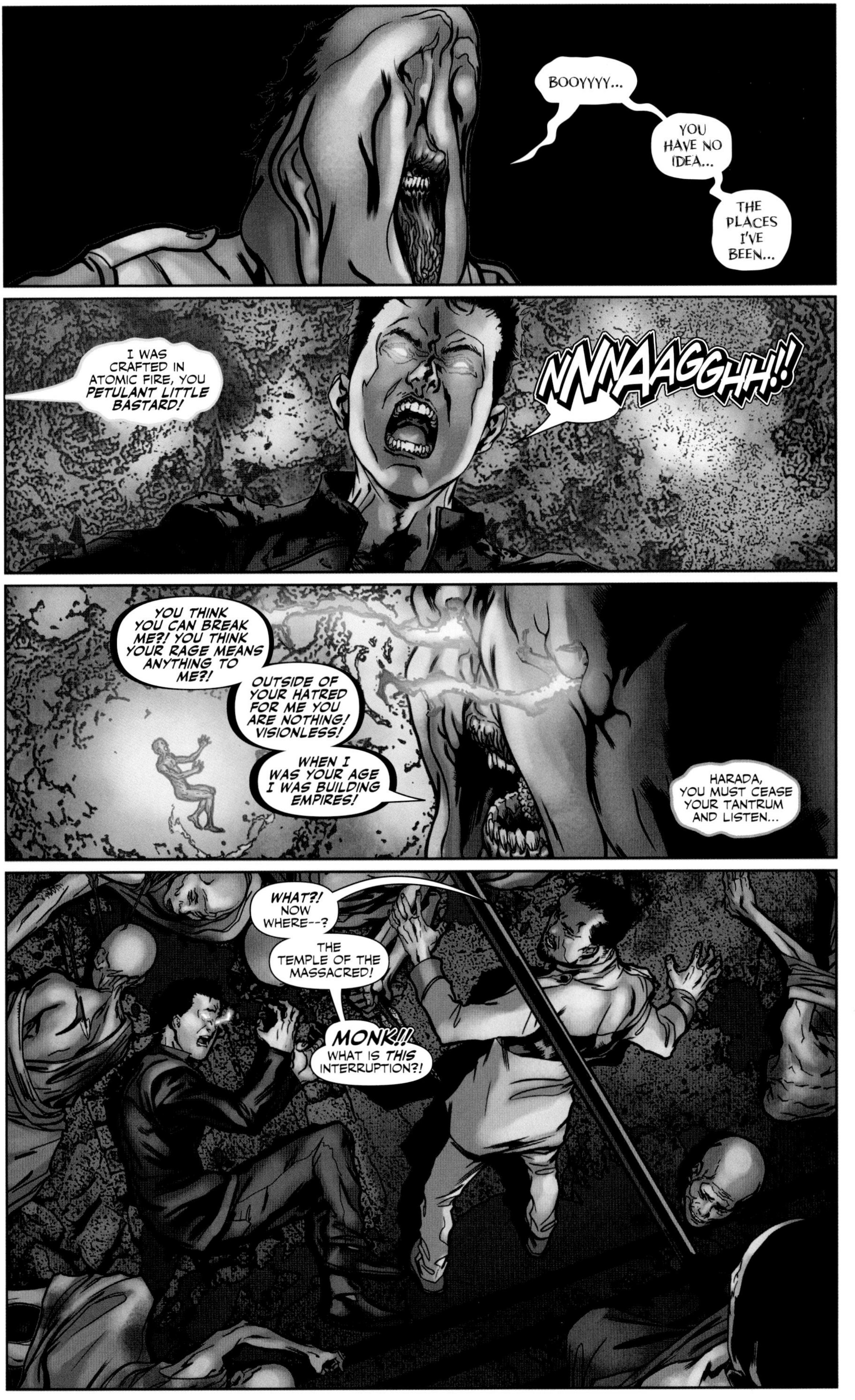
BOOYYYY...
YOU HAVE NO IDEA...
THE PLACES I'VE BEEN...
I WAS CRAFTED IN ATOMIC FIRE, YOU PETULANT LITTLE BASTARD!
NNNAAGGHH!!
YOU THINK YOU CAN BREAK ME?! YOU THINK YOUR RAGE MEANS ANYTHING TO ME?!
OUTSIDE OF YOUR HATRED FOR ME YOU ARE NOTHING! VISIONLESS!
WHEN I WAS YOUR AGE I WAS BUILDING EMPIRES!
HARADA, YOU MUST CEASE YOUR TANTRUM AND LISTEN...
WHAT?! NOW WHERE--?
THE TEMPLE OF THE MASSACRED!
MONK!! WHAT IS THIS INTERRUPTION?!

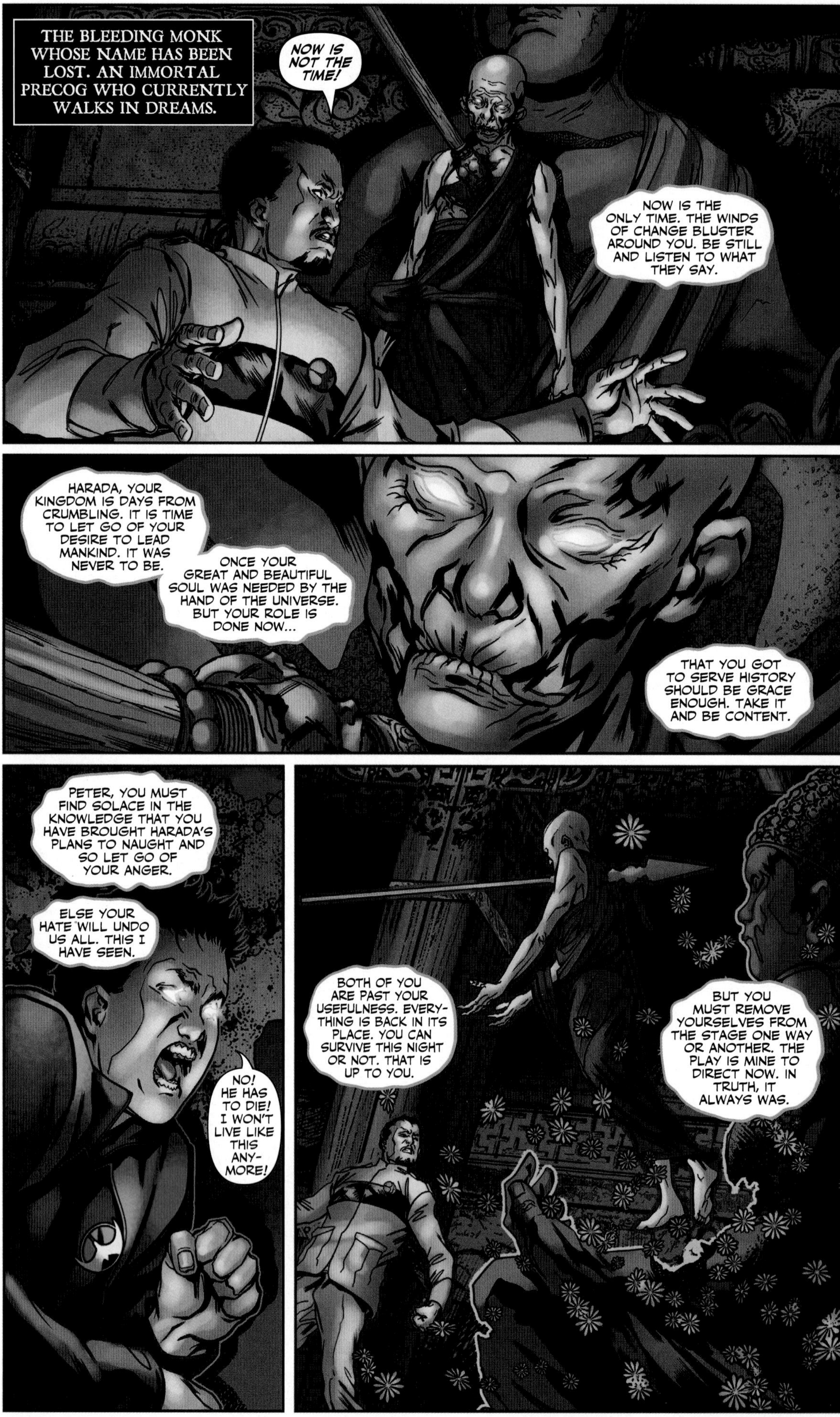
THE BLEEDING MONK WHOSE NAME HAS BEEN LOST. AN IMMORTAL PRECOG WHO CURRENTLY WALKS IN DREAMS.
NOW IS NOT THE TIME!
NOW IS THE ONLY TIME. THE WINDS OF CHANGE BLUSTER AROUND YOU. BE STILL AND LISTEN TO WHAT THEY SAY.
HARADA, YOUR KINGDOM IS DAYS FROM CRUMBLING. IT IS TIME TO LET GO OF YOUR DESIRE TO LEAD MANKIND. IT WAS NEVER TO BE.
ONCE YOUR GREAT AND BEAUTIFUL SOUL WAS NEEDED BY THE HAND OF THE UNIVERSE. BUT YOUR ROLE IS DONE NOW...
THAT YOU GOT TO SERVE HISTORY SHOULD BE GRACE ENOUGH. TAKE IT AND BE CONTENT.
PETER, YOU MUST FIND SOLACE IN THE KNOWLEDGE THAT YOU HAVE BROUGHT HARADA'S PLANS TO NAUGHT AND SO LET GO OF YOUR ANGER.
ELSE YOUR HATE WILL UNDO US ALL. THIS I HAVE SEEN.
NO! HE HAS TO DIE! I WON'T LIVE LIKE THIS ANY-MORE!
BOTH OF YOU ARE PAST YOUR USEFULNESS. EVERY-THING IS BACK IN ITS PLACE. YOU CAN SURVIVE THIS NIGHT OR NOT. THAT IS UP TO YOU.
BUT YOU MUST REMOVE YOURSELVES FROM THE STAGE ONE WAY OR ANOTHER. THE PLAY IS MINE TO DIRECT NOW. IN TRUTH, IT ALWAYS WAS.

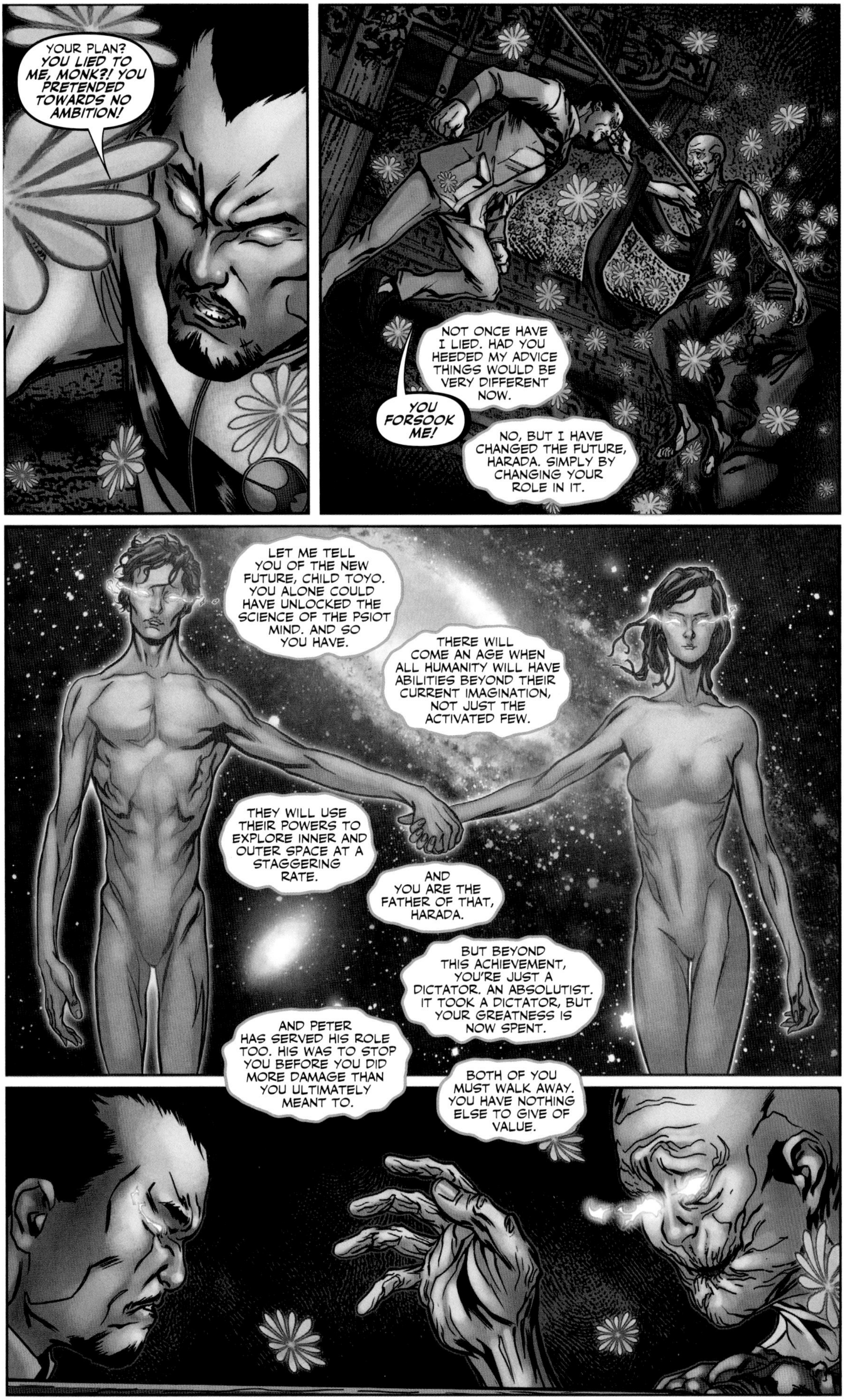
YOUR PLAN? YOU LIED TO ME, MONK?! YOU PRETENDED TOWARDS NO AMBITION!
NOT ONCE HAVE I LIED. HAD YOU HEEDED MY ADVICE THINGS WOULD BE VERY DIFFERENT NOW.
YOU FORSOOK ME!
NO, BUT I HAVE CHANGED THE FUTURE, HARADA. SIMPLY BY CHANGING YOUR ROLE IN IT.
LET ME TELL YOU OF THE NEW FUTURE, CHILD TOYO. YOU ALONE COULD HAVE UNLOCKED THE SCIENCE OF THE PSIOT MIND. AND SO YOU HAVE.
THERE WILL COME AN AGE WHEN ALL HUMANITY WILL HAVE ABILITIES BEYOND THEIR CURRENT IMAGINATION, NOT JUST THE ACTIVATED FEW.
THEY WILL USE THEIR POWERS TO EXPLORE INNER AND OUTER SPACE AT A STAGGERING RATE.
AND YOU ARE THE FATHER OF THAT, HARADA.
BUT BEYOND THIS ACHIEVEMENT, YOU'RE JUST A DICTATOR. AN ABSOLUTIST. IT TOOK A DICTATOR, BUT YOUR GREATNESS IS NOW SPENT.
AND PETER HAS SERVED HIS ROLE TOO. HIS WAS TO STOP YOU BEFORE YOU DID MORE DAMAGE THAN YOU ULTIMATELY MEANT TO.
BOTH OF YOU MUST WALK AWAY. YOU HAVE NOTHING ELSE TO GIVE OF VALUE.

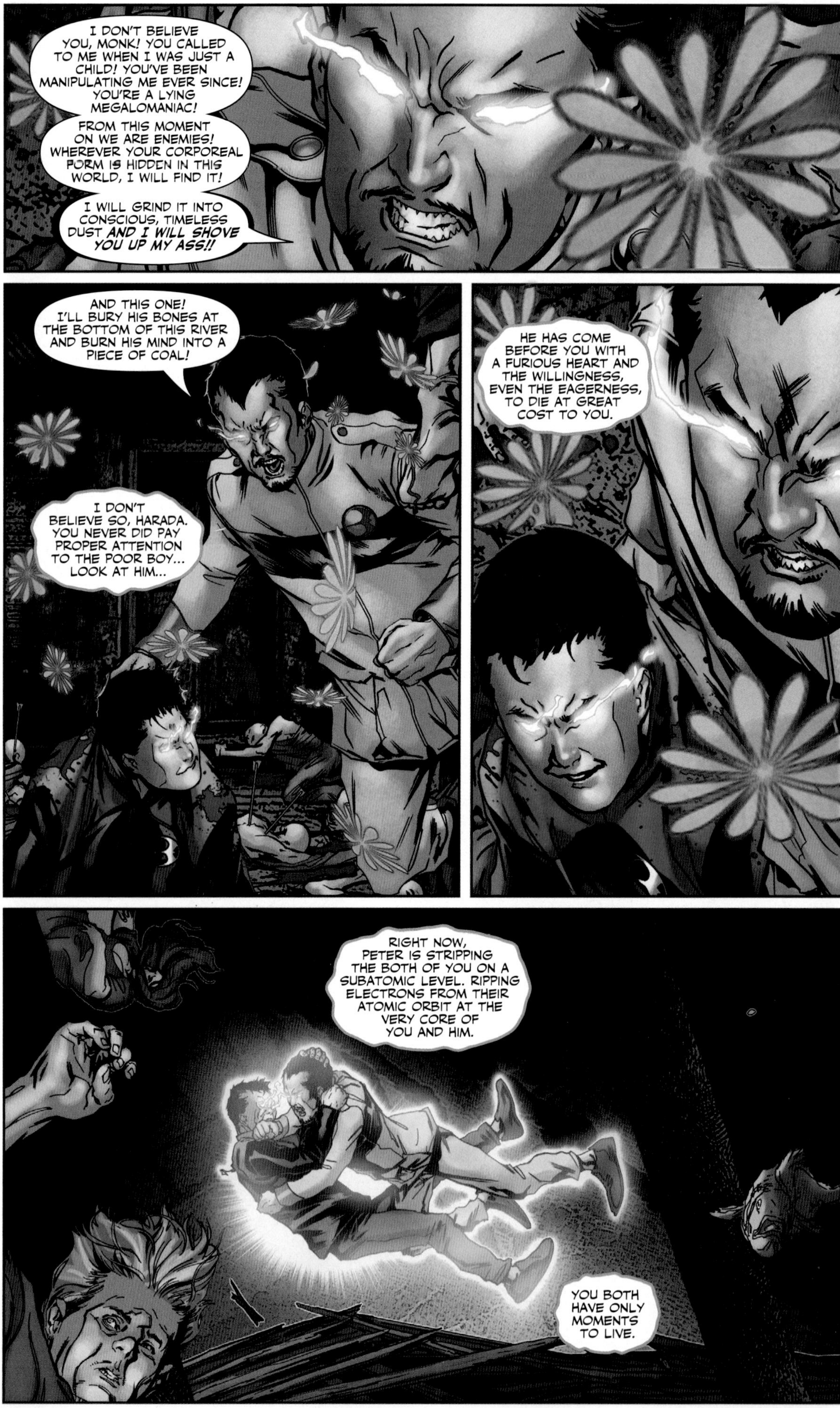

I DON'T BELIEVE YOU, MONK! YOU CALLED TO ME WHEN I WAS JUST A CHILD! YOU'VE BEEN MANIPULATING ME EVER SINCE! YOU'RE A LYING MEGALOMANIAC!
FROM THIS MOMENT ON WE ARE ENEMIES! WHEREVER YOUR CORPOREAL FORM IS HIDDEN IN THIS WORLD, I WILL FIND IT!
I WILL GRIND IT INTO CONSCIOUS, TIMELESS DUST *AND I WILL SHOVE YOU UP MY ASS!!*
AND THIS ONE! I'LL BURY HIS BONES AT THE BOTTOM OF THIS RIVER AND BURN HIS MIND INTO A PIECE OF COAL!
I DON'T BELIEVE SO, HARADA. YOU NEVER DID PAY PROPER ATTENTION TO THE POOR BOY... LOOK AT HIM...
HE HAS COME BEFORE YOU WITH A FURIOUS HEART AND THE WILLINGNESS, EVEN THE EAGERNESS, TO DIE AT GREAT COST TO YOU.
RIGHT NOW, PETER IS STRIPPING THE BOTH OF YOU ON A SUBATOMIC LEVEL. RIPPING ELECTRONS FROM THEIR ATOMIC ORBIT AT THE VERY CORE OF YOU AND HIM.
YOU BOTH HAVE ONLY MOMENTS TO LIVE.

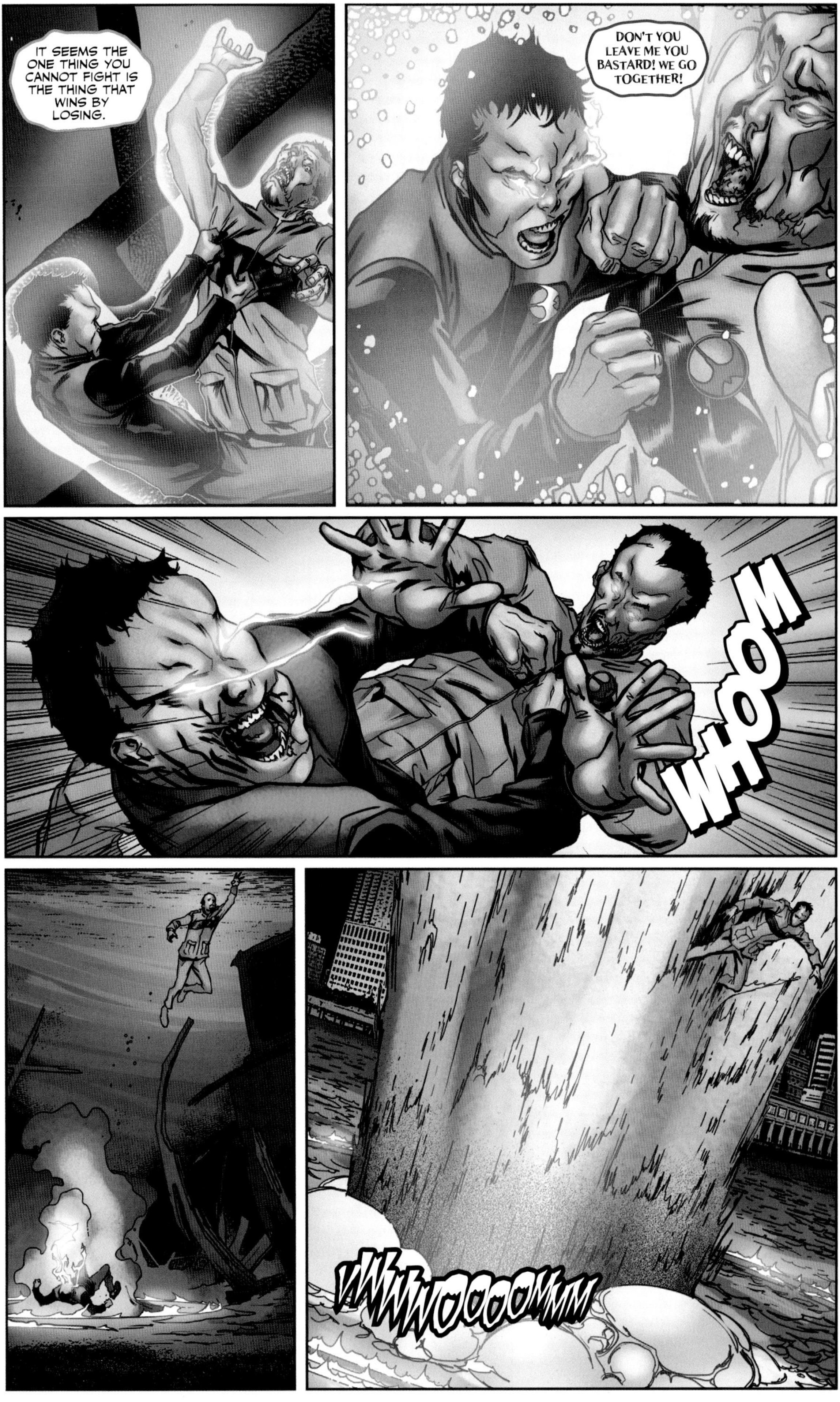
IT SEEMS THE ONE THING YOU CANNOT FIGHT IS THE THING THAT WINS BY LOSING.
DON'T YOU LEAVE ME YOU BASTARD! WE GO TOGETHER!
WHOOM
VMMMWOOOOOMMM

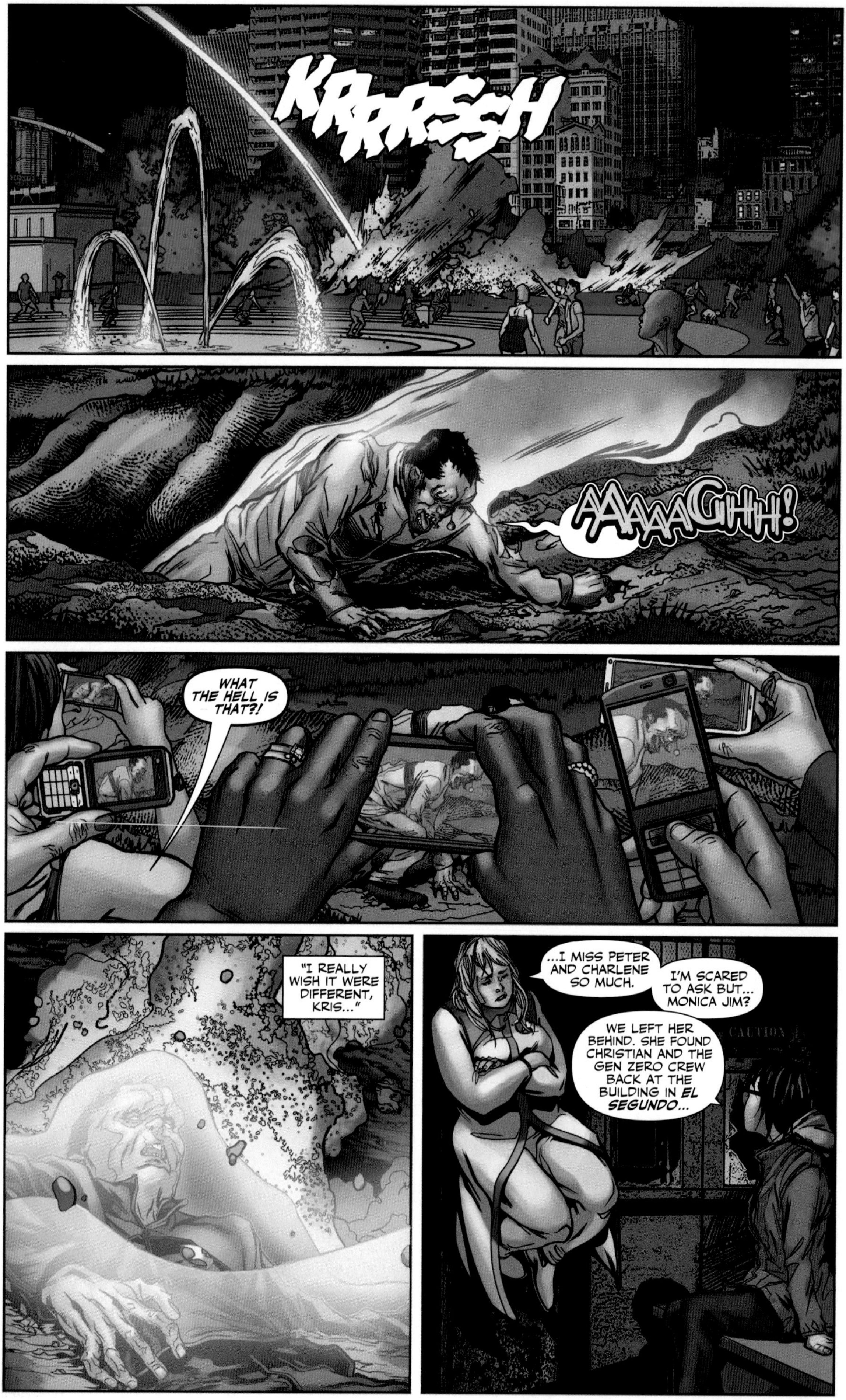
KRRRSSH
AAAAAGHHH!
WHAT THE HELL IS THAT?!
"I REALLY WISH IT WERE DIFFERENT, KRIS..."
...I MISS PETER AND CHARLENE SO MUCH.
I'M SCARED TO ASK BUT... MONICA JIM?
WE LEFT HER BEHIND. SHE FOUND CHRISTIAN AND THE GEN ZERO CREW BACK AT THE BUILDING IN EL SEGUNDO...
CAUTION

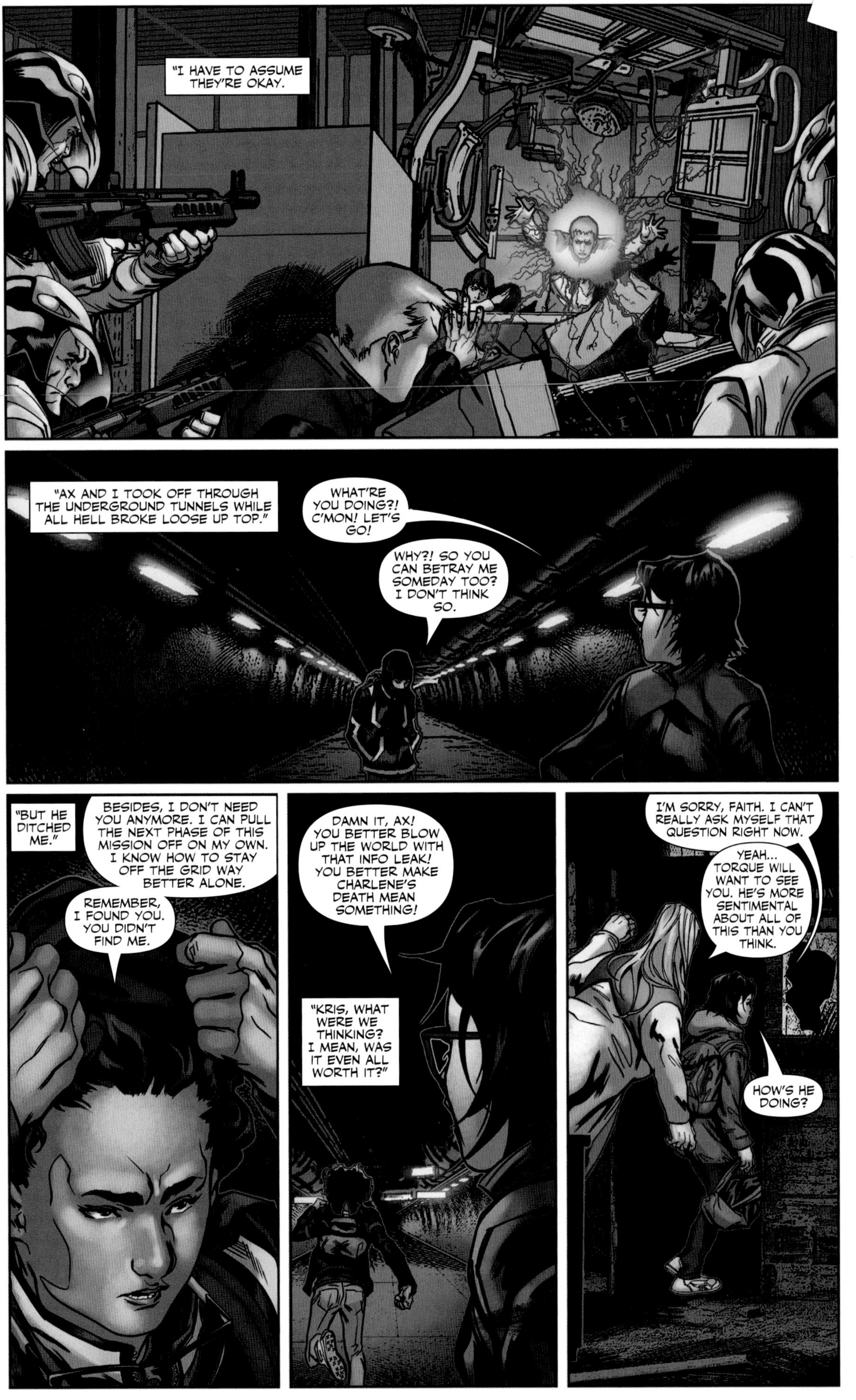
"I HAVE TO ASSUME THEY'RE OKAY.
"AX AND I TOOK OFF THROUGH THE UNDERGROUND TUNNELS WHILE ALL HELL BROKE LOOSE UP TOP."
WHAT'RE YOU DOING?! C'MON! LET'S GO!
WHY?! SO YOU CAN BETRAY ME SOMEDAY TOO? I DON'T THINK SO.
"BUT HE DITCHED ME."
BESIDES, I DON'T NEED YOU ANYMORE. I CAN PULL THE NEXT PHASE OF THIS MISSION OFF ON MY OWN. I KNOW HOW TO STAY OFF THE GRID WAY BETTER ALONE.
REMEMBER, I FOUND YOU. YOU DIDN'T FIND ME.
DAMN IT, AX! YOU BETTER BLOW UP THE WORLD WITH THAT INFO LEAK! YOU BETTER MAKE CHARLENE'S DEATH MEAN SOMETHING!
"KRIS, WHAT WERE WE THINKING? I MEAN, WAS IT EVEN ALL WORTH IT?"
I'M SORRY, FAITH. I CAN'T REALLY ASK MYSELF THAT QUESTION RIGHT NOW.
HOW'S HE DOING?
YEAH... TORQUE WILL WANT TO SEE YOU. HE'S MORE SENTIMENTAL ABOUT ALL OF THIS THAN YOU THINK.

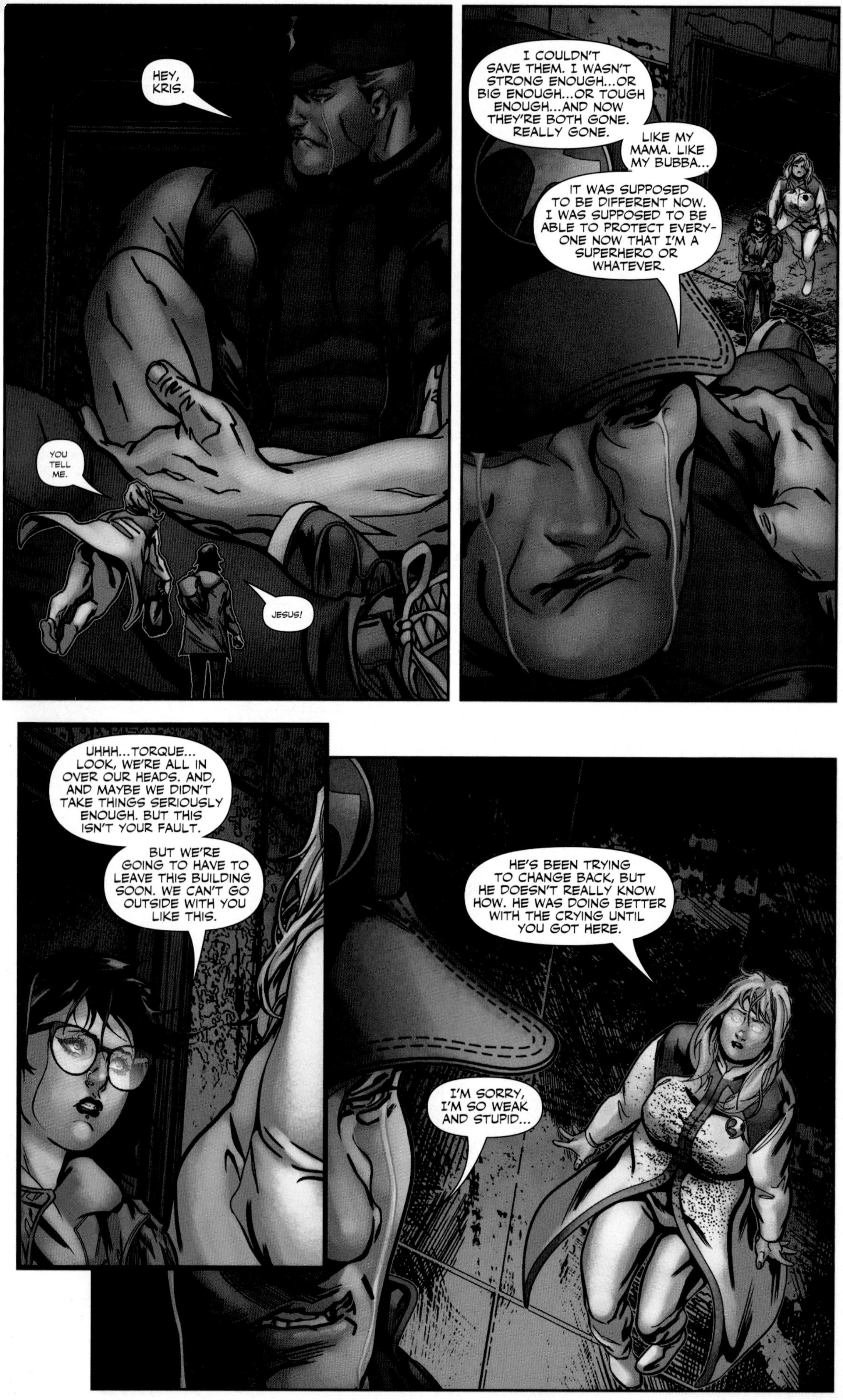
HEY, KRIS.
YOU TELL ME.
JESUS!
I COULDN'T SAVE THEM. I WASN'T STRONG ENOUGH...OR BIG ENOUGH...OR TOUGH ENOUGH...AND NOW THEY'RE BOTH GONE. REALLY GONE.
LIKE MY MAMA. LIKE MY BUBBA...
IT WAS SUPPOSED TO BE DIFFERENT NOW. I WAS SUPPOSED TO BE ABLE TO PROTECT EVERY-ONE NOW THAT I'M A SUPERHERO OR WHATEVER.
UHHH...TORQUE... LOOK, WE'RE ALL IN OVER OUR HEADS. AND, AND MAYBE WE DIDN'T TAKE THINGS SERIOUSLY ENOUGH. BUT THIS ISN'T YOUR FAULT.
BUT WE'RE GOING TO HAVE TO LEAVE THIS BUILDING SOON. WE CAN'T GO OUTSIDE WITH YOU LIKE THIS.
HE'S BEEN TRYING TO CHANGE BACK, BUT HE DOESN'T REALLY KNOW HOW. HE WAS DOING BETTER WITH THE CRYING UNTIL YOU GOT HERE.
I'M SORRY, I'M SO WEAK AND STUPID...

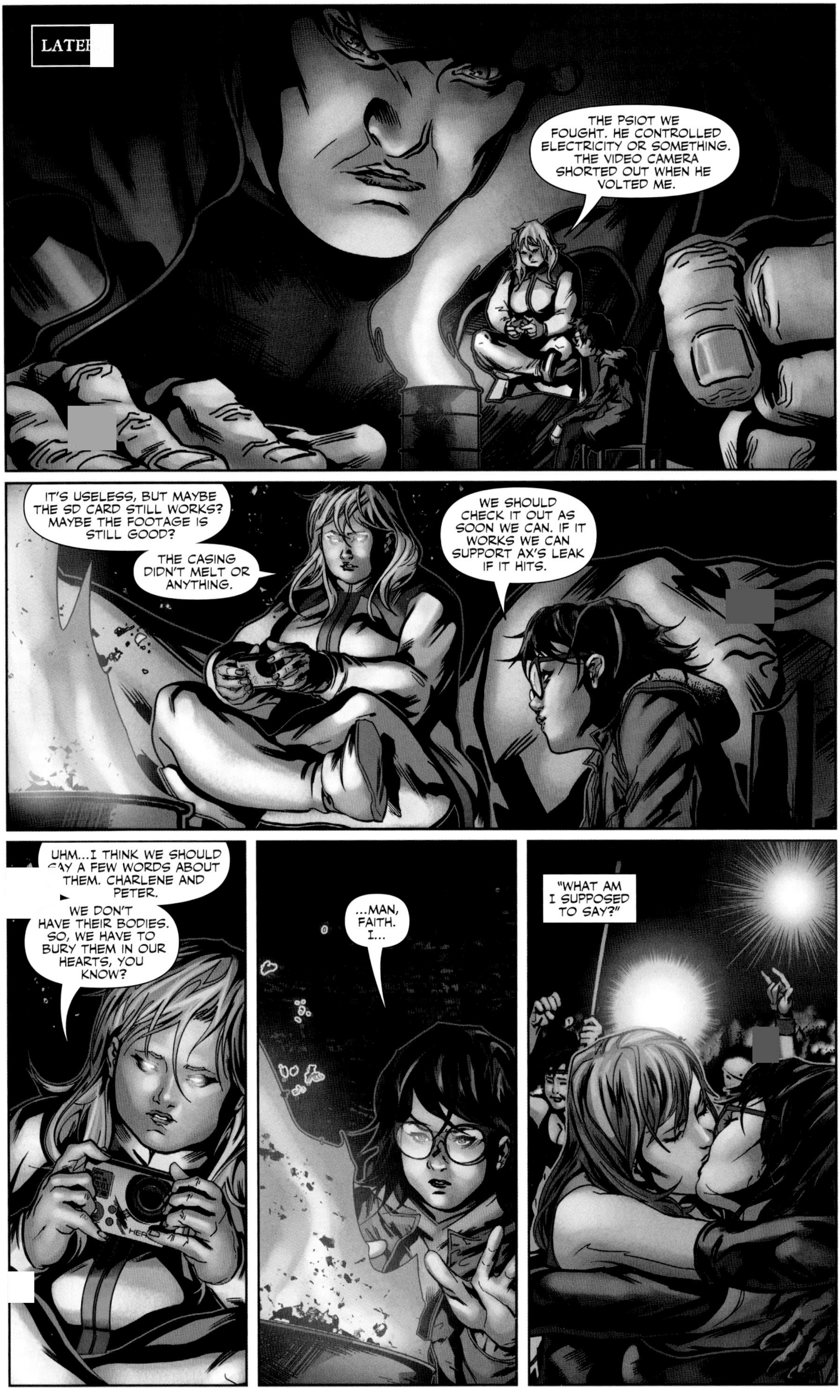
LATE
THE PSIOT WE FOUGHT. HE CONTROLLED ELECTRICITY OR SOMETHING. THE VIDEO CAMERA SHORTED OUT WHEN HE VOLTED ME.
IT'S USELESS, BUT MAYBE THE SD CARD STILL WORKS? MAYBE THE FOOTAGE IS STILL GOOD?
THE CASING DIDN'T MELT OR ANYTHING.
WE SHOULD CHECK IT OUT AS SOON WE CAN. IF IT WORKS WE CAN SUPPORT AX'S LEAK IF IT HITS.
UHM...I THINK WE SHOULD AY A FEW WORDS ABOUT THEM. CHARLENE AND PETER.
WE DON'T HAVE THEIR BODIES. SO, WE HAVE TO BURY THEM IN OUR HEARTS, YOU KNOW?
...MAN, FAITH. I...
"WHAT AM I SUPPOSED TO SAY?"

DID WE--DO WE EVEN REALLY KNOW EACH OTHER AT ALL? ANY OF US?

WHAT?! OF COURSE WE DID! WE DO! WE SAVED EACH OTHER'S LIVES! WE FOUGHT SIDE BY SIDE! WHAT ARE YOU SAYING, KRIS?!

THE RENEGADES ARE THE ONLY PEOPLE I'VE EVER REALLY KNOWN!

I'M NOT GOING TO SIT HERE AND LISTEN TO SOME CRAP-ASS PHILOSOPHICAL ATTEMPT TO EMOTIONALLY DISTANCE YOURSELF FROM THIS!

FAITH, CHILL OUT, OKAY...

TORQUE THINKS IT'S HIS FAULT! BUT IT'S NOT, IS IT?! IT'S YOURS! YOU WANTED TO FIGHT "THE MAN" WAY MORE THAN PETER DID!

I WATCHED YOU USE HIS ADORATION FOR YOU TO MAKE THIS HAPPEN! IN THIS VERY ROOM! SO I KNOW AT LEAST THAT MUCH ABOUT YOU!

I KNOW THAT YOU'RE SELFISH! THAT YOU DON'T LET YOURSELF FEEL ANYTHING REAL SO YOU DON'T HAVE TO FACE YOURSELF! AND I'M SICK OF IT!

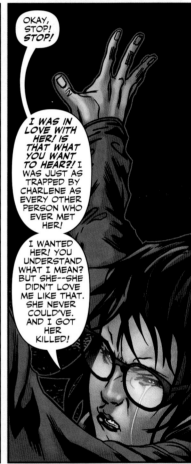

OKAY, STOP! STOP!

I WAS IN LOVE WITH HER! IS THAT WHAT YOU WANT TO HEAR?! I WAS JUST AS TRAPPED BY CHARLENE AS EVERY OTHER PERSON WHO EVER MET HER!

I WANTED HER! YOU UNDERSTAND WHAT I MEAN? BUT SHE--SHE DIDN'T LOVE ME LIKE THAT. SHE NEVER COULD'VE. AND I GOT HER KILLED!

YOU HAPPY?!

SO WHAT? YOU'RE LIKE... A LESBO? OR--?

I SWEAR TO GOD, TORQUE. I DON'T CARE IF YOUR BALLS ARE THE SIZE OF BUICKS RIGHT NOW, I'LL CUT THEM RIGHT OFF IF YOU DON'T SHUT THE *$$% UP!

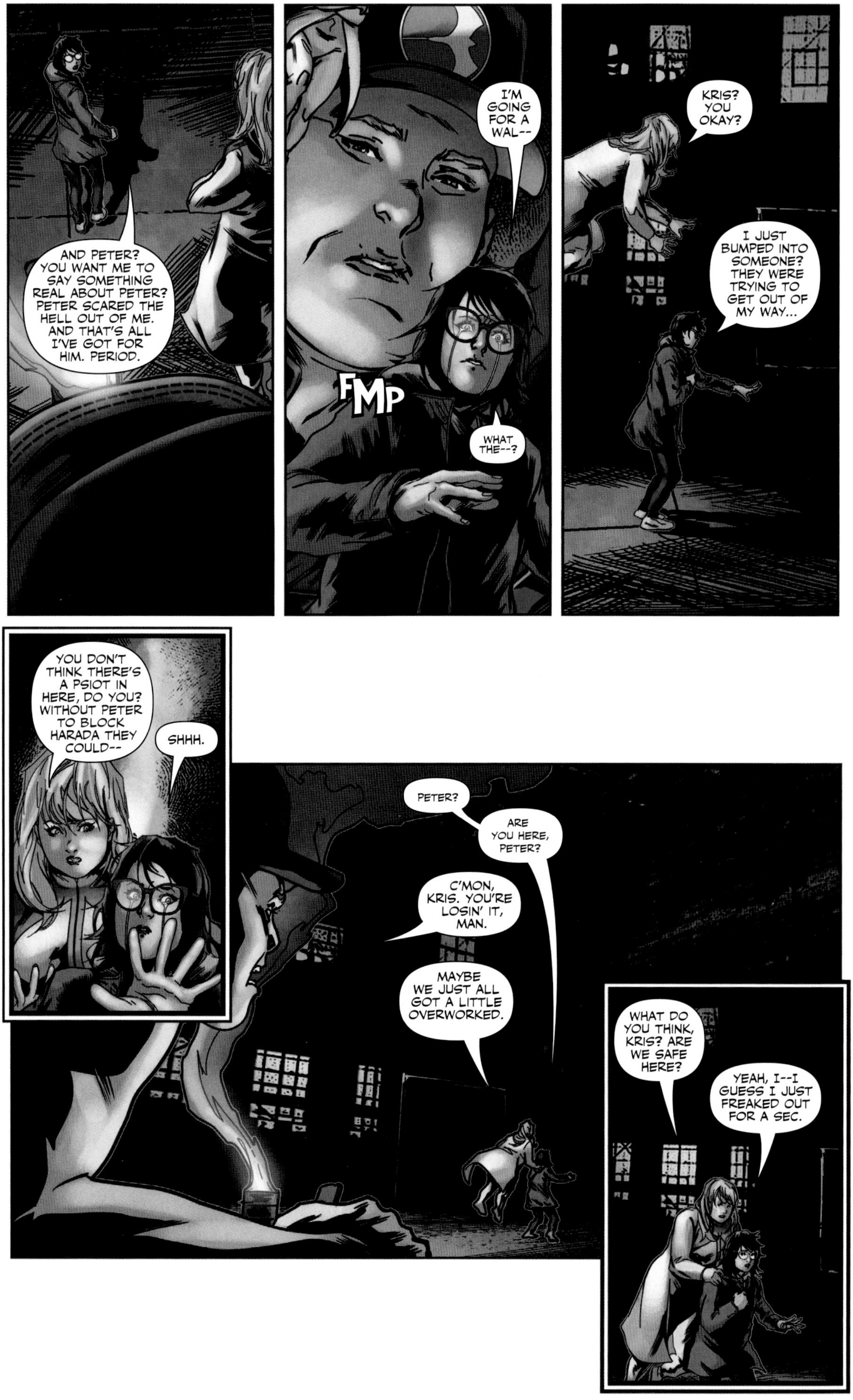
AND PETER? YOU WANT ME TO SAY SOMETHING REAL ABOUT PETER? PETER SCARED THE HELL OUT OF ME. AND THAT'S ALL I'VE GOT FOR HIM. PERIOD.
I'M GOING FOR A WAL--
FMP
WHAT THE--?
KRIS? YOU OKAY?
I JUST BUMPED INTO SOMEONE? THEY WERE TRYING TO GET OUT OF MY WAY...
YOU DON'T THINK THERE'S A PSIOT IN HERE, DO YOU? WITHOUT PETER TO BLOCK HARADA THEY COULD--
SHHH.
PETER?
ARE YOU HERE, PETER?
C'MON, KRIS. YOU'RE LOSIN' IT, MAN.
MAYBE WE JUST ALL GOT A LITTLE OVERWORKED.
WHAT DO YOU THINK, KRIS? ARE WE SAFE HERE?
YEAH, I--I GUESS I JUST FREAKED OUT FOR A SEC.

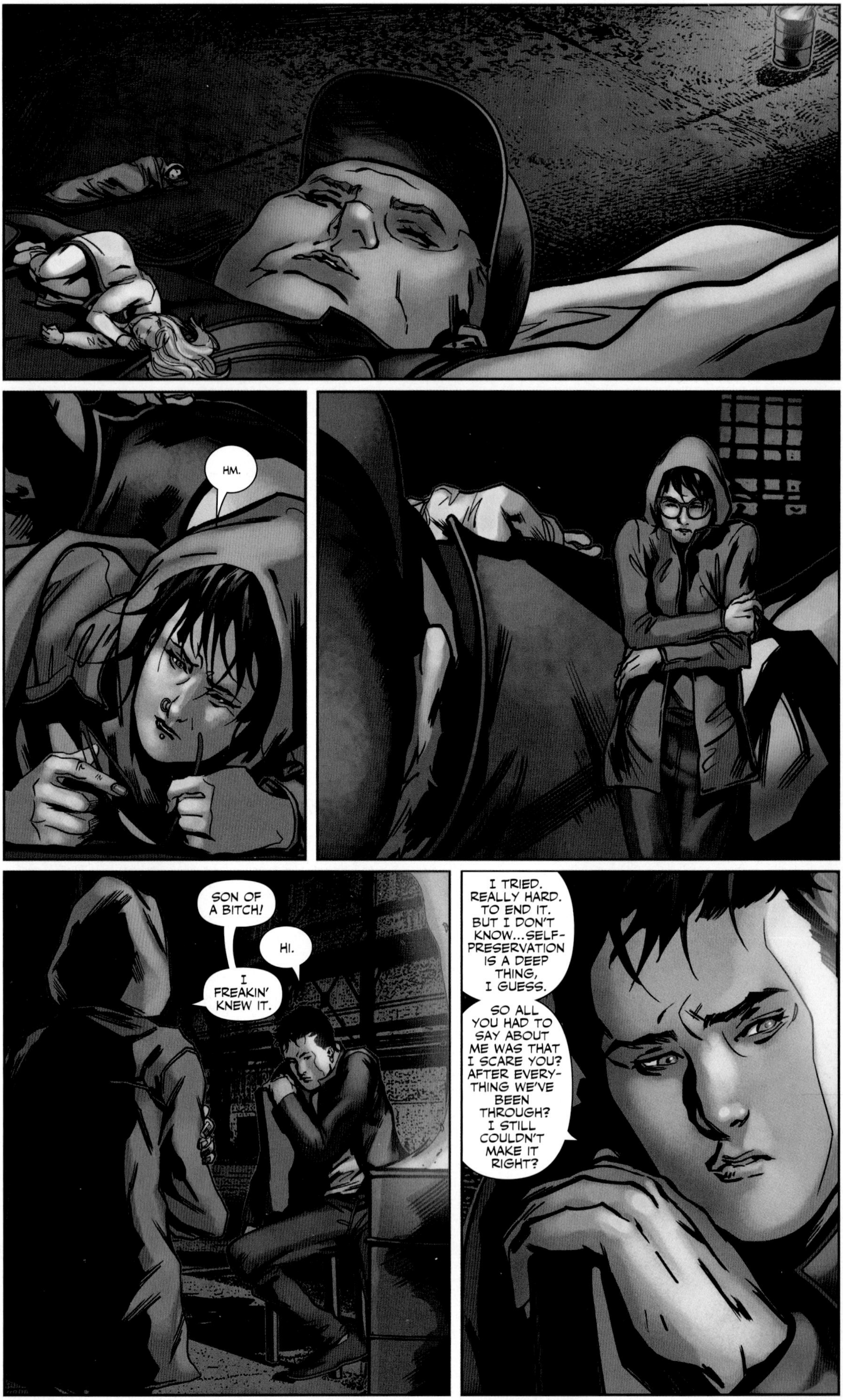
HM.
SON OF A BITCH!
HI.
I FREAKIN' KNEW IT.
I TRIED. REALLY HARD. TO END IT. BUT I DON'T KNOW...SELF-PRESERVATION IS A DEEP THING, I GUESS.
SO ALL YOU HAD TO SAY ABOUT ME WAS THAT I SCARE YOU? AFTER EVERYTHING WE'VE BEEN THROUGH? I STILL COULDN'T MAKE IT RIGHT?

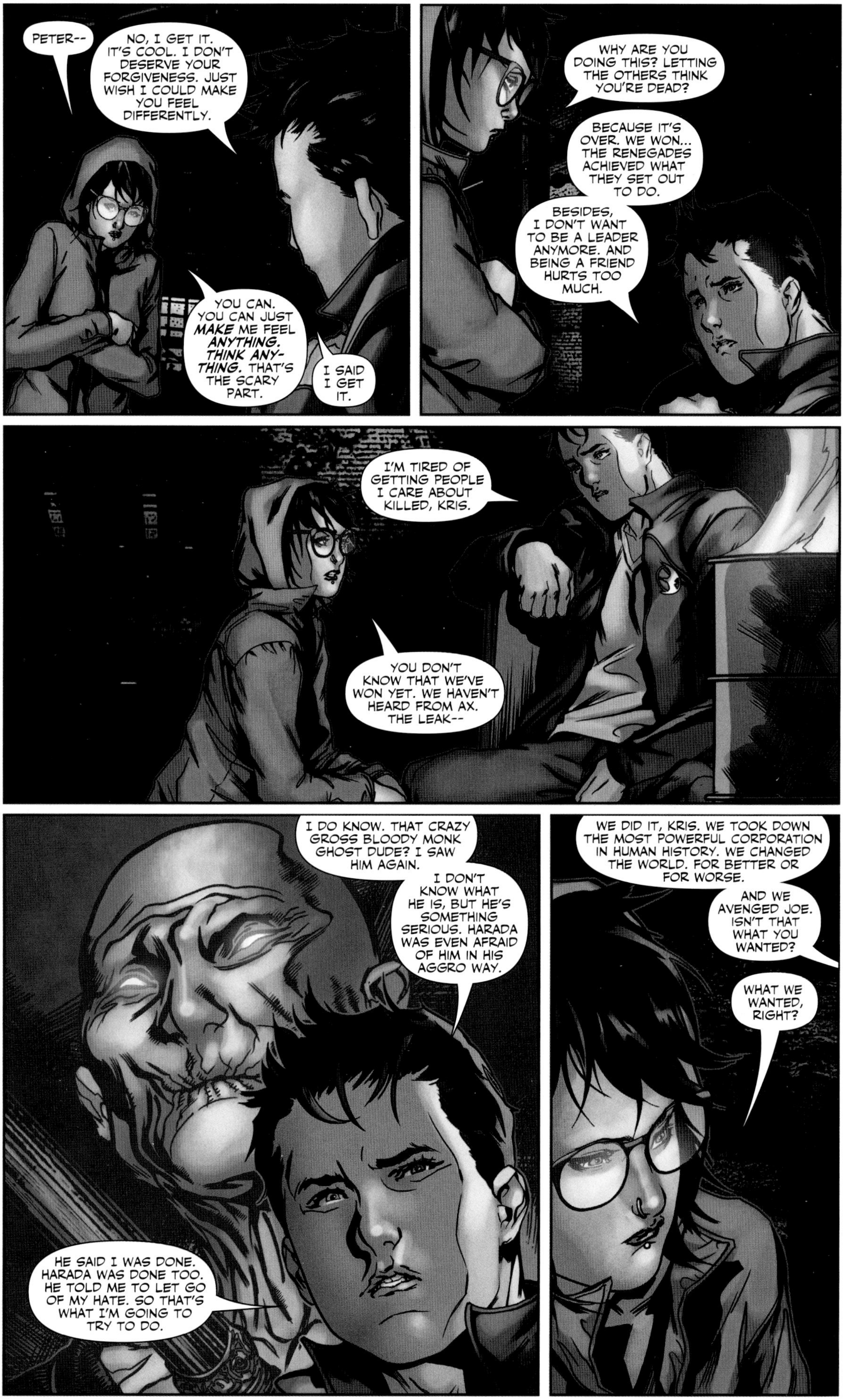
PETER--
NO, I GET IT. IT'S COOL. I DON'T DESERVE YOUR FORGIVENESS. JUST WISH I COULD MAKE YOU FEEL DIFFERENTLY.
YOU CAN. YOU CAN JUST *MAKE* ME FEEL *ANYTHING. THINK ANY-THING.* THAT'S THE SCARY PART.
I SAID I GET IT.
WHY ARE YOU DOING THIS? LETTING THE OTHERS THINK YOU'RE DEAD?
BECAUSE IT'S OVER. WE WON... THE RENEGADES ACHIEVED WHAT THEY SET OUT TO DO.
BESIDES, I DON'T WANT TO BE A LEADER ANYMORE. AND BEING A FRIEND HURTS TOO MUCH.
I'M TIRED OF GETTING PEOPLE I CARE ABOUT KILLED, KRIS.
YOU DON'T KNOW THAT WE'VE WON YET. WE HAVEN'T HEARD FROM AX. THE LEAK--
I DO KNOW. THAT CRAZY GROSS BLOODY MONK GHOST DUDE? I SAW HIM AGAIN.
I DON'T KNOW WHAT HE IS, BUT HE'S SOMETHING SERIOUS. HARADA WAS EVEN AFRAID OF HIM IN HIS AGGRO WAY.
HE SAID I WAS DONE. HARADA WAS DONE TOO. HE TOLD ME TO LET GO OF MY HATE. SO THAT'S WHAT I'M GOING TO TRY TO DO.
WE DID IT, KRIS. WE TOOK DOWN THE MOST POWERFUL CORPORATION IN HUMAN HISTORY. WE CHANGED THE WORLD. FOR BETTER OR FOR WORSE.
AND WE AVENGED JOE. ISN'T THAT WHAT YOU WANTED?
WHAT WE WANTED, RIGHT?

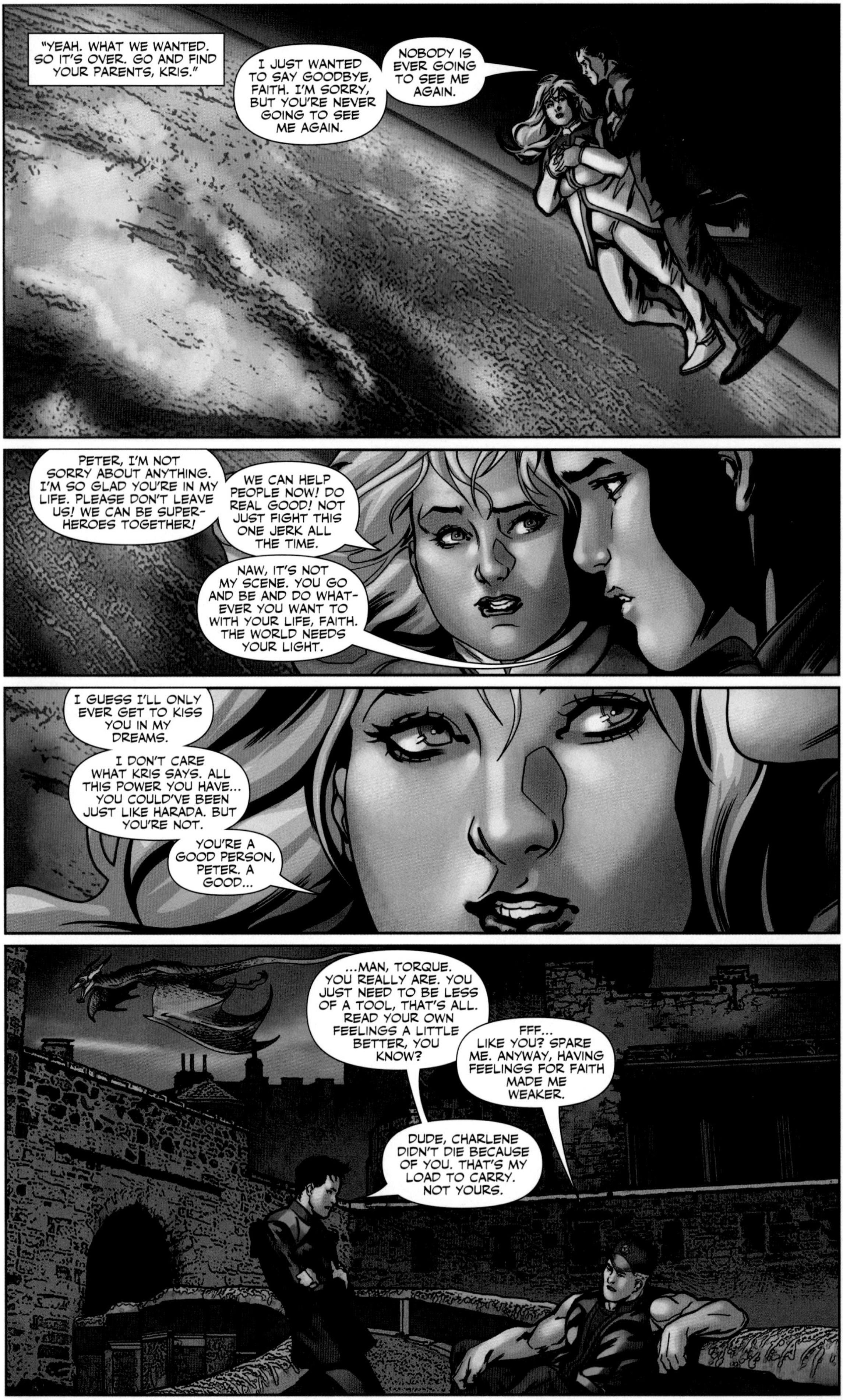
"YEAH. WHAT WE WANTED. SO IT'S OVER. GO AND FIND YOUR PARENTS, KRIS."
I JUST WANTED TO SAY GOODBYE, FAITH. I'M SORRY, BUT YOU'RE NEVER GOING TO SEE ME AGAIN.
NOBODY IS EVER GOING TO SEE ME AGAIN.
PETER, I'M NOT SORRY ABOUT ANYTHING. I'M SO GLAD YOU'RE IN MY LIFE. PLEASE DON'T LEAVE US! WE CAN BE SUPER-HEROES TOGETHER!
WE CAN HELP PEOPLE NOW! DO REAL GOOD! NOT JUST FIGHT THIS ONE JERK ALL THE TIME.
NAW, IT'S NOT MY SCENE. YOU GO AND BE AND DO WHAT-EVER YOU WANT TO WITH YOUR LIFE, FAITH. THE WORLD NEEDS YOUR LIGHT.
I GUESS I'LL ONLY EVER GET TO KISS YOU IN MY DREAMS.
I DON'T CARE WHAT KRIS SAYS. ALL THIS POWER YOU HAVE... YOU COULD'VE BEEN JUST LIKE HARADA. BUT YOU'RE NOT.
YOU'RE A GOOD PERSON, PETER. A GOOD...
...MAN, TORQUE. YOU REALLY ARE. YOU JUST NEED TO BE LESS OF A TOOL, THAT'S ALL. READ YOUR OWN FEELINGS A LITTLE BETTER, YOU KNOW?
FFF... LIKE YOU? SPARE ME. ANYWAY, HAVING FEELINGS FOR FAITH MADE ME WEAKER.
DUDE, CHARLENE DIDN'T DIE BECAUSE OF YOU. THAT'S MY LOAD TO CARRY. NOT YOURS.

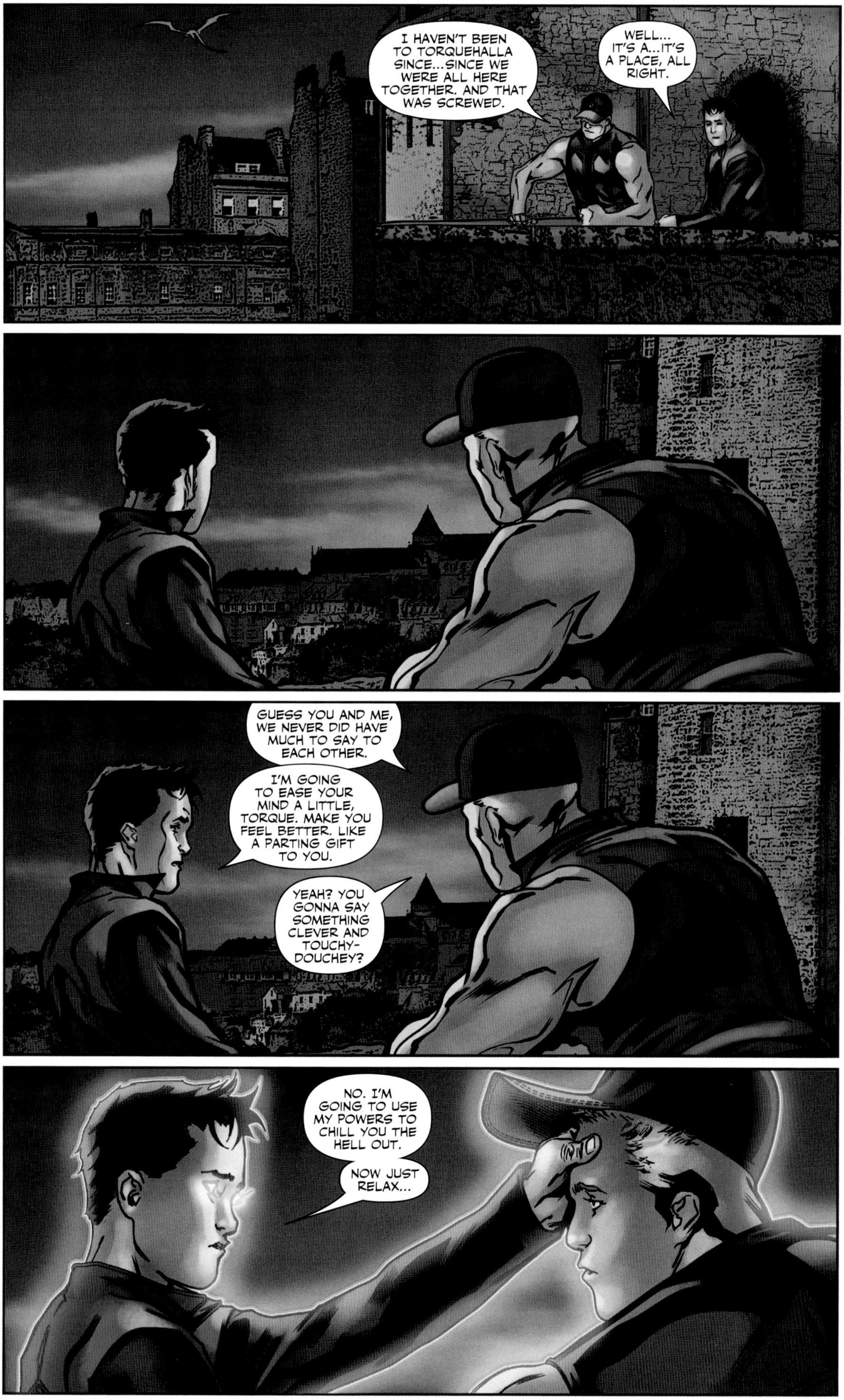
I HAVEN'T BEEN TO TORQUEHALLA SINCE...SINCE WE WERE ALL HERE TOGETHER. AND THAT WAS SCREWED.
WELL... IT'S A...IT'S A PLACE, ALL RIGHT.
GUESS YOU AND ME, WE NEVER DID HAVE MUCH TO SAY TO EACH OTHER.
I'M GOING TO EASE YOUR MIND A LITTLE, TORQUE. MAKE YOU FEEL BETTER. LIKE A PARTING GIFT TO YOU.
YEAH? YOU GONNA SAY SOMETHING CLEVER AND TOUCHY-DOUCHEY?
NO. I'M GOING TO USE MY POWERS TO CHILL YOU THE HELL OUT.
NOW JUST RELAX...

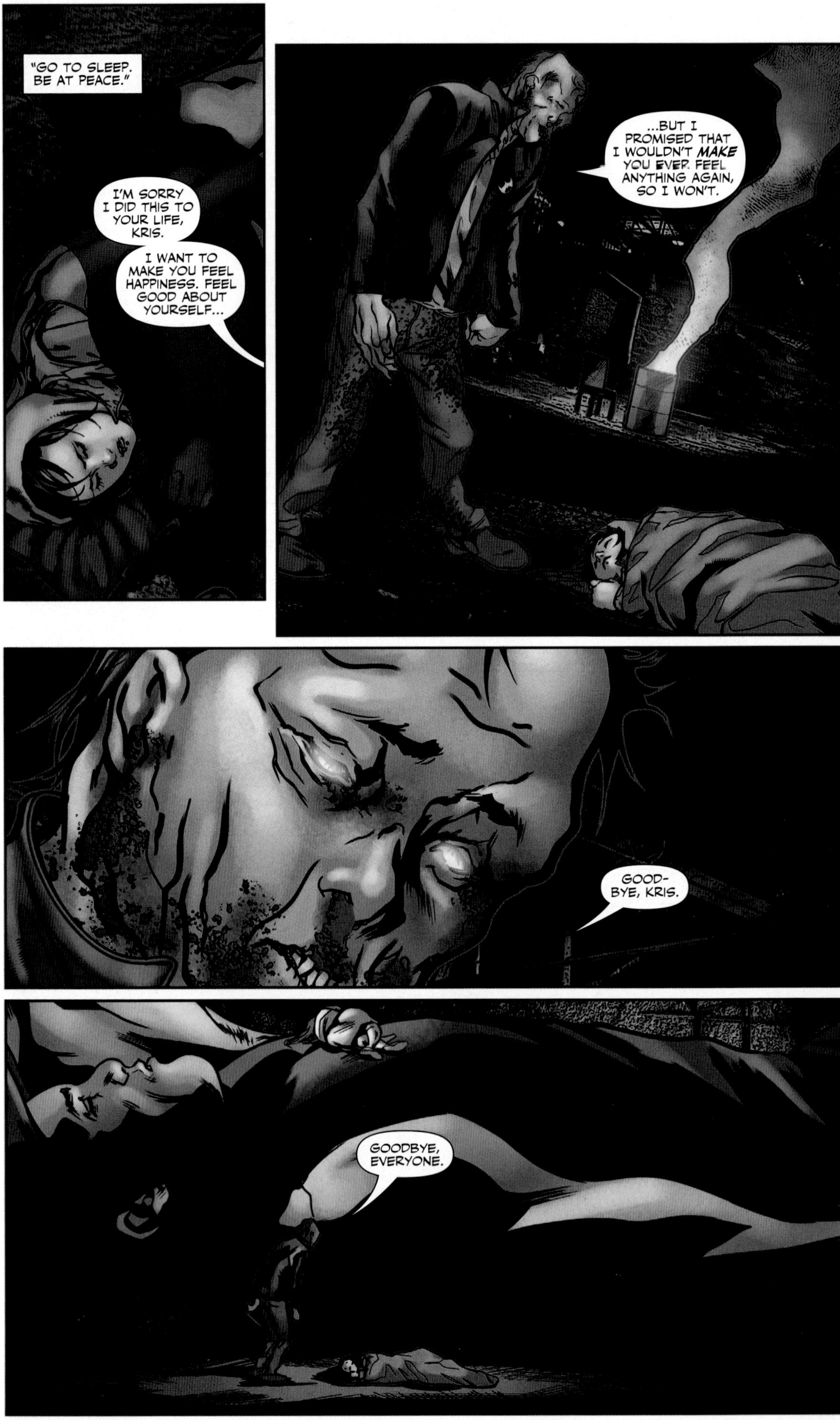
"GO TO SLEEP. BE AT PEACE."
I'M SORRY I DID THIS TO YOUR LIFE, KRIS.
I WANT TO MAKE YOU FEEL HAPPINESS. FEEL GOOD ABOUT YOURSELF...
...BUT I PROMISED THAT I WOULDN'T *MAKE* YOU EVER FEEL ANYTHING AGAIN, SO I WON'T.
GOOD-BYE, KRIS.
GOODBYE, EVERYONE.

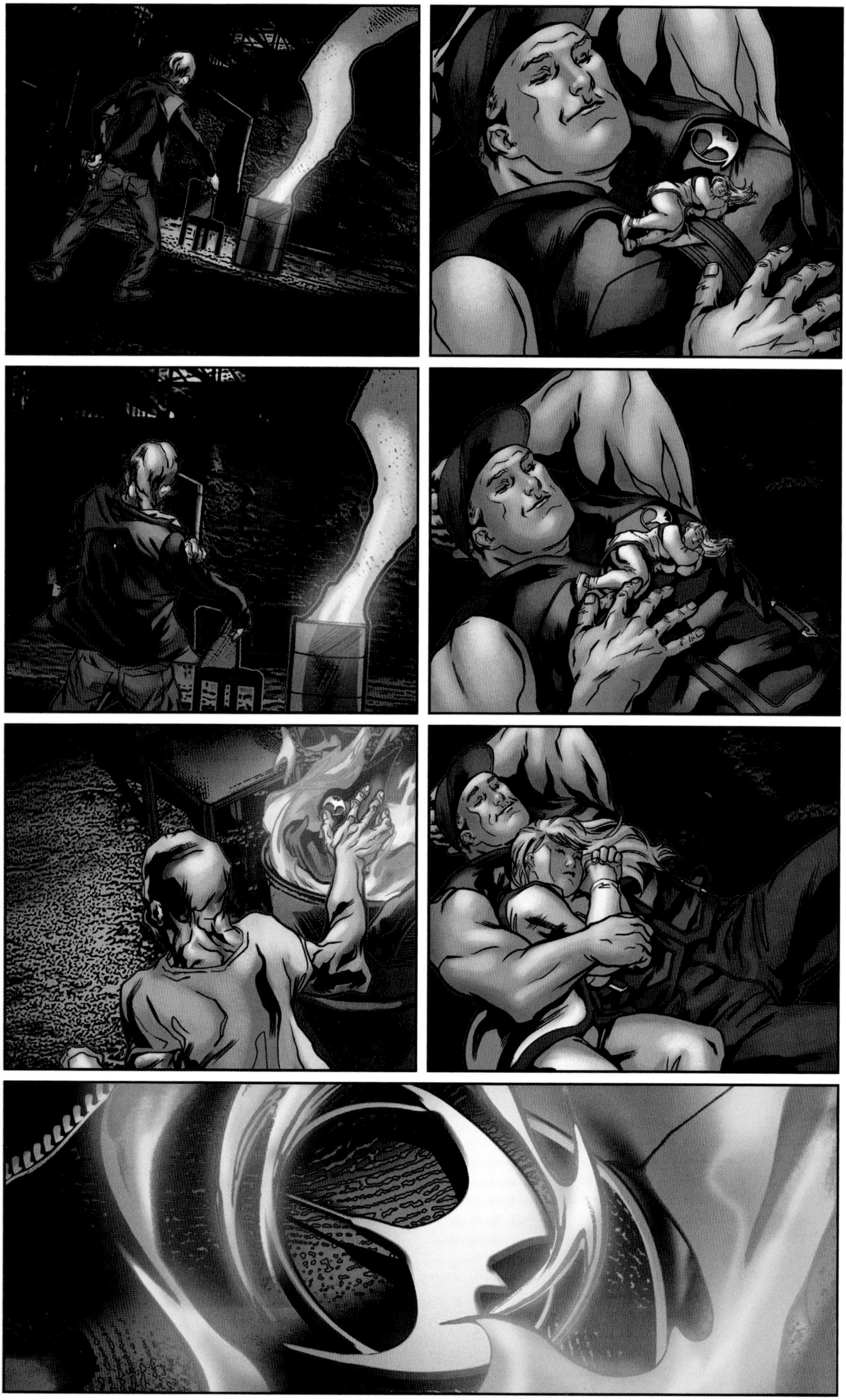

SORRY TO BE CALLING SO LATE, BUT YOU'RE GONNA WANNA SEE THIS...SOMETHING REALLY INSANE IS GOING DOWN.

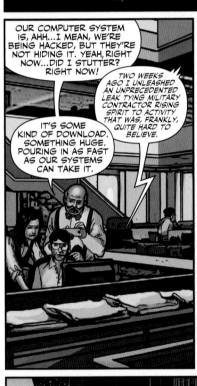

OUR COMPUTER SYSTEM IS, AHH...I MEAN, WE'RE BEING HACKED, BUT THEY'RE NOT HIDING IT. YEAH, RIGHT NOW...DID I STUTTER? RIGHT NOW!

TWO WEEKS AGO I UNLEASHED AN UNPRECEDENTED LEAK TYING MILITARY CONTRACTOR RISING SPIRIT TO ACTIVITY THAT WAS, FRANKLY, QUITE HARD TO BELIEVE.

IT'S SOME KIND OF DOWNLOAD. SOMETHING HUGE. POURING IN AS FAST AS OUR SYSTEMS CAN TAKE IT.

WE JUST CALLED THE GUARDIAN AND THE TIMES OF INDIA. THEY'RE BEING HAMMERED TOO, SAME EXACT THING.

THE WORLD SCOFFED. THEY CALLED ME A FAKE. THOSE FEW THAT BELIEVED IN ME THOUGHT I WAS DEAD. I AM NEITHER.

I AM THE FIRESTARTER.

I MEAN, THIS IS HUGE. WE'VE EVEN GOT VIDEO ON A LOOP COMING IN...

WHAT ONE HUNDRED AND THIRTY-TWO SEPARATE NEWS AGENCIES ACROSS THE PLANET ARE NOW SIMULTANEOUSLY RECEIVING IS THE COMPLETE TRUTH ABOUT MEGA-INDUSTRIALIST TOYO HARADA.

THIS TRUTH, HOWEVER UNIMAGINABLE, IS UNDENIABLE, AND OF HISTORIC PROPORTION. I SUGGEST ALL FREE INFORMATION AGENCIES WORK TOGETHER TO PARSE THROUGH AND DELIVER TO THE PUBLIC THE MAMMOTH AMOUNT OF DATA I'M NOW PROVIDING YOU.

THIS IS THE END OF OUR CHILDHOOD AS A SPECIES. NOW WE MUST CHANGE OUR IDEA OF WHAT IS REAL. AND SO I SAY TO YOU AGAIN...

"YOUR CULTURE IS DEAD. YOUR GOVERNMENTS ARE TIRED. YOUR DREAMS ARE SMALL.

"YOUR ONLY HOPE IS AN END TO SECRETS. AND A NEW ERA OF SELF-GOVERNANCE.

"YOUR DOWNLOAD BEGINS NOW."

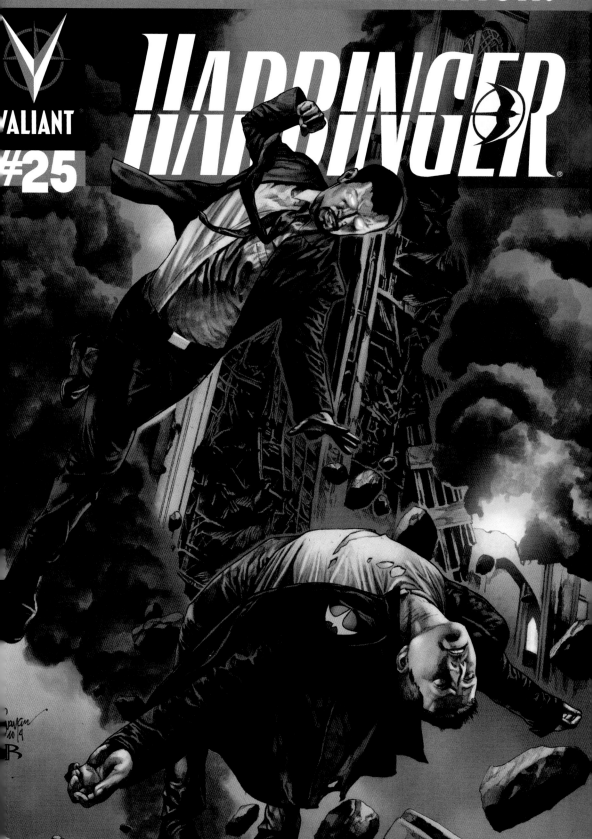

ANNIVERSARY CELEBRATION!

VALIANT

#25

HARBINGER

DEATH OF A RENEGADE: THE WAKE BY JOSHUA DYSART & KHARI EVANS
IN MEMORIAM BY VIVEK J. TIWARY & LEWIS LAROSA
FEATURING DAN GOLDMAN, CLAYTON HENRY, JUSTIN JORDAN, BARRY KITSON, LUCY KNISLEY, RAFER ROBERTS, AND MANY MORE

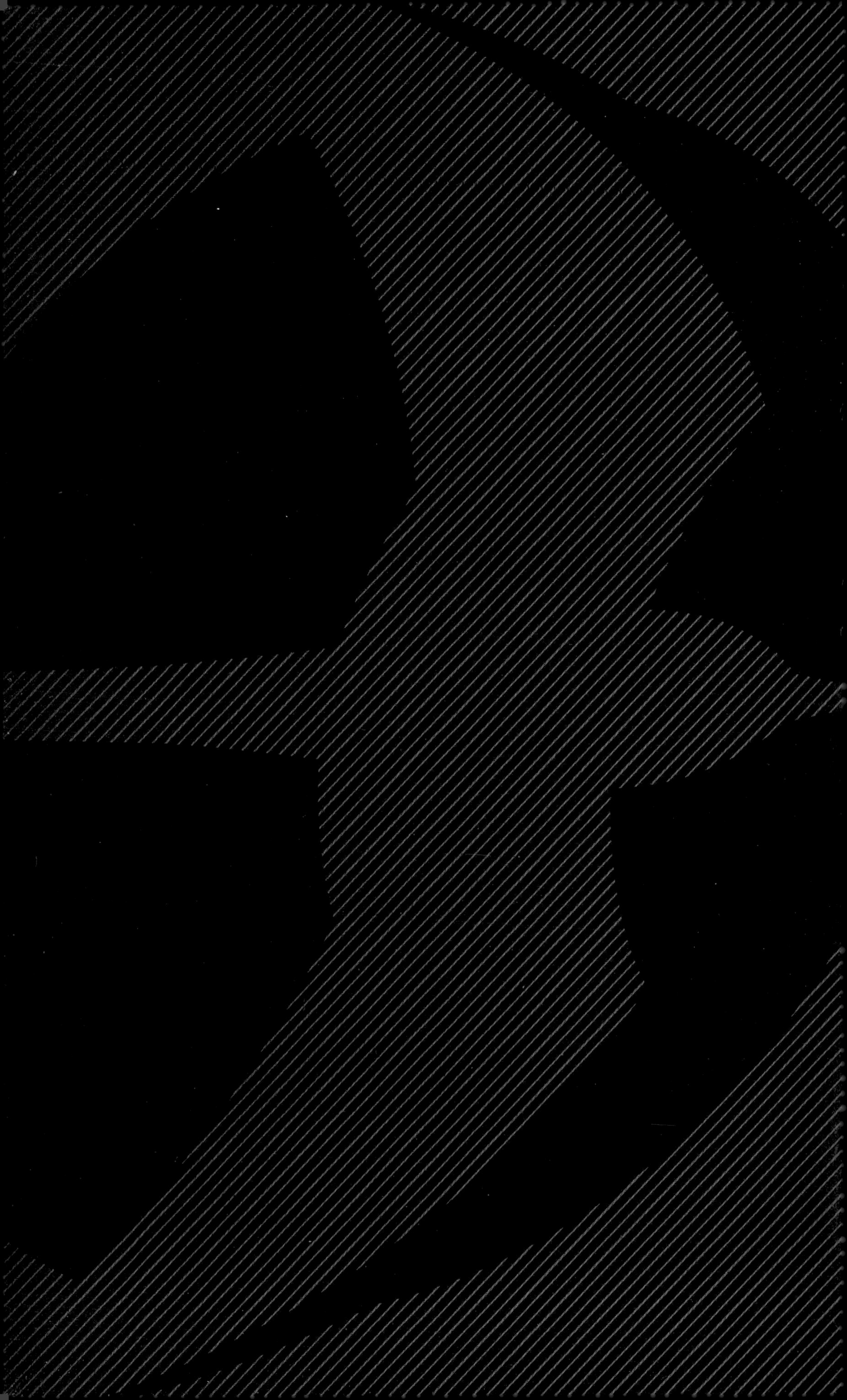

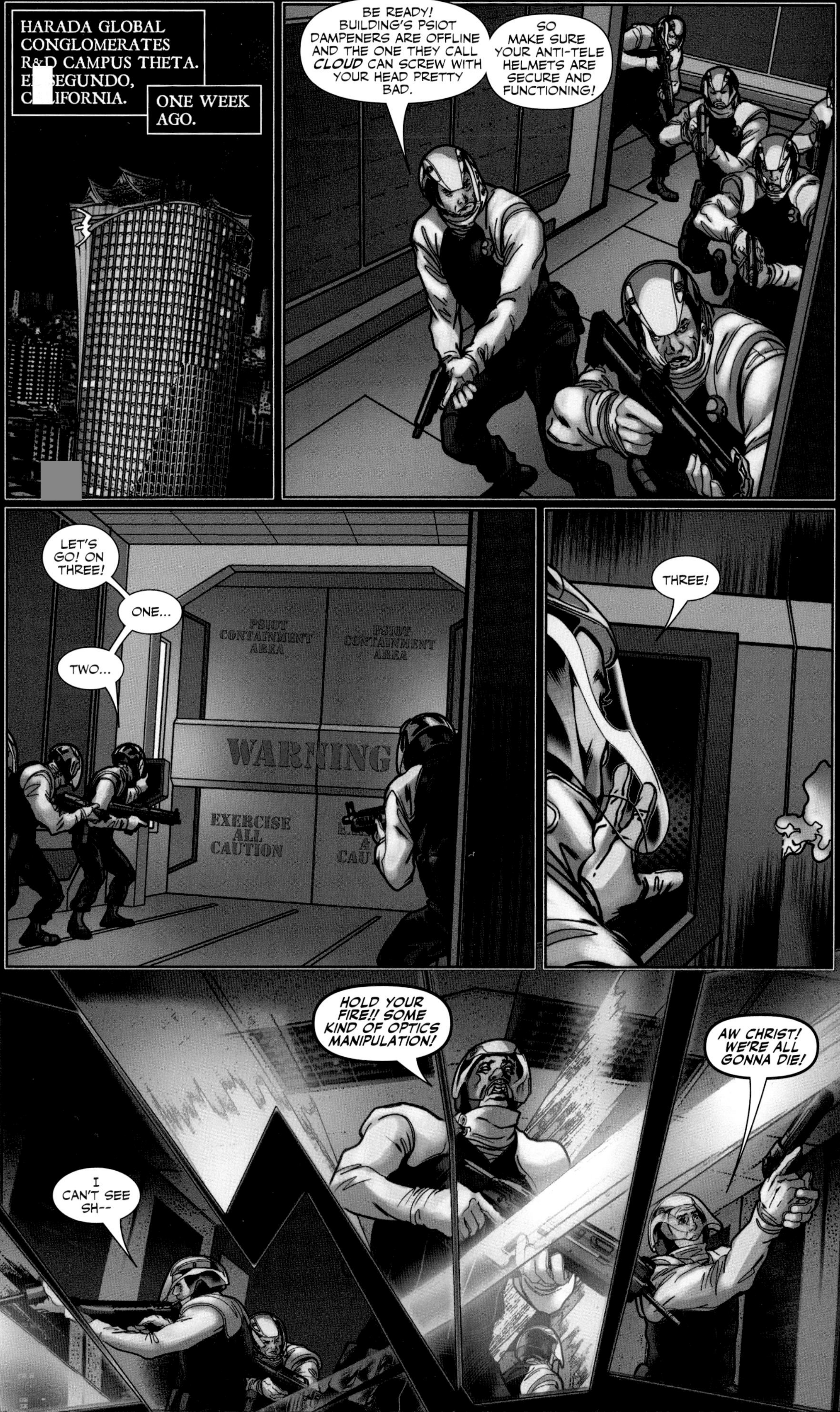
HARADA GLOBAL CONGLOMERATES R&D CAMPUS THETA. E SEGUNDO, C LIFORNIA.
ONE WEEK AGO.
BE READY! BUILDING'S PSIOT DAMPENERS ARE OFFLINE AND THE ONE THEY CALL *CLOUD* CAN SCREW WITH YOUR HEAD PRETTY BAD.
SO MAKE SURE YOUR ANTI-TELE HELMETS ARE SECURE AND FUNCTIONING!
LET'S GO! ON THREE!
ONE...
TWO...
PSIOT CONTAINMENT AREA
PSIOT CONTAINMENT AREA
WARNING
EXERCISE ALL CAUTION
THREE!
HOLD YOUR FIRE!! SOME KIND OF OPTICS MANIPULATION!
AW CHRIST! WE'RE ALL GONNA DIE!
I CAN'T SEE SH--

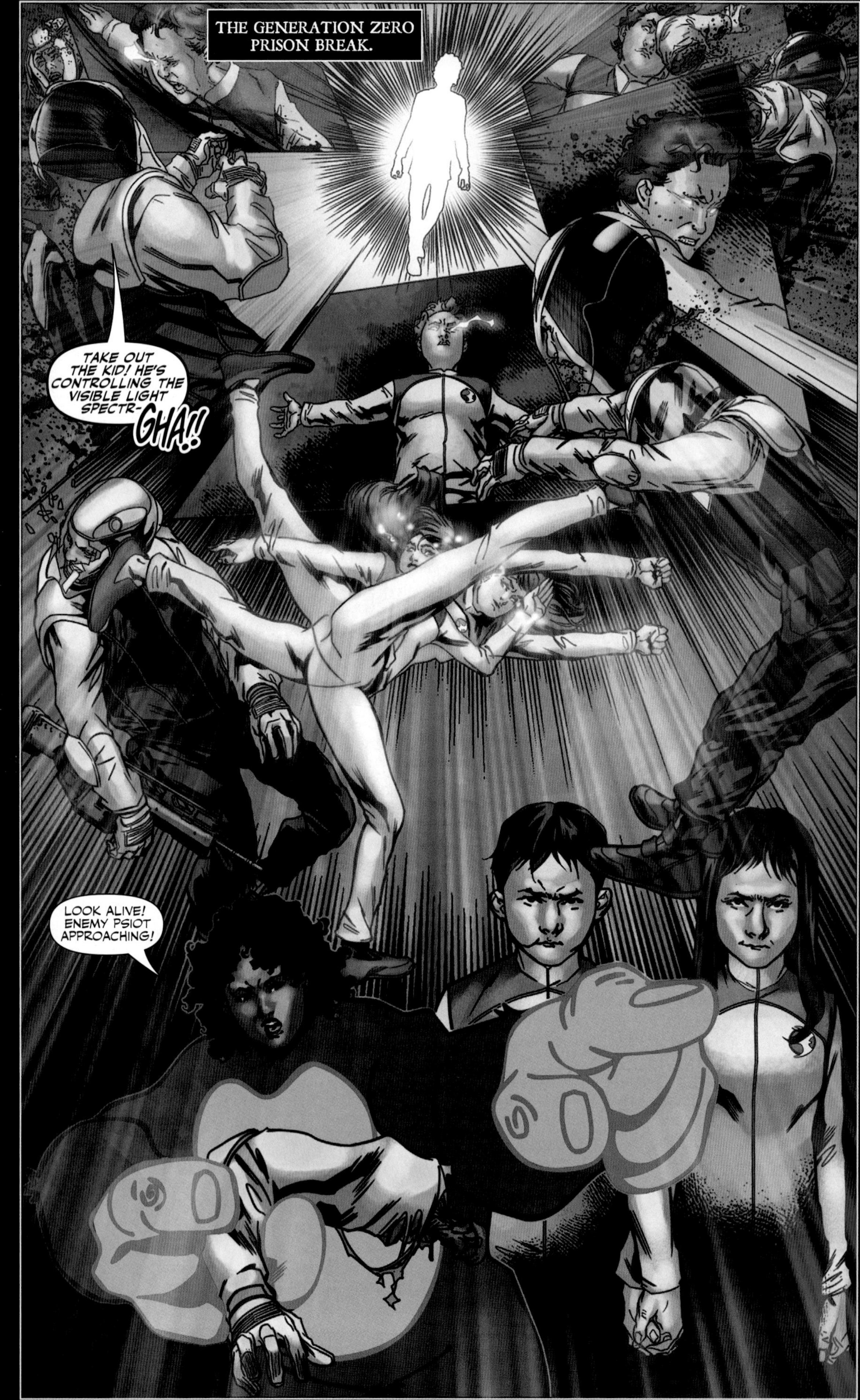
THE GENERATION ZERO PRISON BREAK.
TAKE OUT THE KID! HE'S CONTROLLING THE VISIBLE LIGHT SPECTR-GHA!!
LOOK ALIVE! ENEMY PSIOT APPROACHING!

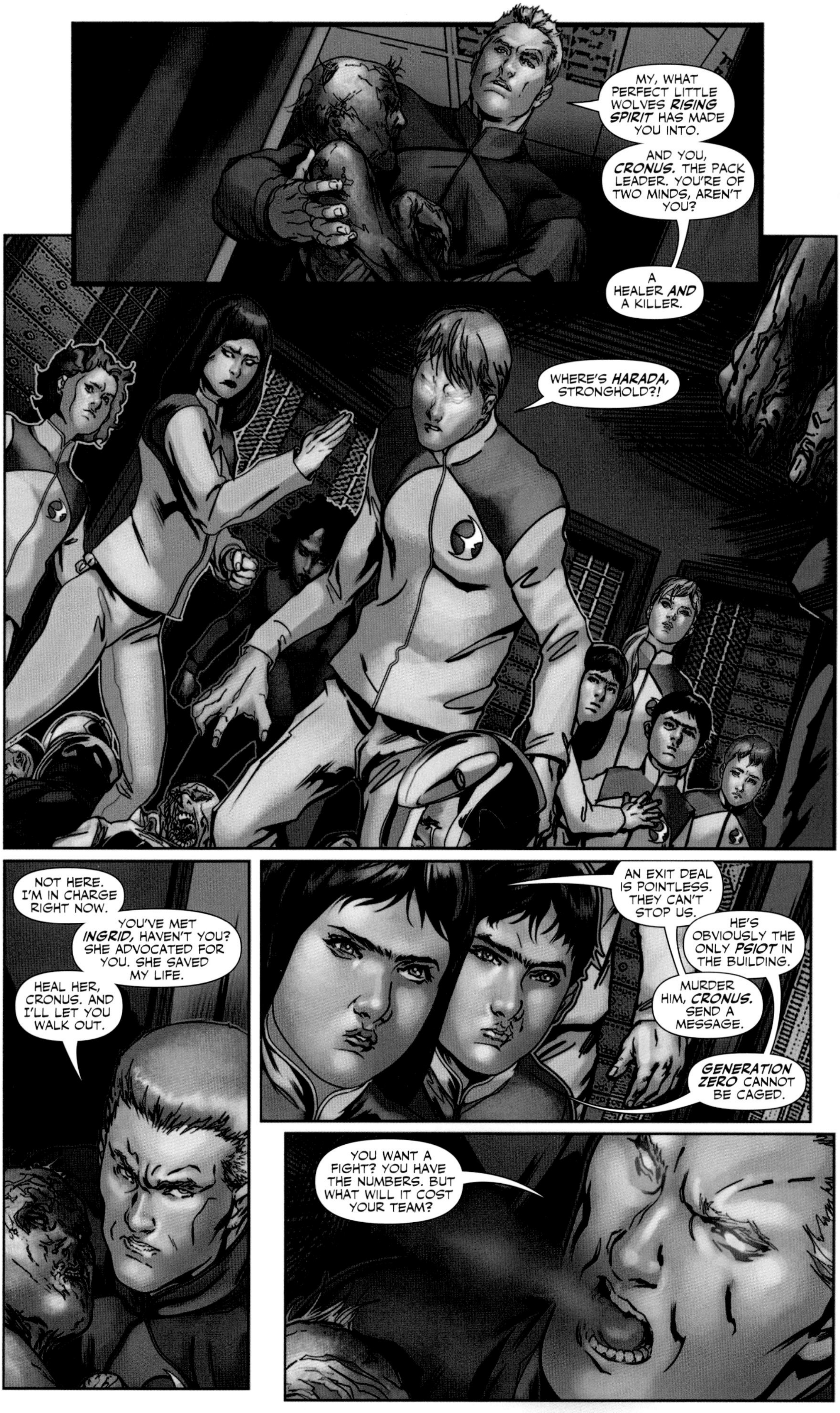
MY, WHAT PERFECT LITTLE WOLVES RISING SPIRIT HAS MADE YOU INTO.
AND YOU, CRONUS. THE PACK LEADER. YOU'RE OF TWO MINDS, AREN'T YOU?
A HEALER AND A KILLER.
WHERE'S HARADA, STRONGHOLD?!
NOT HERE. I'M IN CHARGE RIGHT NOW.
YOU'VE MET INGRID, HAVEN'T YOU? SHE ADVOCATED FOR YOU. SHE SAVED MY LIFE.
HEAL HER, CRONUS. AND I'LL LET YOU WALK OUT.
AN EXIT DEAL IS POINTLESS. THEY CAN'T STOP US.
HE'S OBVIOUSLY THE ONLY PSIOT IN THE BUILDING.
MURDER HIM, CRONUS. SEND A MESSAGE.
GENERATION ZERO CANNOT BE CAGED.
YOU WANT A FIGHT? YOU HAVE THE NUMBERS. BUT WHAT WILL IT COST YOUR TEAM?

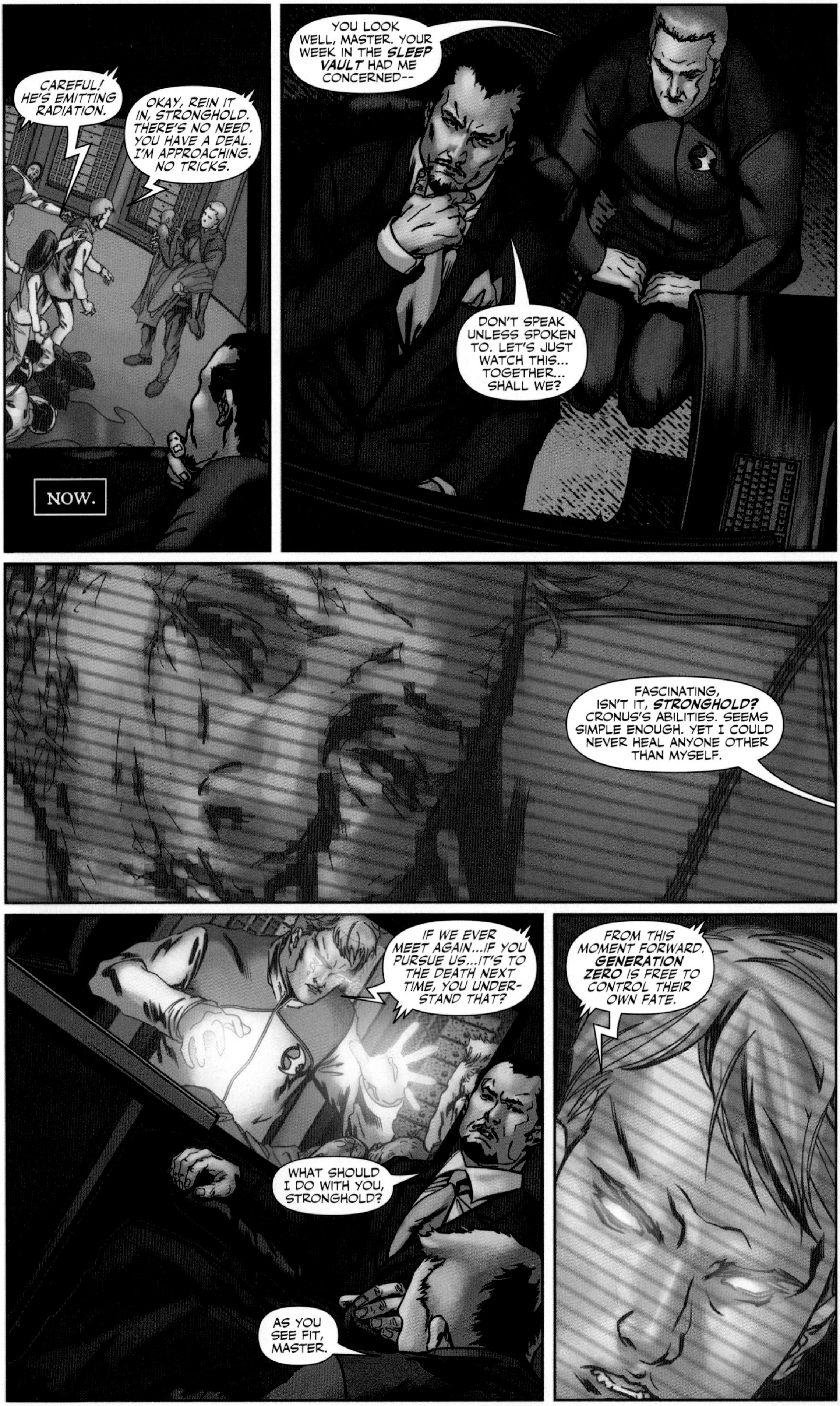
CAREFUL! HE'S EMITTING RADIATION.
OKAY, REIN IT IN, STRONGHOLD. THERE'S NO NEED. YOU HAVE A DEAL. I'M APPROACHING. NO TRICKS.
NOW.
YOU LOOK WELL, MASTER. YOUR WEEK IN THE SLEEP VAULT HAD ME CONCERNED--
DON'T SPEAK UNLESS SPOKEN TO. LET'S JUST WATCH THIS... TOGETHER... SHALL WE?
FASCINATING, ISN'T IT, STRONGHOLD? CRONUS'S ABILITIES. SEEMS SIMPLE ENOUGH. YET I COULD NEVER HEAL ANYONE OTHER THAN MYSELF.
IF WE EVER MEET AGAIN...IF YOU PURSUE US...IT'S TO THE DEATH NEXT TIME, YOU UNDERSTAND THAT?
WHAT SHOULD I DO WITH YOU, STRONGHOLD?
AS YOU SEE FIT, MASTER.
FROM THIS MOMENT FORWARD. GENERATION ZERO IS FREE TO CONTROL THEIR OWN FATE.

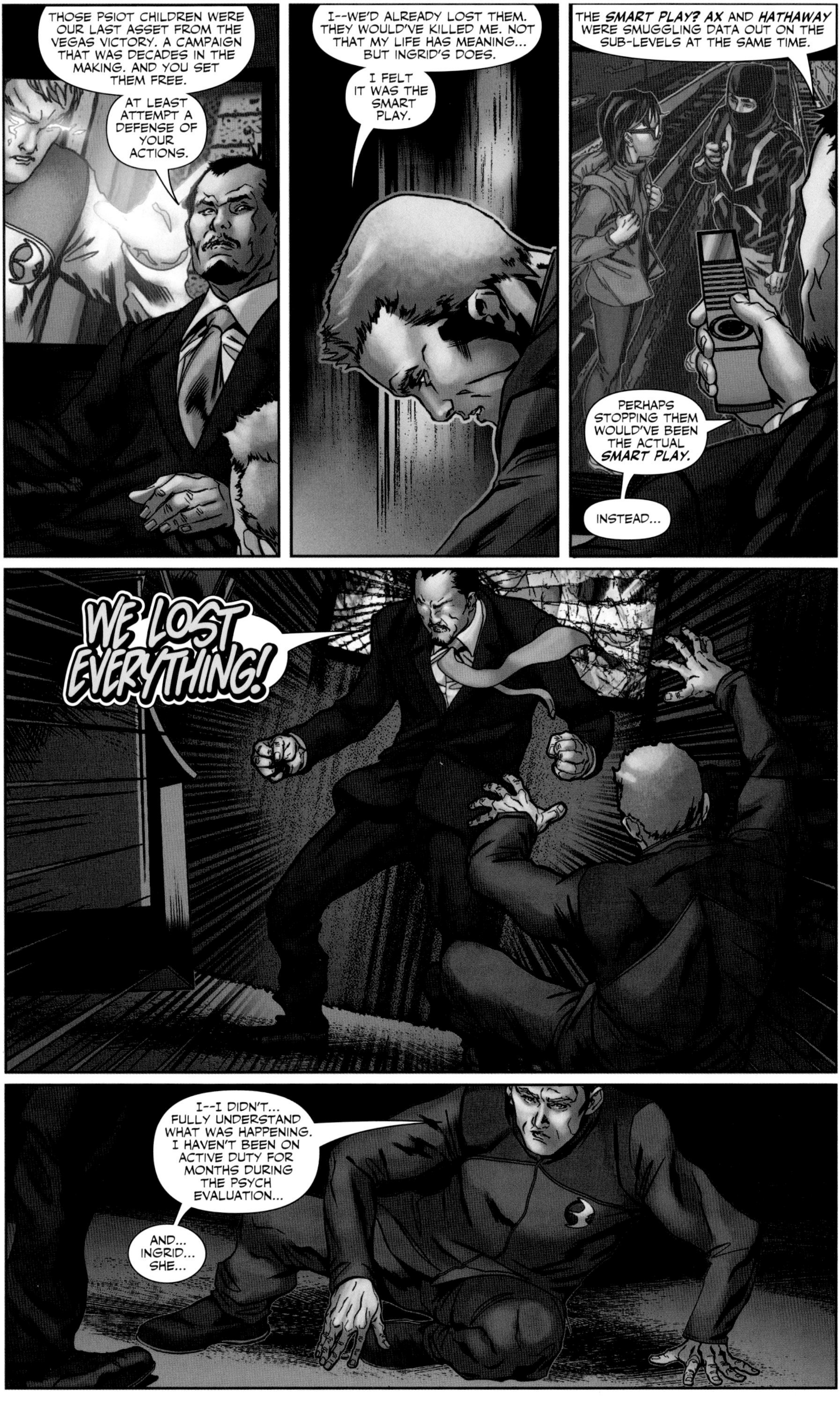
THOSE PSIOT CHILDREN WERE OUR LAST ASSET FROM THE VEGAS VICTORY. A CAMPAIGN THAT WAS DECADES IN THE MAKING. AND YOU SET THEM FREE.
AT LEAST ATTEMPT A DEFENSE OF YOUR ACTIONS.
I--WE'D ALREADY LOST THEM. THEY WOULD'VE KILLED ME. NOT THAT MY LIFE HAS MEANING... BUT INGRID'S DOES.
I FELT IT WAS THE SMART PLAY.
THE *SMART PLAY?* ***AX*** AND ***HATHAWAY*** WERE SMUGGLING DATA OUT ON THE SUB-LEVELS AT THE SAME TIME.
PERHAPS STOPPING THEM WOULD'VE BEEN THE ACTUAL ***SMART PLAY.***
INSTEAD...
WE LOST EVERYTHING!
I--I DIDN'T... FULLY UNDERSTAND WHAT WAS HAPPENING. I HAVEN'T BEEN ON ACTIVE DUTY FOR MONTHS DURING THE PSYCH EVALUATION...
AND... INGRID... SHE...

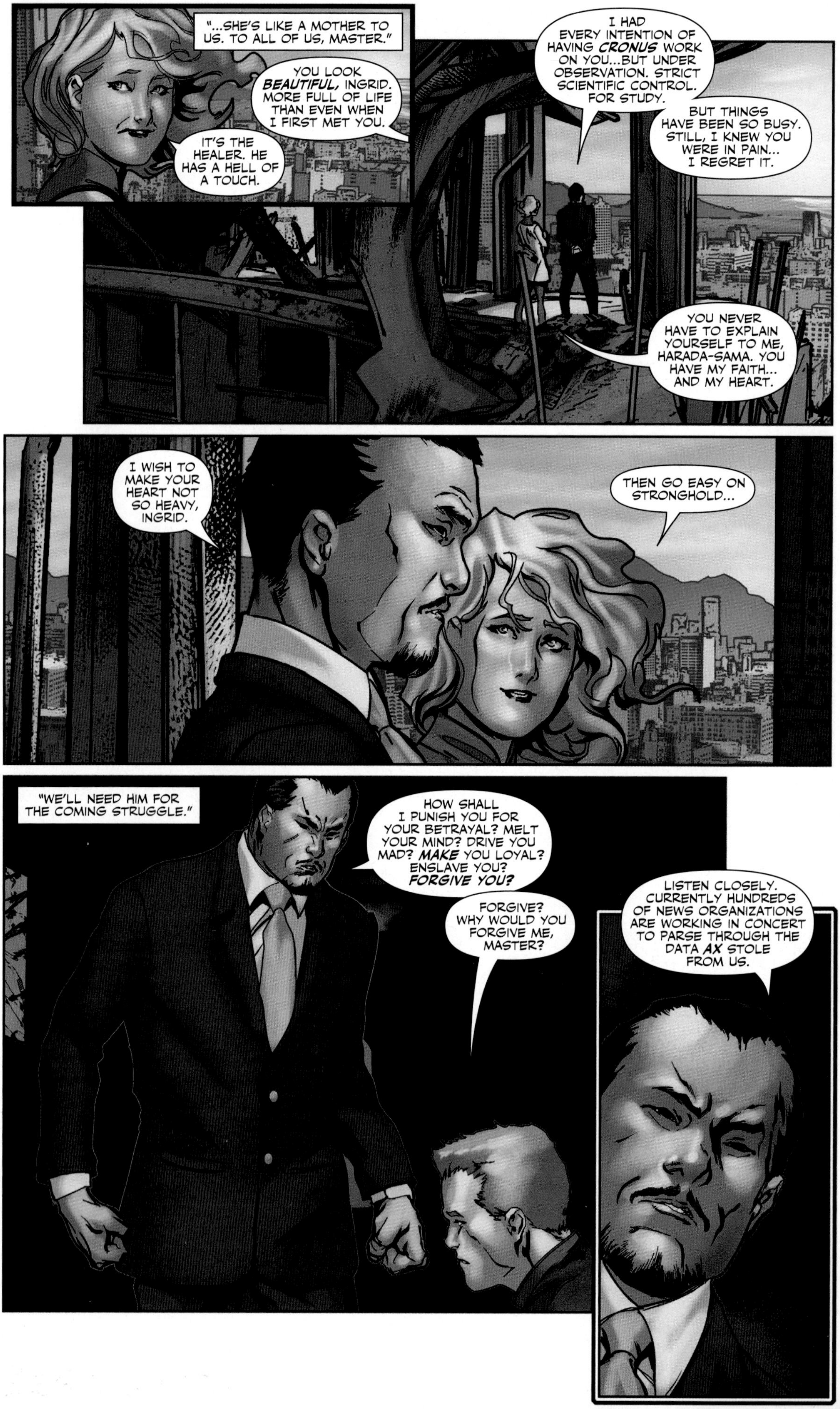
"...SHE'S LIKE A MOTHER TO US. TO ALL OF US, MASTER."
YOU LOOK BEAUTIFUL, INGRID. MORE FULL OF LIFE THAN EVEN WHEN I FIRST MET YOU.
IT'S THE HEALER. HE HAS A HELL OF A TOUCH.
I HAD EVERY INTENTION OF HAVING CRONUS WORK ON YOU...BUT UNDER OBSERVATION. STRICT SCIENTIFIC CONTROL. FOR STUDY.
BUT THINGS HAVE BEEN SO BUSY. STILL, I KNEW YOU WERE IN PAIN... I REGRET IT.
YOU NEVER HAVE TO EXPLAIN YOURSELF TO ME, HARADA-SAMA. YOU HAVE MY FAITH... AND MY HEART.
I WISH TO MAKE YOUR HEART NOT SO HEAVY, INGRID.
THEN GO EASY ON STRONGHOLD...
"WE'LL NEED HIM FOR THE COMING STRUGGLE."
HOW SHALL I PUNISH YOU FOR YOUR BETRAYAL? MELT YOUR MIND? DRIVE YOU MAD? MAKE YOU LOYAL? ENSLAVE YOU? FORGIVE YOU?
FORGIVE? WHY WOULD YOU FORGIVE ME, MASTER?
LISTEN CLOSELY. CURRENTLY HUNDREDS OF NEWS ORGANIZATIONS ARE WORKING IN CONCERT TO PARSE THROUGH THE DATA AX STOLE FROM US.

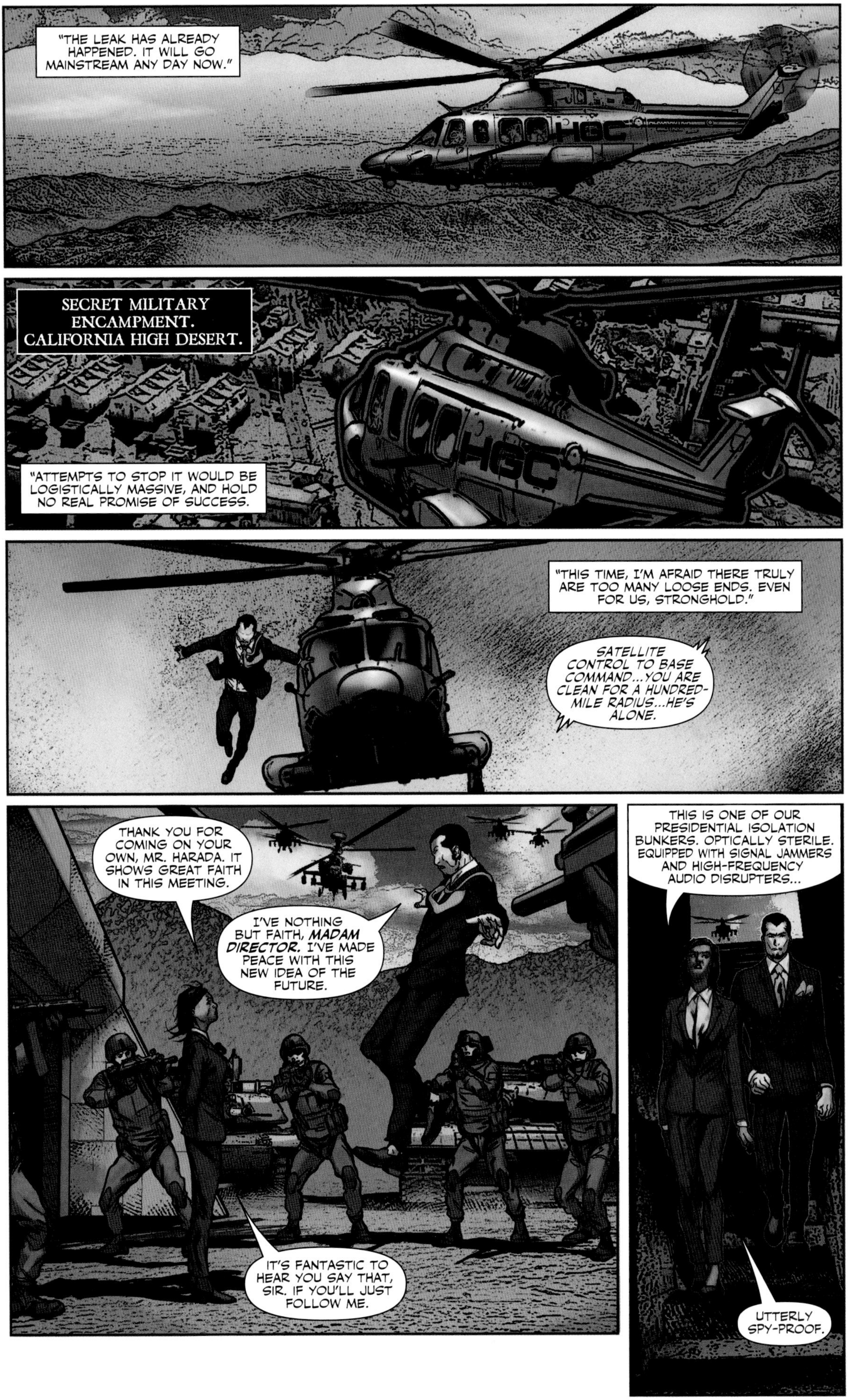
"THE LEAK HAS ALREADY HAPPENED. IT WILL GO MAINSTREAM ANY DAY NOW."
SECRET MILITARY ENCAMPMENT. CALIFORNIA HIGH DESERT.
"ATTEMPTS TO STOP IT WOULD BE LOGISTICALLY MASSIVE, AND HOLD NO REAL PROMISE OF SUCCESS.
"THIS TIME, I'M AFRAID THERE TRULY ARE TOO MANY LOOSE ENDS. EVEN FOR US, STRONGHOLD."
SATELLITE CONTROL TO BASE COMMAND...YOU ARE CLEAN FOR A HUNDRED-MILE RADIUS...HE'S ALONE.
THANK YOU FOR COMING ON YOUR OWN, MR. HARADA. IT SHOWS GREAT FAITH IN THIS MEETING.
I'VE NOTHING BUT FAITH, MADAM DIRECTOR. I'VE MADE PEACE WITH THIS NEW IDEA OF THE FUTURE.
IT'S FANTASTIC TO HEAR YOU SAY THAT, SIR. IF YOU'LL JUST FOLLOW ME.
THIS IS ONE OF OUR PRESIDENTIAL ISOLATION BUNKERS. OPTICALLY STERILE. EQUIPPED WITH SIGNAL JAMMERS AND HIGH-FREQUENCY AUDIO DISRUPTERS...
UTTERLY SPY-PROOF.

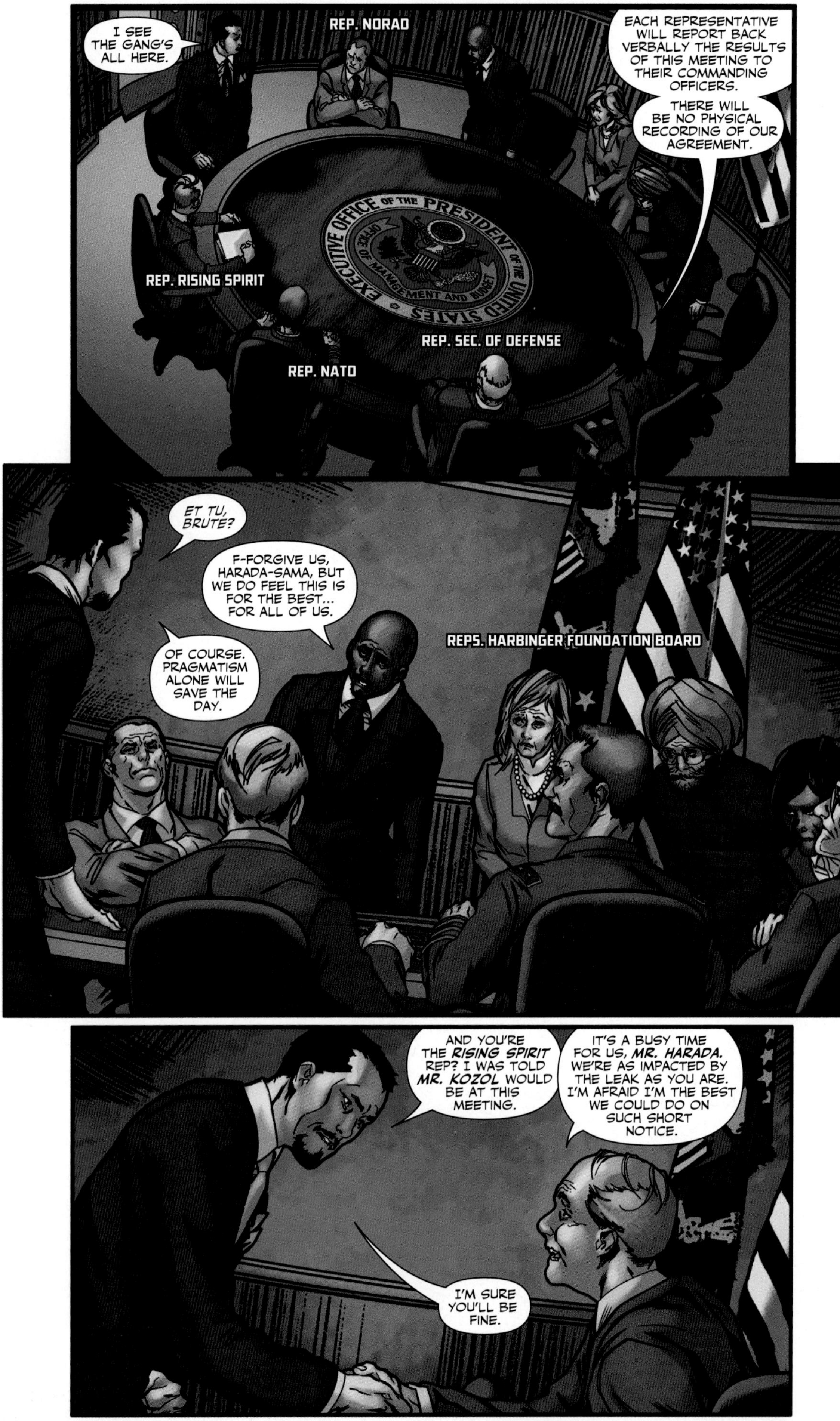
I SEE THE GANG'S ALL HERE.
REP. NORAD
EACH REPRESENTATIVE WILL REPORT BACK VERBALLY THE RESULTS OF THIS MEETING TO THEIR COMMANDING OFFICERS.
THERE WILL BE NO PHYSICAL RECORDING OF OUR AGREEMENT.
EXECUTIVE OFFICE OF THE PRESIDENT OF THE UNITED STATES
OFFICE OF MANAGEMENT AND BUDGET
REP. RISING SPIRIT
REP. SEC. OF DEFENSE
REP. NATO
ET TU, BRUTE?
F-FORGIVE US, HARADA-SAMA, BUT WE DO FEEL THIS IS FOR THE BEST... FOR ALL OF US.
OF COURSE. PRAGMATISM ALONE WILL SAVE THE DAY.
REPS. HARBINGER FOUNDATION BOARD
AND YOU'RE THE RISING SPIRIT REP? I WAS TOLD MR. KOZOL WOULD BE AT THIS MEETING.
IT'S A BUSY TIME FOR US, MR. HARADA. WE'RE AS IMPACTED BY THE LEAK AS YOU ARE. I'M AFRAID I'M THE BEST WE COULD DO ON SUCH SHORT NOTICE.
I'M SURE YOU'LL BE FINE.

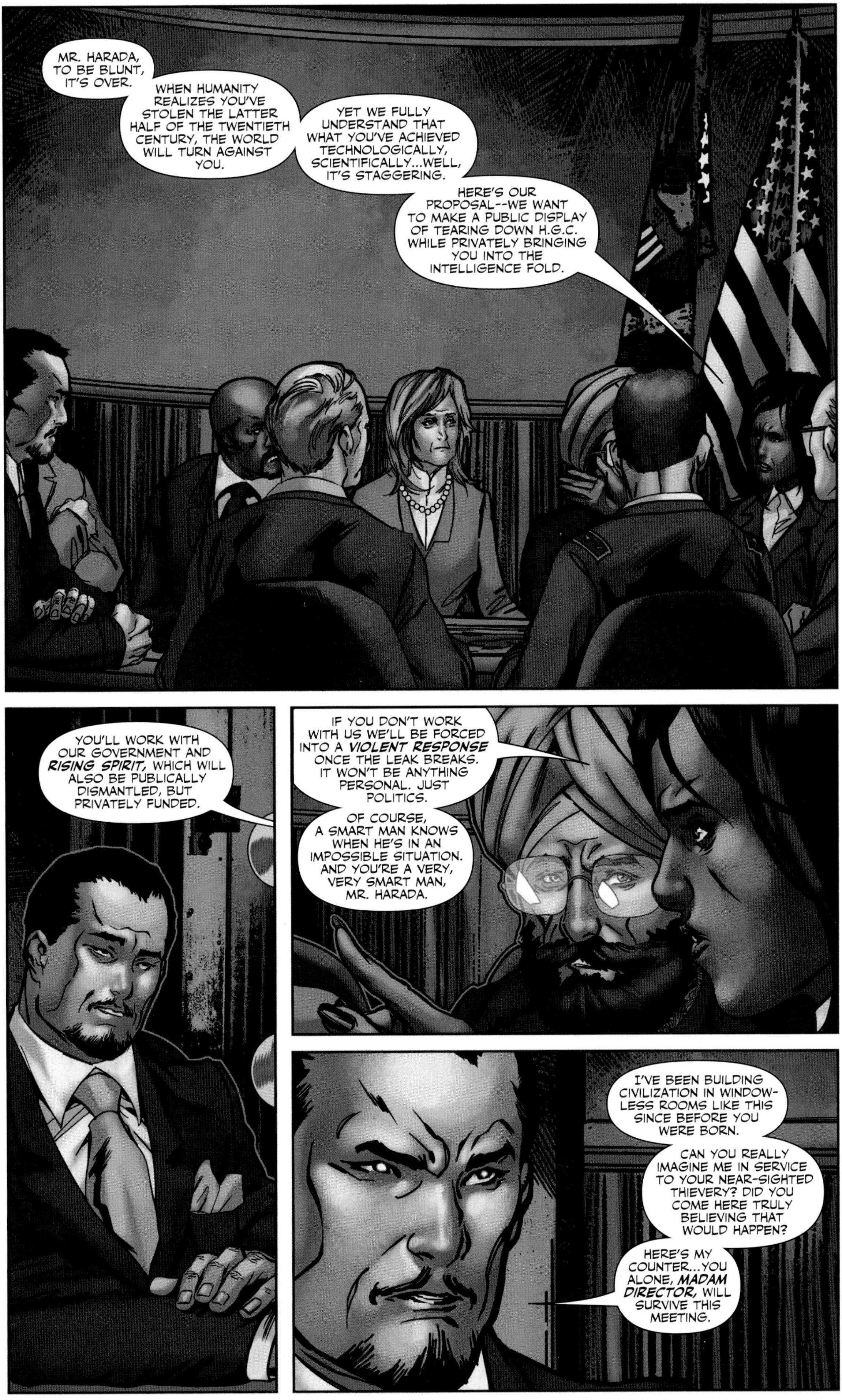
MR. HARADA, TO BE BLUNT, IT'S OVER.
WHEN HUMANITY REALIZES YOU'VE STOLEN THE LATTER HALF OF THE TWENTIETH CENTURY, THE WORLD WILL TURN AGAINST YOU.
YET WE FULLY UNDERSTAND THAT WHAT YOU'VE ACHIEVED TECHNOLOGICALLY, SCIENTIFICALLY...WELL, IT'S STAGGERING.
HERE'S OUR PROPOSAL--WE WANT TO MAKE A PUBLIC DISPLAY OF TEARING DOWN H.G.C. WHILE PRIVATELY BRINGING YOU INTO THE INTELLIGENCE FOLD.
YOU'LL WORK WITH OUR GOVERNMENT AND *RISING SPIRIT,* WHICH WILL ALSO BE PUBLICALLY DISMANTLED, BUT PRIVATELY FUNDED.
IF YOU DON'T WORK WITH US WE'LL BE FORCED INTO A ***VIOLENT RESPONSE*** ONCE THE LEAK BREAKS. IT WON'T BE ANYTHING PERSONAL. JUST POLITICS.
OF COURSE, A SMART MAN KNOWS WHEN HE'S IN AN IMPOSSIBLE SITUATION. AND YOU'RE A VERY, VERY SMART MAN, MR. HARADA.
I'VE BEEN BUILDING CIVILIZATION IN WINDOW-LESS ROOMS LIKE THIS SINCE BEFORE YOU WERE BORN.
CAN YOU REALLY IMAGINE ME IN SERVICE TO YOUR NEAR-SIGHTED THIEVERY? DID YOU COME HERE TRULY BELIEVING THAT WOULD HAPPEN?
HERE'S MY COUNTER...YOU ALONE, ***MADAM DIRECTOR,*** WILL SURVIVE THIS MEETING.

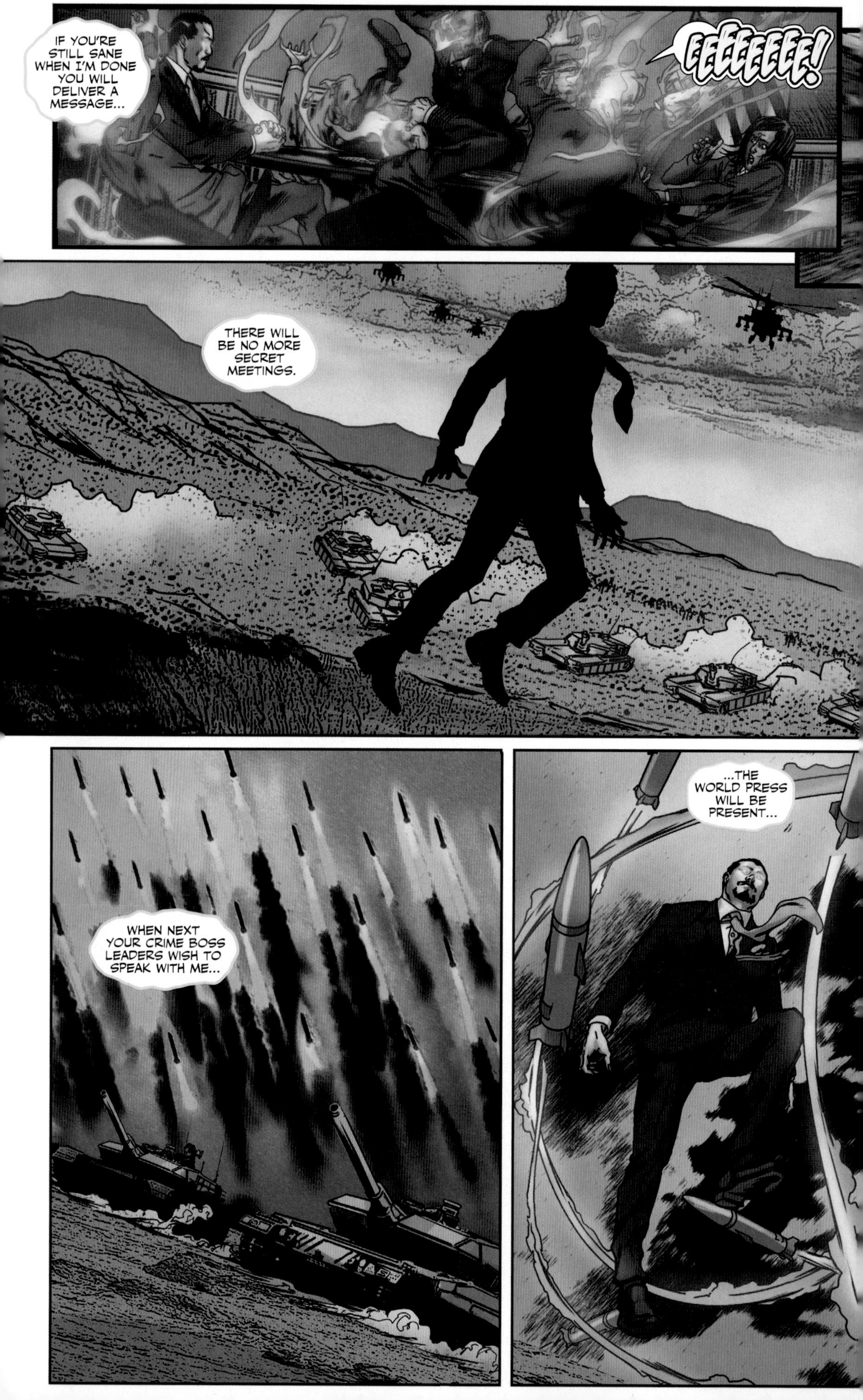
IF YOU'RE STILL SANE WHEN I'M DONE YOU WILL DELIVER A MESSAGE...
EEEEEEEE!
THERE WILL BE NO MORE SECRET MEETINGS.
WHEN NEXT YOUR CRIME BOSS LEADERS WISH TO SPEAK WITH ME...
...THE WORLD PRESS WILL BE PRESENT...

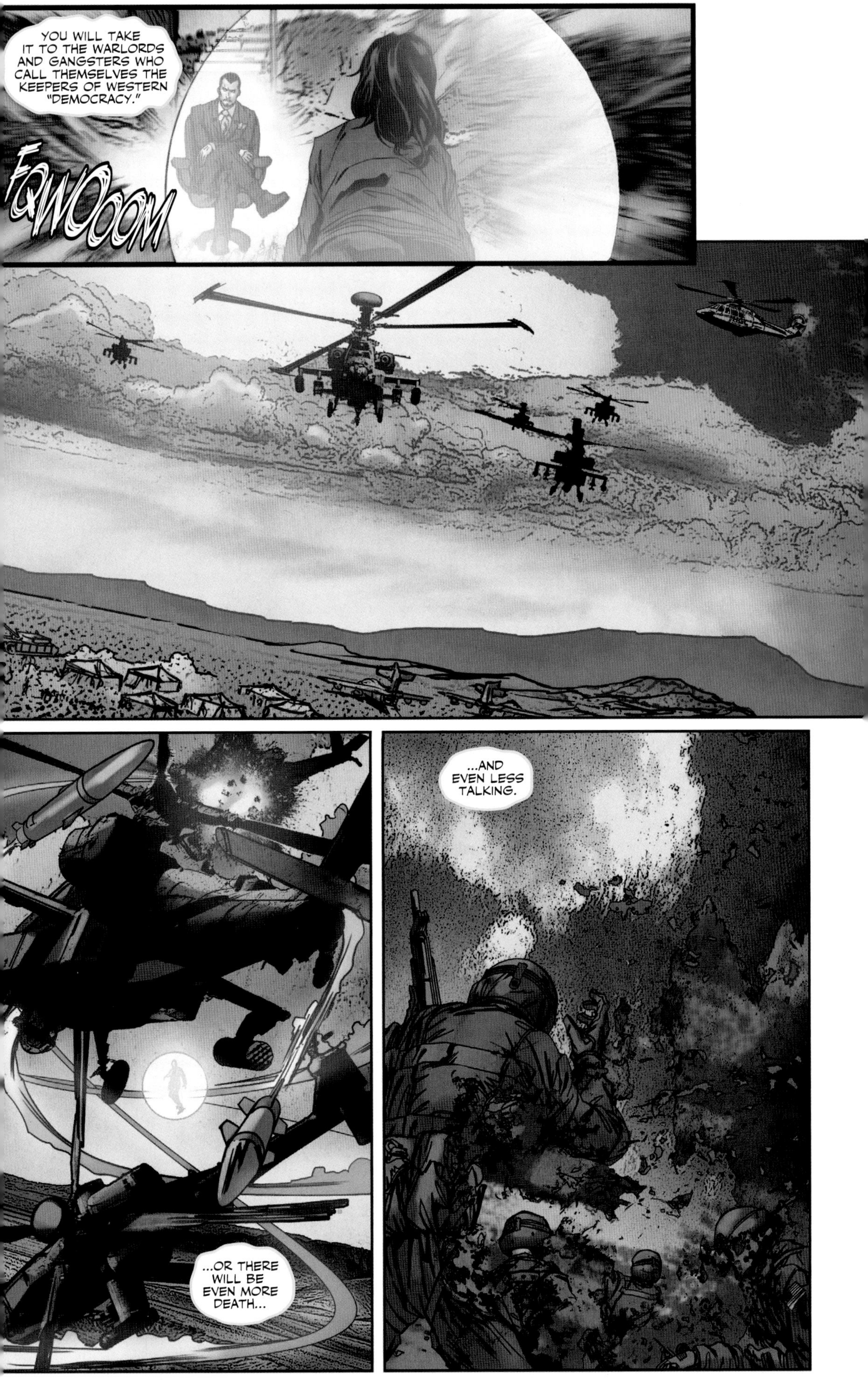
YOU WILL TAKE IT TO THE WARLORDS AND GANGSTERS WHO CALL THEMSELVES THE KEEPERS OF WESTERN "DEMOCRACY."
FQWOOOM
...OR THERE WILL BE EVEN MORE DEATH...
...AND EVEN LESS TALKING.

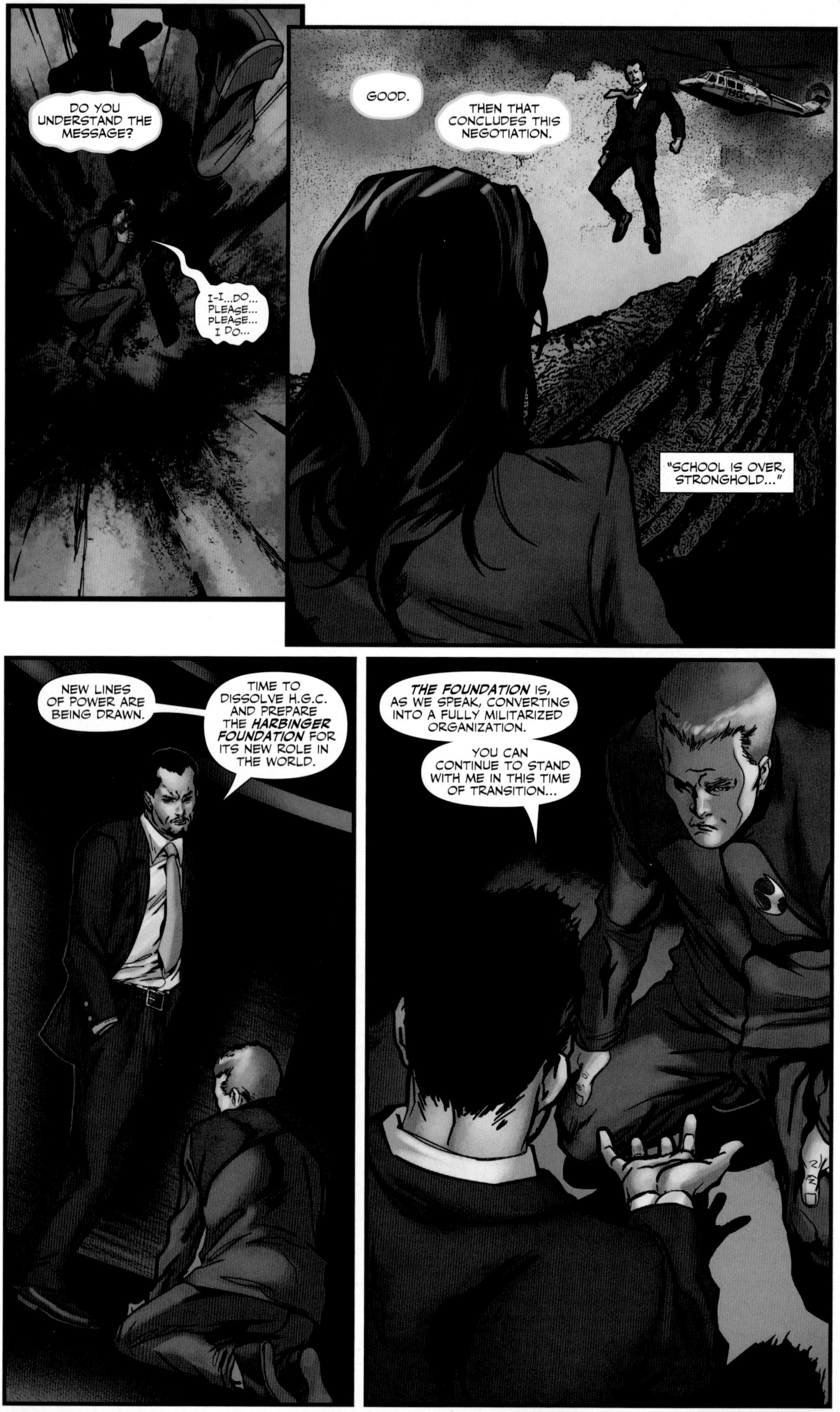
DO YOU UNDERSTAND THE MESSAGE?
I-I...DO... PLEASE... PLEASE... I DO...
GOOD.
THEN THAT CONCLUDES THIS NEGOTIATION.
"SCHOOL IS OVER, STRONGHOLD..."
NEW LINES OF POWER ARE BEING DRAWN.
TIME TO DISSOLVE H.G.C. AND PREPARE THE HARBINGER FOUNDATION FOR ITS NEW ROLE IN THE WORLD.
THE FOUNDATION IS, AS WE SPEAK, CONVERTING INTO A FULLY MILITARIZED ORGANIZATION.
YOU CAN CONTINUE TO STAND WITH ME IN THIS TIME OF TRANSITION...

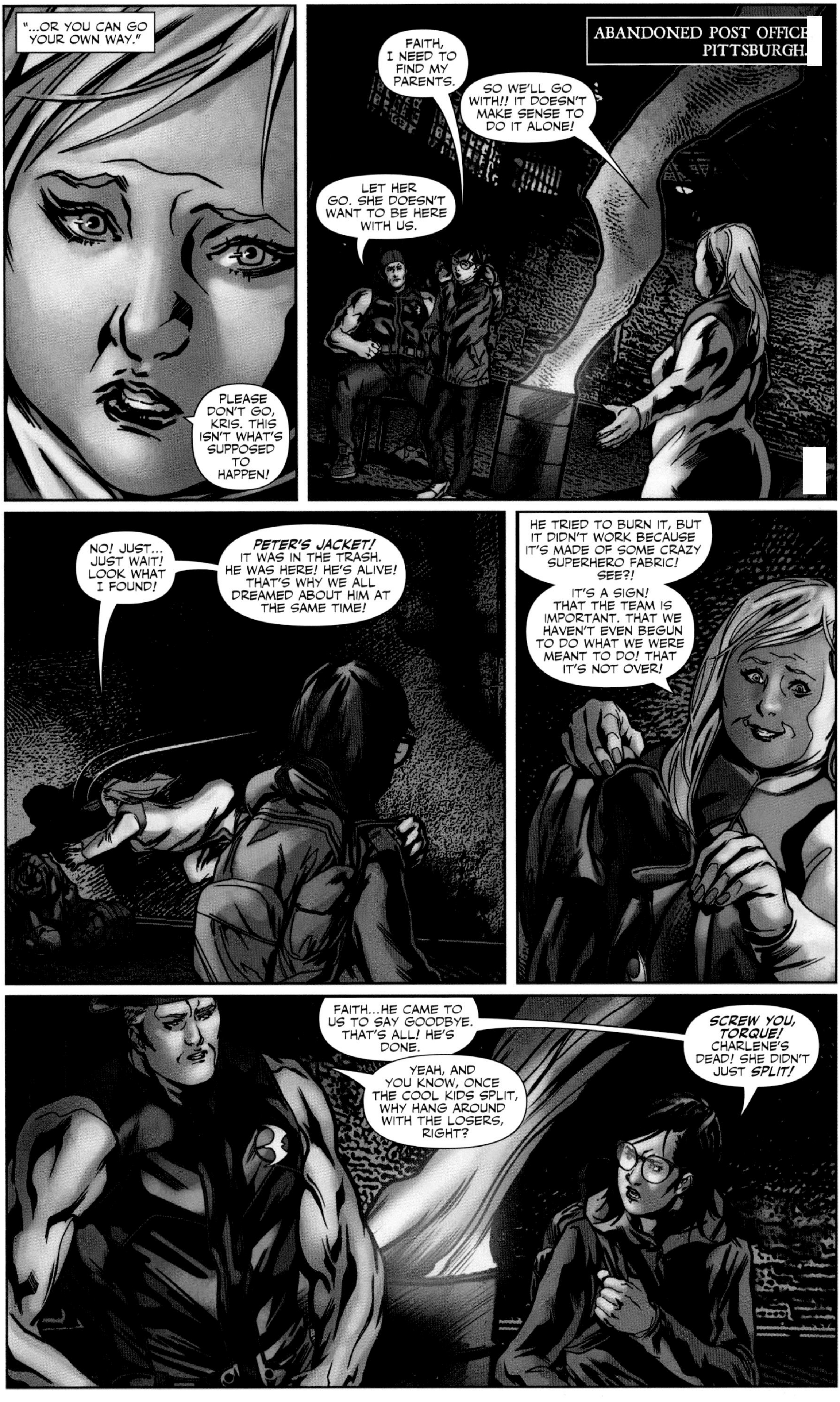
"...OR YOU CAN GO YOUR OWN WAY."
PLEASE DON'T GO, KRIS. THIS ISN'T WHAT'S SUPPOSED TO HAPPEN!
ABANDONED POST OFFICE PITTSBURGH
FAITH, I NEED TO FIND MY PARENTS.
SO WE'LL GO WITH!! IT DOESN'T MAKE SENSE TO DO IT ALONE!
LET HER GO. SHE DOESN'T WANT TO BE HERE WITH US.
NO! JUST... JUST WAIT! LOOK WHAT I FOUND!
PETER'S JACKET! IT WAS IN THE TRASH. HE WAS HERE! HE'S ALIVE! THAT'S WHY WE ALL DREAMED ABOUT HIM AT THE SAME TIME!
HE TRIED TO BURN IT, BUT IT DIDN'T WORK BECAUSE IT'S MADE OF SOME CRAZY SUPERHERO FABRIC! SEE?!
IT'S A SIGN! THAT THE TEAM IS IMPORTANT. THAT WE HAVEN'T EVEN BEGUN TO DO WHAT WE WERE MEANT TO DO! THAT IT'S NOT OVER!
FAITH...HE CAME TO US TO SAY GOODBYE. THAT'S ALL! HE'S DONE.
YEAH, AND YOU KNOW, ONCE THE COOL KIDS SPLIT, WHY HANG AROUND WITH THE LOSERS, RIGHT?
SCREW YOU, TORQUE! CHARLENE'S DEAD! SHE DIDN'T JUST SPLIT!

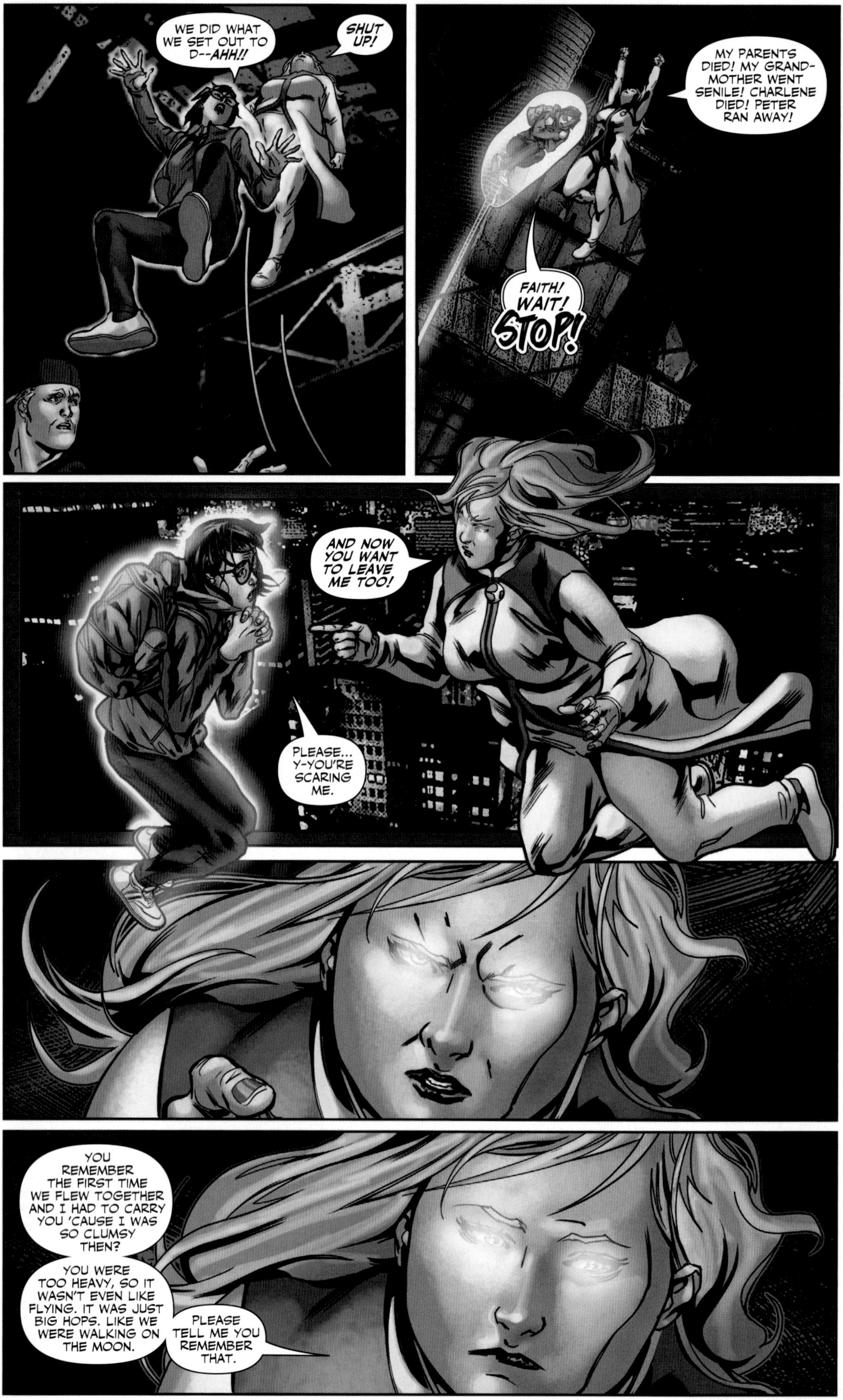
WE DID WHAT WE SET OUT TO D--AHH!!
SHUT UP!
MY PARENTS DIED! MY GRAND-MOTHER WENT SENILE! CHARLENE DIED! PETER RAN AWAY!
FAITH! WAIT! STOP!
AND NOW YOU WANT TO LEAVE ME TOO!
PLEASE... Y-YOU'RE SCARING ME.
YOU REMEMBER THE FIRST TIME WE FLEW TOGETHER AND I HAD TO CARRY YOU 'CAUSE I WAS SO CLUMSY THEN?
YOU WERE TOO HEAVY, SO IT WASN'T EVEN LIKE FLYING. IT WAS JUST BIG HOPS. LIKE WE WERE WALKING ON THE MOON.
PLEASE TELL ME YOU REMEMBER THAT.

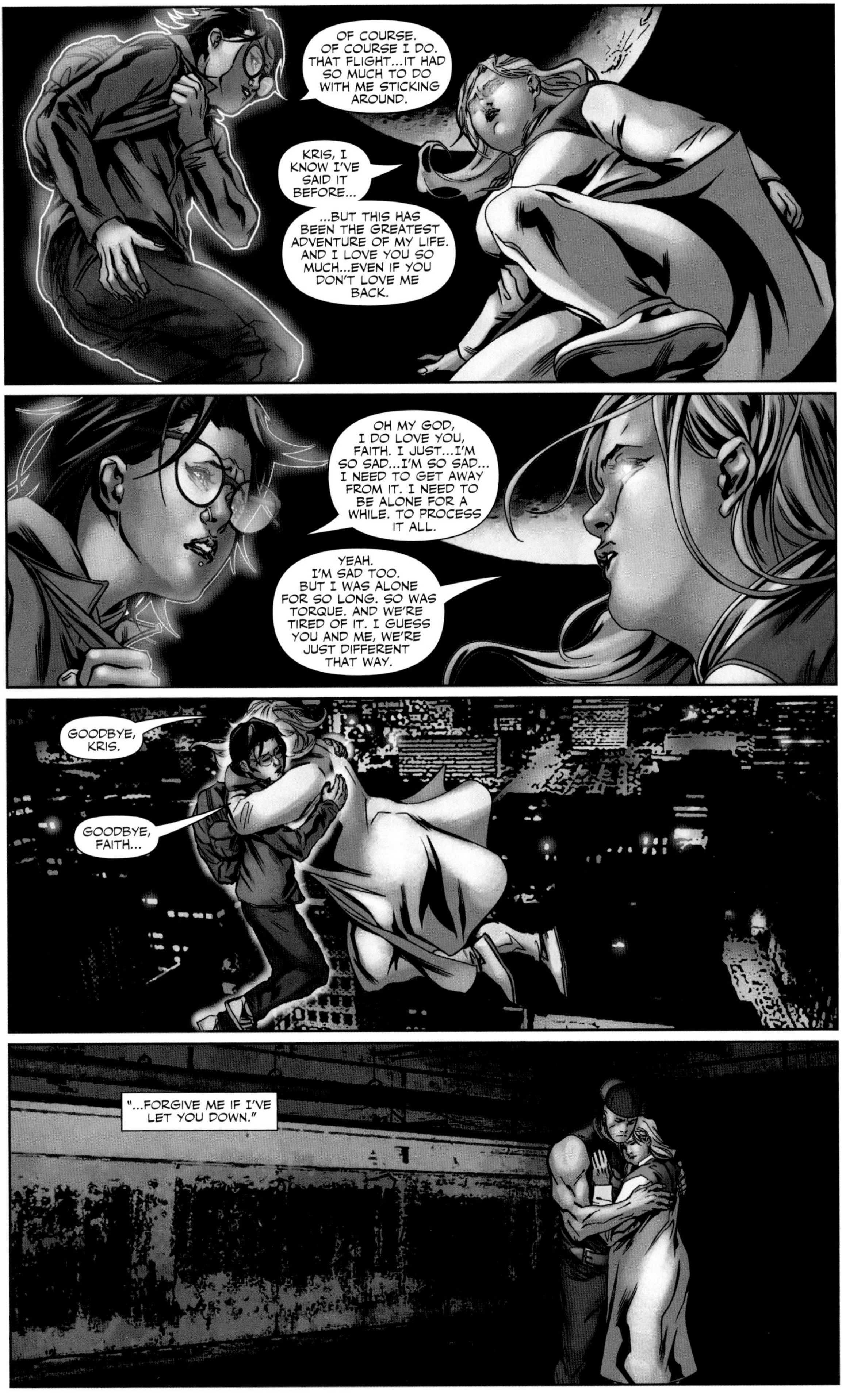
OF COURSE. OF COURSE I DO. THAT FLIGHT...IT HAD SO MUCH TO DO WITH ME STICKING AROUND.
KRIS, I KNOW I'VE SAID IT BEFORE...
...BUT THIS HAS BEEN THE GREATEST ADVENTURE OF MY LIFE. AND I LOVE YOU SO MUCH...EVEN IF YOU DON'T LOVE ME BACK.
OH MY GOD, I DO LOVE YOU, FAITH. I JUST...I'M SO SAD...I'M SO SAD... I NEED TO GET AWAY FROM IT. I NEED TO BE ALONE FOR A WHILE. TO PROCESS IT ALL.
YEAH. I'M SAD TOO. BUT I WAS ALONE FOR SO LONG. SO WAS TORQUE. AND WE'RE TIRED OF IT. I GUESS YOU AND ME, WE'RE JUST DIFFERENT THAT WAY.
GOODBYE, KRIS.
GOODBYE, FAITH...
"...FORGIVE ME IF I'VE LET YOU DOWN."

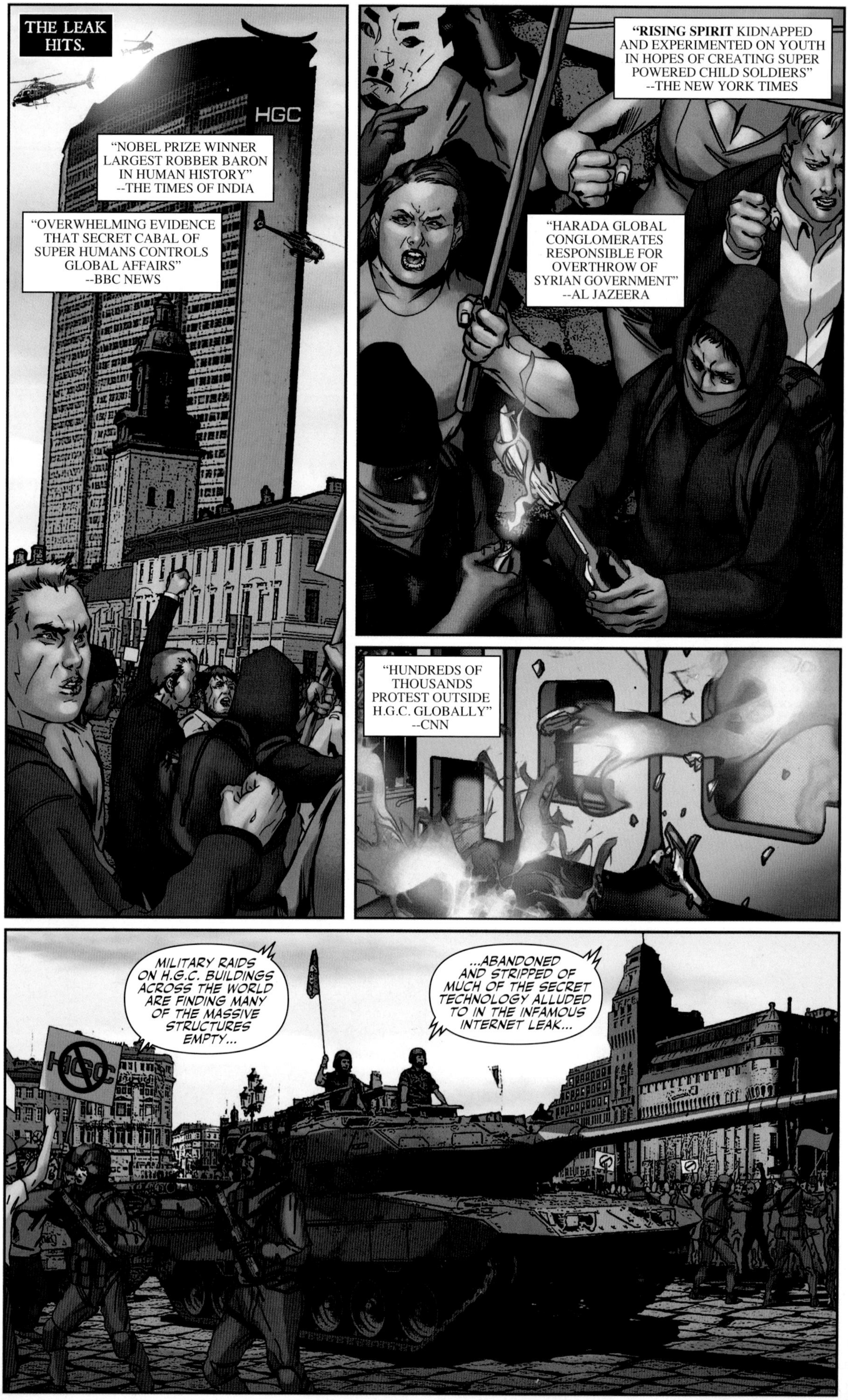
THE LEAK HITS.
"NOBEL PRIZE WINNER LARGEST ROBBER BARON IN HUMAN HISTORY" --THE TIMES OF INDIA
"OVERWHELMING EVIDENCE THAT SECRET CABAL OF SUPER HUMANS CONTROLS GLOBAL AFFAIRS" --BBC NEWS
HGC
"RISING SPIRIT KIDNAPPED AND EXPERIMENTED ON YOUTH IN HOPES OF CREATING SUPER POWERED CHILD SOLDIERS" --THE NEW YORK TIMES
"HARADA GLOBAL CONGLOMERATES RESPONSIBLE FOR OVERTHROW OF SYRIAN GOVERNMENT" --AL JAZEERA
"HUNDREDS OF THOUSANDS PROTEST OUTSIDE H.G.C. GLOBALLY" --CNN
MILITARY RAIDS ON H.G.C. BUILDINGS ACROSS THE WORLD ARE FINDING MANY OF THE MASSIVE STRUCTURES EMPTY...
...ABANDONED AND STRIPPED OF MUCH OF THE SECRET TECHNOLOGY ALLUDED TO IN THE INFAMOUS INTERNET LEAK...
HGC

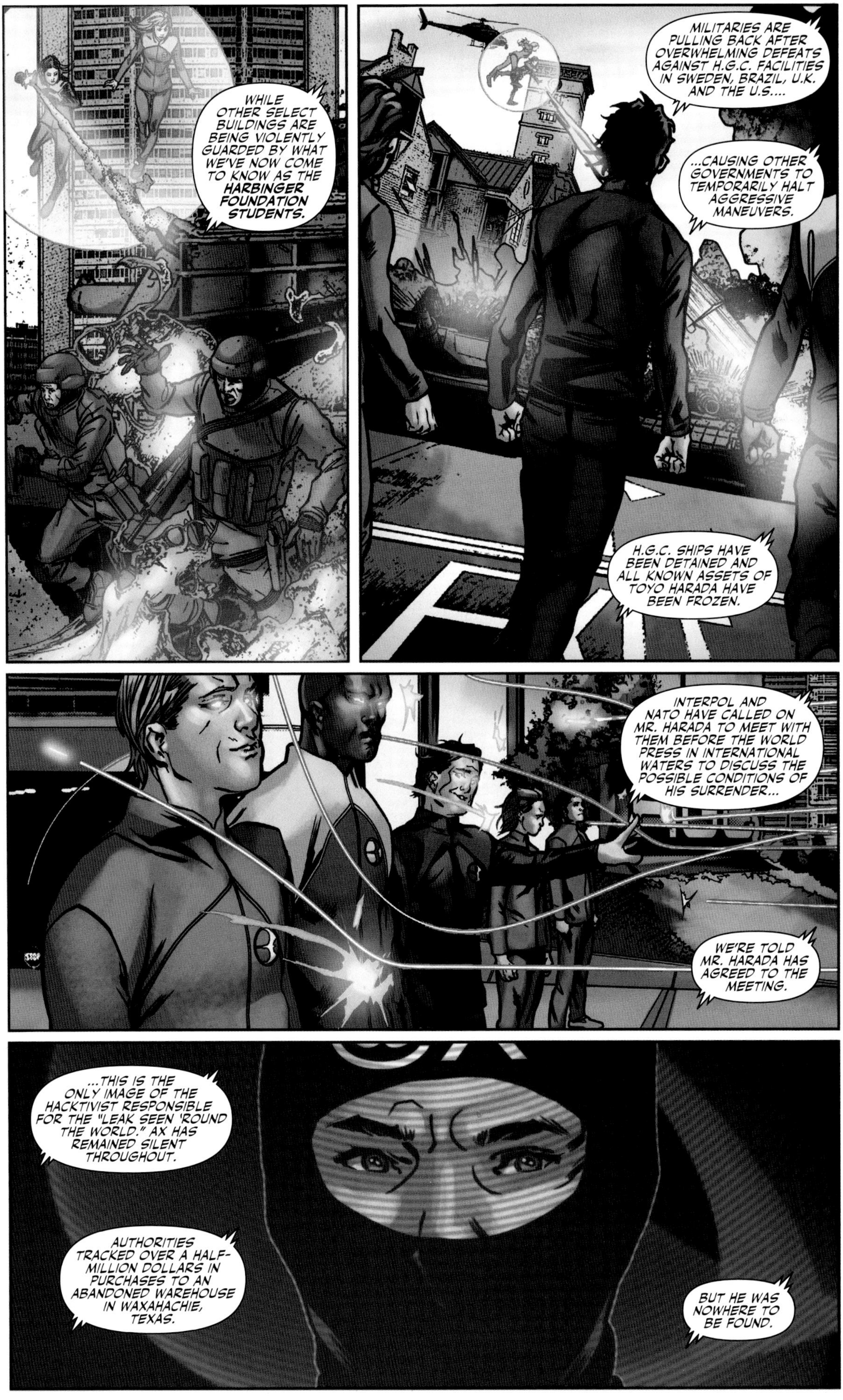
WHILE OTHER SELECT BUILDINGS ARE BEING VIOLENTLY GUARDED BY WHAT WE'VE NOW COME TO KNOW AS THE **HARBINGER FOUNDATION STUDENTS.**
MILITARIES ARE PULLING BACK AFTER OVERWHELMING DEFEATS AGAINST H.G.C. FACILITIES IN SWEDEN, BRAZIL, U.K. AND THE U.S....
...CAUSING OTHER GOVERNMENTS TO TEMPORARILY HALT AGGRESSIVE MANEUVERS.
H.G.C. SHIPS HAVE BEEN DETAINED AND ALL KNOWN ASSETS OF TOYO HARADA HAVE BEEN FROZEN.
INTERPOL AND NATO HAVE CALLED ON MR. HARADA TO MEET WITH THEM BEFORE THE WORLD PRESS IN INTERNATIONAL WATERS TO DISCUSS THE POSSIBLE CONDITIONS OF HIS SURRENDER...
WE'RE TOLD MR. HARADA HAS AGREED TO THE MEETING.
...THIS IS THE ONLY IMAGE OF THE HACKTIVIST RESPONSIBLE FOR THE "LEAK SEEN 'ROUND THE WORLD." AX HAS REMAINED SILENT THROUGHOUT.
AUTHORITIES TRACKED OVER A HALF-MILLION DOLLARS IN PURCHASES TO AN ABANDONED WAREHOUSE IN WAXAHACHIE, TEXAS.
BUT HE WAS NOWHERE TO BE FOUND.

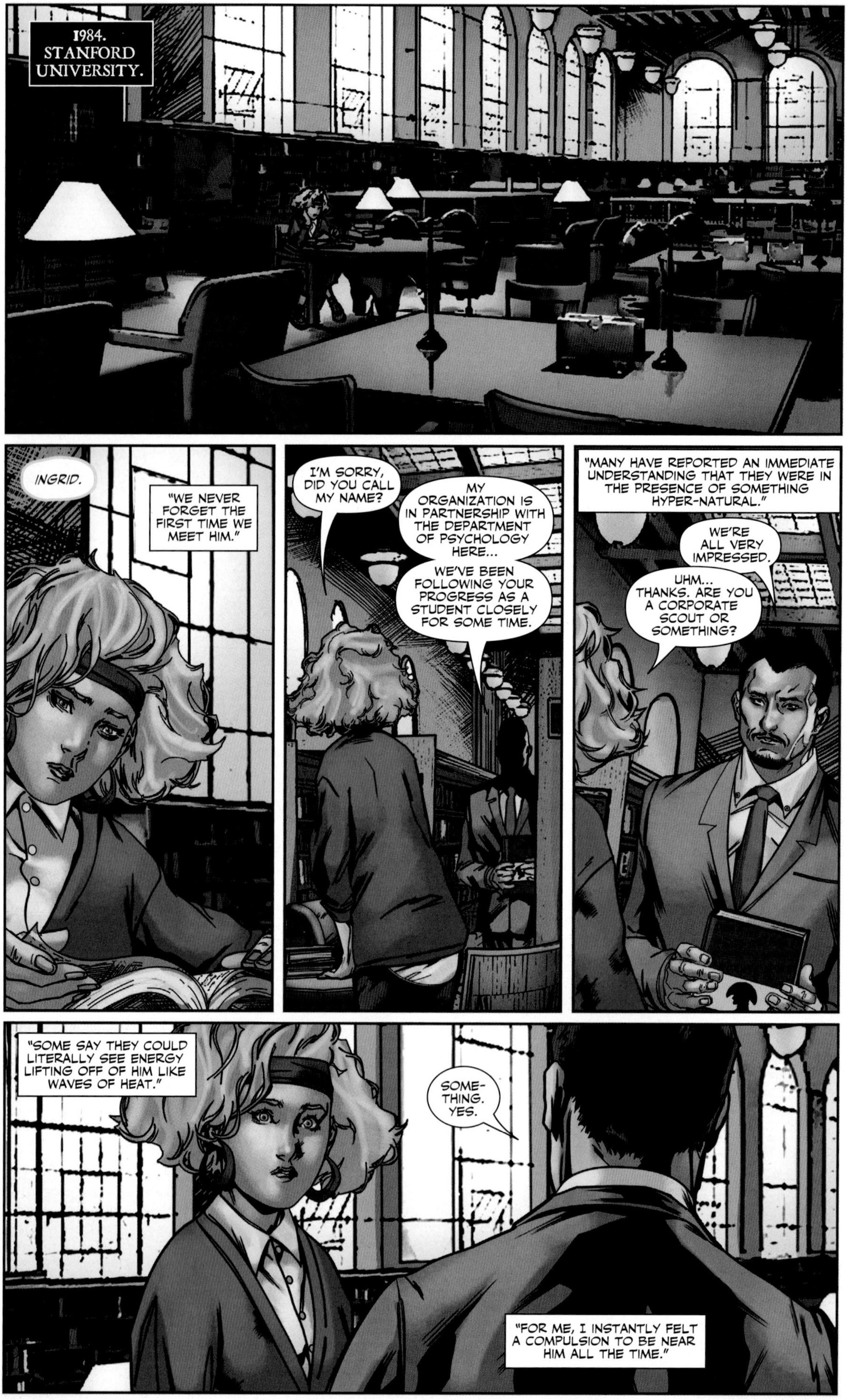
1984.
STANFORD UNIVERSITY.
INGRID.
"WE NEVER FORGET THE FIRST TIME WE MEET HIM."
I'M SORRY, DID YOU CALL MY NAME?
MY ORGANIZATION IS IN PARTNERSHIP WITH THE DEPARTMENT OF PSYCHOLOGY HERE...
WE'VE BEEN FOLLOWING YOUR PROGRESS AS A STUDENT CLOSELY FOR SOME TIME.
"MANY HAVE REPORTED AN IMMEDIATE UNDERSTANDING THAT THEY WERE IN THE PRESENCE OF SOMETHING HYPER-NATURAL."
WE'RE ALL VERY IMPRESSED.
UHM... THANKS. ARE YOU A CORPORATE SCOUT OR SOMETHING?
"SOME SAY THEY COULD LITERALLY SEE ENERGY LIFTING OFF OF HIM LIKE WAVES OF HEAT."
SOME-THING. YES.
"FOR ME, I INSTANTLY FELT A COMPULSION TO BE NEAR HIM ALL THE TIME."

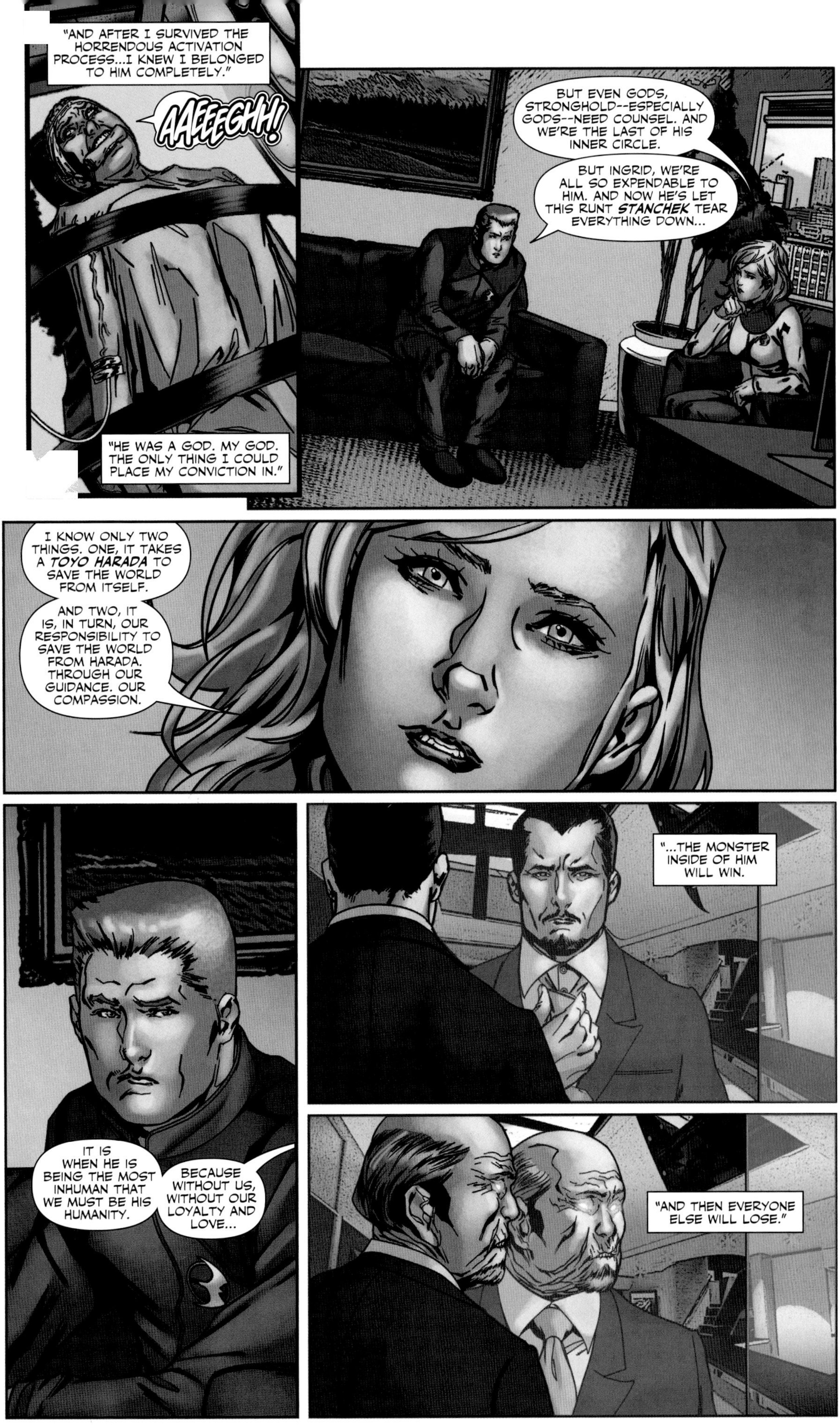
"AND AFTER I SURVIVED THE HORRENDOUS ACTIVATION PROCESS...I KNEW I BELONGED TO HIM COMPLETELY."
AAEEEGHH!
"HE WAS A GOD. MY GOD. THE ONLY THING I COULD PLACE MY CONVICTION IN."
BUT EVEN GODS, STRONGHOLD--ESPECIALLY GODS--NEED COUNSEL. AND WE'RE THE LAST OF HIS INNER CIRCLE.
BUT INGRID, WE'RE ALL SO EXPENDABLE TO HIM. AND NOW HE'S LET THIS RUNT STANCHEK TEAR EVERYTHING DOWN...
I KNOW ONLY TWO THINGS. ONE, IT TAKES A TOYO HARADA TO SAVE THE WORLD FROM ITSELF.
AND TWO, IT IS, IN TURN, OUR RESPONSIBILITY TO SAVE THE WORLD FROM HARADA. THROUGH OUR GUIDANCE. OUR COMPASSION.
IT IS WHEN HE IS BEING THE MOST INHUMAN THAT WE MUST BE HIS HUMANITY.
BECAUSE WITHOUT US, WITHOUT OUR LOYALTY AND LOVE...
"...THE MONSTER INSIDE OF HIM WILL WIN.
"AND THEN EVERYONE ELSE WILL LOSE."

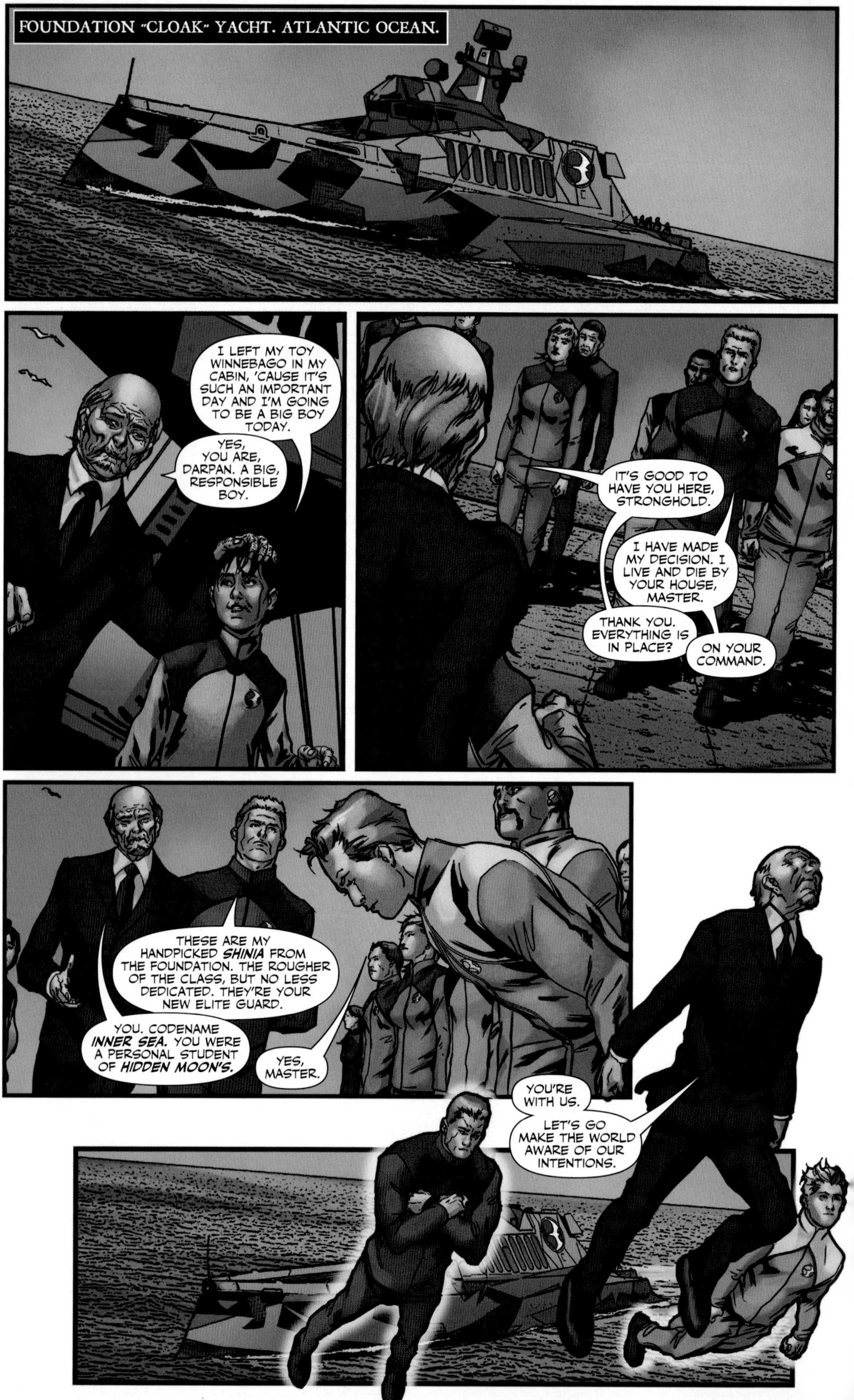
FOUNDATION "CLOAK" YACHT. ATLANTIC OCEAN.
I LEFT MY TOY WINNEBAGO IN MY CABIN, 'CAUSE IT'S SUCH AN IMPORTANT DAY AND I'M GOING TO BE A BIG BOY TODAY.
YES, YOU ARE, DARPAN. A BIG, RESPONSIBLE BOY.
IT'S GOOD TO HAVE YOU HERE, STRONGHOLD.
I HAVE MADE MY DECISION. I LIVE AND DIE BY YOUR HOUSE, MASTER.
THANK YOU. EVERYTHING IS IN PLACE?
ON YOUR COMMAND.
THESE ARE MY HANDPICKED SHINIA FROM THE FOUNDATION. THE ROUGHER OF THE CLASS, BUT NO LESS DEDICATED. THEY'RE YOUR NEW ELITE GUARD.
YOU. CODENAME INNER SEA. YOU WERE A PERSONAL STUDENT OF HIDDEN MOON'S.
YES, MASTER.
YOU'RE WITH US.
LET'S GO MAKE THE WORLD AWARE OF OUR INTENTIONS.

JESUS CHRIST... I DON'T KNOW IF YOU CAN SEE THIS ON *EOTS,* CARRIER BUSH. BUT IT'S A HELL OF A THING.

WELCOMING TEAM, YOU SHOULD BE IN VISUAL RANGE AT ANY MOMENT. OVER.

ROGER THAT, CARRIER BUSH. OVER.

GOT 'EM COMING IN FROM THE WEST.

"THIS IS ANDREA RODRIGUEZ REPORTING FROM THE SUPERCARRIER *U.S.S. GEORGE H.W. BUSH...*

"...HERE TO WITNESS THE AGREED-UPON AND SCHEDULED SURRENDER OF MULTI-BILLIONAIRE C.E.O. *TOYO HARADA.*"

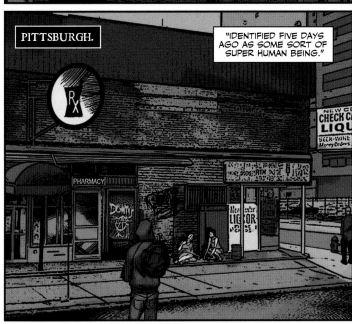

PITTSBURGH.

"IDENTIFIED FIVE DAYS AGO AS SOME SORT OF SUPER HUMAN BEING."

DING

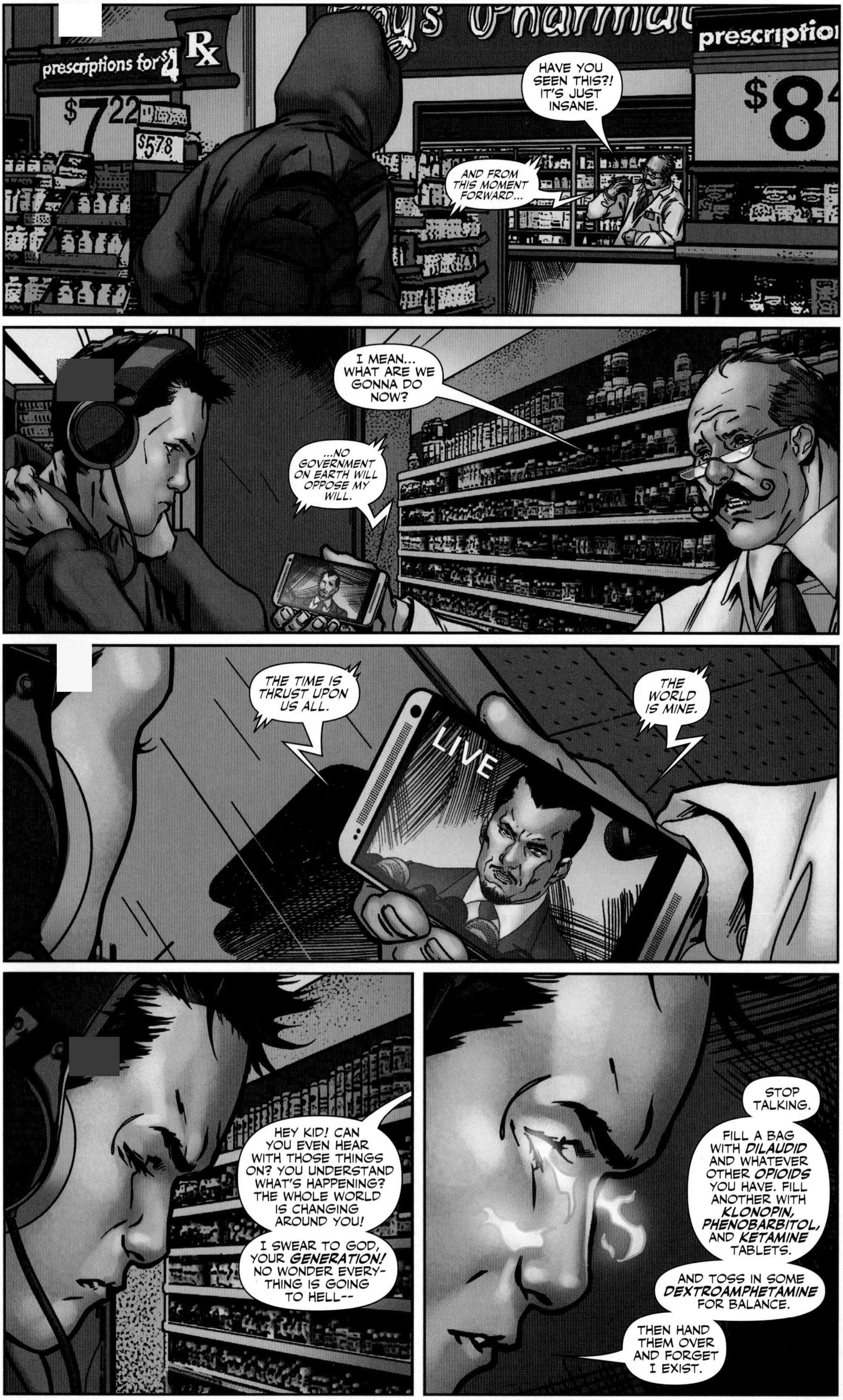
prescriptions for $4
$7.22
$5.78
prescription
$8
HAVE YOU SEEN THIS?! IT'S JUST INSANE.
AND FROM THIS MOMENT FORWARD...
I MEAN... WHAT ARE WE GONNA DO NOW?
...NO GOVERNMENT ON EARTH WILL OPPOSE MY WILL.
THE TIME IS THRUST UPON US ALL.
LIVE
THE WORLD IS MINE.
HEY KID! CAN YOU EVEN HEAR WITH THOSE THINGS ON? YOU UNDERSTAND WHAT'S HAPPENING? THE WHOLE WORLD IS CHANGING AROUND YOU!
I SWEAR TO GOD, YOUR *GENERATION!* NO WONDER EVERY-THING IS GOING TO HELL--
STOP TALKING.
FILL A BAG WITH *DILAUDID* AND WHATEVER OTHER *OPIOIDS* YOU HAVE. FILL ANOTHER WITH *KLONOPIN, PHENOBARBITOL,* AND *KETAMINE* TABLETS.
AND TOSS IN SOME *DEXTROAMPHETAMINE* FOR BALANCE.
THEN HAND THEM OVER AND FORGET I EXIST.

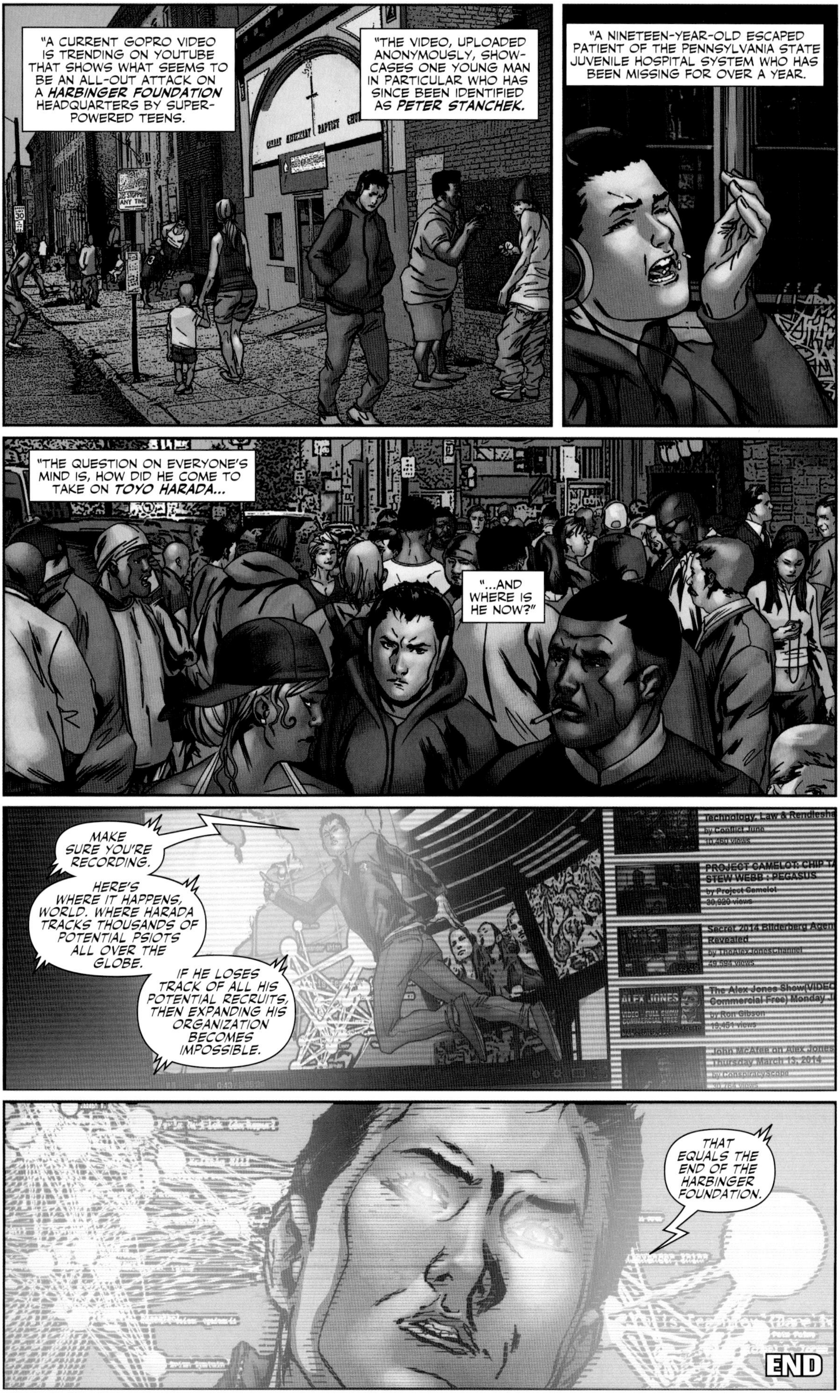

"A CURRENT GOPRO VIDEO IS TRENDING ON YOUTUBE THAT SHOWS WHAT SEEMS TO BE AN ALL-OUT ATTACK ON A HARBINGER FOUNDATION HEADQUARTERS BY SUPER-POWERED TEENS.
"THE VIDEO, UPLOADED ANONYMOUSLY, SHOWCASES ONE YOUNG MAN IN PARTICULAR WHO HAS SINCE BEEN IDENTIFIED AS PETER STANCHEK.
"A NINETEEN-YEAR-OLD ESCAPED PATIENT OF THE PENNSYLVANIA STATE JUVENILE HOSPITAL SYSTEM WHO HAS BEEN MISSING FOR OVER A YEAR.
"THE QUESTION ON EVERYONE'S MIND IS, HOW DID HE COME TO TAKE ON TOYO HARADA...
"...AND WHERE IS HE NOW?"
MAKE SURE YOU'RE RECORDING.
HERE'S WHERE IT HAPPENS, WORLD. WHERE HARADA TRACKS THOUSANDS OF POTENTIAL PSIOTS ALL OVER THE GLOBE.
IF HE LOSES TRACK OF ALL HIS POTENTIAL RECRUITS, THEN EXPANDING HIS ORGANIZATION BECOMES IMPOSSIBLE.
Technology, Law & Rendlesha
by Conflict June
PROJECT CAMELOT: CHIP TA
STEW WEBB : PEGASUS
by Project Camelot
Secret 2014 Bilderberg Agen
Revealed
by TheAlexJonesChannel
The Alex Jones Show(VIDEO
Commercial Free) Monday J
by Ron Gibson
John McAfee on Alex Jones
Thursday March 13, 2014
by ConspiracyScope
THAT EQUALS THE END OF THE HARBINGER FOUNDATION.
END

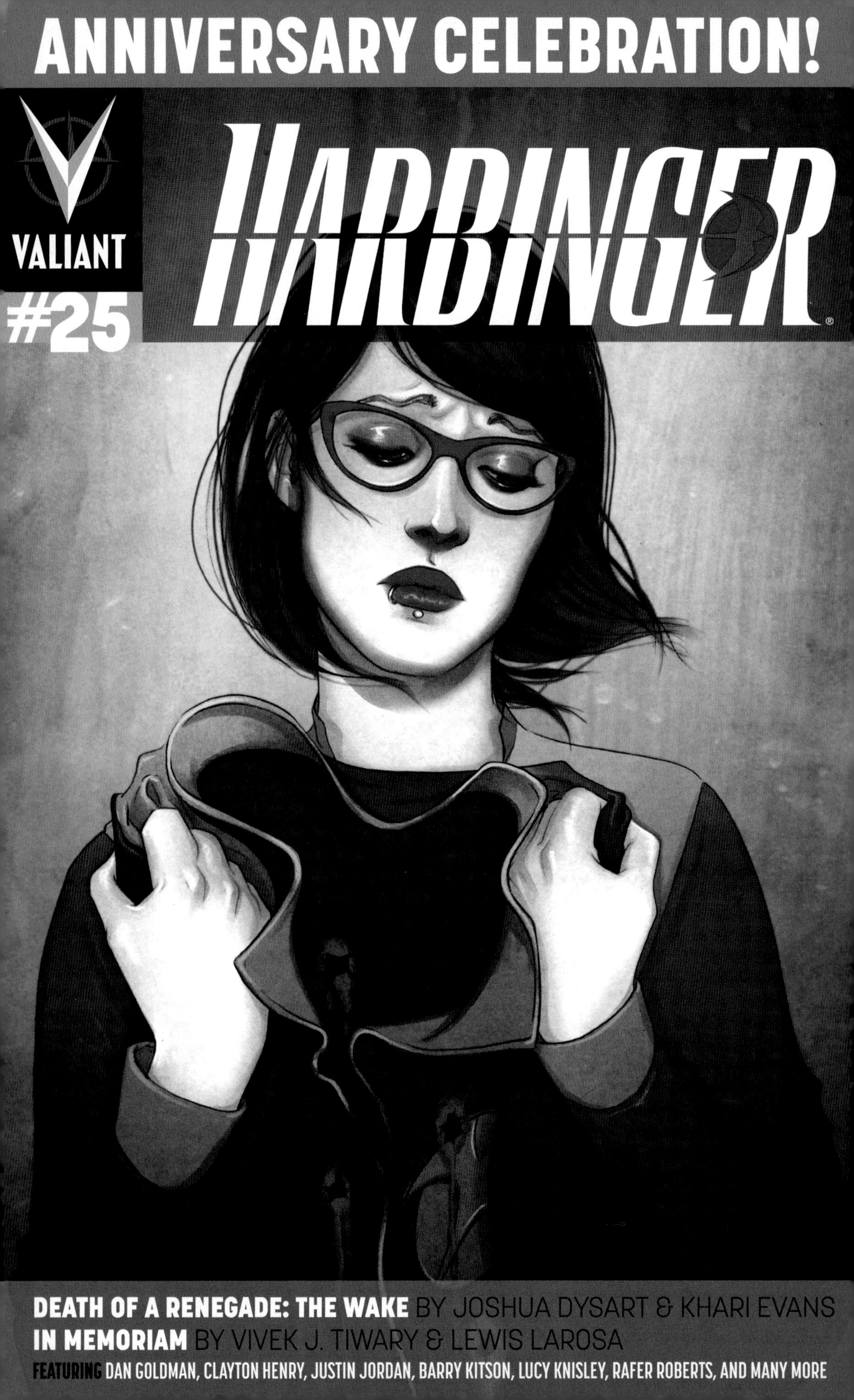
ANNIVERSARY CELEBRATION!
VALIANT
#25
HARBINGER®
DEATH OF A RENEGADE: THE WAKE BY JOSHUA DYSART & KHARI EVANS
IN MEMORIAM BY VIVEK J. TIWARY & LEWIS LAROSA
FEATURING DAN GOLDMAN, CLAYTON HENRY, JUSTIN JORDAN, BARRY KITSON, LUCY KNISLEY, RAFER ROBERTS, AND MANY MORE

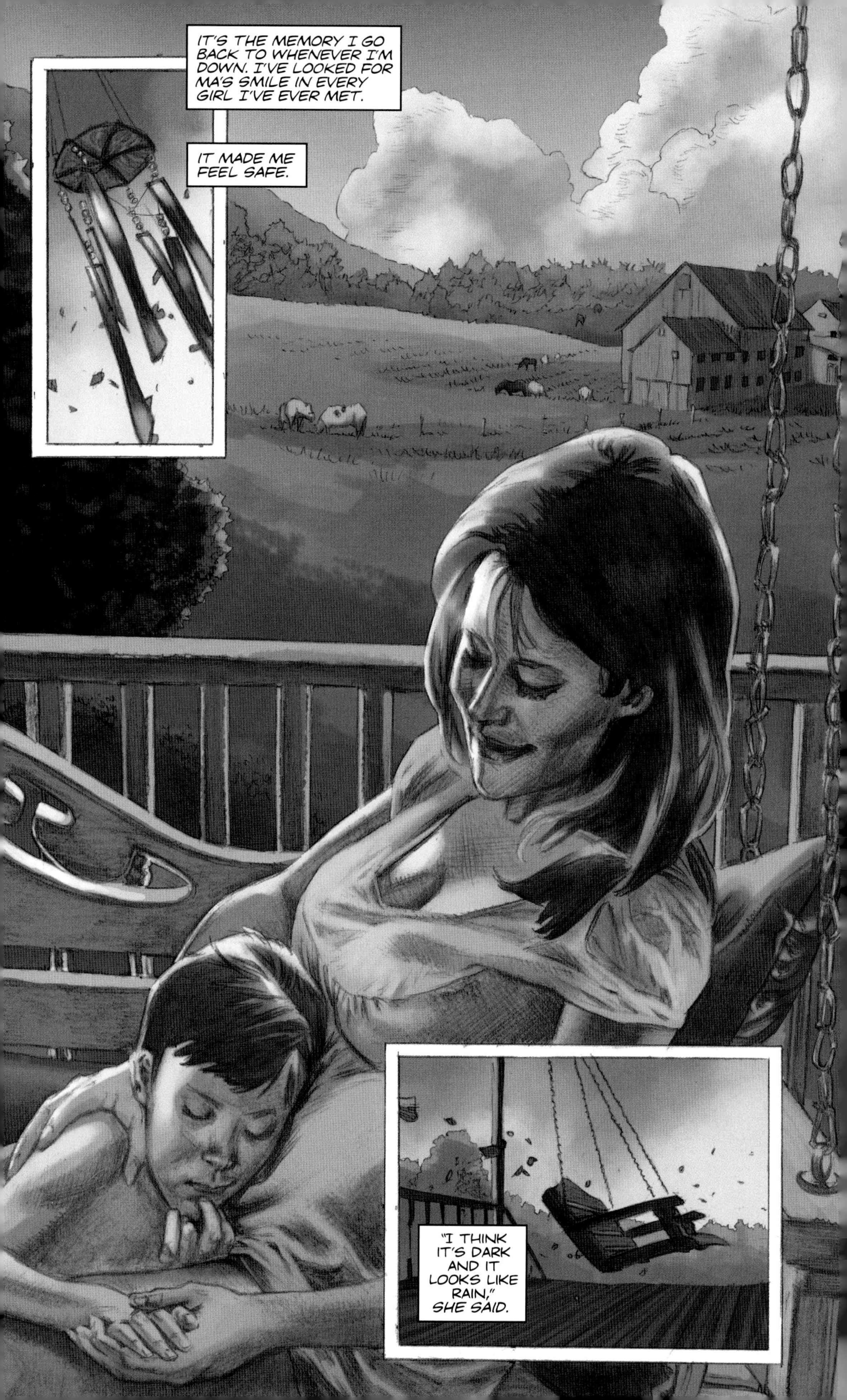
IT'S THE MEMORY I GO BACK TO WHENEVER I'M DOWN. I'VE LOOKED FOR MA'S SMILE IN EVERY GIRL I'VE EVER MET.
IT MADE ME FEEL SAFE.
"I THINK IT'S DARK AND IT LOOKS LIKE RAIN," SHE SAID.

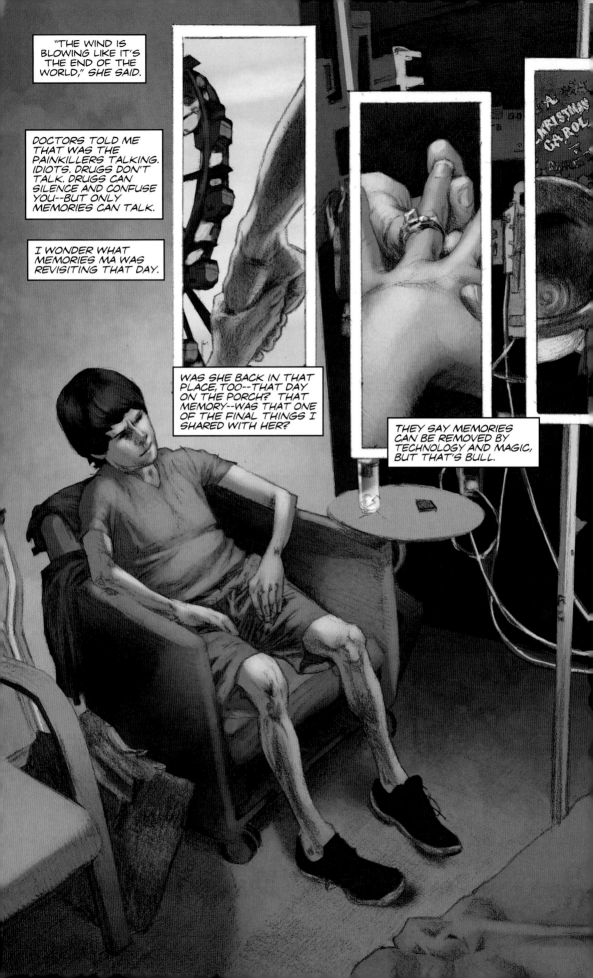

"THE WIND IS BLOWING LIKE IT'S THE END OF THE WORLD," SHE SAID.

DOCTORS TOLD ME THAT WAS THE PAINKILLERS TALKING. IDIOTS. DRUGS DON'T TALK. DRUGS CAN SILENCE AND CONFUSE YOU--BUT ONLY MEMORIES CAN TALK.

I WONDER WHAT MEMORIES MA WAS REVISITING THAT DAY.

WAS SHE BACK IN THAT PLACE, TOO--THAT DAY ON THE PORCH? THAT MEMORY--WAS THAT ONE OF THE FINAL THINGS I SHARED WITH HER?

THEY SAY MEMORIES CAN BE REMOVED BY TECHNOLOGY AND MAGIC, BUT THAT'S BULL.

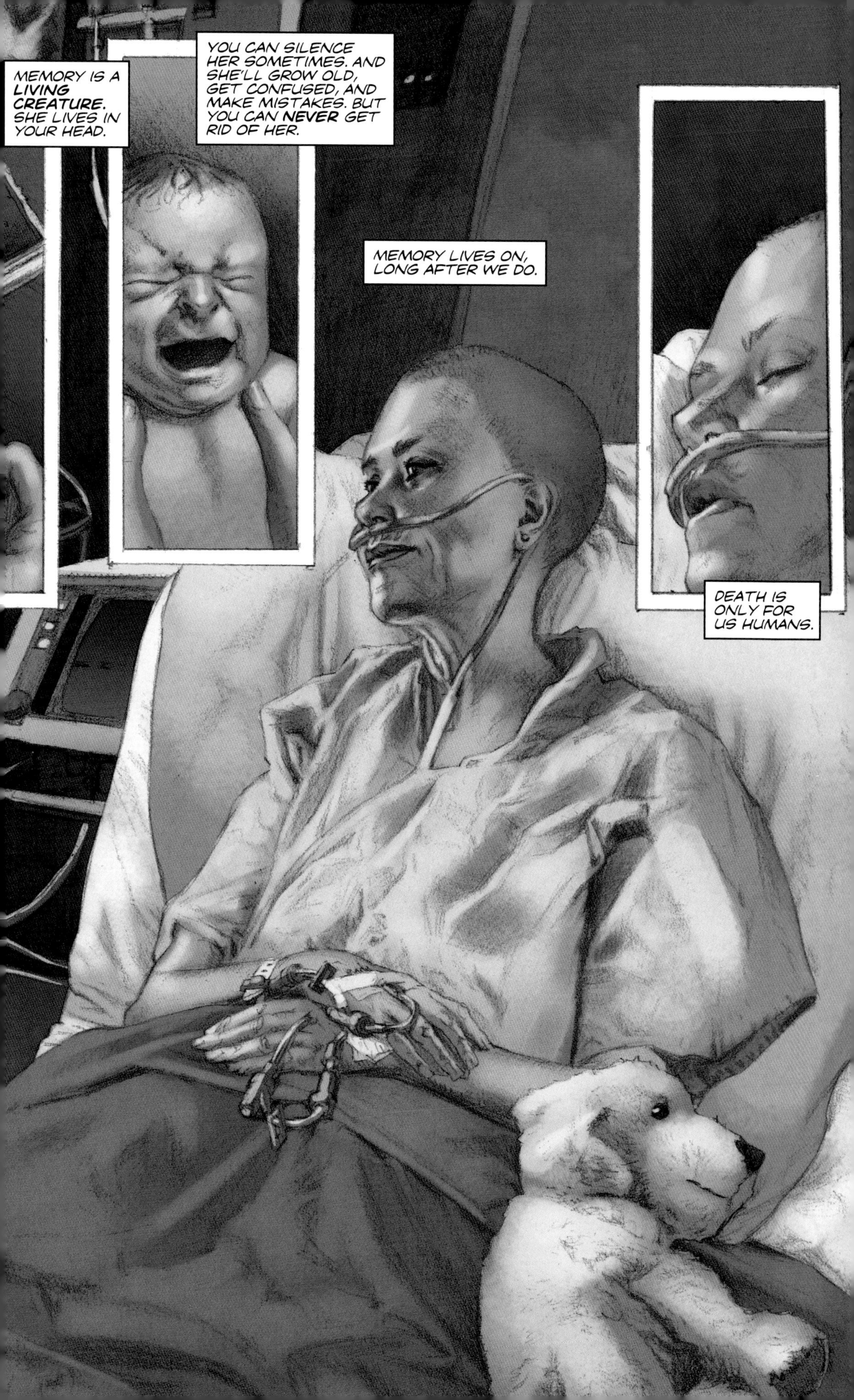
MEMORY IS A **LIVING CREATURE.** SHE LIVES IN YOUR HEAD.
YOU CAN SILENCE HER SOMETIMES. AND SHE'LL GROW OLD, GET CONFUSED, AND MAKE MISTAKES. BUT YOU CAN **NEVER** GET RID OF HER.
MEMORY LIVES ON, LONG AFTER WE DO.
DEATH IS ONLY FOR US HUMANS.

DAD DIED LONG BEFORE, AND I'VE GOT NO BROTHERS OR SISTERS. SO MA LEFT ME TRULY ALONE.

UNTIL I MET PETER STANCHEK.

MY BEST FRIEND.

PETER TOLD ME WHEN HE WAS A KID, HE HURT ANOTHER BOY ON THE PLAYGROUND.

THE BOY WAS A BULLY, SO HE DESERVED IT.

BUT IT WAS AN ACCIDENT. PETER DIDN'T MEAN TO HURT HIM.

AND THAT BOY GREW UP...

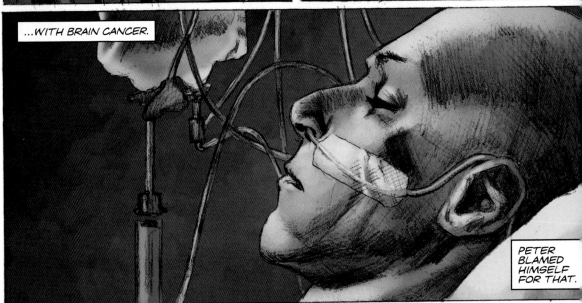

...WITH BRAIN CANCER.

PETER BLAMED HIMSELF FOR THAT.

HE KEPT TABS ON THAT BOY. SO WHEN WE FOUND OUT HE WAS DYING, I MADE PETER GO TO HIM. EVEN THOUGH WE WERE ON THE RUN--

I REMEMBER PETER'S FEAR AND CONFUSION. HE TOLD THE DOCTORS TO MAKE THAT BOY BETTER--

I KNEW IT WAS WORTH THE RISK.

AND HE COULDN'T UNDERSTAND WHY THEY WOULDN'T DO WHAT HE ASKED.

I KNEW EXACTLY HOW HE FELT.

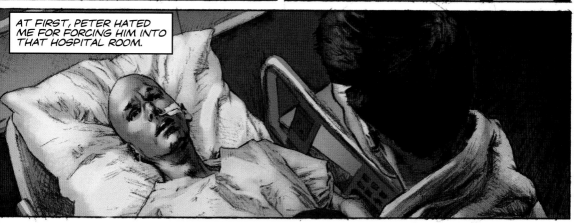

AT FIRST, PETER HATED ME FOR FORCING HIM INTO THAT HOSPITAL ROOM.

BUT WE TOOK THAT BOY INTO A MEMORY...

...AND I HELPED PETER THAT DAY.

LIKE PETER HELPED ME...

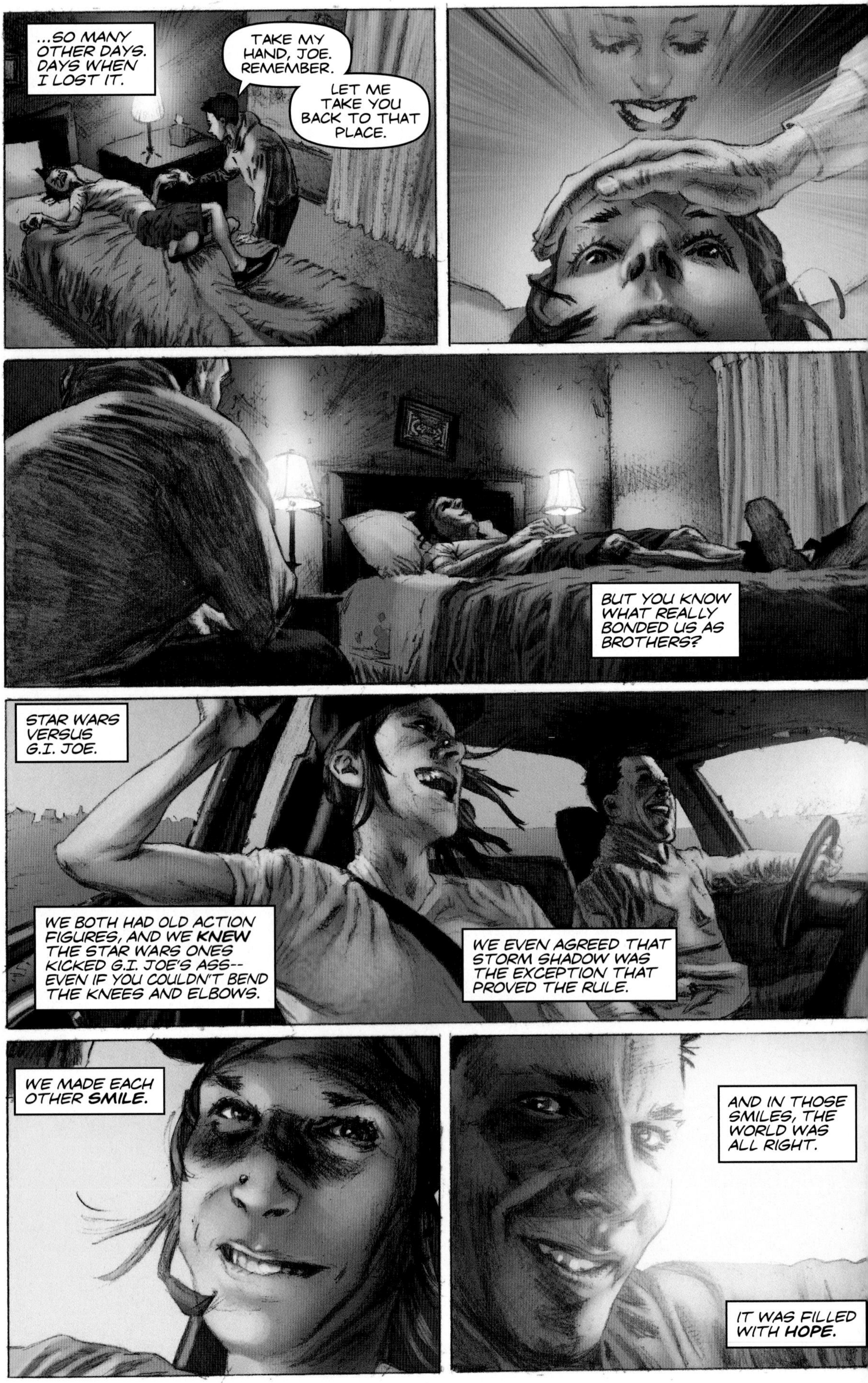
...SO MANY OTHER DAYS. DAYS WHEN I LOST IT.
TAKE MY HAND, JOE. REMEMBER.
LET ME TAKE YOU BACK TO THAT PLACE.
BUT YOU KNOW WHAT REALLY BONDED US AS BROTHERS?
STAR WARS VERSUS G.I. JOE.
WE BOTH HAD OLD ACTION FIGURES, AND WE **KNEW** THE STAR WARS ONES KICKED G.I. JOE'S ASS-- EVEN IF YOU COULDN'T BEND THE KNEES AND ELBOWS.
WE EVEN AGREED THAT STORM SHADOW WAS THE EXCEPTION THAT PROVED THE RULE.
WE MADE EACH OTHER **SMILE**.
AND IN THOSE SMILES, THE WORLD WAS ALL RIGHT.
IT WAS FILLED WITH **HOPE**.

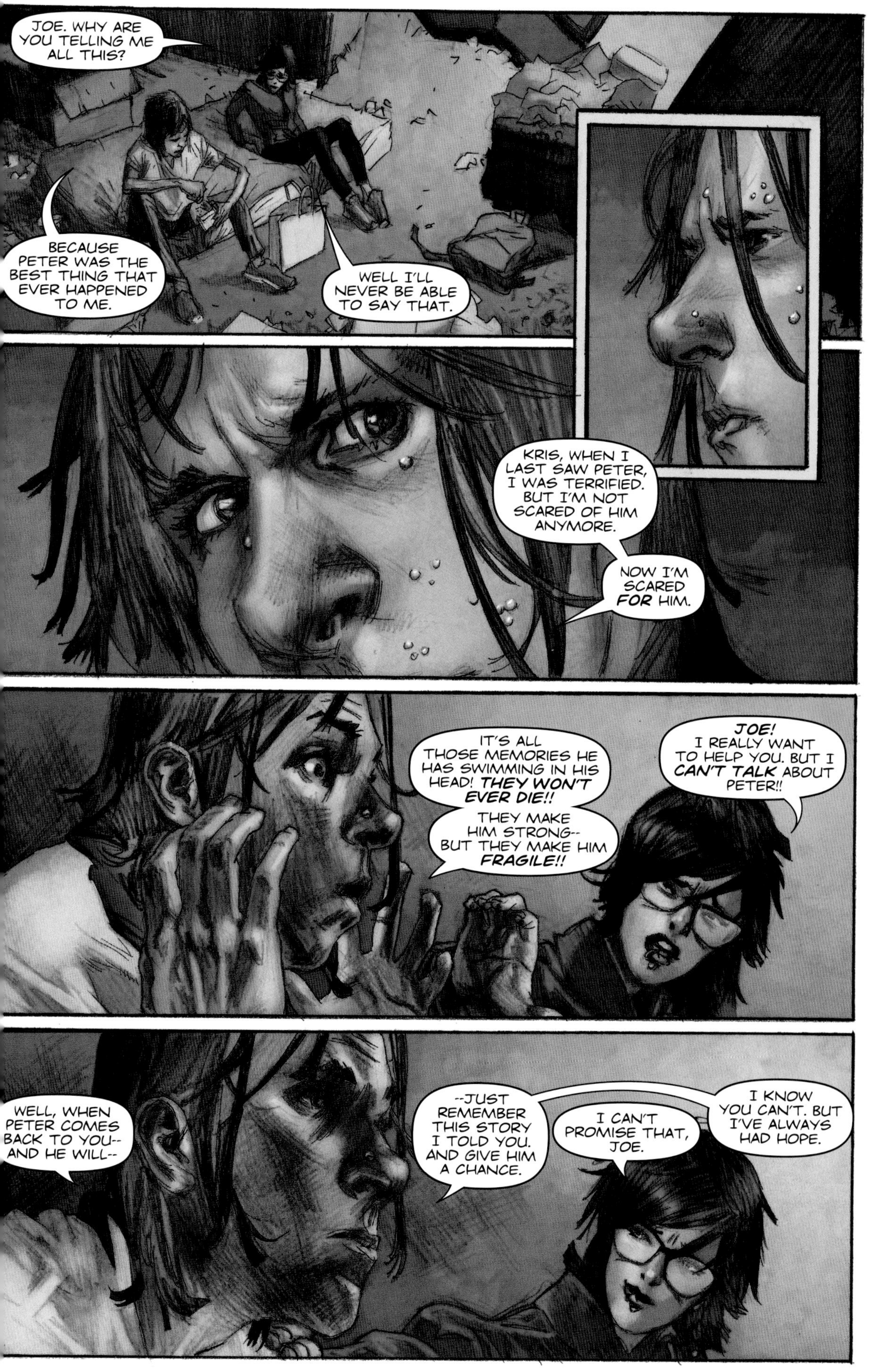
JOE. WHY ARE YOU TELLING ME ALL THIS?
BECAUSE PETER WAS THE BEST THING THAT EVER HAPPENED TO ME.
WELL I'LL NEVER BE ABLE TO SAY THAT.
KRIS, WHEN I LAST SAW PETER, I WAS TERRIFIED. BUT I'M NOT SCARED OF HIM ANYMORE.
NOW I'M SCARED **FOR** HIM.
IT'S ALL THOSE MEMORIES HE HAS SWIMMING IN HIS HEAD! ***THEY WON'T EVER DIE!!***
THEY MAKE HIM STRONG-- BUT THEY MAKE HIM ***FRAGILE!!***
JOE! I REALLY WANT TO HELP YOU. BUT I ***CAN'T TALK*** ABOUT PETER!!
WELL, WHEN PETER COMES BACK TO YOU-- AND HE WILL--
--JUST REMEMBER THIS STORY I TOLD YOU. AND GIVE HIM A CHANCE.
I CAN'T PROMISE THAT, JOE.
I KNOW YOU CAN'T. BUT I'VE ALWAYS HAD HOPE.

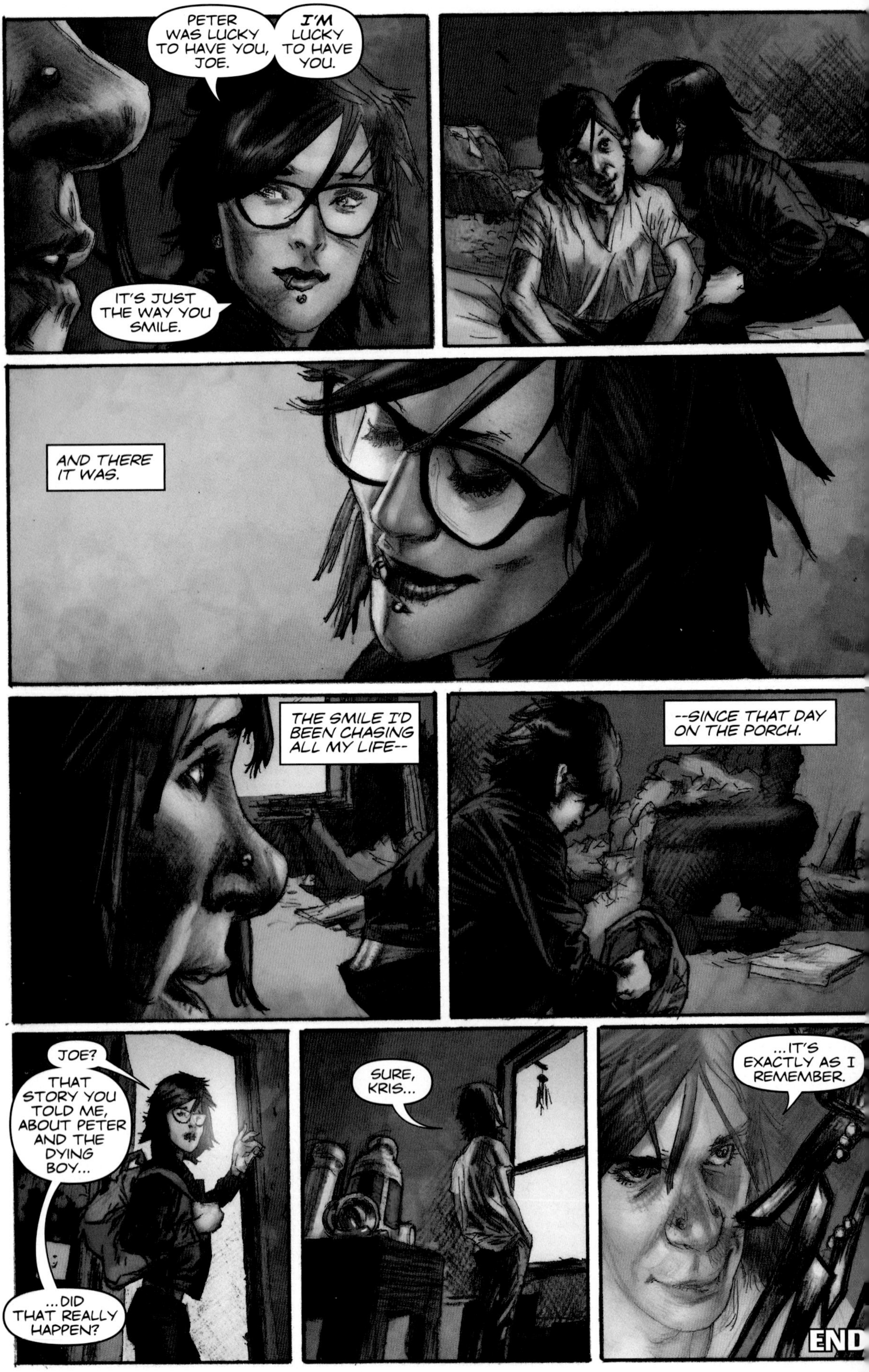
PETER WAS LUCKY TO HAVE YOU, JOE.
I'M LUCKY TO HAVE YOU.
IT'S JUST THE WAY YOU SMILE.
AND THERE IT WAS.
THE SMILE I'D BEEN CHASING ALL MY LIFE--
--SINCE THAT DAY ON THE PORCH.
JOE?
THAT STORY YOU TOLD ME, ABOUT PETER AND THE DYING BOY...
...DID THAT REALLY HAPPEN?
SURE, KRIS...
...IT'S EXACTLY AS I REMEMBER.
END

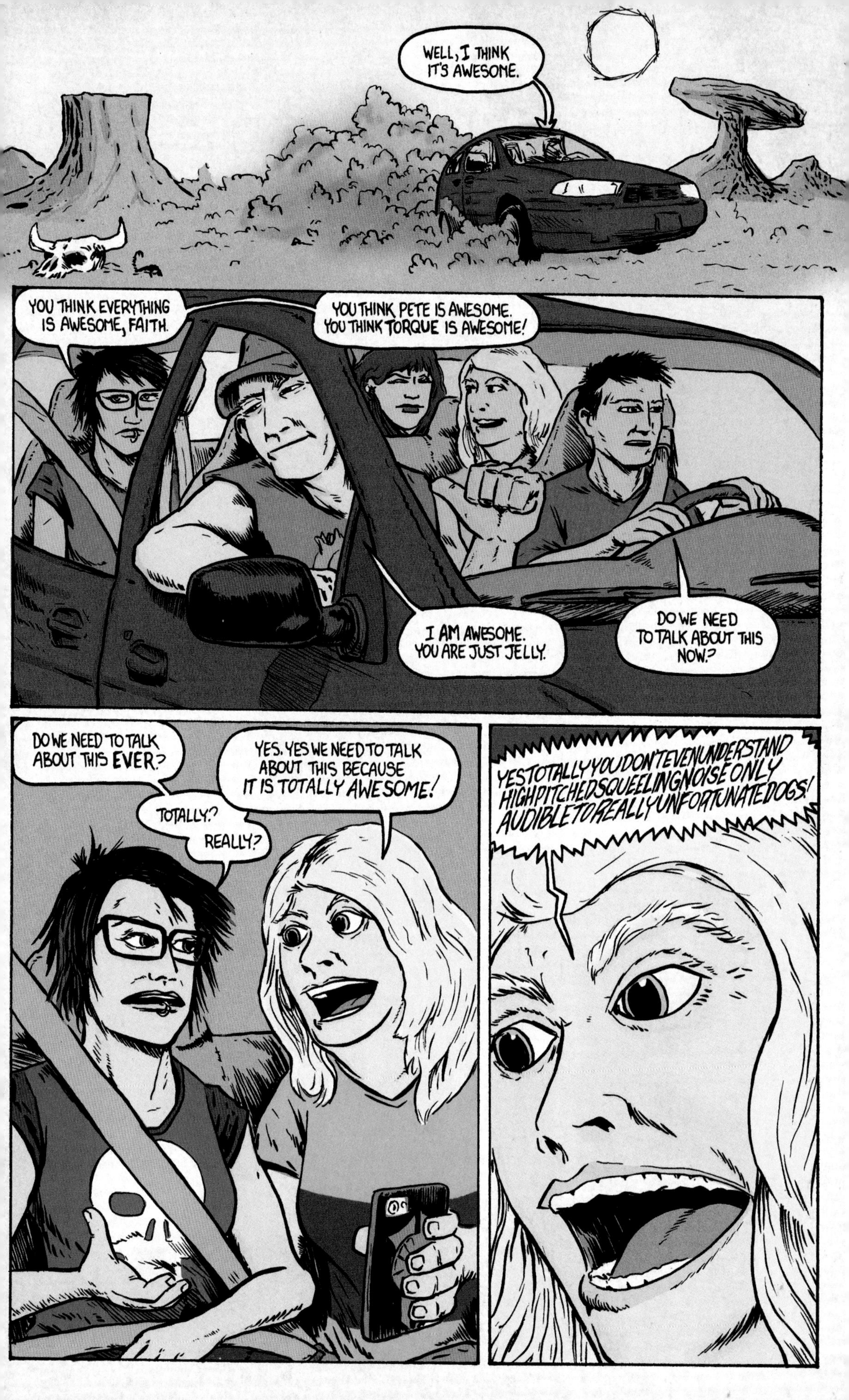
WELL, I THINK IT'S AWESOME.
YOU THINK EVERYTHING IS AWESOME, FAITH.
YOU THINK PETE IS AWESOME. YOU THINK TORQUE IS AWESOME!
I AM AWESOME. YOU ARE JUST JELLY.
DO WE NEED TO TALK ABOUT THIS NOW?
DO WE NEED TO TALK ABOUT THIS EVER?
TOTALLY?
REALLY?
YES. YES WE NEED TO TALK ABOUT THIS BECAUSE IT IS TOTALLY AWESOME!
YESTOTALLYYOUDON'TEVENUNDERSTAND HIGHPITCHEDSQUEELINGNOISE ONLY AUDIBLETOREALLYUNFORTUNATEDOGS!

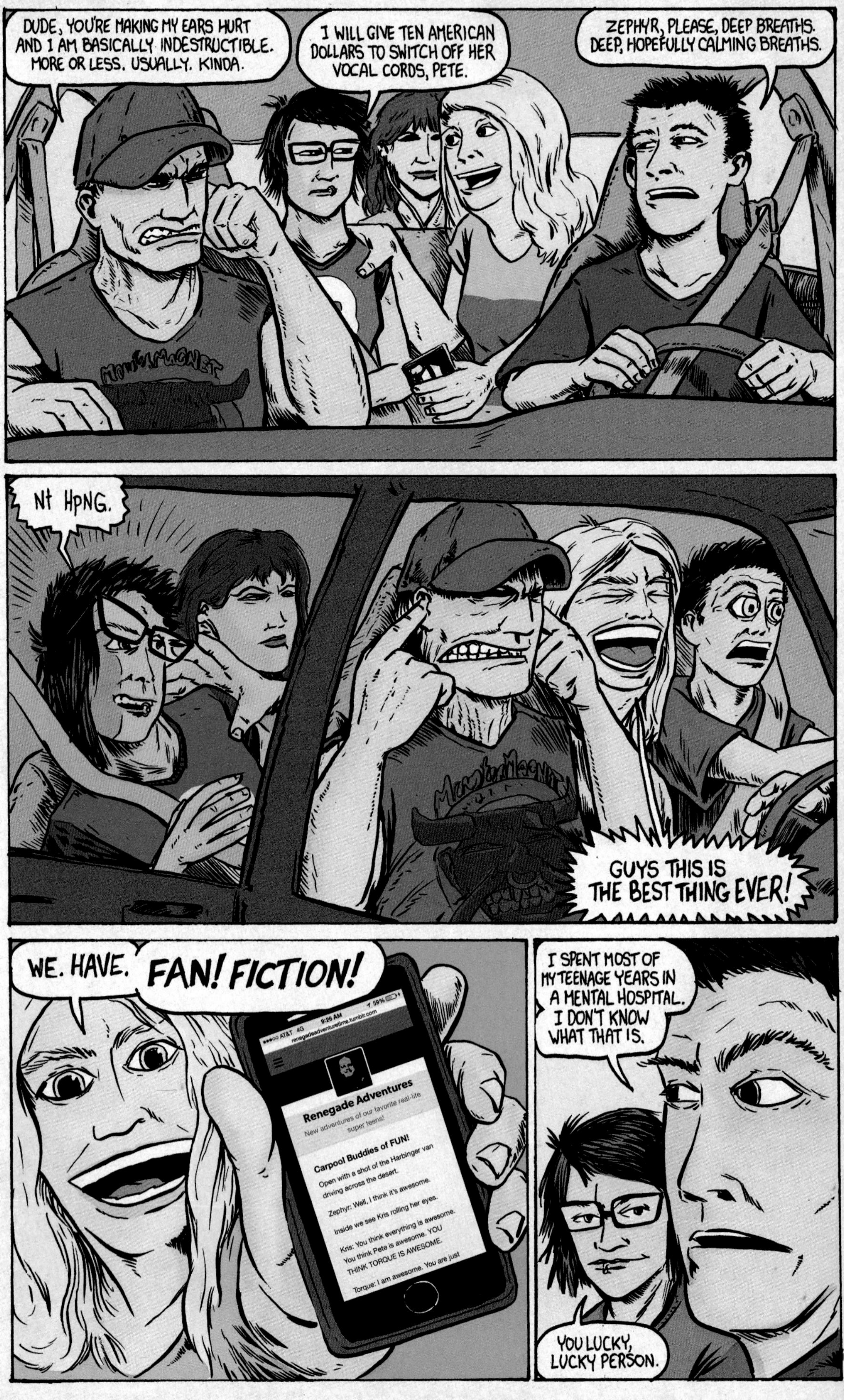
DUDE, YOU'RE MAKING MY EARS HURT AND I AM BASICALLY INDESTRUCTIBLE. MORE OR LESS. USUALLY. KINDA.
I WILL GIVE TEN AMERICAN DOLLARS TO SWITCH OFF HER VOCAL CORDS, PETE.
ZEPHYR, PLEASE, DEEP BREATHS. DEEP, HOPEFULLY CALMING BREATHS.
Nt HpNG.
GUYS THIS IS THE BEST THING EVER!
WE. HAVE.
FAN! FICTION!
renegadeadventuretime.tumblr.com
Renegade Adventures
New adventures of our favorite real-life super teens!
Carpool Buddies of FUN!
Open with a shot of the Harbinger van driving across the desert.
Zephyr: Well, I think it's awesome.
Inside we see Kris rolling her eyes.
Kris: You think everything is awesome. You think Pete is awesome. YOU THINK TORQUE IS AWESOME.
Torque: I am awesome. You are just
I SPENT MOST OF MY TEENAGE YEARS IN A MENTAL HOSPITAL. I DON'T KNOW WHAT THAT IS.
YOU LUCKY, LUCKY PERSON.

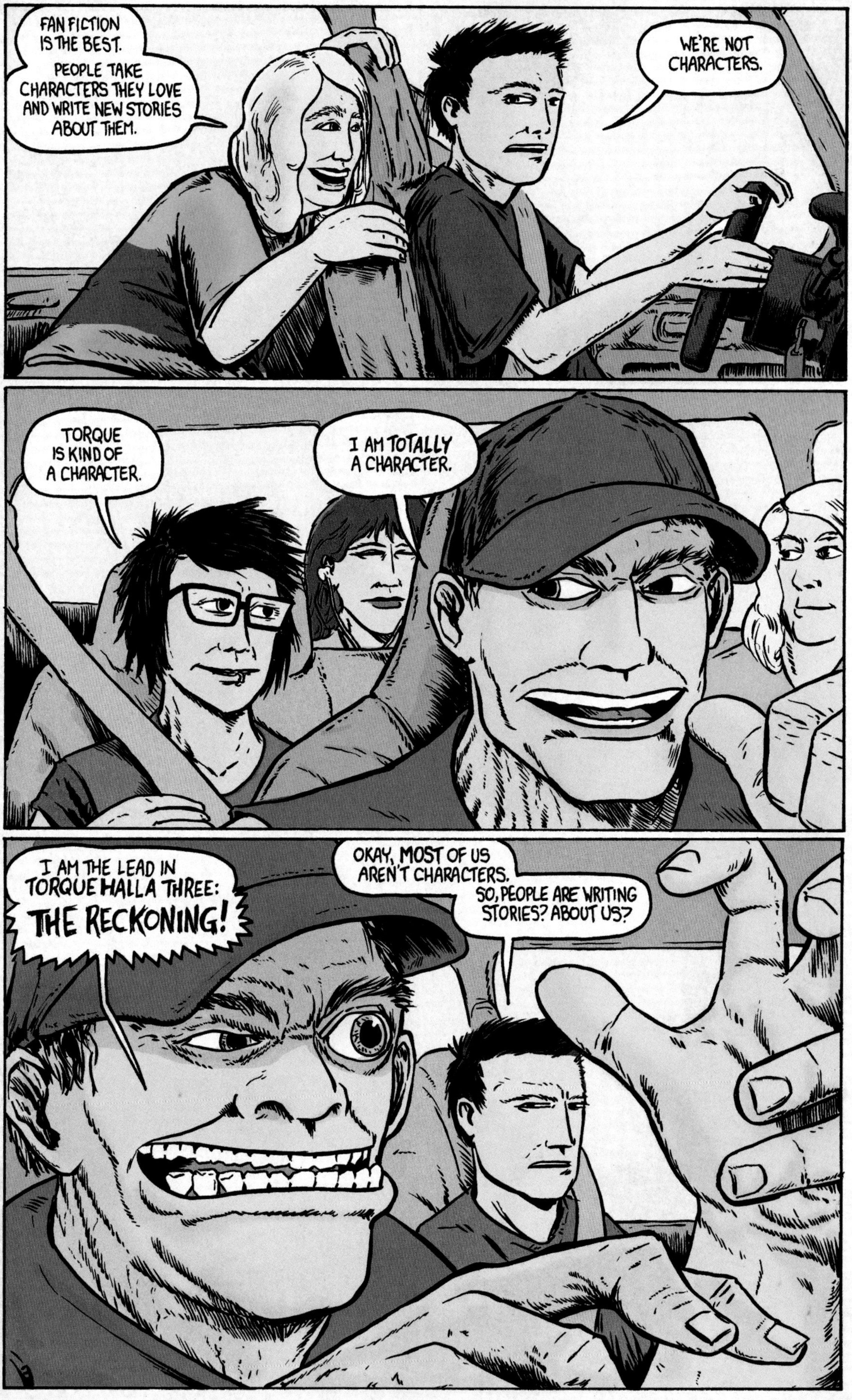
FAN FICTION IS THE BEST.
PEOPLE TAKE CHARACTERS THEY LOVE AND WRITE NEW STORIES ABOUT THEM.
WE'RE NOT CHARACTERS.
TORQUE IS KIND OF A CHARACTER.
I AM TOTALLY A CHARACTER.
I AM THE LEAD IN TORQUE HALLA THREE:
THE RECKONING!
OKAY, MOST OF US AREN'T CHARACTERS.
SO, PEOPLE ARE WRITING STORIES? ABOUT US?

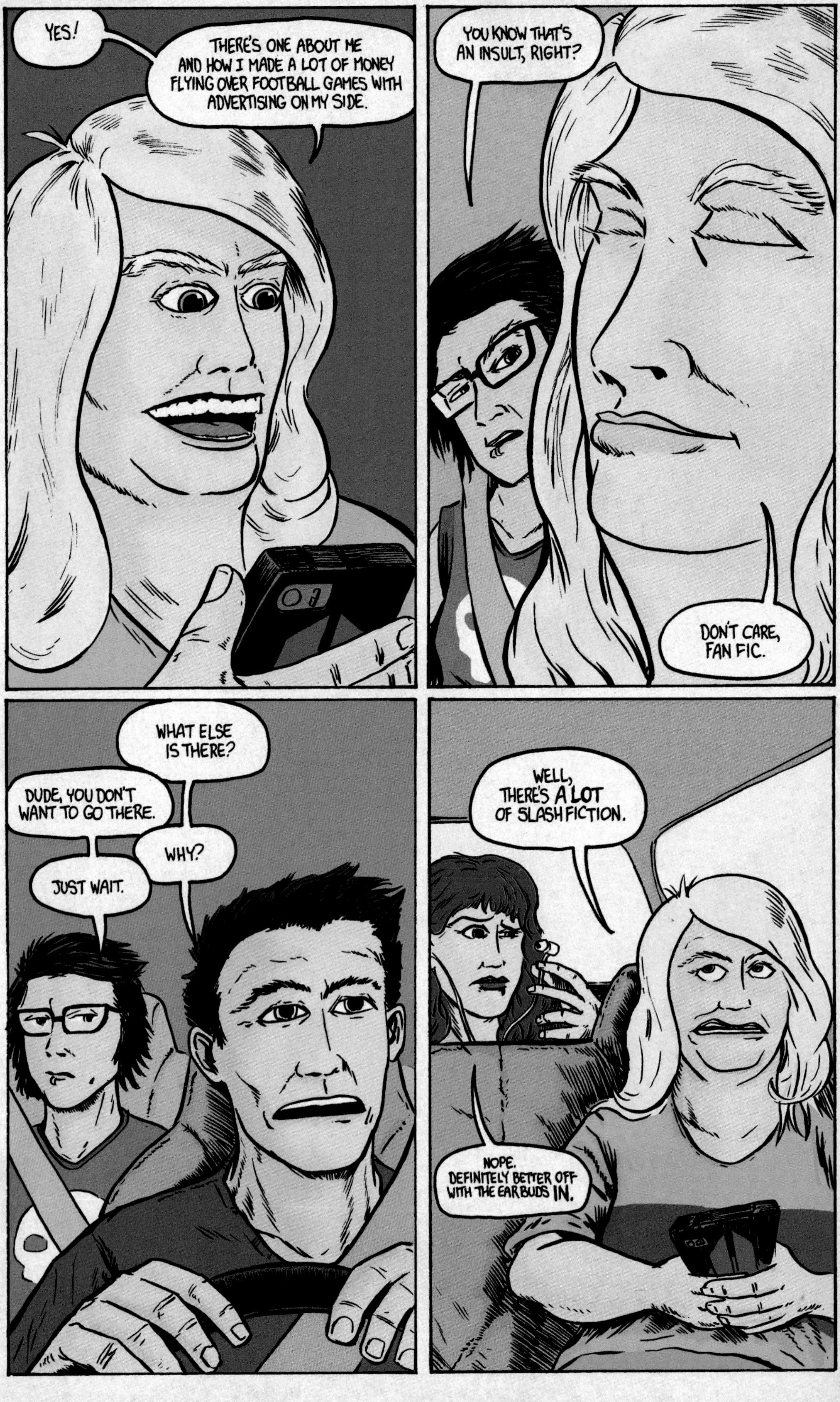
YES!
THERE'S ONE ABOUT ME AND HOW I MADE A LOT OF MONEY FLYING OVER FOOTBALL GAMES WITH ADVERTISING ON MY SIDE.
YOU KNOW THAT'S AN INSULT, RIGHT?
DON'T CARE, FAN FIC.
WHAT ELSE IS THERE?
DUDE, YOU DON'T WANT TO GO THERE.
WHY?
JUST WAIT.
WELL, THERE'S A LOT OF SLASH FICTION.
NOPE. DEFINITELY BETTER OFF WITH THE EAR BUDS IN.

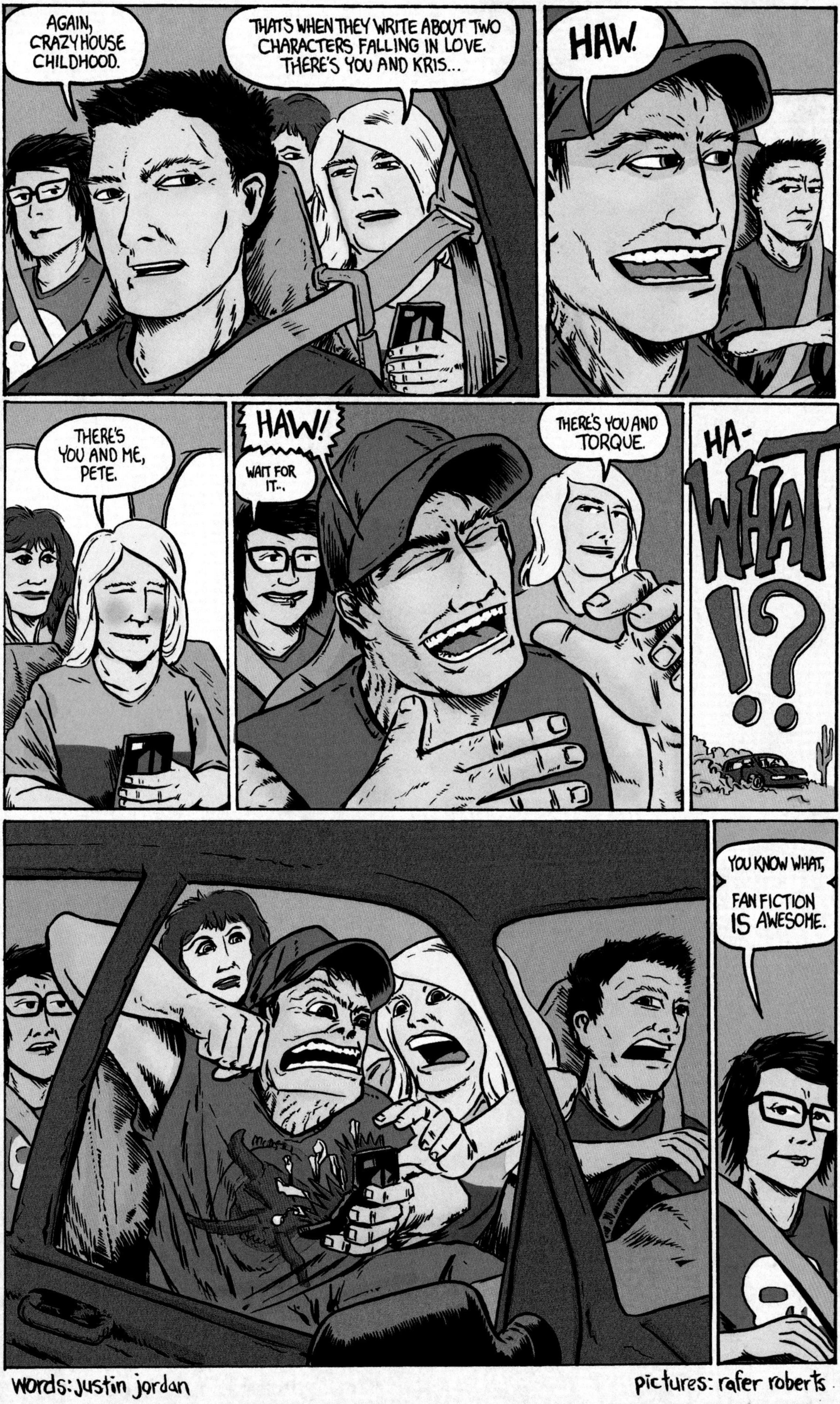
AGAIN, CRAZYHOUSE CHILDHOOD.
THAT'S WHEN THEY WRITE ABOUT TWO CHARACTERS FALLING IN LOVE. THERE'S YOU AND KRIS...
HAW.
THERE'S YOU AND ME, PETE.
HAW!
WAIT FOR IT...
THERE'S YOU AND TORQUE.
HA-WHAT!?
YOU KNOW WHAT,
FAN FICTION IS AWESOME.

words: justin jordan

pictures: rafer roberts

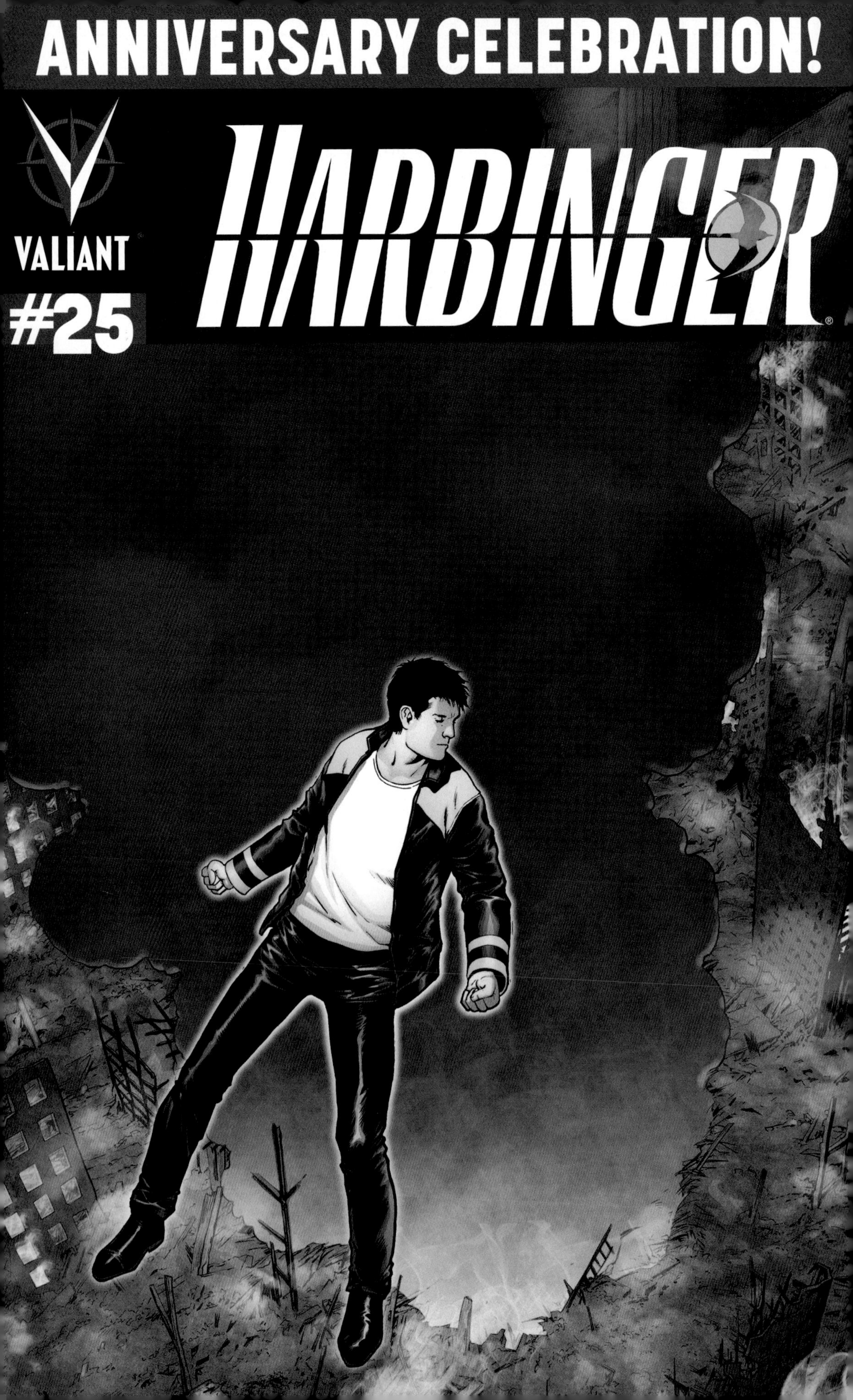

ANNIVERSARY CELEBRATION!
VALIANT
#25
HARBINGER

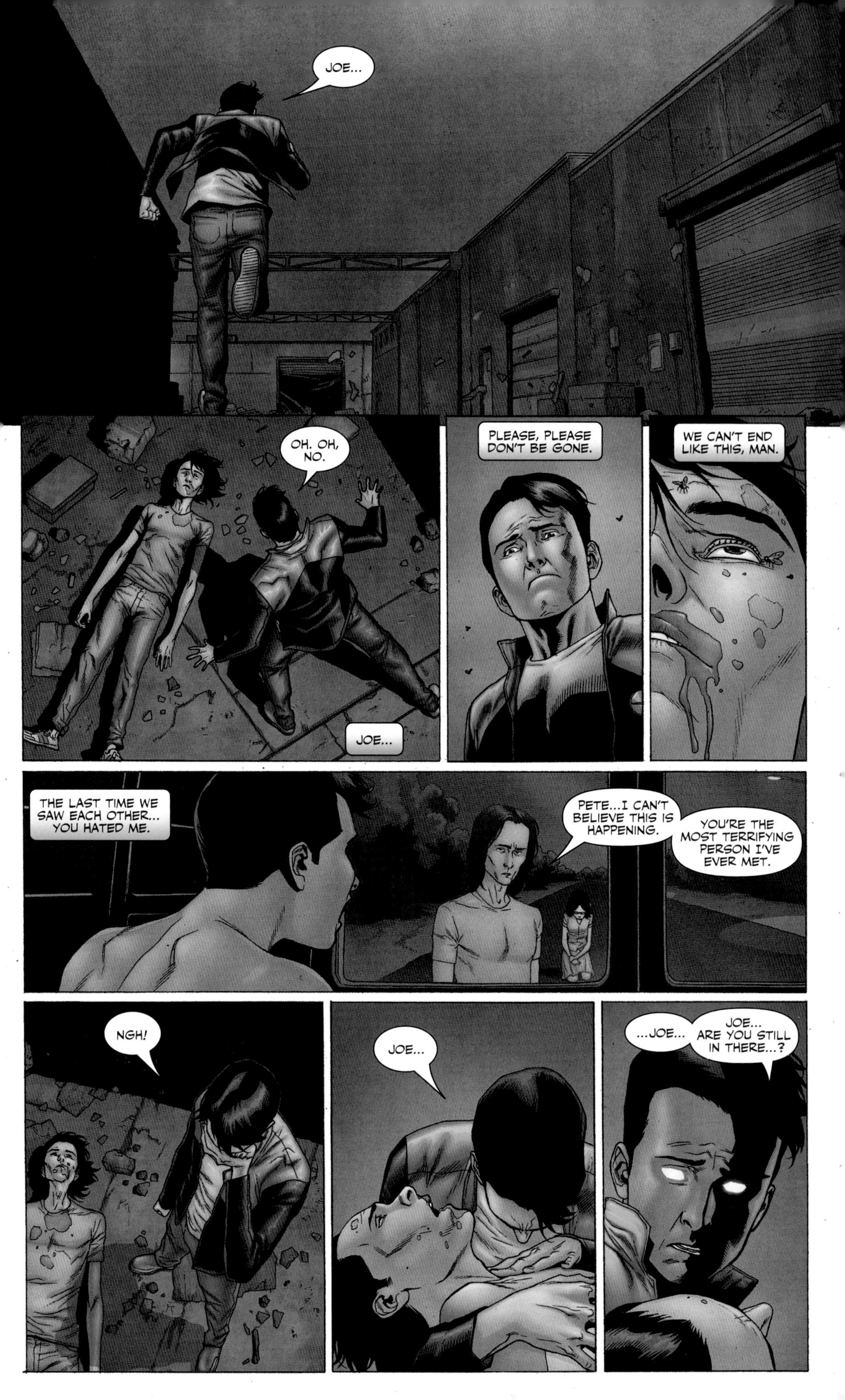
JOE...
OH. OH, NO.
JOE...
PLEASE, PLEASE DON'T BE GONE.
WE CAN'T END LIKE THIS, MAN.
THE LAST TIME WE SAW EACH OTHER... YOU HATED ME.
PETE...I CAN'T BELIEVE THIS IS HAPPENING.
YOU'RE THE MOST TERRIFYING PERSON I'VE EVER MET.
NGH!
JOE...
...JOE...
JOE... ARE YOU STILL IN THERE...?

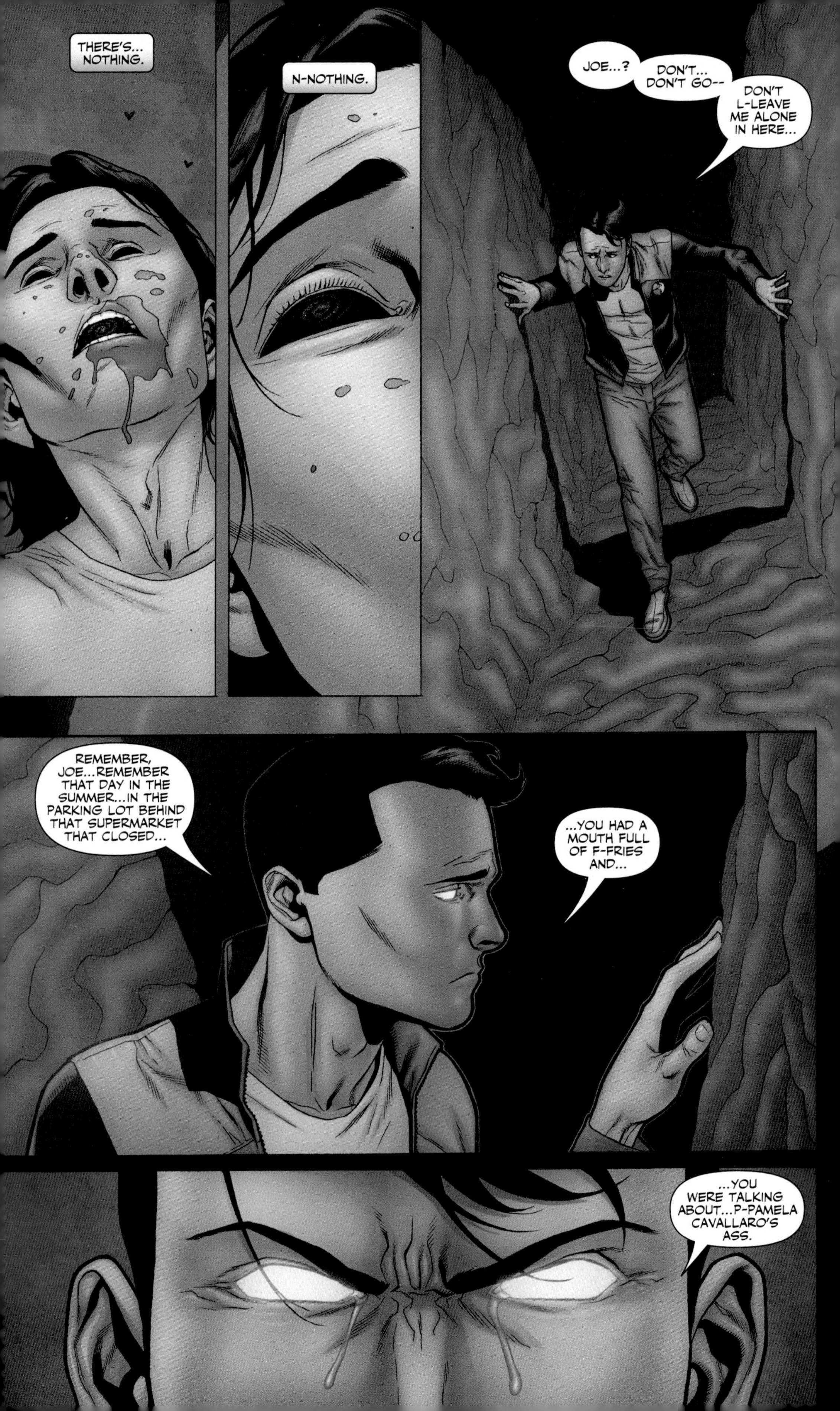

THERE'S... NOTHING.
N-NOTHING.
JOE...?
DON'T... DON'T GO--
DON'T L-LEAVE ME ALONE IN HERE...
REMEMBER, JOE...REMEMBER THAT DAY IN THE SUMMER...IN THE PARKING LOT BEHIND THAT SUPERMARKET THAT CLOSED...
...YOU HAD A MOUTH FULL OF F-FRIES AND...
...YOU WERE TALKING ABOUT...P-PAMELA CAVALLARO'S ASS.

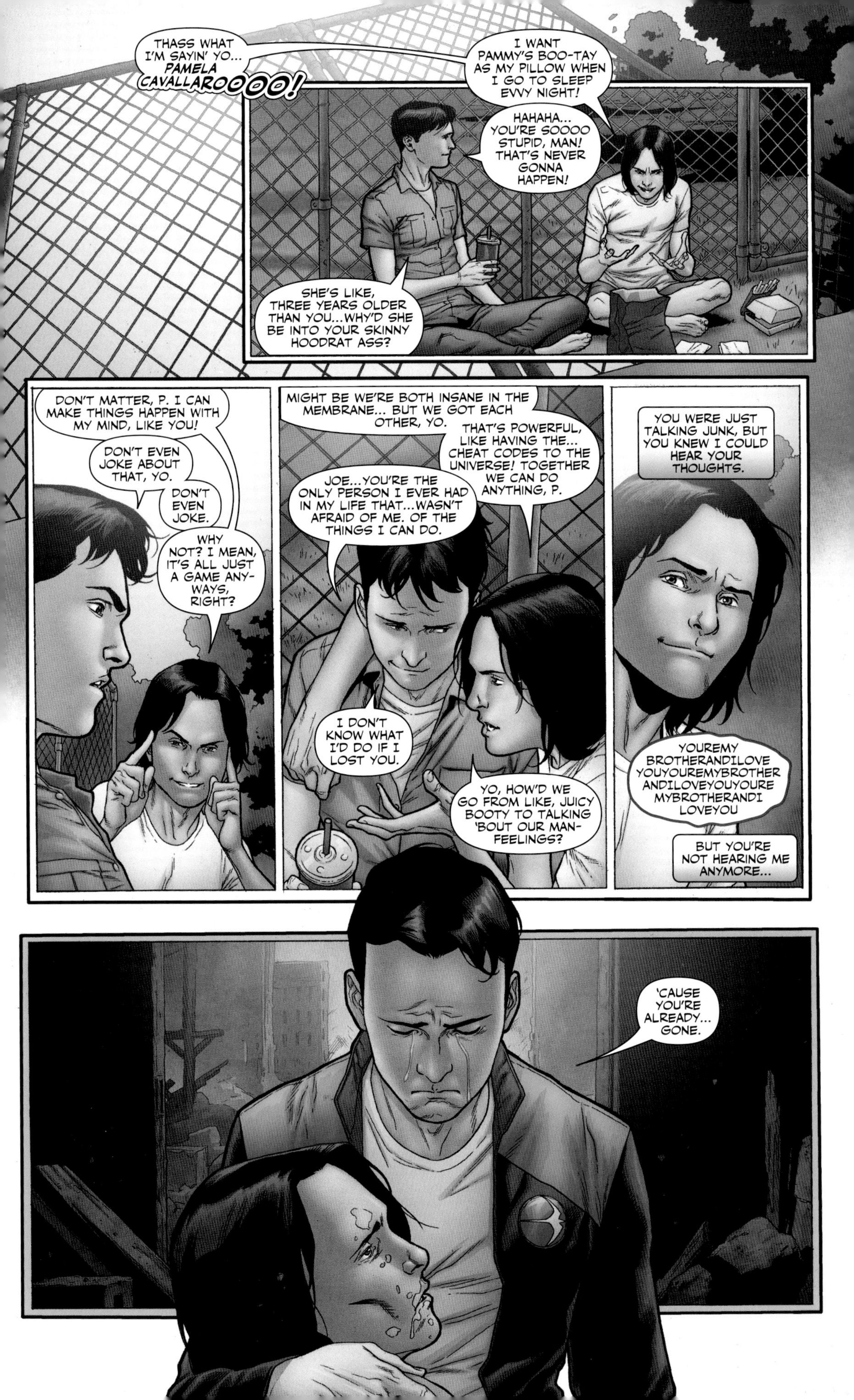
THASS WHAT I'M SAYIN' YO... PAMELA CAVALLAROOOOO!
I WANT PAMMY'S BOO-TAY AS MY PILLOW WHEN I GO TO SLEEP EVVY NIGHT!
HAHAHA... YOU'RE SOOOO STUPID, MAN! THAT'S NEVER GONNA HAPPEN!
SHE'S LIKE, THREE YEARS OLDER THAN YOU...WHY'D SHE BE INTO YOUR SKINNY HOODRAT ASS?
DON'T MATTER, P. I CAN MAKE THINGS HAPPEN WITH MY MIND, LIKE YOU!
DON'T EVEN JOKE ABOUT THAT, YO.
DON'T EVEN JOKE.
WHY NOT? I MEAN, IT'S ALL JUST A GAME ANY-WAYS, RIGHT?
MIGHT BE WE'RE BOTH INSANE IN THE MEMBRANE... BUT WE GOT EACH OTHER, YO.
THAT'S POWERFUL, LIKE HAVING THE... CHEAT CODES TO THE UNIVERSE! TOGETHER WE CAN DO ANYTHING, P.
JOE...YOU'RE THE ONLY PERSON I EVER HAD IN MY LIFE THAT...WASN'T AFRAID OF ME. OF THE THINGS I CAN DO.
I DON'T KNOW WHAT I'D DO IF I LOST YOU.
YO, HOW'D WE GO FROM LIKE, JUICY BOOTY TO TALKING 'BOUT OUR MAN-FEELINGS?
YOU WERE JUST TALKING JUNK, BUT YOU KNEW I COULD HEAR YOUR THOUGHTS.
YOUREMY BROTHERANDILOVE YOUYOUREMYBROTHER ANDILOVEYOUYOURE MYBROTHERANDI LOVEYOU
BUT YOU'RE NOT HEARING ME ANYMORE...
'CAUSE YOU'RE ALREADY... GONE.

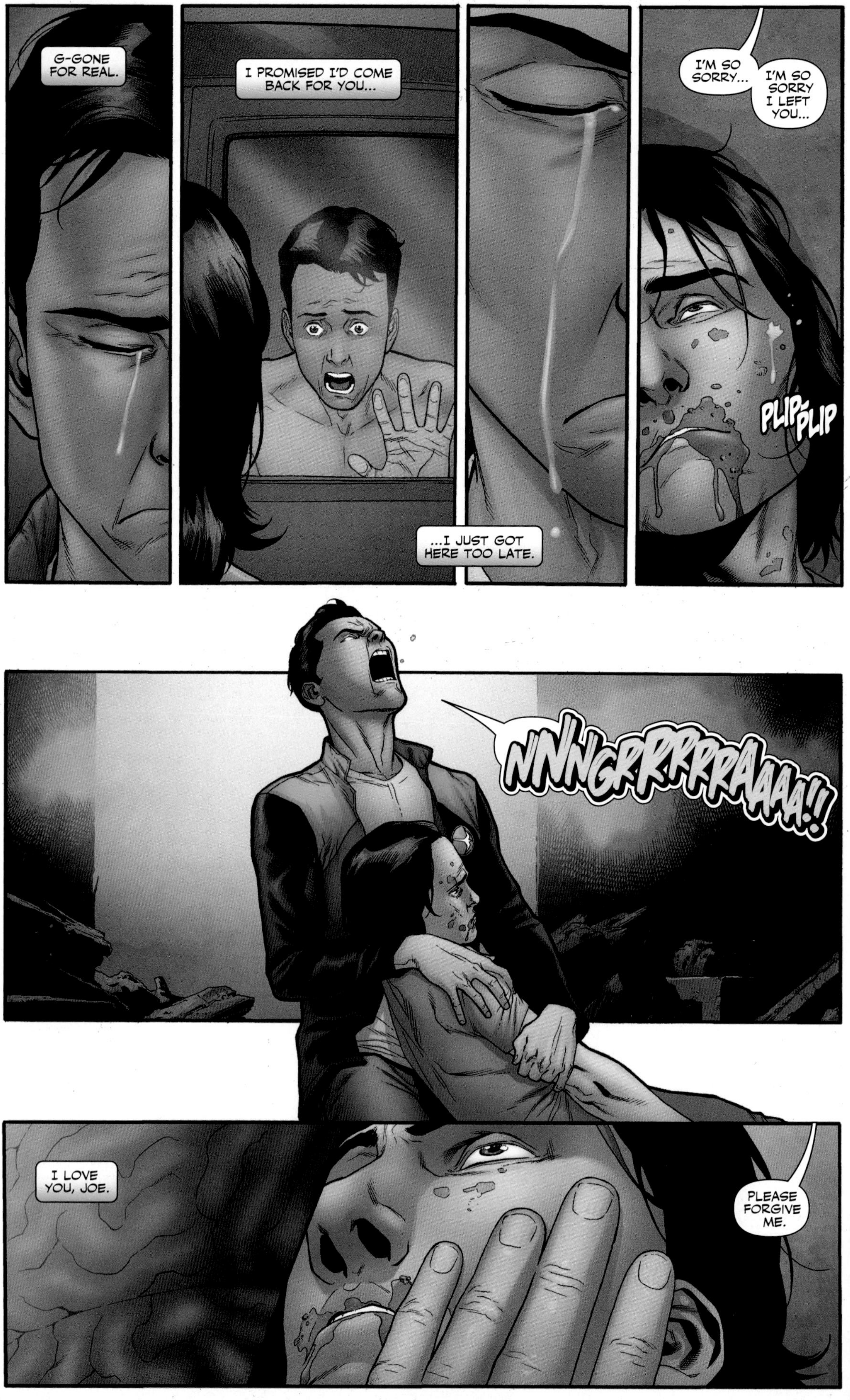
G-GONE FOR REAL.
I PROMISED I'D COME BACK FOR YOU...
...I JUST GOT HERE TOO LATE.
I'M SO SORRY...
I'M SO SORRY I LEFT YOU...
PLIP-PLIP
NNNGRRRRRAAAA!!
I LOVE YOU, JOE.
PLEASE FORGIVE ME.

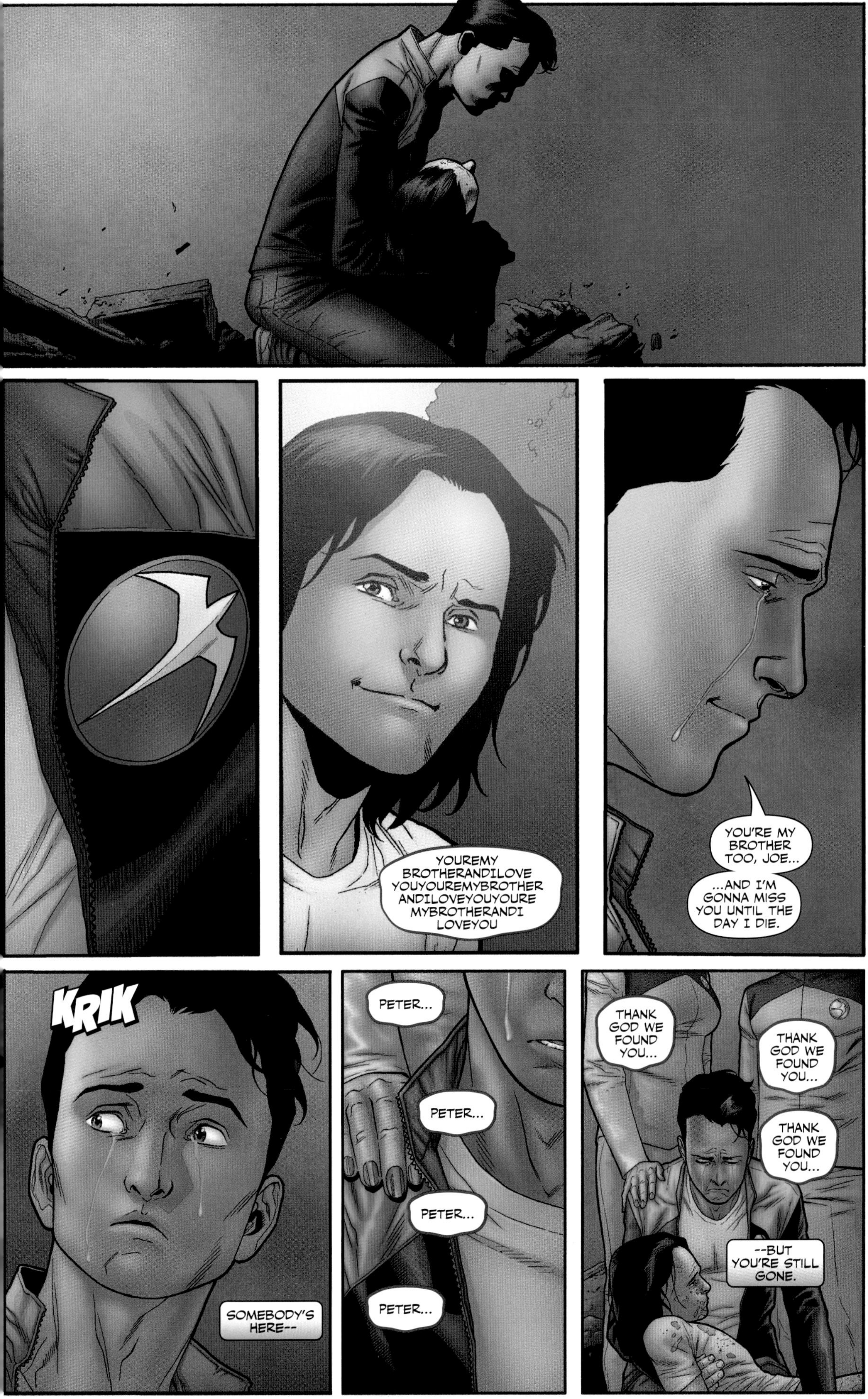
YOUREMY BROTHERANDILOVE YOUYOUREMYBROTHER ANDILOVEYOUYOURE MYBROTHERANDI LOVEYOU
YOU'RE MY BROTHER TOO, JOE...
...AND I'M GONNA MISS YOU UNTIL THE DAY I DIE.
KRIK
SOMEBODY'S HERE--
PETER...
PETER...
PETER...
PETER...
THANK GOD WE FOUND YOU...
THANK GOD WE FOUND YOU...
THANK GOD WE FOUND YOU...
--BUT YOU'RE STILL GONE.

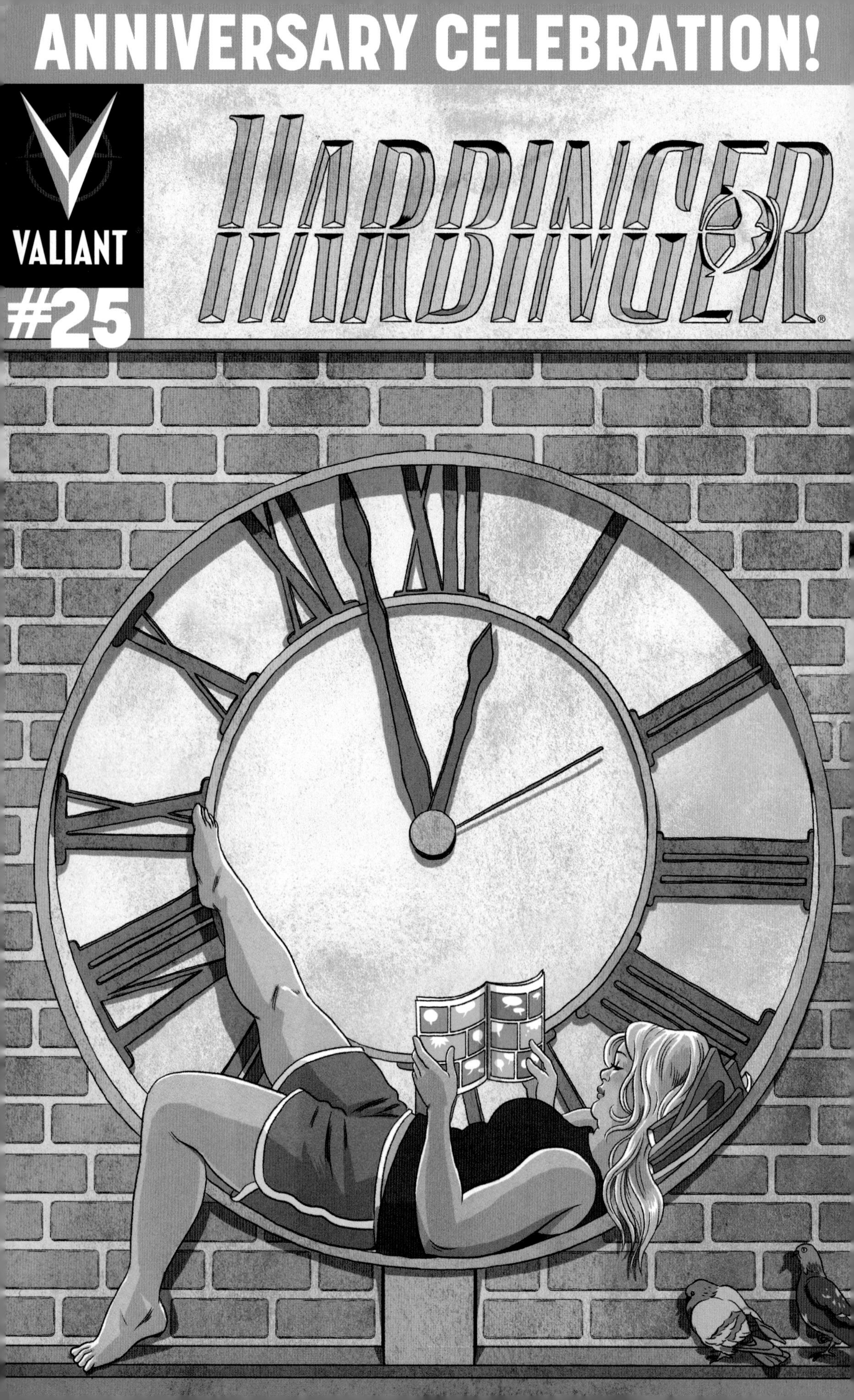
ANNIVERSARY CELEBRATION!
VALIANT
#25
HARBINGER®

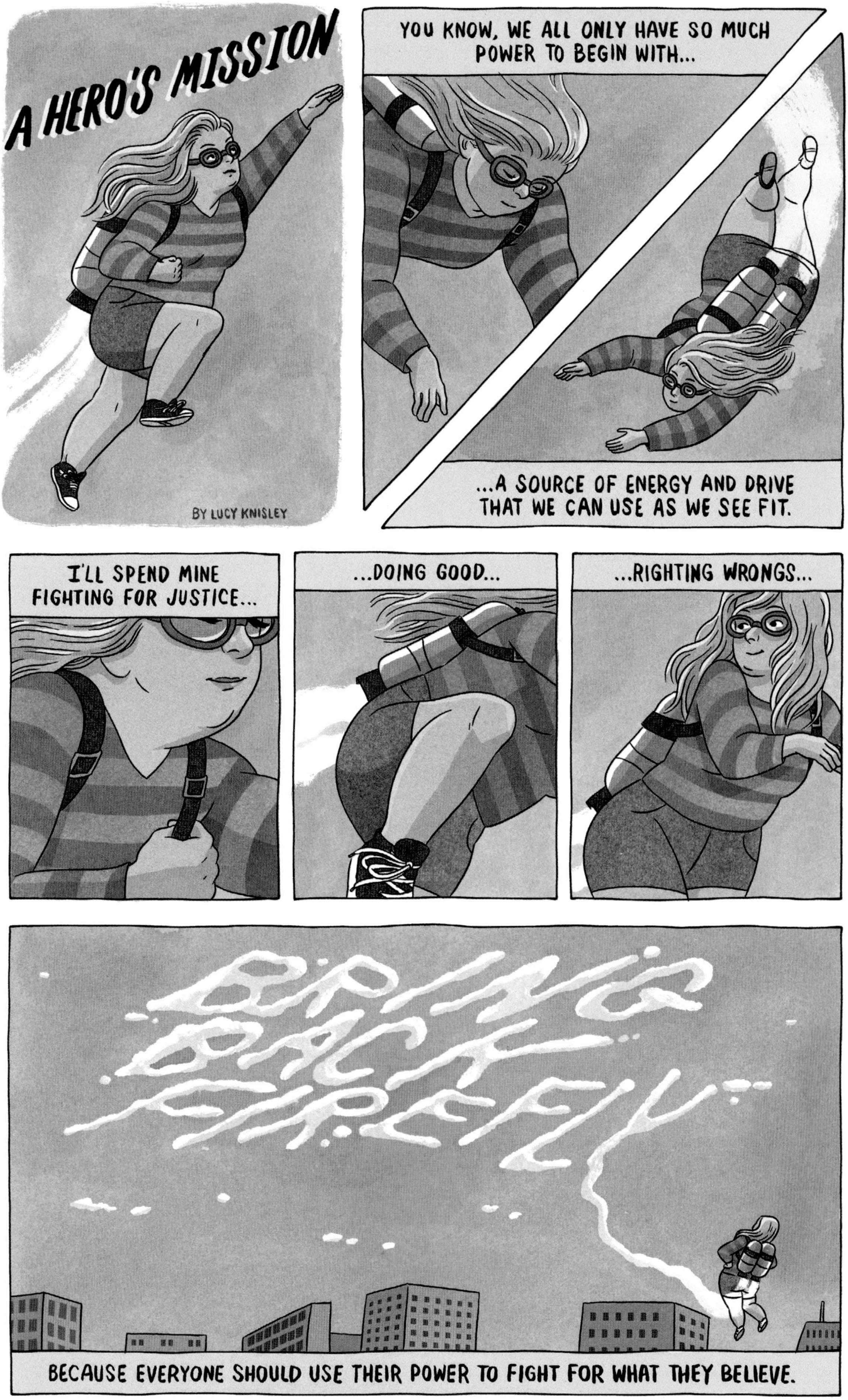
A HERO'S MISSION
BY LUCY KNISLEY
YOU KNOW, WE ALL ONLY HAVE SO MUCH POWER TO BEGIN WITH...
...A SOURCE OF ENERGY AND DRIVE THAT WE CAN USE AS WE SEE FIT.
I'LL SPEND MINE FIGHTING FOR JUSTICE...
...DOING GOOD...
...RIGHTING WRONGS...
BRING BACK FIREFLY
BECAUSE EVERYONE SHOULD USE THEIR POWER TO FIGHT FOR WHAT THEY BELIEVE.

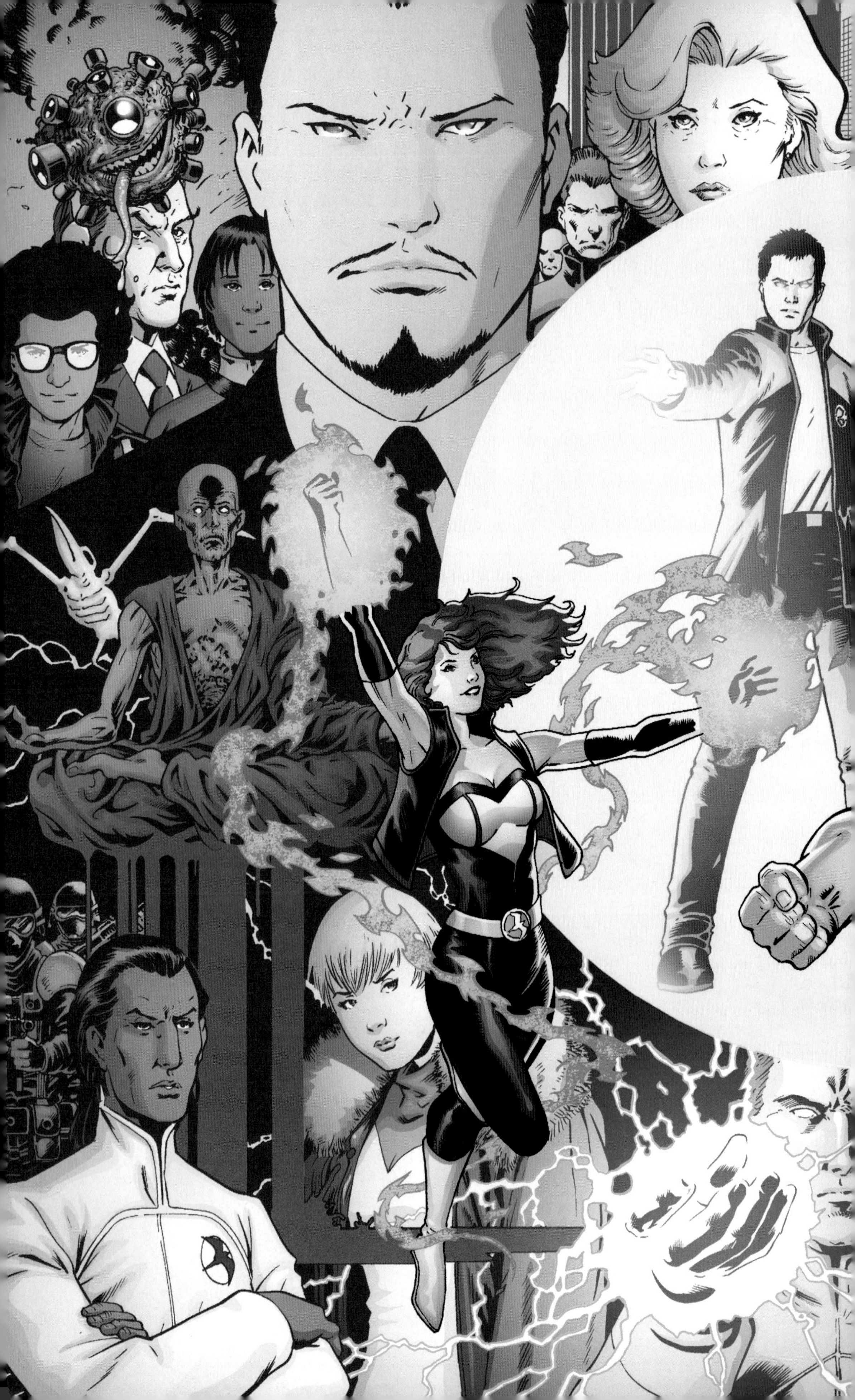

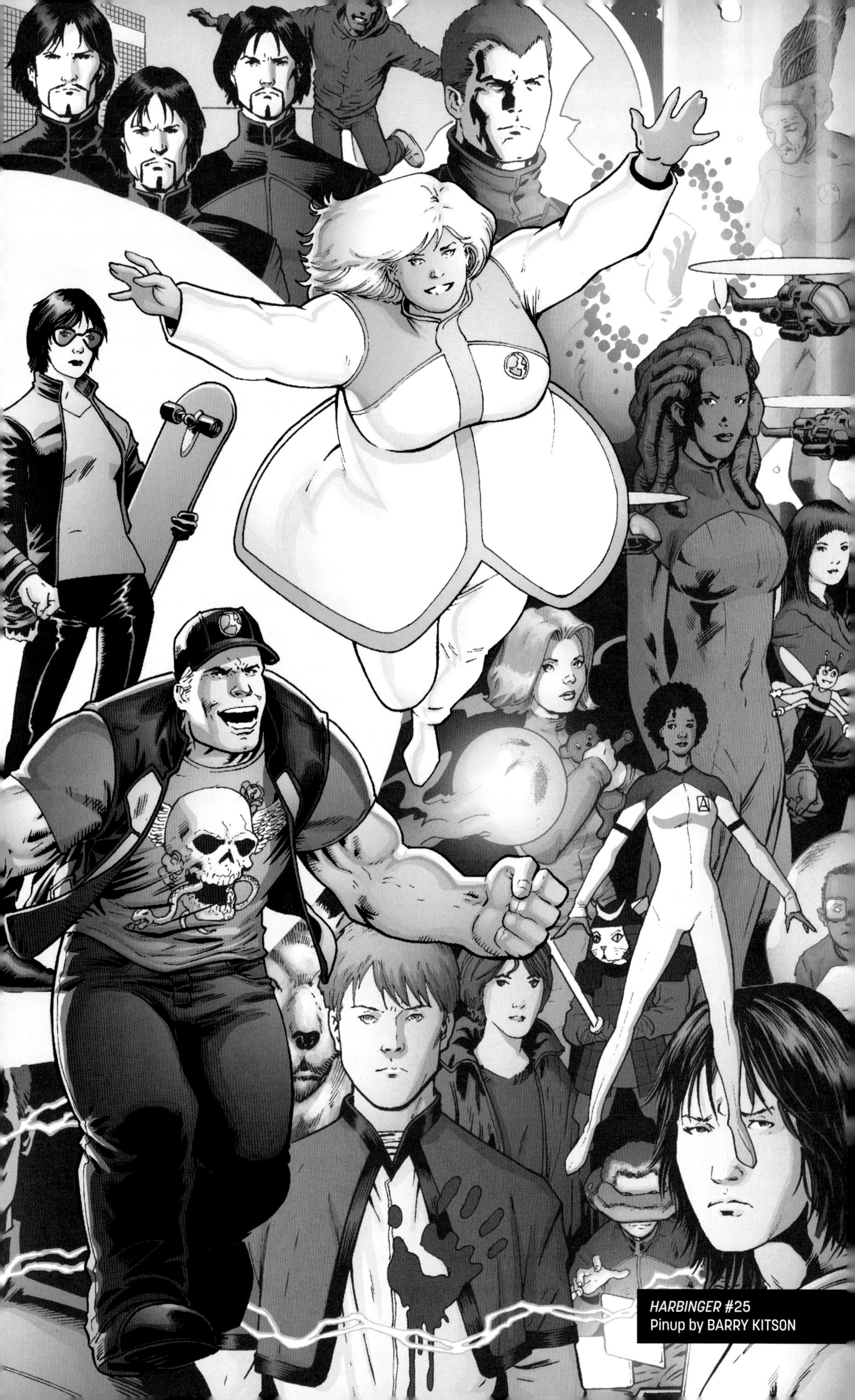

HARBINGER #25
Pinup by BARRY KITSON

HARBINGER COVER GALLERY

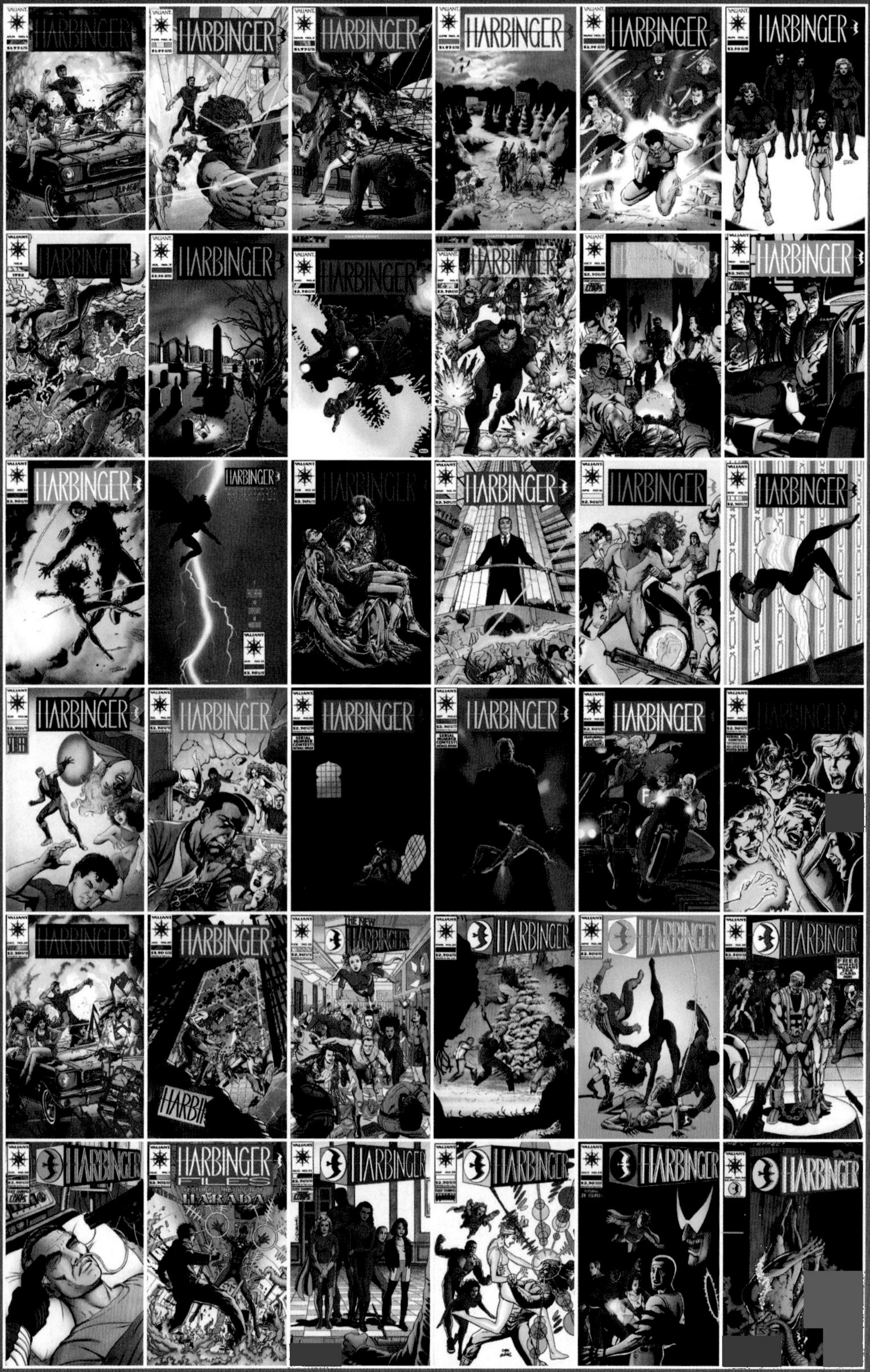

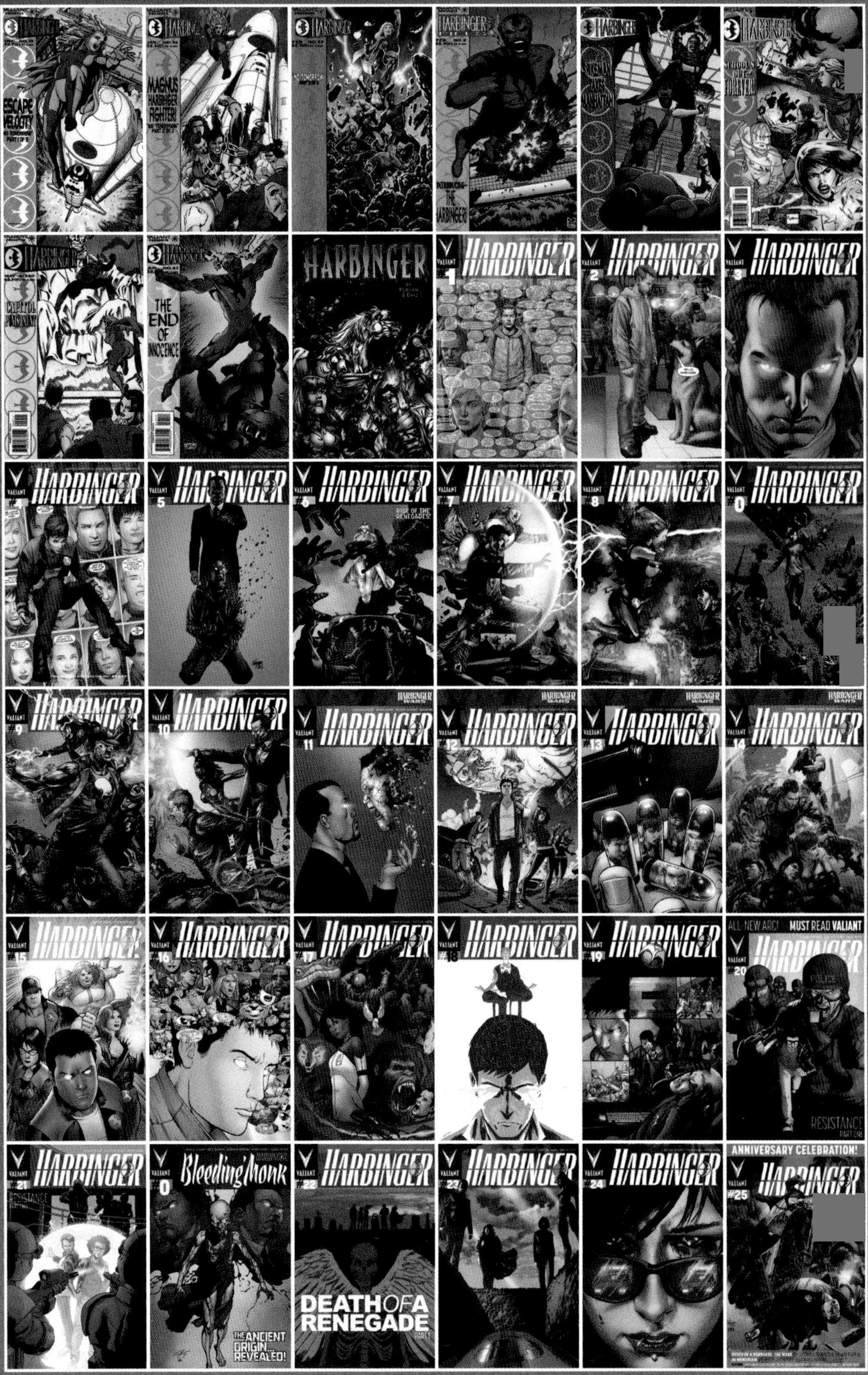
HARBINGER
ESCAPE VELOCITY
HARBINGER
MAGNUS HARBINGER FIGHTER!
HARBINGER
HARBINGER
INTRODUCING THE HARBINGER
HARBINGER
HARBINGER
SCHOOL'S OUT FOREVER!
HARBINGER
HARBINGER
THE END OF INNOCENCE
HARBINGER
HARBINGER 1
HARBINGER 2
HARBINGER 3
HARBINGER
HARBINGER 5
HARBINGER 6
RISE OF THE RENEGADES!
HARBINGER 7
HARBINGER 8
HARBINGER 0
HARBINGER 9
HARBINGER 10
HARBINGER WARS
HARBINGER 11
HARBINGER WARS
HARBINGER 12
HARBINGER WARS
HARBINGER 13
HARBINGER WARS
HARBINGER 14
HARBINGER 15
HARBINGER 16
HARBINGER 17
HARBINGER 18
HARBINGER 19
ALL-NEW ARC!
MUST READ VALIANT
HARBINGER 20
RESISTANCE
HARBINGER 21
RESISTANCE
Bleeding Monk 0
THE ANCIENT ORIGIN... REVEALED!
HARBINGER 22
DEATH OF A RENEGADE
HARBINGER 23
HARBINGER 24
ANNIVERSARY CELEBRATION!
HARBINGER #25

GALLERY

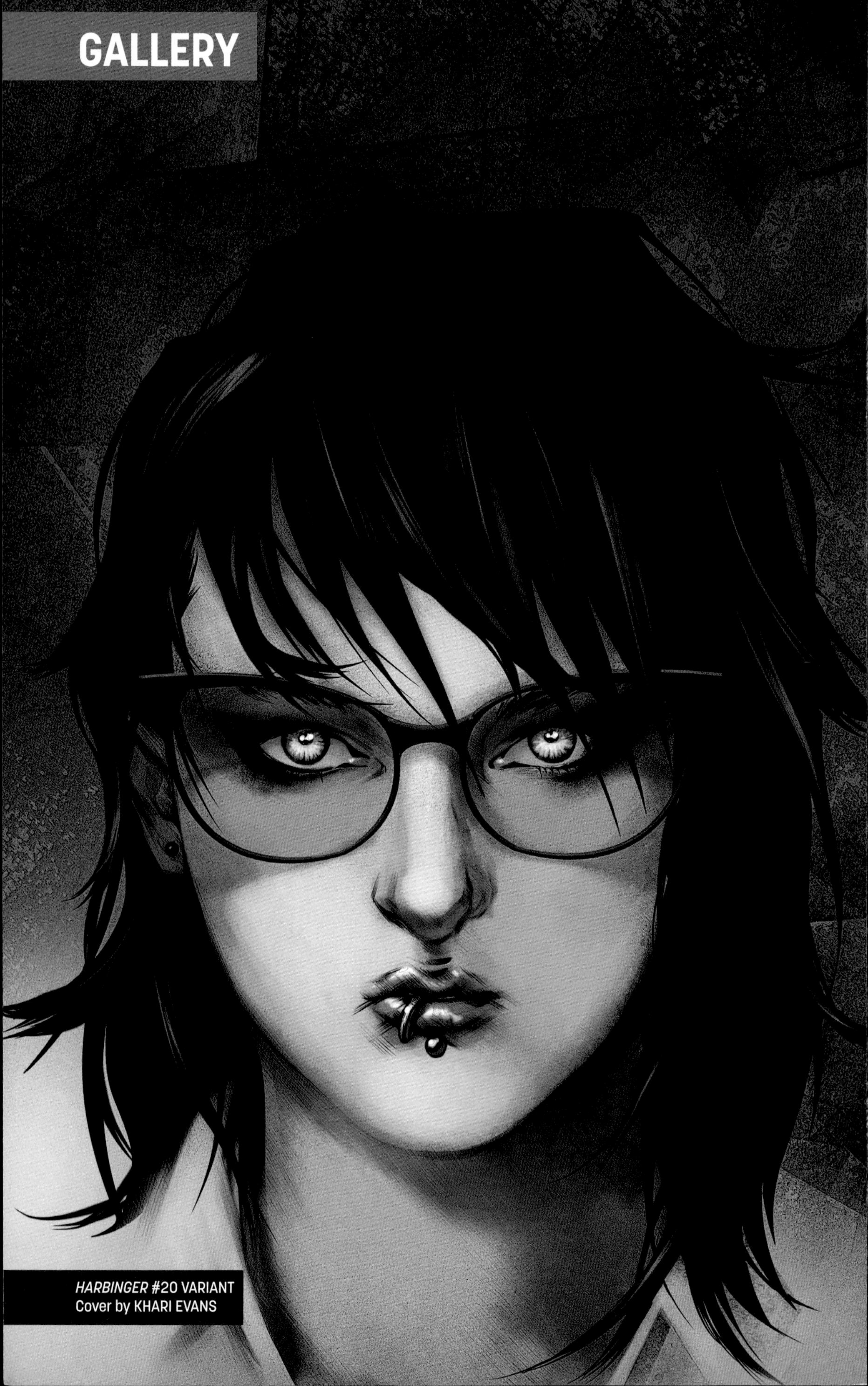

HARBINGER #20 VARIANT
Cover by KHARI EVANS

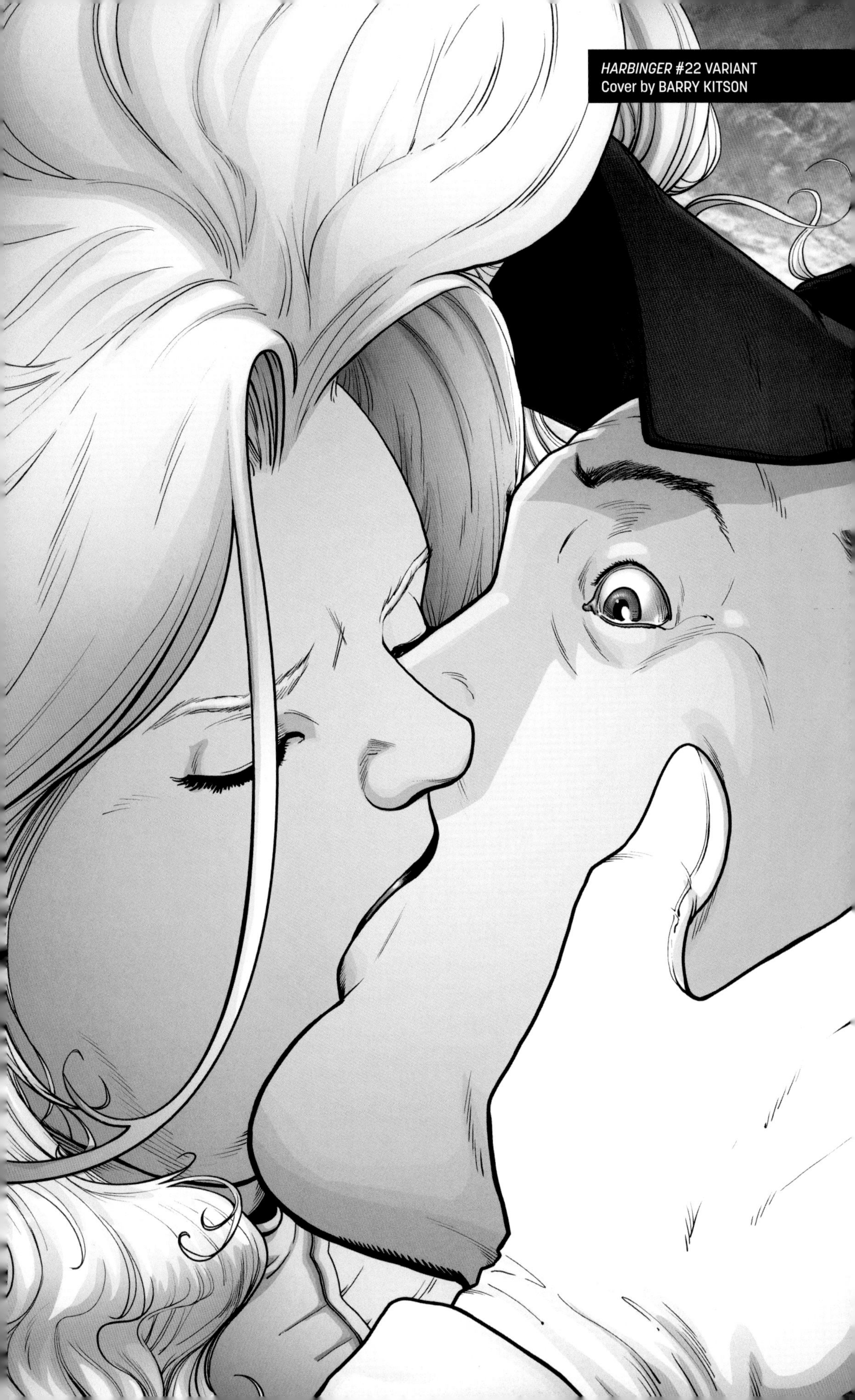

HARBINGER #22 VARIANT
Cover by BARRY KITSON

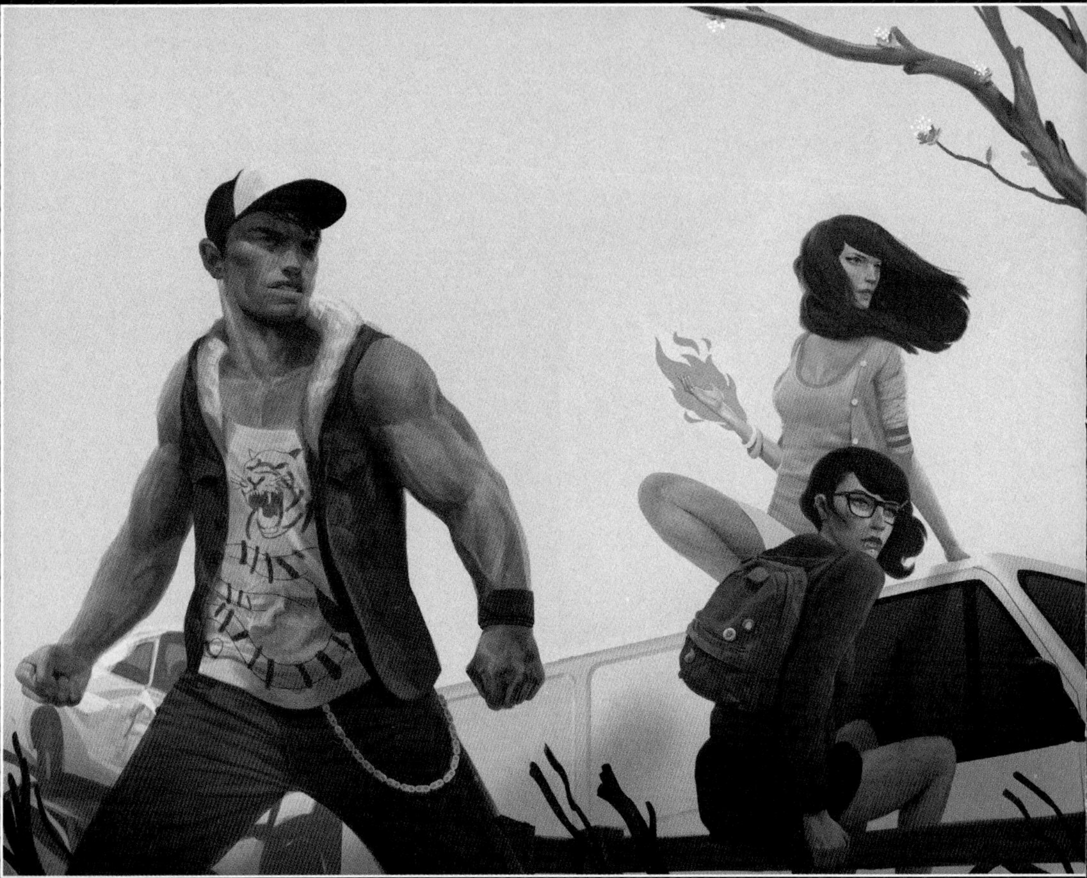

HARBINGER #23, *HARBINGER* #20 PULLBOX EXCLUSIVE,
HARBINGER #21, and *HARBINGER* #22 INTERLOCKING VARIANT
Covers by ZACH MONTOYA

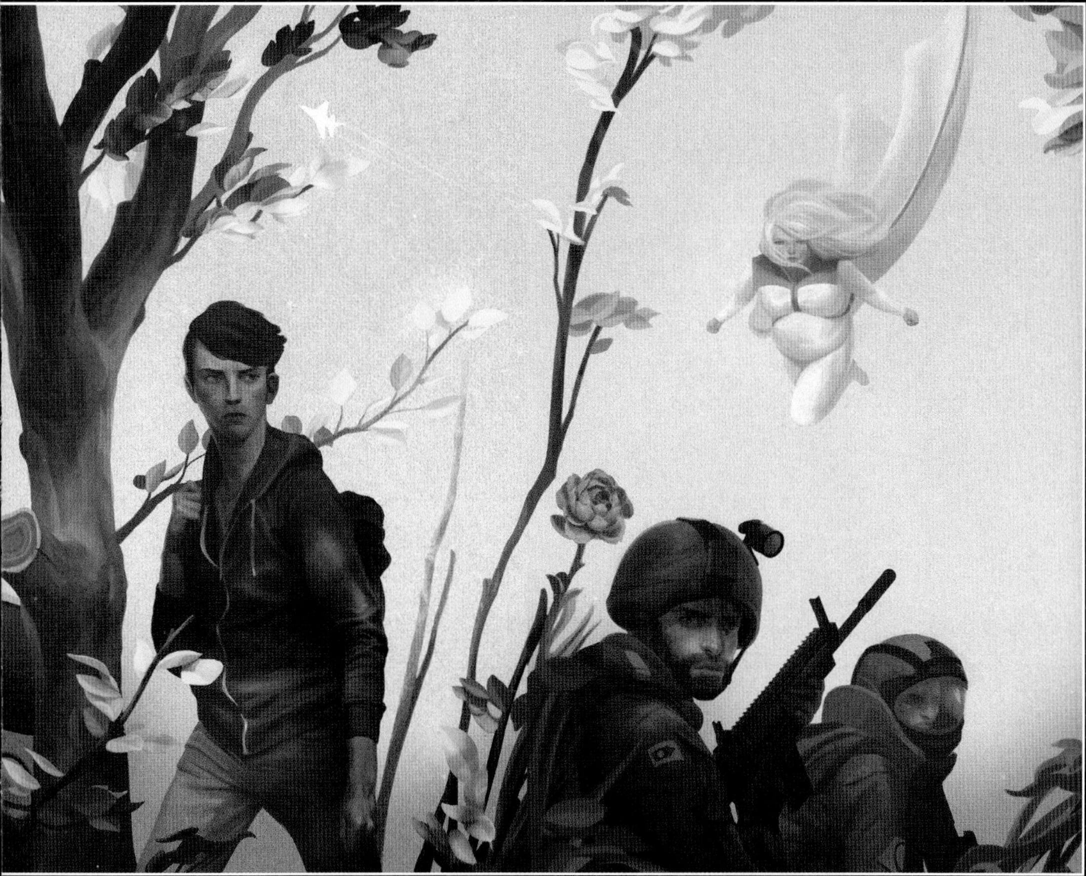

HARBINGER #23 VARIANT
Cover by KHARI EVANS

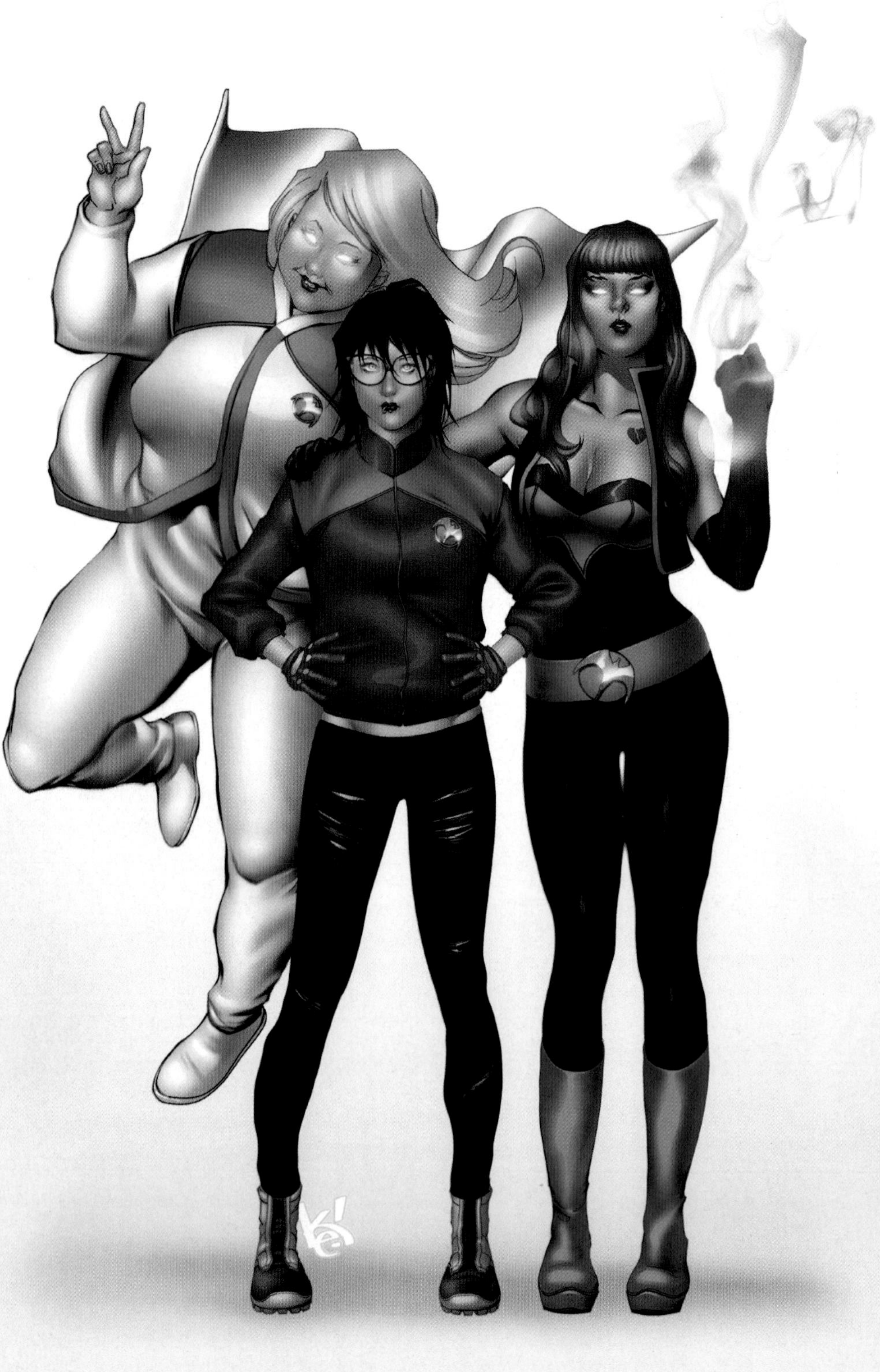

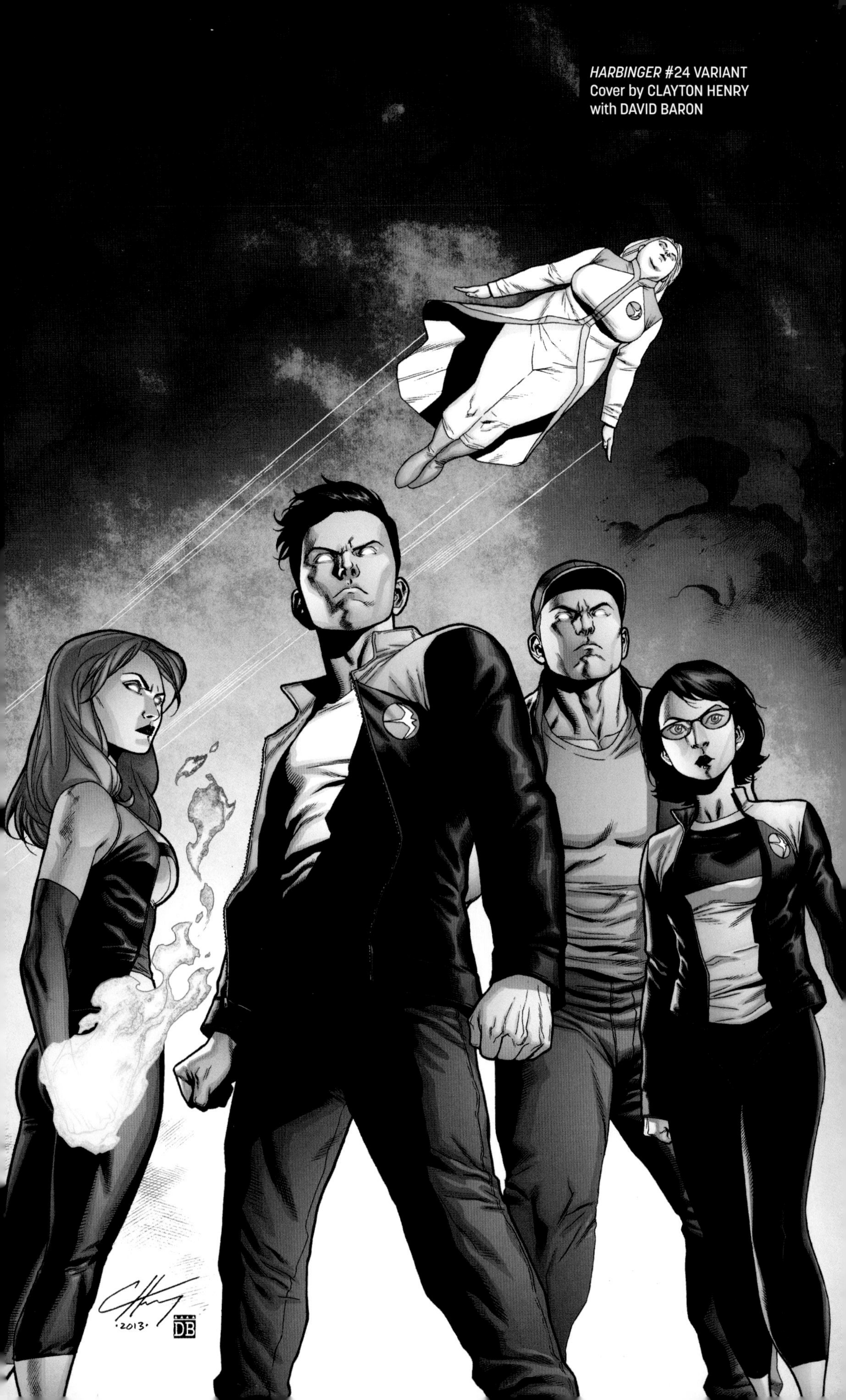
·2013·
DB

HARBINGER #24 VARIANT
Cover by CLAYTON HENRY
with DAVID BARON

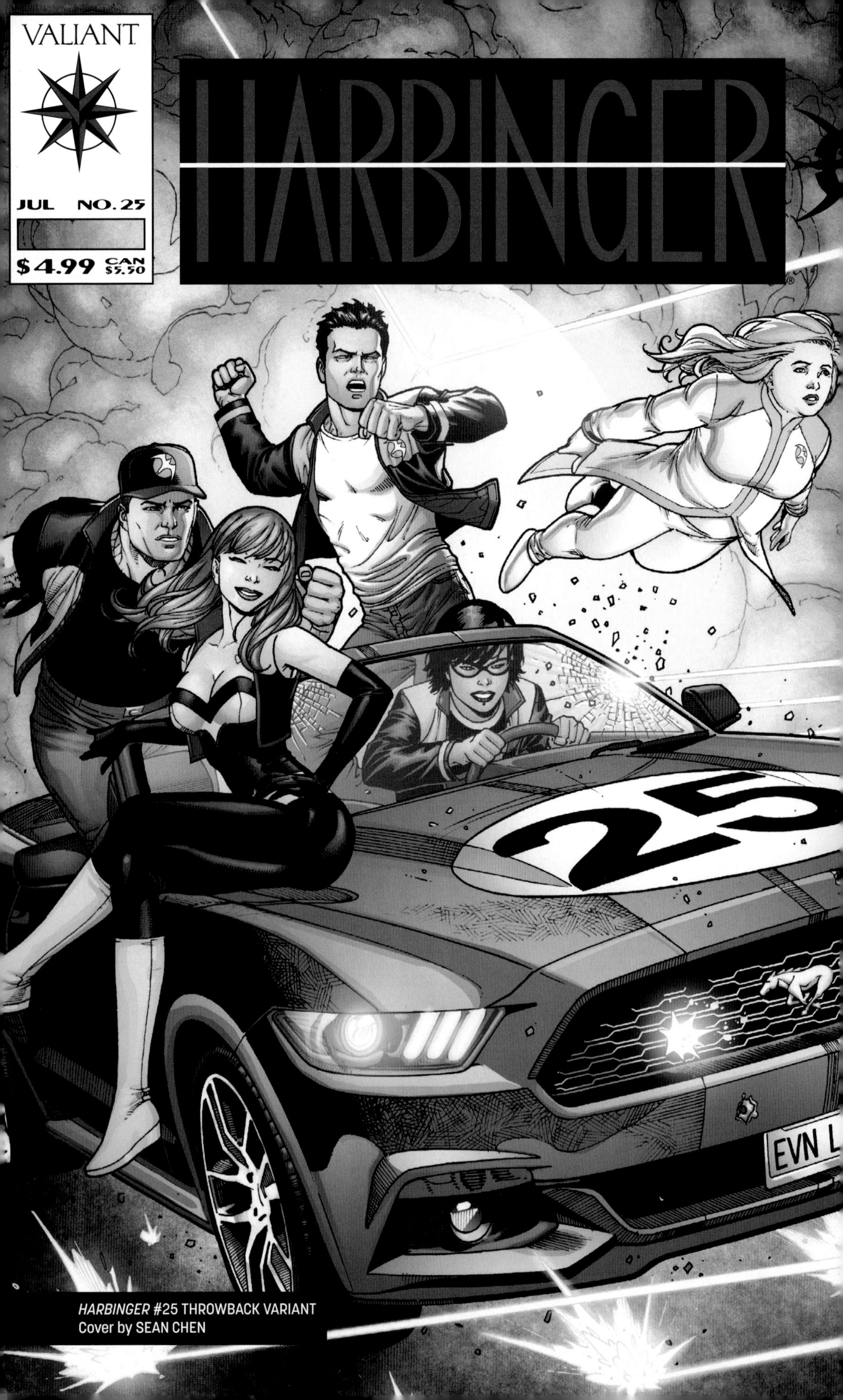
VALIANT
HARBINGER
JUL NO. 25
$4.99 CAN $5.50
25
EVN L

HARBINGER #25 THROWBACK VARIANT
Cover by SEAN CHEN

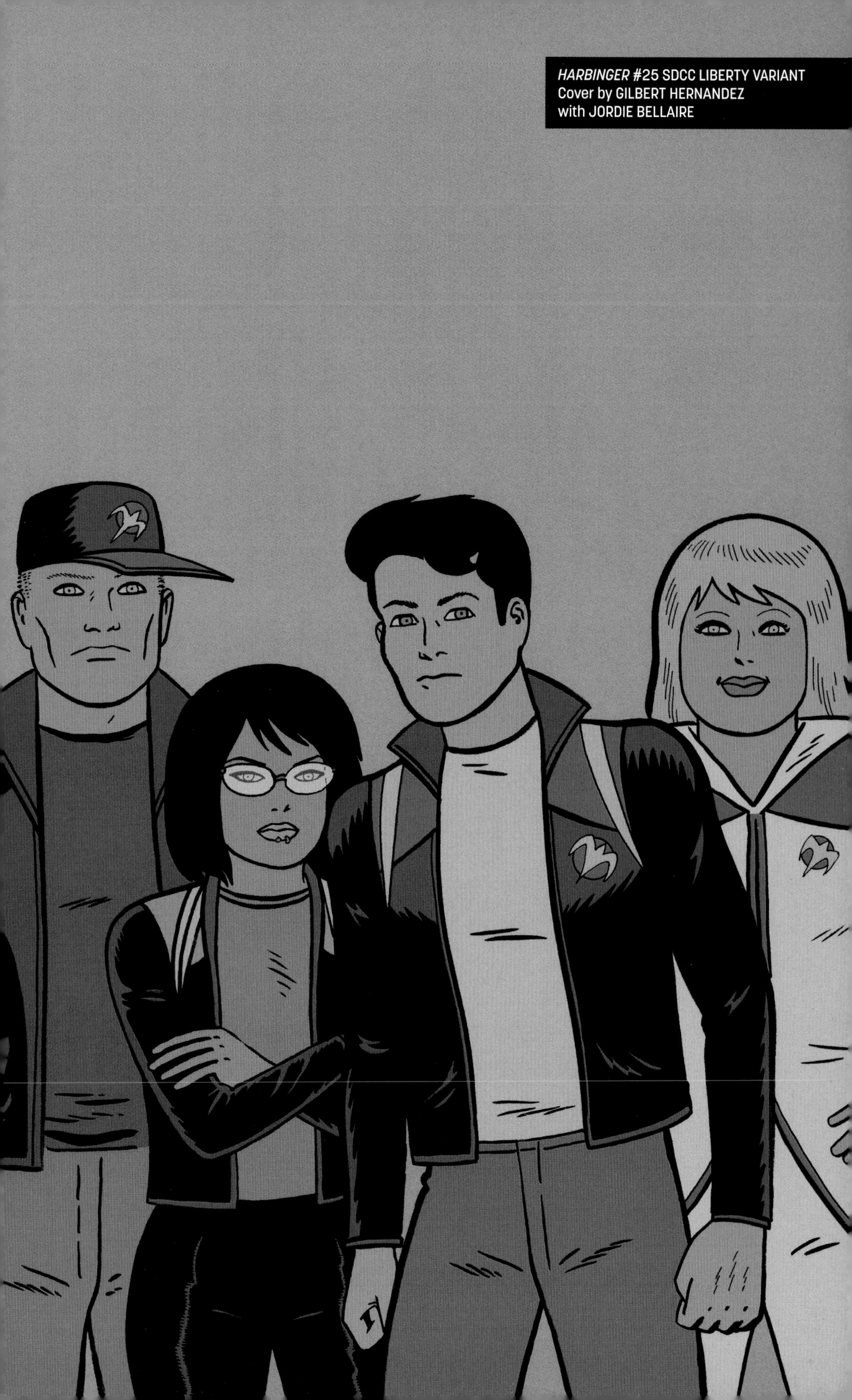

HARBINGER #25 SDCC LIBERTY VARIANT
Cover by GILBERT HERNANDEZ
with JORDIE BELLAIRE

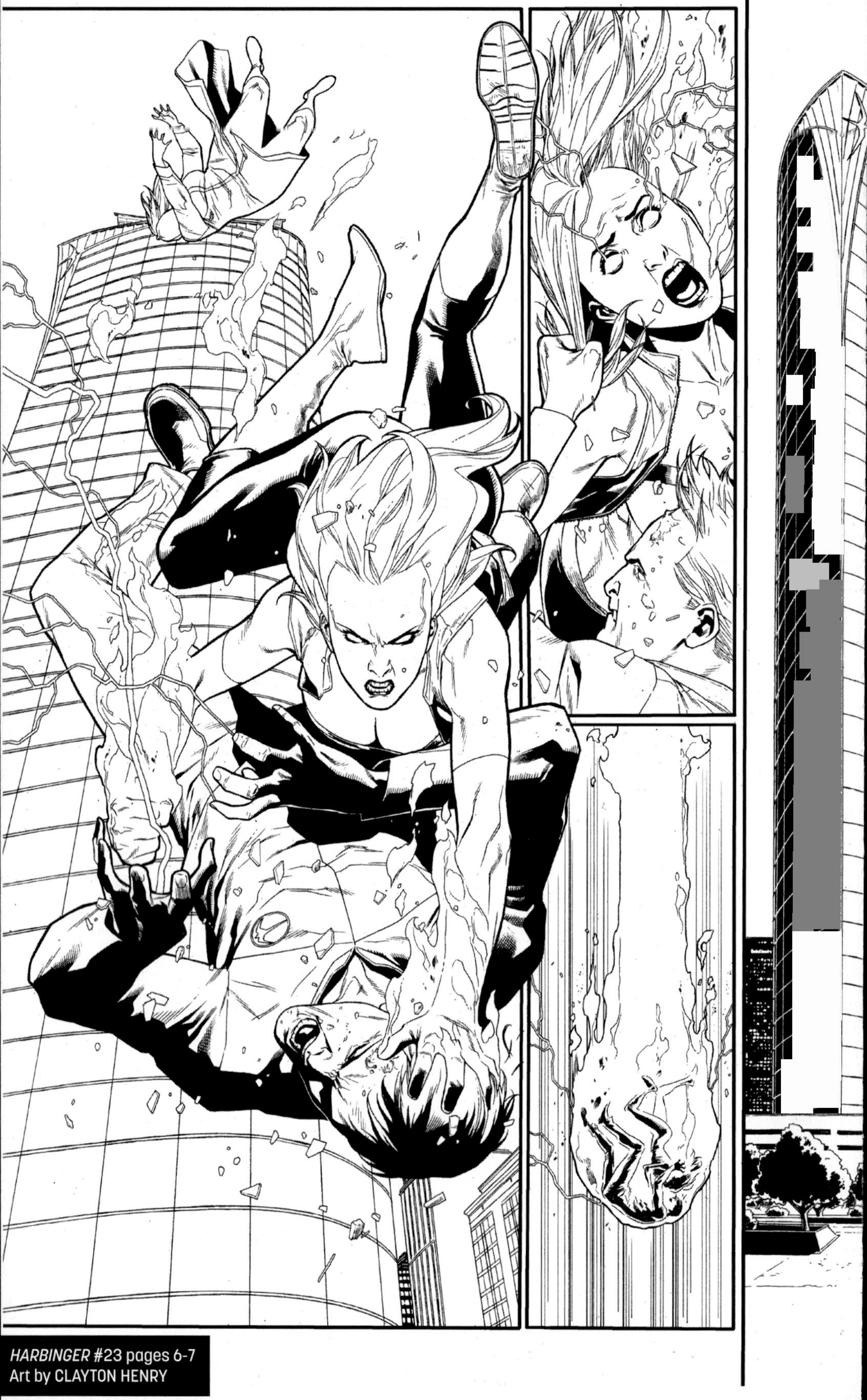

HARBINGER #23 pages 6-7
Art by CLAYTON HENRY

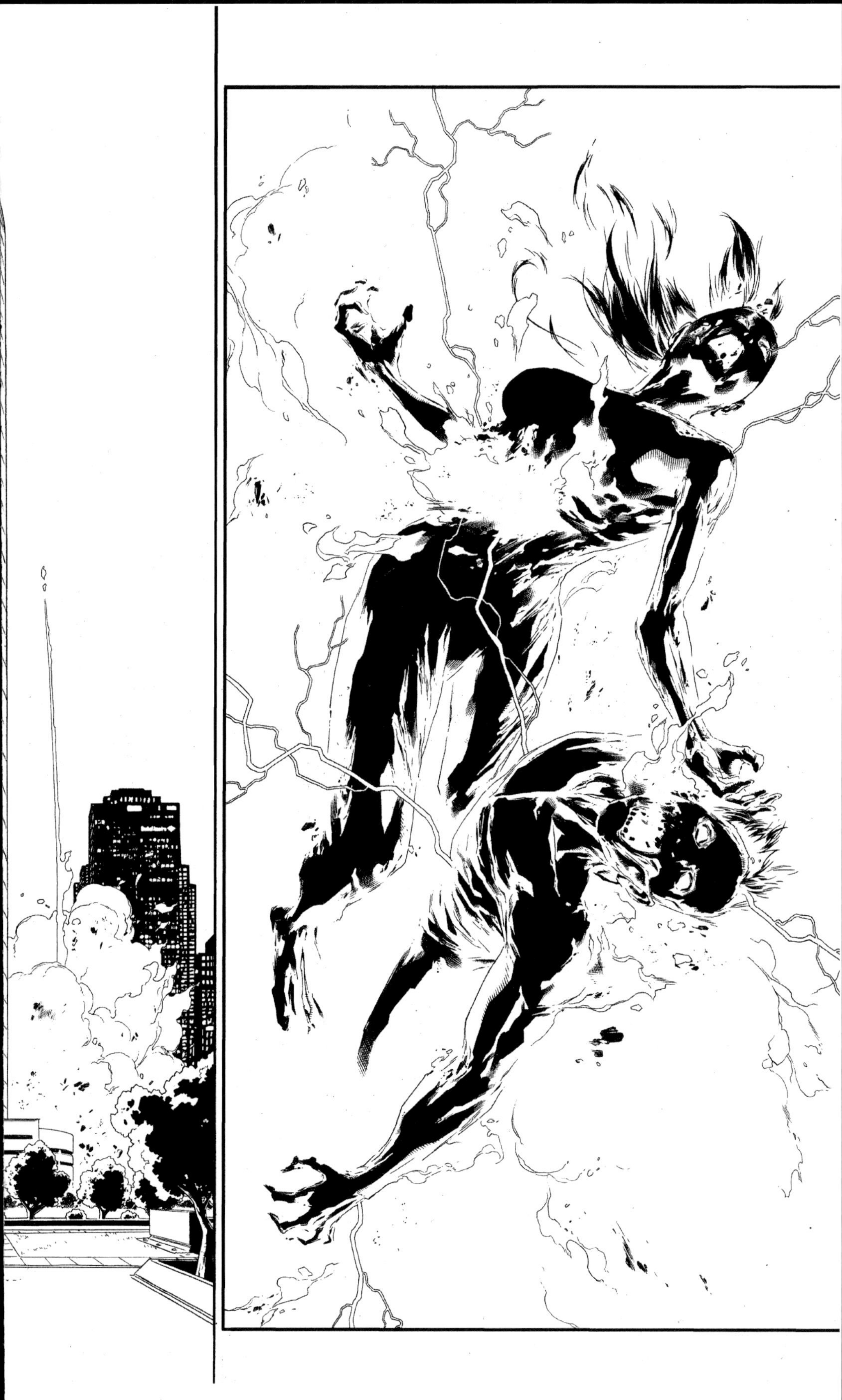

VALIANT®

DELUXE HARDCOVERS

ROBERT VENDITTI | CARY NORD | LEE GARBETT
TREVOR HAIRSINE | STEFANO GAUDIANO | MOOSE BAUMANN
VALIANT
X-O MANOWAR
DELUXE EDITION 1

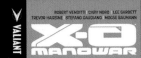

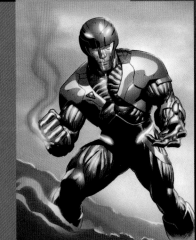

X-O MANOWAR DELUXE EDITION BOOK 1

Writer: Robert Venditti | Artists: Cary Nord, Lee Garbett, and Trevor Hairsine
ISBN: 9781939346100 | Diamond Code: AUG131497 | Price: $39.99 |
Format: Oversized HC

Aric of Dacia, a fifth-century Visigoth armed with the universe's most powerful weapon, is all that stands between the Earth and all-out annihilation at the hands of the alien race that abducted him from his own time. Stranded in the modern day, X-O Manowar's battle against the Vine will take him into the shadows with the lethal operative known as Ninjak–and launch a quest for vengeance that will bring an alien empire to its knees. The Vine destroyed Aric's world. Now he will give them war.

Collecting X-O MANOWAR #1-14 and more than 20 pages of bonus materials!

JOSHUA DYSART | KHARI EVANS | TREVOR HAIRSINE
MICO SUAYAN | IAN HANNIN
VALIANT
HARBINGER
DELUXE EDITION 1

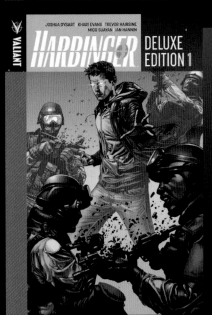

HARBINGER DELUXE EDITION BOOK 1

Writer: Joshua Dysart | Artists: Khari Evans, Trevor Hairsine, Barry Kitson, and Lee Garbett
ISBN: 9781939346131 | Diamond Code: SEP131373 | Price: $39.99 | Format: Oversized HC

Outside the law. Inside your head. You've never met a team of super-powered teenagers quite like the Renegades. Skipping across the country in a desperate attempt to stay one step ahead of the authorities, psionically powered teenager Peter Stanchek only has one option left–run. But he won't have to go it alone. As the shadowy corporation known as the Harbinger Foundation draws close on all sides, Peter will have to find and recruit other unique individuals like himself...other troubled, immensely powerful youths with abilities beyond their control. Their mission? Bring the fight back to the Harbinger Foundation's founder Toyo Harada–and dismantle his global empire brick by brick...

Collecting HARBINGER #0-14 and more than 20 pages of bonus materials!

DUANE SWIERCZYNSKI | MANUEL GARCIA
BARRY KITSON | ARTURO LOZZI | STEFANO GAUDIANO
VALIANT
BLOODSHOT
DELUXE EDITION 1

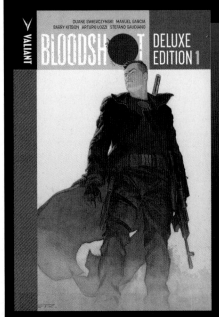

BLOODSHOT DELUXE EDITION BOOK 1

Writer: Duane Swierczynski | Artists: Manuel García, Barry Kitson, Matthew Clark, and Arturo Lozzi
ISBN: 9781939346216 | Diamond Code: JAN141376 | Price: $39.99 | Format: Oversized HC

You have no name, just a project designation. They call you Bloodshot, but the voices inside your head call you "daddy, "sir," "commander," "comrade"–whatever it takes to motivate you to get the job done. But after so many missions and so many lives, you're finally ready to confront your handlers at Project Rising Spirit and find out who you really are. You'd better move quickly, though, because your former masters don't like it when a billion-dollar weapons project goes rogue. And wherever you go, all hell is sure to follow...

Collecting BLOODSHOT #1-13 and more than 20 pages of bonus materials!

VALIANT® DELUXE HARDCOVERS

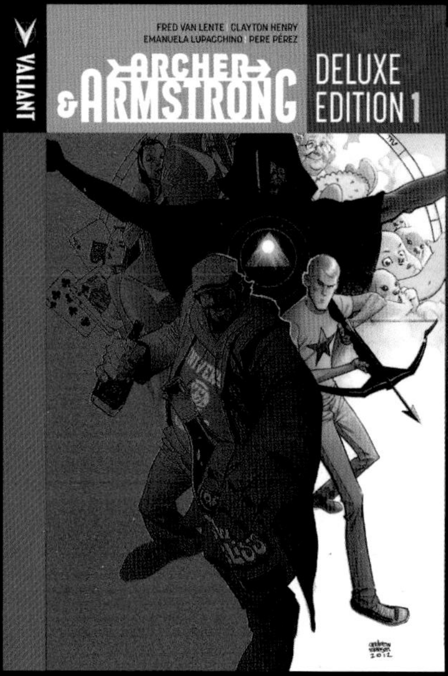
VALIANT
FRED VAN LENTE | CLAYTON HENRY
EMANUELA LUPACCHINO | PERE PÉREZ
ARCHER & ARMSTRONG
DELUXE EDITION 1

ARCHER & ARMSTRONG DELUXE EDITION BOOK 1

Writer: Fred Van Lente | Artists: Clayton Henry, Emanuela Lupacchino, Pere Pérez, and Álvaro Martínez
ISBN: 9781939346223 | Diamond Code: FEB141484 | Price: $39.99 | Format: Oversized HC

Join one of the most acclaimed adventures in comics as naive teenage assassin Obadiah Archer and the fun-loving, hard-drinking immortal called Armstrong unite to stop a plot ten thousand years in the making! From the lost temples of ancient Sumeria to modern-day Wall Street, Area 51, and beyond, Valiant's conspiracy-smashing adventurers are going on a globe-trotting quest to bring down the unholy coalition of cultists known as the Sect–and stop each of history's most notorious conspiracies from remaking the world in their own insane image.

Collecting ARCHER & ARMSTRONG #0-13 and more than 20 pages of bonus materials!

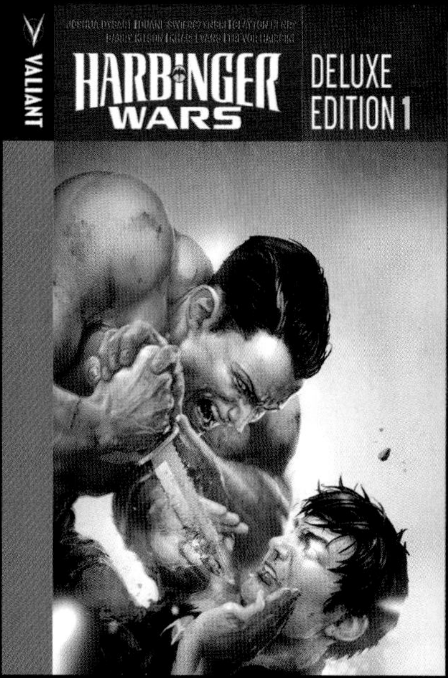
VALIANT
HARBINGER WARS
DELUXE EDITION 1

HARBINGER WARS DELUXE EDITION

Writer: Joshua Dysart & Duane Swierczynski | Artists: Clayton Henry, Pere Pérez, Barry Kitson, Khari Evans, Trevor Hairsine, Mico Suayan, and Clayton Crain
ISBN: 9781939346322 | Diamond Code: MAR141422 | **Price: $39.99 | Format: Oversized HC**

Re-presenting Valiant's best-selling crossover event in complete chronological order!

When an untrained and undisciplined team of super-powered test subjects escapes from Project Rising Spirit and onto the Vegas Strip, Bloodshot and the Harbinger Renegades will find themselves locked in battle against a deadly succession of opponents–and each other. As the combined forces of the H.A.R.D. Corps, Bloodshot, and omega-level telekinetic Toyo Harada all descend on Las Vegas to vie for control of Rising Spirit's deadliest assets, the world is about to discover the shocking price of an all-out superhuman conflict...and no one will escape unscathed. Who will survive the Harbinger Wars?

Collecting HARBINGER WARS #1-4, HARBINGER #11-14, BLOODSHOT #10-13, material from the HARBINGER WARS SKETCHBOOK, and more than 20 pages of bonus materials!

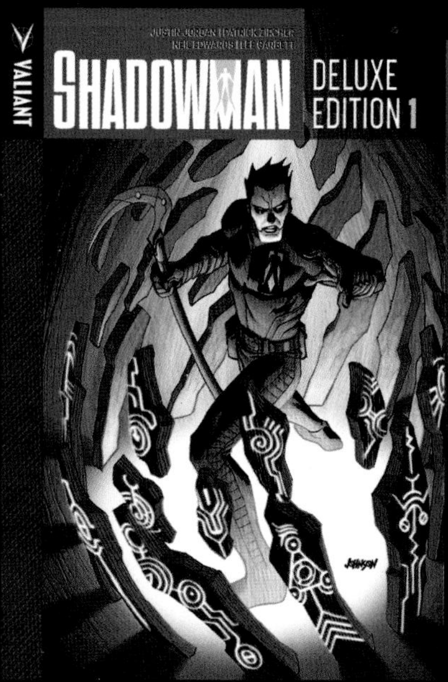
VALIANT
JUSTIN JORDAN | PATRICK ZIRCHER
NEIL EDWARDS | LEE GARBETT
SHADOWMAN
DELUXE EDITION 1

SHADOWMAN DELUXE EDITION BOOK 1

Writers: Justin Jordan and Patrick Zircher | Artists: Patrick Zircher, Neil Edwards, Lee Garbett, Diego Bernard, Roberto de la Torre, Mico Suayan, and Lewis LaRosa
ISBN: 9781939346438 | Price: $39.99 | Format: Oversized HC | COMING SOON

There are a million dreams in the Big Easy. But now its worst nightmare is about to come true. As the forces of darkness prepare to claim New Orleans as their own, Jack Boniface must accept the legacy he was born to uphold. As Shadowman, Jack is about to become the only thing that stands between his city and an army of unspeakable monstrosities from beyond the night. But what is the true cost of the Shadowman's otherworldly power? And can Jack master his new abilities before Master Darque brings down the wall between reality and the otherwordly dimension known only as the Deadside?

Collecting SHADOWMAN #0-10 and more than 20 pages of bonus materials!

VALIANT® TRADE PAPERBACKS

VALIANT
TO KILL A KING
UNITY

UNITY VOL. 1: TO KILL A KING
ISBN: 9781939346261 | Diamond Code: JAN141356 | Price: $14.99 | Format: TP

UNITY VOL. 2: TRAPPED BY WEBNET
ISBN: 97819393463461 | Diamond Code: MAY141658 | Price: $14.99 | Format: TP

VALIANT
BY THE SWORD
X-O
MANOWAR

X-O MANOWAR VOL. 1: BY THE SWORD
ISBN: 9780979640995 | Diamond Code: OCT121241 | Price: $9.99 | Format: TP

X-O MANOWAR VOL. 2: ENTER NINJAK
ISBN: 9780979640940 | Diamond Code: JAN131306 | Price: $14.99 | Format: TP

X-O MANOWAR VOL. 3: PLANET DEATH
ISBN: 9781939346087 | Diamond Code: JUN131325 | Price: $14.99 | Format: TP

X-O MANOWAR VOL. 4: HOMECOMING
ISBN: 9781939346179 | Diamond Code: OCT131347 | Price: $14.99 | Format: TP

X-O MANOWAR VOL. 5: AT WAR WITH UNITY
ISBN: 9781939346247 | Diamond Code: FEB141472 | Price: $14.99 | Format: TP

X-O MANOWAR VOL. 6: PRELUDE TO ARMOR HUNTERS
ISBN: 9781939346407 | Diamond Code: JUN141513 | Price: $14.99 | Format: TP

VALIANT
SETTING THE WORLD ON FIRE
BLOODSHOT

BLOODSHOT VOL. 1: SETTING THE WORLD ON FIRE
ISBN: 9780979640964 | Diamond Code: DEC121274 | Price: $9.99 | Format: TP

BLOODSHOT VOL. 2: THE RISE AND THE FALL
ISBN: 9781939346032| Diamond Code: APR131280 | Price: $14.99 | Format: TP

BLOODSHOT VOL. 3: HARBINGER WARS
ISBN: 9781939346124 | Diamond Code: AUG131494 | Price: $14.99 | Format: TP

BLOODSHOT VOL. 4: H.A.R.D. CORPS
ISBN: 9781939346193 | Diamond Code: NOV131275 | Price: $14.99 | Format: TP

BLOODSHOT VOL. 5: GET SOME!
ISBN: 9781939346315 | Diamond Code: JUN141514 | Price: $14.99 | Format: TP

VALIANT
SWORD OF THE WILD
ETERNAL WARRIOR

ETERNAL WARRIOR VOL. 1: SWORD OF THE WILD
ISBN: 9781939346209 | Diamond Code: NOV131271 | Price: $9.99 | Format: TP

ETERNAL WARRIOR VOL. 2: ETERNAL EMPEROR
ISBN: 9781939346292 | Diamond Code: APR141439 | Price: $14.99 | Format: TP

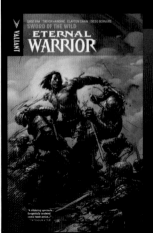

VALIANT TRADE PAPERBACKS

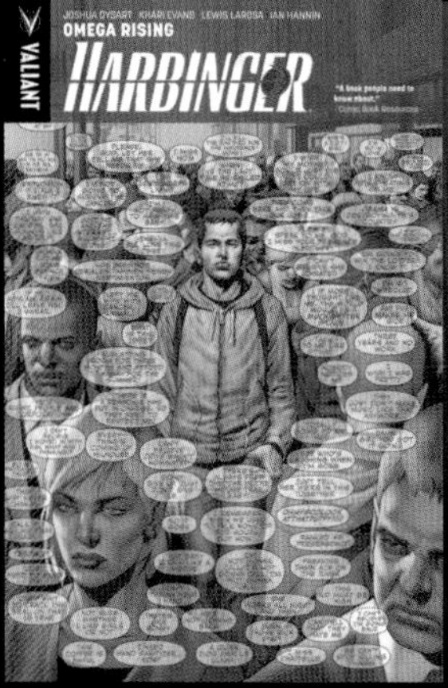
VALIANT
JOSHUA DYSART | KHARI EVANS | LEWIS LAROSA | IAN HANNIN
OMEGA RISING
HARBINGER

HARBINGER VOL. 1: OMEGA RISING
ISBN: 9780979640957 | Diamond Code: NOV121345 | Price: $9.99 | Format: TP

HARBINGER VOL. 2: RENEGADES
ISBN: 9781939346025 | Diamond Code: MAR131332 | Price: $14.99 | Format: TP

HARBINGER WARS (MINI-SERIES)
ISBN: 9781939346094 | Diamond Code: JUL131325 | Price: $14.99 | Format: TP

HARBINGER VOL. 3: HARBINGER WARS
ISBN: 9781939346117 | Diamond Code: JUL131326 | Price: $14.99 | Format: TP

HARBINGER VOL. 4: PERFECT DAY
ISBN: 9781939346155 | Diamond Code: DEC131331 | Price: $14.99 | Format: TP

HARBINGER VOL. 5: DEATH OF A RENEGADE
ISBN: 9781939346339 | Diamond Code: JUL141498 | Price:$19.99 | Format: TP

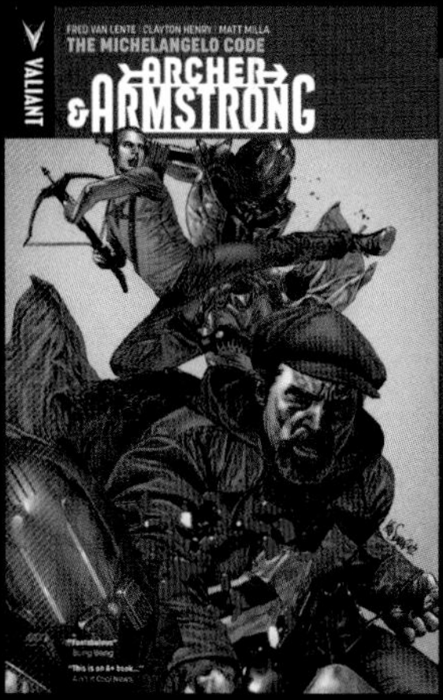
VALIANT
FRED VAN LENTE | CLAYTON HENRY | MATT MILLA
THE MICHELANGELO CODE
ARCHER & ARMSTRONG

ARCHER & ARMSTRONG VOL. 1: THE MICHELANGELO CODE
ISBN: 9780979640988 | Diamond Code: JAN131309 | Price: $14.99 | Format: TP

ARCHER & ARMSTRONG VOL. 2: WRATH OF THE ETERNAL WARRIOR
ISBN: 9781939346049 | Diamond Code: MAY131314 | Price: $14.99 | Format: TP

ARCHER & ARMSTRONG VOL. 3: FAR FARAWAY
ISBN: 9781939346148 | Diamond Code: OCT131350 | Price: $14.99 | Format: TP

ARCHER & ARMSTRONG VOL. 4: SECT CIVIL WAR
ISBN: 9781939346254 | Diamond Code: DEC131317 | Price: $14.99 | Format: TP

ARCHER & ARMSTRONG VOL. 5: MISSION: IMPROBABLE
ISBN: 9781939346353 | Diamond Code: APR141438 | Price: $14.99 | Format: TP

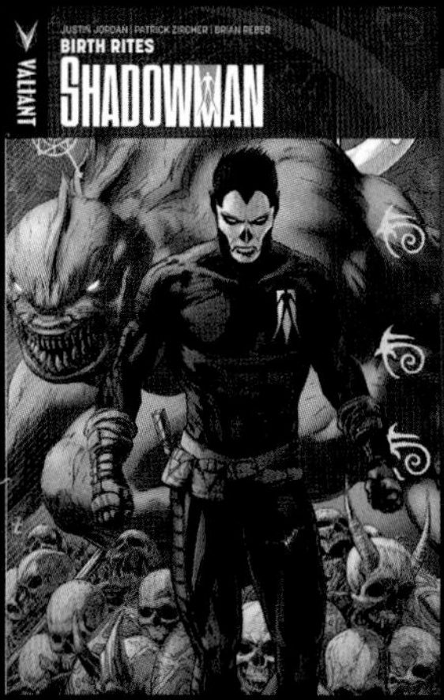
VALIANT
JUSTIN JORDAN | PATRICK ZIRCHER | BRIAN REBER
BIRTH RITES
SHADOWMAN

SHADOWMAN VOL. 1: BIRTH RITES
ISBN: 9781939346001 | Diamond Code: FEB131168 | Price: $9.99 | Format: TP

SHADOWMAN VOL. 2: DARQUE RECKONING
ISBN: 9781939346056 | Diamond Code: AUG131482 | Price: $14.99 | Format: TP

SHADOWMAN VOL. 3: DEADSIDE BLUES
ISBN: 9781939346162 | Diamond Code: NOV131282 | Price: $14.99 | Format: TP

SHADOWMAN VOL. 4: FEAR, BLOOD, AND SHADOWS
ISBN: 9781939346278 | Diamond Code: MAR141410 | Price: $14.99 | Format: TP

SHADOWMAN VOL. 5: END TIMES
ISBN: 9781939346377 | Diamond Code: JUN141515 | Price: $14.99 | Format: TP

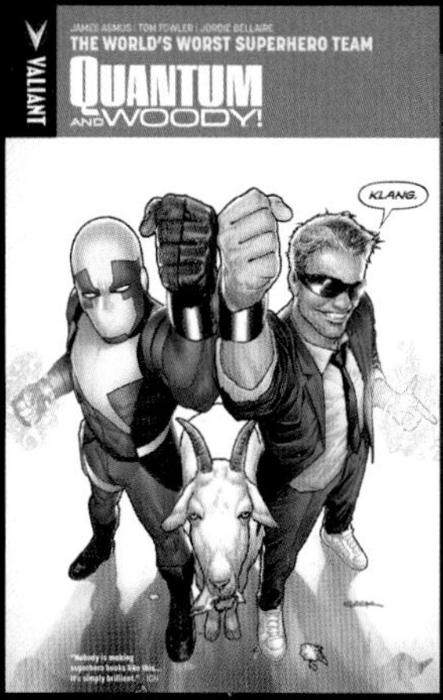
VALIANT
JAMES ASMUS | TOM FOWLER | JORDIE BELLAIRE
THE WORLD'S WORST SUPERHERO TEAM
QUANTUM AND WOODY!
KLANG.

QUANTUM AND WOODY VOL. 1: THE WORLD'S WORST SUPERHERO TEAM
ISBN: 9781939346186 | Diamond Code: SEP131374 | Price: $9.99 | Format: TP

QUANTUM AND WOODY VOL. 2: IN SECURITY
ISBN: 9781939346230 | Diamond Code: JAN141365 | Price: $14.99 | Format: TP

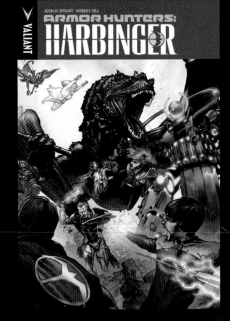